THE CAMBRIDGE COMP

DUNS SCOTUS

Each volume in this series of companions to major philosophers contains specially commissioned essays by an international team of scholars, together with a substantial bibliography, and will serve as a reference work for students and nonspecialists. One aim of the series is to dispel the intimidation such readers often feel when faced with the work of a difficult and challenging thinker.

John Duns Scotus (1265/6–1308) was (along with Aquinas and Ockham) one of the three principal figures in medieval philosophy and theology, with an influence on modern thought arguably even greater than that of Aquinas. The essays in this volume systematically survey the full range of Scotus's thought. They take care to explain the technical details of his writing in lucid terms and demonstrate the relevance of his work to contemporary philosophical debate.

New readers will find this the most convenient and accessible guide to Scotus currently available. Advanced students and specialists will find a conspectus of recent developments in the interpretation of Scotus.

Thomas Williams is Associate Professor of Philosophy at the University of Iowa.

CAMBRIDGE COMPANIONS TO PHILOSOPHY:

AQUINAS   *Edited by* NORMAN KRETZMANN *and*
ELEONORE STUMP
HANNAH ARENDT   *Edited by* DANA VILLA
ARISTOTLE   *Edited by* JONATHAN BARNES
AUGUSTINE   *Edited by* ELEONORE STUMP *and*
NORMAN KRETZMANN
BACON   *Edited by* MARKKU PELTONEN
DESCARTES   *Edited by* JOHN COTTINGHAM
EARLY GREEK PHILOSOPHY   *Edited by* A. A. LONG
FEMINISM IN PHILOSOPHY   *Edited by* MIRANDA
FRICKER *and* JENNIFER HORNSBY
FOUCAULT   *Edited by* GARY GUTTING
FREUD   *Edited by* JEROME NEU
GADAMER   *Edited by* ROBERT DOSTAL
GALILEO   *Edited by* PETER MACHAMER
GERMAN IDEALISM   *Edited by* KARL AMERIKS
HABERMAS   *Edited by* STEPHEN K. WHITE
HEGEL   *Edited by* FREDERICK BEISER
HEIDEGGER   *Edited by* CHARLES GUIGNON
HOBBES   *Edited by* TOM SORELL
HUME   *Edited by* DAVID FATE NORTON
HUSSERL   *Edited by* BARRY SMITH *and*
DAVID WOODRUFF SMITH
WILLIAM JAMES   *Edited by* RUTH ANNA PUTNAM
KANT   *Edited by* PAUL GUYER
KIERKEGAARD   *Edited by* ALASTAIR HANNAY *and*
GORDON MARINO
LEIBNIZ   *Edited by* NICHOLAS JOLLEY
LOCKE   *Edited by* VERE CHAPPELL
MALEBRANCHE   *Edited by* STEPHEN NADLER
MARX   *Edited by* TERRELL CARVER
MILL   *Edited by* JOHN SKORUPSKI
NEWTON   *Edited by* I. BERNARD COHEN *and*
GEORGE E. SMITH
NIETZSCHE   *Edited by* BERND MAGNUS *and*
KATHLEEN HIGGINS
OCKHAM   *Edited by* PAUL VINCENT SPADE
PLATO   *Edited by* RICHARD KRAUT
PLOTINUS   *Edited by* LLOYD P. GERSON
ROUSSEAU   *Edited by* PATRICK RILEY
SARTRE   *Edited by* CHRISTINA HOWELLS
SCHOPENHAUER   *Edited by* CHRISTOPHER JANAWAY
SPINOZA   *Edited by* DON GARRETT
WITTGENSTEIN   *Edited by* HANS SLUGA *and*
DAVID STERN

The Cambridge Companion to
DUNS SCOTUS

Edited by

Thomas Williams
University of Iowa

CAMBRIDGE
UNIVERSITY PRESS

PUBLISHED BY THE PRESS SYNDICATE OF THE UNIVERSITY OF CAMBRIDGE
The Pitt Building, Trumpington Street, Cambridge, United Kingdom

CAMBRIDGE UNIVERSITY PRESS
The Edinburgh Building, Cambridge CB2 2RU, UK
40 West 20th Street, New York, NY 10011-4211, USA
477 Williamstown Road, Port Melbourne, VIC 3207, Australia
Ruiz de Alarcón 13, 28014 Madrid, Spain
Dock House, The Waterfront, Cape Town 8001, South Africa

http://www.cambridge.org

© Cambridge University Press 2003

First published 2003

Printed in the United States of America

Typeface Trump Medieval 10/13pt.   *System* LaTeX 2_ε [TB]

A catalog record for this book is available from the British Library.

Library of Congress Cataloging in Publication Data
The Cambridge companion to Duns Scotus / edited by Thomas Williams.
    p.   cm. – (Cambridge companions to philosophy)
    Includes bibliographical references and index.
    ISBN 0-521-63205-6 – ISBN 0-521-63563-2 (pbk.)
    1. Duns Scotus, John, ca. 1266–1308.   I. Williams, Thomas, 1967–
II. Series.
B765.D74 C35   2002
189'.4 – dc21   2002070898

ISBN 0 521 63205 6 hardback
ISBN 0 521 63563 2 paperback

CONTENTS

vii

CONTRIBUTORS

TODD BATES is a doctoral student in the Department of Philosophy at the University of Pennsylvania.

RICHARD CROSS is Tutorial Fellow in Theology, Oriel College, University of Oxford. He is the author of *The Physics of Duns Scotus: The Scientific Context of a Theological Vision*, *Duns Scotus* (Great Medieval Thinkers), and *The Metaphysics of the Incarnation: Thomas Aquinas to Duns Scotus*, all published by Oxford University Press, and has written numerous articles on medieval theology, philosophy, and science, on Patristic and Reformation theology, and on the philosophy of religion.

BONNIE KENT is Associate Professor of Philosophy at the University of California at Irvine and the author of *Virtues of the Will: The Transformation of Ethics in the Late Thirteenth Century*. Her articles include "Moral Provincialism," "Moral Growth and the Unity of the Virtues," and "Augustine's Ethics" in *The Cambridge Companion to Augustine*.

PETER KING is Professor of Philosophy and Medieval Studies at the University of Toronto. He is translator of *John Buridan's Logic: The Treatise on Supposition, The Treatise on Consequences* and of *Augustine: Against the Academicians and The Teacher* and author of other publications on medieval philosophy.

NEIL LEWIS is Associate Professor of Philosophy at Georgetown University. He is author of several articles on medieval philosophy, including an edition of Robert Grosseteste's *De libero arbitrio*. His research focuses on the development of medieval philosophy in Britain. Currently he is editing several works by Grosseteste and is a

ix

member of the editorial team, led by Professor Rega Wood, preparing editions of the works of Richard Rufus of Cornwall.

WILLIAM E. MANN is Marsh Professor of Intellectual and Moral Philosophy at the University of Vermont. He has written extensively on topics in medieval philosophy and the philosophy of religion. His recent articles include "Augustine on Evil and Original Sin" in *The Cambridge Companion to Augustine* and "Abelard's Ethics: The Inside Story" in *The Cambridge Companion to Abelard*.

HANNES MÖHLE is Wissenschaftlicher Assistent in the Philosophisches Seminar of the Universität Bonn. He is the author of *Ethik als scientia practica nach Johannes Duns Scotus: Eine philosophische Grundlegung* and coeditor of the forthcoming edition of the *Theoremata*.

TIMOTHY B. NOONE is Associate Professor of Philosophy at The Catholic University of America and the present director of the Scotus Project, an editorial team currently editing the *Opera philosophica* of Duns Scotus. He is one of the coeditors of the three volumes of the *Opera* that have already appeared and the author of many articles on Franciscan philosophy in the Middle Ages.

CALVIN G. NORMORE is Professor of Philosophy at the University of California at Los Angeles. His publications include "Ockham on Mental Language," "Some Aspects of Ockham's Logic" in *The Cambridge Companion to Ockham*, and Chapter 18 ("Future Contingents") in *The Cambridge History of Later Medieval Philosophy*.

ROBERT PASNAU is Assistant Professor of Philosophy at the University of Colorado, Boulder. He is the author of *Thomas Aquinas on Human Nature* and *Theories of Cognition in the Later Middle Ages*, both published by Cambridge.

DOMINIK PERLER is Professor of Philosophy at the University of Basel, Switzerland. He is the author of *Der propositionale Wahrheitsbegriff im 14. Jahrhundert*, *Repräsentation bei Descartes* and *Theorien der Intentionalität im Mittelalter* and is the editor of *Ancient and Medieval Theories of Intentionality*.

JAMES F. ROSS is Professor of Philosophy and Law at the University of Pennsylvania. He is the author of *Philosophical Theology* and

Portraying Analogy, as well as numerous articles in medieval philosophy, metaphysics, and the philosophy of religion.

THOMAS WILLIAMS is Associate Professor of Philosophy at the University of Iowa. He is translator of Augustine's *On Free Choice of the Will* and Anselm's *Monologion and Proslogion* and *Three Philosophical Dialogues: On Truth, On Freedom of Choice, On the Fall of the Devil*. His recent articles include contributions to the *Cambridge Companions* to Augustine, Anselm, Abelard, and Medieval Philosophy.

ABBREVIATIONS AND METHOD OF CITATION

WORKS OF SCOTUS

References to the works of Scotus are given as follows:

Add.	*Additiones magnae*
Coll.	*Collationes oxonienses et parisienses*
De primo princ.	*De primo principio*
In De an.	*Quaestiones super libros De anima*
In Metaph.	*Quaestiones super libros Metaphysicorum Aristotelis*
In Periherm. I	*Quaestiones in I et II librum Perihermeneias*
In Periherm. II	*Octo Quaestiones in duos libros Perihermeneias*
In Porph.	*Quaestiones in librum Porphyrii Isagoge*. This is the same work that is often referred to as *Super Universalia Porphyrii*, as it is known in the Wadding edition.
In Praed.	*Quaestiones super Praedicamenta Aristotelis*
In Soph. El.	*Quaestiones in libros Elenchorum*
Lect.	*Lectura*
Ord.	*Ordinatio.* Some authors use *Op. Ox.* (= *Opus Oxoniense*) for the parts that have not yet been critically edited.
Quodl.	*Quaestiones Quodlibetales*
Rep.	*Reportatio parisiensis*
Theor.	*Theoremata*

References are given using standard internal divisions, using "prol." for Prologue, "d." for distinction, "q." for question, and "n." for paragraph number. Citations of modern editions are given only where they offer a more precise reference. They are identified as follows:

Bonaventure   *Opera philosophica.* 1997–. Saint Bonaventure, NY: The Franciscan Institute.

Vatican   *Opera Omnia.* 1950–. Vatican City: Vatican Polyglot Press.

Wadding   *Opera Omnia.* 1639. Edited by Luke Wadding. Lyon: Laurentius Durand. Photoreprint, Hildesheim: Georg Olms, 1968.

OTHER AUTHORS

References to Aristotle's works are given according to the following abbreviations:

Cat.	*Categories*
De an.	*De anima*
De gen. et corr.	*De generatione et corruptione*
Metaph.	*Metaphysics*
Nic. Eth.	*Nicomachean Ethics*
Peri herm.	*Peri hermeneias (De interpretatione)*
Phys.	*Physics*
Post. An.	*Posterior Analytics*
Soph. El.	*Sophistical Refutations*
Top.	*Topics*

References to the *Summa Theologiae* of Thomas Aquinas are given as *ST* followed by part, question, and article. IaIIae = First Part of the Second Part; IIaIIae = Second Part of the Second Part. *Summa Contra Gentiles* is abbreviated *SCG*.

OTHER ABBREVIATIONS

AL	*Aristoteles Latinus*
CSEL	*Corpus Scriptorum Ecclesiasticorum Latinorum*
PG	*Patrologia Graeca*
PL	*Patrologia Latina*
ad	response to an objection
in corp.	*in corpore* (in the author's response to the question)

DUNS SCOTUS IN ENGLISH TRANSLATION

Complete Works

De primo princ., Wolter 1966
In Metaph., Etzkorn and Wolter 1997
Quodl., Alluntis and Wolter 1975

Selections

(An asterisk indicates that only a part of the text is translated.)

Add.

1, d. 33, q. 2*: Bosley and Tweedale 1997, 329–34 (misidentified as
Rep. 1, d. 33, q. 2)

Lect.

prol., pars 4, qq. 1–2*: Wolter 1986, 127–43
1, d. 2, pars 1, qq. 1–2: Wolter 1966, 157–89

Ord.

prol., pars 1, q. un.: Wolter 1951
1, d. 2, pars 1, q. 1: Wolter 1987, 35–81
1, d. 2, pars 1, q. 3: Wolter 1987, 83–95
1, d. 3, pars 1, q. 1: Wolter 1987, 14–33
1, d. 3, pars 1, q. 3*: Wolter 1987, 4–8
1, d. 3, pars 1, q. 4: Wolter 1987, 97–132
1, d. 8, pars 1, q. 3*: Wolter 1987, 2–3
1, d. 17, pars 1, qq. 1–2, nn. 62–6: Wolter 1986, 207–9
1, d. 38, pars 2 and d. 39, qq. 1–5: Bosley and Tweedale 1997, 284–300

1, d. 42: Bosley and Tweedale 1997, 65–8
1, d. 43*: Bosley and Tweedale 1997, 68–9
1, d. 44: Wolter 1986, 255–61
1, d. 48: Wolter 1986, 235–7
2, d. 1, q. 3: Bosley and Tweedale 1997, 215–30
2, d. 3, pars 1, qq. 1–6: Spade 1994, 57–113
2, d. 6, q. 2*: Wolter 1986, 463–77
2, d. 7, q. un.*: Wolter 1986, 219–25
2, d. 39, qq. 1–2: Wolter 1986, 197–205
2, d. 40, q. un.: Wolter 1986, 225–9
2, d. 41, q. un.: Wolter 1986, 229–35
2, d. 42, qq. 1–4, nn 10–11: Wolter 1986, 173–5
2, d. 43, q. 2: Wolter 1986, 477–9
2, d. 44, q. un.: Wolter 1986, 459–63
3, d. 17, q. un.*: Wolter 1986, 181–3
3, d. 26, q. un.*: Wolter 1986, 179–81
3, d. 27, q. un.*: Wolter 1986, 423–47
3, d. 28, q. un.*: Wolter 1986, 447–55
3, d. 29, q. un.: Wolter 1986, 455–7
3, d. 33, q. un.: Wolter 1986, 319–47
3, d. 34, q. un.: Wolter 1986, 347–77
3, d. 36, q. un.: Wolter 1986, 377–421
3, d. 37, q. un.: Wolter 1986, 269–87
3, d. 38, q. un.: Wolter 1986, 481–501
3, d. 39, q. un.: Wolter 1986, 501–19
4, d. 15, q. 2*: Wolter 1986, 311–17
4, d. 17, q. un.*: Wolter 1986, 263–9
4, d. 21, q. 2*: Wolter 1986, 519–21
4, d. 29, q. un.*: Wolter 1986, 175–7
4, d. 33, q. 1: Wolter 1986, 289–97
4, d. 33, q. 3: Wolter 1986, 297–311
4, d. 36, q. 1: Wolter 1986, 523–33
4, d. 43, q. 2: Wolter 1987, 134–62
4, d. 46, q. 1: Wolter 1986, 239–55
4, d. 49, qq. 9–10*: Wolter 1986, 183–97

Rep.

1A, prol., q. 3*: Wolter 1987, 9–12
1A, d. 2, qq. 1–4: Wolter and Adams 1982

Introduction

The Life and Works
of John Duns the Scot

We know very little with certainty about the details of Scotus's life and the chronology of his writings, and the evidence and arguments used to establish what we do know are sometimes forbiddingly complex. I make no attempt here to lay out all the speculations or even to adjudicate all the controversies. What follows is therefore a partial and inevitably controversial account of Scotus's life and works. It would, I believe, command wide acceptance among students of Scotus; I indicate some points of dispute in the text and offer extensive references for those who want to explore these matters in more detail.[1]

I. SCOTUS'S LIFE

As a guide through the complexities of the narrative that follows, I first offer a chronology in tabular form. AY stands for academic year, a period extending from early October to late June.

23 December 1265– 17 March 1266	John Duns born in Duns, Scotland, a few miles from the English border
17 March 1291	Ordained to the priesthood at Saint Andrew's Priory, Northampton, England
AY 1300–01	Took part in a disputation under Philip of Bridlington
26 July 1300	Was one of twenty-two candidates presented to the Bishop of Lincoln for faculties to hear confessions in the Franciscan church at Oxford

AY 1302–03	Lectured at Paris on the *Sentences* of Peter Lombard
June 1303	Expelled from France, along with eighty other friars, for taking the pope's side in a dispute with the French king; most likely returned to Oxford
April 1304	Allowed to return to France; resumed lectures on the *Sentences*
18 November 1304	Appointed regent master of theology for the Franciscans at Paris by Gonsalvus of Spain
early 1305	Incepted as master
Advent 1306 or Lent 1307	Disputed the *Quodlibetal Questions*
October 1307	Took up duties as *lector* at the Franciscan *studium* at Cologne
8 November 1308	Died at Cologne

The first definite date we have for Scotus's life is that of his ordination to the priesthood in the Order of Friars Minor – the Franciscans – at Saint Andrew's Priory in Northampton, England, on 17 March 1291. The minimum age for ordination was twenty-five, so we can conclude that Scotus was born before 17 March 1266. But how much before? The conjecture, plausible but by no means certain, is that Scotus would have been ordained as early as canonically permitted. Since the Bishop of Lincoln (the diocese that included Oxford, where Scotus was studying, as well as St. Andrew's Priory) had ordained priests in Wycombe on 23 December 1290, we can place Scotus's birth between 23 December 1265 and 17 March 1266.

It seems likely that Scotus began his studies with the Franciscans at Oxford at a very young age. The history written by John Mair (or John Major) in 1521 says that "When [Scotus] was no more than a boy, but had been already grounded in grammar, he was taken by two Scottish Minorite [i.e., Franciscan] friars to Oxford, for at that time there existed no university in Scotland. By the favour of those friars he lived in the convent of the Minorites at Oxford."[2] A. G. Little[3] reports that it was typical for boys to begin their studies at Oxford when they were as young as ten or twelve years old. And Scotus himself, in a remark that many have quite naturally taken as a reflection on his own early training, notes that "these days boys are taught and trained forthwith in matters pertaining to the clergy or the divine office, so nowadays a boy of thirteen years is more adequately instructed in such matters than a twenty-five-year-old peasant might have been in the primitive church."[4]

Direct evidence about Scotus's theological education at Oxford is hard to come by. One commonly accepted chronology assumes that he followed the typical course of training for university students.[5] That course would require that after completing his preliminary studies in the faculty of arts Scotus would spend six academic years studying theology. In his seventh and eighth years he would have learned to serve as opponent, and in his ninth year as respondent, in disputations. In his tenth year he would have prepared his lectures on the *Sentences* of Peter Lombard, to be delivered in the following year. In his twelfth year he would have been required to lecture on the Bible, and in his final year to dispute under various masters. Now we know that Scotus participated in a disputation under Philip Bridlington during Bridlington's year of regency, which was the academic year 1300–01.[6] This fact would suggest that Scotus's final year of training at Oxford was 1300–01. If so, we could conclude that Scotus began his theological study in 1288, served as opponent in 1294–96 and as respondent in 1296–97, prepared his lectures on the *Sentences* in 1297–98, delivered them in 1298–99, and lectured on the Bible in 1299–1300. After his studies were completed in 1301, a further year would be required before Scotus was qualified to read the *Sentences* at Paris; Brampton therefore concludes that "He must have taught in an unknown convent in England as a lector."[7]

Unfortunately, the assumption on which this chronology rests – that Scotus would have followed the typical university course leading to the mastership in theology – is very likely false. The university regulations establishing that course applied to secular masters, not to members of the mendicant orders, who were granted a number of dispensations from the sequence prescribed for secular degree candidates.[8] Indeed, the Franciscan educational system allowed enough flexibility at various levels of study that it is impossible to reconstruct a year-by-year chronology of Scotus's studies, or even to determine exactly when they began.

We do, however, have some good evidence relating to the final stages of his academic career at Oxford. We know, for example, that Scotus was in Oxford in July 1300, when the English provincial,

Hugh of Hertilpole, asked Bishop Dalderby to license one "Johannes Douns," along with 21 others, to hear confessions at the Franciscan church at Oxford.[9] As Wolter notes,[10] it seems highly improbable that Hugh would have presented Scotus for faculties to hear confessions in the Oxford church if he had assigned Scotus to go to Paris for the fall term, which would have started only about ten weeks later. So it is reasonable to conclude that Scotus remained in Oxford through 1300–01.

Further evidence is found in a statement Scotus makes in the prologue to his *Ordinatio*. Having argued that the long endurance of the Church testifies to its divine authority, he considers the objection that Islam has also endured for many centuries:

If an objection is raised concerning the permanence of the sect of Mohammed, I reply: that sect began more than six hundred years after the law of Christ, and, God willing, it will shortly be brought to an end, since it has been greatly weakened in the year of Christ 1300, and many of its believers are dead and still more have fled, and a prophecy current among them states that their sect is to be brought to an end.[11]

What Scotus has in mind here is the defeat of the Sultan of Egypt by Turks allied with the Christians of Armenia and Georgia on 23 December 1299. News of that defeat probably reached Oxford in June of 1300, but the excitement it generated proved to be short lived. Now this passage occurs in the second part of the Prologue to the *Ordinatio*, the revised version of his Oxford lectures, but it has no predecessor in the *Lectura*, which gives the actual text of the lectures he had delivered some time earlier. The obvious conclusion to draw is that Scotus was just beginning to revise his Oxford lectures in the summer or early fall of 1300 and that the lectures themselves had been given some time earlier.[12]

Scotus began lecturing on the *Sentences* at the University of Paris in October 1302. In the spring of 1303 he probably participated in the disputation between the Franciscan Regent Master, Gonsalvus of Spain, and the Dominican Meister Eckhart. Around that time the campaign of King Philip IV ("the Fair") of France to call a general council to depose Pope Boniface VIII moved into high gear. Beginning in March Philip secured the support, first of the French nobility, then of nearly all the higher clergy, and finally of the University of Paris and the chapter of Notre Dame. As Little continues the story, "On 24 June a great anti-papal demonstration was organized in the gardens of the Louvre; the mendicant friars attended in procession, and the meeting was addressed by Bertold of St. Denys, bishop of Orleans and ex-chancellor of the university, and by two Friars Preachers and two Friars Minor."[13] The next day royal commissioners visited the Franciscan convent and asked each friar individually whether he consented to the king's proposals. Eighty-four Franciscans, nearly all French, were listed as agreeing to the king's appeal; eighty-seven, mostly foreigners, dissented. Among the dissenters were Scotus and Gonsalvus. The king ordered the dissident friars to leave France within three days.

We are not absolutely certain where Scotus went during his exile from France. Some have suggested Cambridge, since it appears that Scotus lectured at Cambridge at some point.[14] But most scholars find it more probable to suppose that he returned to Oxford, and the Vatican editors believe that the so-called *Lectura completa*, a set of lectures given at Oxford on Book 3 of the *Sentences*, dates from Scotus's exile.[15] In any event, the exile was not long. Boniface VIII died on October 11, and the new pope, Benedict XI, made peace with Philip. In April 1304 Philip permitted Scotus and the rest of the friars to return to Paris. Scotus probably resumed his lectures with Book 4 of the *Sentences*.

Some time early in the academic year 1304–05 Scotus acted as respondent in the formal disputation that was part of the inception of Gilles de Ligny. (*Inception* is the name for the academic exercises by which a bachelor theologian received the doctorate and was promoted to master.) Shortly thereafter, on 18 November, the Franciscan Minister-General, Gonsalvus of Spain, sent a letter to the Minister-Provincial of France asking that Scotus be put next in line for such promotion: "I assign to you John the Scot, of whose praiseworthy life, outstanding knowledge, and most subtle intelligence I have been made fully aware, partly through long experience and partly through his reputation, which has spread everywhere."[16] Scotus incepted as master early in 1305. It was around this time that Scotus disputed with the Dominican William Peter Godinus on the principle of individuation.[17] In either Advent 1306 or Lent 1307 he conducted a quodlibetal disputation.

According to tradition, Scotus's time in Paris came to a sudden and unexpected end when the Minister-General transferred him to the Franciscan *studium* at Cologne. Whether this story of a hasty removal is true or not, it is certainly the case that Scotus's successor at Paris is known to have been master at least as early as 25 October 1307, and Scotus is listed as "lector of Cologne" in a document dated 20 February 1308,[18] so it is likely that Scotus began teaching in Cologne in October 1307 and continued through the rest of the academic year. In default of hard evidence, various speculations, ranging from the fantastic to the mundane, have been proposed to explain why Scotus was transferred out of the far more prestigious University of Paris at the height of his career. One of the more ingenious explanations was that of Callebaut,[19] who argued that Scotus was in danger because of his opposition to the French king's vigorous measures to suppress the Knights Templar, measures enthusiastically supported by John of Pouilly, who had accused Scotus of heresy for his defense of the Immaculate Conception and expressed the desire to attack Scotus "not by arguments but in some other way" (*non argumentis sed aliter*). So, according to Callebaut, Gonsalvus sent Scotus to Cologne to be out of the way of danger. A more matter-of-fact explanation was suggested by Longpré, who noted that it was common for the Franciscans to send their star theologians from one house to another.[20] But whatever his reason for being in Cologne, he was not to be there long. He died at Cologne in 1308; the date is traditionally given as November 8. He was buried in the Franciscan church in Cologne, where today his remains rest in an ornate sarcophagus bearing the Latin epitaph that has been associated with his burial place for centuries:

Scotia me genuit,	Scotland bore me,
Anglia me suscepit,	England received me,
Gallia me docuit,	France taught me,
Colonia me tenet.	Cologne holds me.

II. SCOTUS'S WORKS

What follows is a discussion of Scotus's works in a rough chronological order (since no precise order can be given). For each work I indicate the best available edition, if any. (Note that the Wadding edition of 1639 is not a critical edition and must therefore be used with care; the Bonaventure and Vatican editions are critical editions.)

More detailed discussions of the nature, authenticity, authority, and chronology of Scotus's works can be found in the critical prefaces to Volumes 1 and 3 of the Bonaventure edition and Volumes 1, 4, 6, 7, 8, 17, and 19 of the Vatican edition.

Quaestiones super Porphyrii Isagogem	edition: Bonaventure 1
Quaestiones in librum Praedicamentorum	edition: Bonaventure 1
Quaestiones in I et II librum Perihermeneias	edition: Wadding 1 (Bonaventure, in progress)
Octo quaestiones in duos libros Perihermeneias	edition: Wadding 1 (Bonaventure, in progress)
Quaestiones in libros Elenchorum	edition: Wadding 1 (Bonaventure, in progress)

These works are collectively known as the *parva logicalia*, or "little logical works." They have traditionally been dated to early in Scotus's career, possibly as early as 1295, although the evidence currently available does not permit any definitive dating. There is substantial evidence that these are genuine works of Scotus.[21] The manuscript tradition for each of these works contains ascriptions to Scotus. Antonius Andreas, an early and generally faithful follower of Scotus, includes summaries of Scotus's questions on the *Isagoge* and *Praedicamenta* in his own works. And Adam Wodeham, who is noted for his accurate citations of Scotus, twice cites the questions on the *Perihermenias* in his *Lectura secunda*.

Lectura	edition (Books 1 and 2): Vatican 16–19
	edition (Book 3): not yet edited

The *Lectura* contains Scotus's notes for the lectures he gave on Books 1 and 2 of the *Sentences* as a bachelor theologian at Oxford. It is therefore his earliest theological work, and since the later revision of these lectures, the *Ordinatio*, was never completed, it is the only Oxford commentary we have on certain parts of the *Sentences*. For example, Scotus never dictated a revised version of Book 2, dd. 15–25, and the Vatican edition of the *Ordinatio* does not contain questions on those distinctions.

We also have a set of lecture notes on Book 3, the *Lectura completa*, which exists in only three manuscripts and has not yet been edited. These lectures were also given at Oxford, but later, possibly during Scotus's exile from Paris in 1303–04. We have no *Lectura* at all on Book 4. Some have argued that Scotus never lectured on Book 4 at Oxford, but Wolter suggests that "the total absence of any Oxford lectures on Bks. III and IV before Scotus went to Paris may be a consequence of the destructive raids on the university libraries of England in 1535 and 1550."[22]

Quaestiones super   edition: Bonaventure (in progress)
libros De anima

Although some scholars deny the authenticity of the question-commentary on Aristotle's *De anima*, the attributions to Scotus in the manuscript tradition and its explicit citation by Adam Wodeham provide strong evidence in favor of its authenticity. Further discussion of the authenticity and dating of the work should be sought in the forthcoming critical edition.

Quaestiones super libros   edition: Bonaventure 3–4
Metaphysicorum Aristotelis

The editors of the critical edition say that "this work of the Subtle Doctor has come down to us in a disorderly state,"[23] with questions ordered differently in different manuscripts, single manuscripts in multiple hands, questions transcribed more than once in a single manuscript, and the ordering of paragraphs within questions varying from one manuscript to another. Nevertheless, they say, "the meaning of the text which has come down to us is rarely compromised."[24]

The *Questions on the Metaphysics* have traditionally been dated early, a tradition that the Vatican editors follow,[25] but the editors of the critical edition argue that no single dating is possible for the entire work: "we suggest that these questions were composed and revised over an extended period of time and that certain questions stem from a period late in Scotus's career."[26] Indeed, detailed textual analysis by Dumont, Noone, and the editors themselves strongly suggests that Books 7 through 9 date in their present form to late in Scotus's career; Wolter notes that Book 7 must date between Book 2 of the *Ordinatio* and Book 2 of the *Reportatio*.[27] On the other hand, Richard Cross argues that Book 5 of the *Questions on the Metaphysics* must predate the *Lectura*, and therefore that the first five books should all be dated to before 1300.[28]

Scotus also wrote an *Expositio* on Aristotle's *Metaphysics*, which is now lost. The *Expositio super libros Metaphysicorum Aristotelis* printed as Scotus's in the Wadding edition is the work of Antonius Andreas.

| *Ordinatio* | edition (Books 1 and 2): Vatican 1–8 |
| | edition (Books 3 and 4): Wadding 6–10 |

An *ordinatio* is a text that the instructor himself has set in order in preparation for publication (i.e., copying by the official university scribes and distribution to the booksellers). Scotus's *Ordinatio* is his revision of the lectures he gave as a bachelor at Oxford, based on the *Lectura*. We can clearly discern at least two layers of revision. The initial revision was begun in the summer of 1300 and left incomplete when Scotus departed for Paris in 1302; it probably did not get much past Book 2. Further revisions were made in Paris; we know that Scotus was still dictating questions for Book 4 as late as 1304, as well as updating the parts he had already revised while still at Oxford. These updates were usually in the form of marginal additions or interpolated texts that reflected what Scotus taught in Paris. Our picture of the nature and extent of the second layer of revisions is, however, still murky, in part because the Vatican edition of the *Ordinatio* is complete only through the end of Book 2, and no critical edition of the Paris *Reportatio* is available at all (see *Reportatio parisiensis*, below). Much further study is needed to understand just how much the *Ordinatio* represents the views Scotus held at Oxford and how much he revised it to reflect developments in his views while in Paris. At present, however, the most plausible view would seem to be that of Wolter, who wrote that it is a

serious and inexcusable mistake for scholars writing on Scotus today to regard his *Ordinatio* as a seamless garment rather than a work begun in Oxford and left unfinished when he left Paris for Cologne. It is particularly unwise to consider the basic text of the eleven volumes of the Vatican edition so far printed as necessarily representative of his final views simply because parts were updated with a view to what he taught later in Paris.[29]

And Wolter argues persuasively that *Ordinatio* 1 "is simply a more mature expression of his early views, and needs to be supplemented by the later positions he held which can be found in the reports of his lectures at Cambridge and Paris."[30]

Collationes oxonienses   edition: Wadding 3; Harris 1927, 2:371–8;
    et parisienses   Balić 1929; three as yet unedited

The *Collationes* represent disputations in which Scotus participated at Oxford and Paris. Dumont notes that "The *Collationes* are
perhaps the least studied of Scotus's theological works, yet the fact
that Scotus himself refers to them several times in the course of re-
vising his *Ordinatio* indicates their importance."[31] He argues that
the Oxford *Collationes* were disputed either during Scotus's exile
from Paris in 1303–04 or at some time between 1305 and his death
in 1308.[32] The Paris *Collationes* were presumably disputed at various
times between 1302 and 1307.

Reportatio parisiensis   edition: see below

A *reportatio* is a student report of a lecture. We have several *reportationes* of Scotus's lectures at Paris, and the relationship among
the various versions is unclear. There are also questions about the
order in which he commented on the *Sentences*. One plausible view
is that he commented sequentially on all four books in the academic
year 1302–03, being interrupted near the end by his exile from Paris,
and resuming with Book 4 upon his return in the spring of 1304.
There are future-tense references in Book 4 to topics he will treat in
Book 3, presumably in the academic year 1304–05, when he may have
given another complete course of lectures on the *Sentences*. The one
clear fact is that Scotus himself personally examined a *reportatio* of
his lectures on Book 1, which is therefore known as the *Reportatio
examinata*. Since this work represents Scotus's most mature commentary on the matters treated in *Sentences* 1, it is of paramount
importance in understanding his thought and its development. Unfortunately, it has not yet been edited. What the Wadding edition
prints as *Reportatio* 1 is actually Book 1 of the *Additiones magnae*.

The Vatican editors[33] identify the following versions of the *Reportatio*:

On Book 1:
   Reportatio 1A (the *Reportatio*   edition: not yet edited
     examinata)
   Reportatio 1B   edition: Paris 1517
   Reportatio 1C (now identified as the   edition: not yet edited
     Reportatio cantabrigiensis)

Reportatio 1D	edition: not yet edited
Reportatio 1E[34]	edition: not yet edited
On Book 2:	
Reportatio 2A	edition: Wadding 11
Reportatio 2B (a shorter version and the principal source for *Additiones* 2)	edition: not yet edited
On Book 3:	
Reportatio 3A	edition: Wadding 11
Reportatio 3B, 3C, 3D	edition: not yet edited
On Book 4:	
Reportatio 4A	edition: Wadding
Reportatio 4B	edition: Paris 1518
Additiones magnae	edition (Book 1): Wadding 11 (misidentified there as *Reportatio* 1) edition (Book 2): not yet edited

The *Additiones magnae* on Books 1 and 2 of the *Sentences* were compiled by William of Alnwick, Scotus's companion and secretary, from Scotus's lectures at both Oxford and Paris, but principally from the latter. (In fact, some manuscripts call the *Additiones* "Lectura Parisiensis.") They were most likely produced between 1312 and 1325.[35] The Vactican editors take a dim view of Alnwick's faithfulness to the mind of Scotus, at least as regards the *Additiones* on Book 2, d. 25,[36] but their opinion is not generally shared, and surely Dumont is correct in saying that the evidence available to us "gives every indication that the Additiones are faithful to Scotus."[37] Three manuscripts of *Additiones* 2 contain an *explicit* attributing the *Additiones* to Scotus and identifying Alnwick not as their author but as their compiler:

Here conclude the Additions to the second book of Master John Duns, extracted by Master William of Alnwick of the Order of Friars Minor from the Paris and Oxford lectures of the aforesaid Master John.[38]

In their earliest appearances, the *Additiones* were identified as an appendix to Scotus's *Ordinatio*, but they gradually came to be inserted into the *Ordinatio* itself to supply material where Scotus had left the *Ordinatio* incomplete – a process that attests to the belief of Scotus's contemporaries and immediate successors in the authenticity of the *Additiones*. Furthermore, the *Additiones* are cited in the early four-teenth century as an authentic work of Scotus, in particular by Adam Wodeham. So although the precise occasion or purpose of Alnwick's compilation is not clear, there is overwhelming evidence that the *Additiones* represent the teaching of Scotus himself.

Quaestiones Quodlibetales   edition: Alluntis 1963

It was part of the duty of a regent master to conduct quodlibetal disputations, so called because "they could be about any topic what-ever (*de quolibet*) and could be initiated by any member of the audi-ence (*a quolibet*)."[39] Scotus's *Quodlibetal Questions* were disputed in either Advent 1306 or Lent 1307. Scotus then revised the ques-tions, completing the revision up through the last question, q. 21.

De primo principio   edition: Wolter 1966

This short treatise in natural theology, once taken to be an early work, is now generally believed to be one of Scotus's later works, and perhaps his very latest. About one half of it is taken verbatim from Book 1 of the *Ordinatio*. Wolter observes that

A careful analysis of the [manuscripts] leads one to conclude that Scotus had considerable secretarial help in composing the final draft. He seems to have contented himself with sketching the main outlines of the treatise and entrusted his personal amanuensis or other scribes with the task of filling in the substance of the work from those sections of the *Ordinatio* he had indicated. This would explain why certain words were deleted that should have been copied, or conversely why words or phrases were added that could hardly have been intended when the amanuensis on occasion obviously strayed beyond the section Scotus wanted copied. It would also account for the unusual turn of phrase, or other stylistic differences between this and Scotus's other writings.[40]

The resulting text is accordingly sometimes obscure, and *De primo principio* is therefore best read in conjunction with the parallel treat-ments in the *Ordinatio* and the *Reportatio examinata*.

Theoremata   edition: Wadding 3

Near the end of *De primo principio* Scotus notes that he has been discussing metaphysical conclusions about God, reached through natural reason, and he announces his intention to provide a companion volume treating matters of faith. Some have identified this companion volume with the so-called *tractatus de creditis*, Theorems 14 to 16 of the *Theoremata*. This identification is, however, difficult to maintain in the face of apparent doctrinal discrepancies between *De primo principio* and the *tractatus de creditis*. Largely because of such discrepancies, the authenticity of the *Theoremata* is highly disputed. In my view, the balance of the evidence demands that we reject the attribution of this work to Scotus, but the matter is by no means settled.[41]

NOTES

1 The account that follows relies on Wolter 1993, 1995, 1996; S. Dumont 1996, 2001; Noone 1995; and the introductions to the critical editions of Scotus's works (see the chart of editions, below). I am grateful to Timothy B. Noone for his helpful remarks on an earlier draft of this essay.

2 Major 1892, 206; quoted in Wolter 1993, 6.

3 Little 1892, 191.

4 *Ord.* 4, d. 25, q. 2, n. 2

5 The classic statement of this chronology is in Brampton 1964. It has been defended by Allan B. Wolter, most notably in Wolter 1995, and widely accepted by other writers.

6 Brampton 1964, 17–8.

7 Brampton 1964, 17.

8 Roest 2000, 100. Roest's study offers an excellent overview of the development of the Franciscan educational system.

9 Hugh met in person with Bishop Dalderby at Dorchester-on-Thames on 26 July 1300. The Bishop thought the request for 22 licenses was wildly excessive for a single church and selected only eight of the friars. Scotus was not among them.

10 Wolter 1995, 187–8.

11 *Ord.* prol., pars 2, q. un., n. 112.

12 The Vatican editors, however, date the lectures to 1300–01. See Vatican 19:33*, and cf. Brampton 1964, 8–9, and Wolter 1996, 45–7.

13 Little 1932, 575.

14 Scotus refers to his Cambridge lecture at *Ord.* 1, d. 4, n. 1. See *Reportatio* 1C, below. It is also possible that Scotus lectured at Cambridge some time before going to Paris in 1302.

15 Vatican 19:33*.
16 Little 1892, 220. Note that the adjective *subtle* had come to be associated with Scotus even during his lifetime, although I know of no appearance of the epithet "Subtle Doctor" until a few years after his death.
17 See Noone 1995, 394–5. An edition of this disputation is printed in Stroick 1974, 581–608.
18 Little 1932, 582; Wolter 1993, 12.
19 Callebaut 1928.
20 Wolter 1993, 13.
21 For a more detailed examination of this evidence and a discussion of the dating of the logical works, see Bonaventure 1:xxvi–xxxi. The other logical works that appear as Scotus's in the Wadding edition are inauthentic.
22 Wolter 1993, 34.
23 Bonaventure 3:xxxiii.
24 Bonaventure 3:xxxvii.
25 Vatican 19:41*–2*.
26 Bonaventure 3:xlii.
27 S. Dumont 1995; Noone 1995; Wolter 1996, 52.
28 Cross 1998, 245–6.
29 Wolter 1996, 39–40.
30 Wolter 1996, 50.
31 S. Dumont 1996, 69.
32 Both dates pose certain problems. For a thorough discussion of the evidence, see S. Dumont 1996.
33 Vatican 1:144*–9*, 7:4*–5*.
34 *Reportatio* 1E is thought by many to be an amalgam of Henry Harclay's lectures and Scotus's own work. But see Balić 1939, 2:4–9.
35 For the arguments that establish these dates, see Wolter 1996, 44.
36 Vatican 19:39*–40*, note 3.
37 S. Dumont 2001, 767; see also Balić 1927, 101–3, and Wolter 1996, 44–5.
38 *Expliciunt Additiones secundi libri magistri Iohannis Duns extractae per magistrum Gillermum de Alnwick de ordine fratrum minorum de Lectura Parisiensi et Oxoniensi pracedicti magistri Iohannis.* The wording given here is that of Oxford, Balliol College, MS 208, f. 40v. Vat. lat. 876, f. 310v, and Berlin, Staatsbibliothek, Lat. Fol. MS 928, f. 35vb, have similar *explicits*.
39 Kenny and Pinborg 1982, 22.
40 Wolter 1966, x–xi.
41 For a different view, see Ross and Bates, ch. 6 in this volume, sec. II.

1   Scotus on Metaphysics

This chapter discusses Scotus's metaphysics under six headings: the nature of metaphysics itself as a discipline (Section I); identity and distinctness (Section II); the extent and scope of the Aristotelian categories (Section III); causality and essential orders (Section IV); matter, form, and the composite of matter and form (Section V); and a brief return to the nature of metaphysics (Section VI). Some metaphysical topics are not treated here but in other chapters of this volume: space and time (Chapter 2), universals and individuation (Chapter 3), and modality (Chapter 4). Scotus's proof of God's existence, discussed in Section IV, is examined in Chapter 6.

I. METAPHYSICS AS THE SCIENCE OF BEING

I.1. Theoretical Science

Scotus holds that there are exactly three real theoretical sciences, pursued for their own sake, that are open to us in our present life: metaphysics, mathematics, and physics (*In Metaph.* 6, q. 1, nn. 43–6). Each qualification is important. The requirement that such sciences be "real" that is, concerned with things in the world rather than our concepts of them – excludes logic, which is the normative science of how we are to think about things, and thus concerned with concepts. The requirement that such sciences be pursued for their own sake excludes ethics, whose primary goal is to direct and regulate the will. The requirement that we can attain such knowledge in the condition of our present life, where we can only know things through sense perception and hence have no direct epistemic access to principles or to immaterial beings, rules out theology in the strict sense

15

as well as a properly axiomatic metaphysics; we can however construct a 'natural' theology and metaphysics within our limitations.[1] Mathematics and physics are defined in terms of material substance. Mathematics deals with material substances in their material aspect, namely, in terms of their purely quantitative features (which they have in virtue of their matter) and whatever is consequent upon those features. Physics on the other hand deals with material substances in their formal aspect, since form is the source of their specific operations as well as motion, rest, and other attributes open to sense perception.[2] Other theoretical sciences dealing with material substance, for example, astronomy, optics, music (as the theory of harmonic proportions), biology, and the like, will be subordinate to them.

Metaphysics, however, is not defined in terms of immaterial substance. Instead, Scotus identifies the subject of metaphysics as being *qua* being.[3] This is partly due to our lack of direct access to immaterial substance, as noted previously (*In Metaph.* 6, q. 1, n. 56). But there are other reasons to reject the claim that metaphysics is properly about God or about substance, the traditional alternatives.[4] Strictly speaking, the object of metaphysical study should be reality, · in general, which includes God and substance but other things in addition (creatures and accidents, respectively). Scotus makes this line of argument precise with the notion of a *primary object*, which in its turn requires the notion of a *per se object*.

I.2. The Primary Object of a Science

The *per se* object of something is that to which it applies by its nature. For example, when Jones sees a black sheep, his power of vision is actualized by the particular blackness of the sheep's wool, which is therefore the *per se* object of his seeing; the sheep itself is "seen" only accidentally or incidentally. Likewise, the *per se* object of building is the house that is built; the builder may also become strong through his physical labor, but health is not what building is about by definition, even if it is a result of construction. Hence, *per se* objects are particular items in the world: the blackness of the sheep's wool, the newly built house.

The primary object of something is the most general nonrelational feature, or set of features, in virtue of which its *per se* object counts as its *per se* object.[5] The primary object must be nonrelational, since otherwise, it risks being empty. For to say that Jones's vision is actualized by anything visible is true but trivial, since *visible* is a relational term that means "able to actualize the faculty of vision." The primary object must equally be general: to say that Jones sees the blackness of the sheep's wool in virtue of its blackness is also true and also trivial; we can sense green things as well as black ones.[6] Yet we cannot see everything in the category of Quality. Hence, the most informative characterization of what can be seen is *color*, the primary object of sight. Analogously, the primary object of geometry is *figure* rather than (say) *triangle*.

Scotus holds, then, that the primary object of metaphysics is *being* – that the human intellect in its present condition is able to have knowledge of being as such.[7] Hence, the primary object of the human intellect is *being*, an alternative formulation Scotus discusses at some length.[8] We are, in a sense, natural metaphysicians. Not that such knowledge comes to us easily! Yet we are naturally suited to have it: a view Scotus finds implicit in the opening remark of Aristotle's *Metaphysics* that all men desire by nature to know (980[a]21).[9]

Scotus rejects the traditional claims about the subject of metaphysics. For the primary object must, by definition, be truly predicable of anything falling under it as a *per se* object.[10] Thus if substance were its primary object, metaphysics would not deal with accidents at all, since accidents are not substances (even if existentially dependent on them). But this is clearly false. Likewise, God cannot be the primary object of metaphysics, for not everything is God. However, there is a straightforward sense in which anything capable of real existence is a being. In *Quodl.* q. 3, n. 6, Scotus distinguishes several senses of 'being' or 'thing', the broadest of which is whatever does not include a contradiction. He explicitly says that being thus broadly conceived is the proper subject of metaphysics (*Quodl.* q. 3, n. 9). God, angels, and substances are all considered in metaphysics to the extent that they are beings, but they are no more the primary object of metaphysics than triangles are of geometry.

Scotus admits that God and substance are special to metaphysics in another sense, however. For substance is more of a being than accident, and God is more complete and perfect – the words are the same in Latin – than any other being. *Qua* beings they are treated alike, but there is an ascending scale of completeness that makes the study of substance more fruitful for metaphysics than the study of accidents, and so much the more for God.[11] Again, metaphysics investigates the way beings are related to one another, and, since everything depends on God, in some sense God could be called the main subject of metaphysics.[12] But neither of these proposals is to be confused with Scotus's fundamental thesis that the primary object of metaphysics is *being*.

I.3. The Univocity of 'Being'

To defend his thesis, Scotus has to show that there is a uniform nontrivial sense in which everything considered by metaphysics can be said to be a being, and that the human intellect is equipped to know being as such. He addresses both by defending the univocity of 'being'.[13] There is, Scotus maintains, a single unified notion of being[14] that applies equally to substance and accident (and generally to all ten categories), as well as to God and creatures, which serves to ground metaphysics as a science. The two arguments he seems to have found the most compelling are as follows.

First, we can be certain of one concept while doubting another. We can, for example, be certain that God is a being but doubt whether God is finite or infinite, or even material or immaterial. This shows that the notion of being is different from that of finite and infinite being, of which it is predicated, and hence is univocal to both.[15]

Second, Scotus argues that in our present condition all our knowledge derives from sense perception, and this leads only to simple concepts that have a content in common with that which inspires them. Hence, there is no basis for forming simple analogous concepts. Furthermore, we do possess a simple concept of being, since otherwise we would have no conception of substance. Since it is not sensed directly, substance would be entirely unknown and not even a "something I know not what" unless there were a simple concept common to it and accidents (which are sensed directly).[16] But the only concept that could serve this purpose is the concept of being. A similar line of reasoning can be applied to God and creatures. Hence, we either have to admit that God and substance are entirely unknown, or grant that 'being' is univocal. Since the former is clearly unacceptable, the latter must hold.

These arguments establish that we have a univocal concept of being. However, they do not show that it is the primary object of our intellect, since it has yet to be established that this concept covers everything: that it is "adequate" in the sense that it is univocally predicable *in quid* of whatever the intellect can grasp.[17] Here some care is required, for Scotus thinks that, strictly speaking, no concept is adequate in the sense called for, although our concept of being comes closest.[18] It turns out that 'being' is not univocally predicable *in quid* of either ultimate differentiae or the proper attributes of being (*passiones entis*), although it is predicable of each of them *in quale* (n. 151). Let's look at his reasoning.

A differentia is *ultimate* if it does not itself have a differentia. Most familiar examples of differentiae are composite: substances are differentiated into animate and inanimate by 'living', for example, which itself can be resolved into the different kinds of living – life characterized by nutritive and reproductive functions only, life characterized by the further powers of locomotion, and so on. Only when we reach differentiae that are not themselves further decomposable will we have reached the ultimate differentiae, which are therefore purely qualitative. Scotus, however, leaves open the identification of which differentiae are ultimate.[19] Now Scotus offers two proofs that 'being' is not univocally predicated *in quid* of ultimate differentiae. First, if 'being' is univocally predicable of two distinct differentiae, these differentiae must be beings that are themselves distinguished from one another by proper differentiating features, which, in their turn, are distinct differentiae (since the original pair were distinct). If these latter differentiae include being quidditatively, the same line of reasoning applies to them. Therefore, to avoid an infinite regress, there must be some indecomposable differentiae that do not include being quidditatively, that is, differentiae of which 'being' is not predicated *in quid* (n. 132).[20] Second, just as a composite being is composed of act and potency, so too a composite concept is composed of an actual and potential concept, that is, a determinable and a determining concept. Since every concept not irreducibly simple is resolvable into irreducibly simple concepts, we only need to consider the latter. They must likewise be composed of determinable and determining elements. But since they are irreducibly simple, neither component can be further decomposed. Hence, an irreducibly simple concept must consist of two indecomposable concepts. One is purely determinable, with nothing determining it, namely, being; the other has nothing determinable in it but is purely determining, namely, an ultimate differentia. By definition, being cannot be predicated *in quid* of the latter (n. 133).

A proper attribute is a feature that includes its subject in its definition, though not conversely.[21] For instance, *odd* is a proper attribute of number, since in explaining what 'odd' means we need to speak of number, but we can explain 'number' without speaking of odd or even (despite the fact that every number is necessarily odd or even). Hence, a proper attribute does not belong to the essence of its subject, even if it is conjoined to it necessarily, as the property *risible* is necessarily present in all human beings. Scotus identifies three proper attributes of being: *one*, *true*, and *good*. These features are coextensive with being, but each adds something distinctive to the notion of a being, something apart from being itself. What each one is, then, involves something other than being itself, and so 'being' cannot be predicated *in quid* of its proper attributes (n. 134).[22]

Scotus concludes that we can say that being is the primary object of the intellect and the proper subject of metaphysics only with the qualification that ultimate differentiae and the proper attributes of being are included not quidditatively but in a derivative fashion. Indeed, 'being' is predicable *in quale* of them. Furthermore, since ultimate differentiae are constituents of beings (although purely qualitative in themselves), and the proper attributes of being characterize all beings as such, Scotus says that they are "virtually" contained under being.[23] Hence, the primary object of metaphysics is *being*, which is predicable, essentially or denominatively, of all there is.

There remains a serious challenge to Scotus's account of metaphysics. Two things are *different* when there is some real common factor that is combined in each item with a real distinguishing element. Such is the case with coordinate species under their proximate genus: they share the genus as a real common factor, but each is set apart from the other by the presence of a differentia, which, in combination with the genus, produces each species. Two things are *diverse* when there is no real common factor and hence no foundation for a distinguishing element. Such is, traditionally, the case with the ten categories: they are diverse from one another, since they do not share any real common factor. Their diversity is the result of the ontological gaps between them. Equally, God and creatures were thought to be diverse, since there was no reality common to them; the distance between the finite and the infinite seemed unbridgeable.

Now Scotus's account of metaphysics seems to replace the ontological diversity among the ten categories, and between God and creature, with mere difference. On the one hand, if 'being' is univocally predicable *in quid* of the ten categories, then it seems as though it will be the supreme genus above them all.[24] But Aristotle and Porphyry were taken to offer cogent arguments against there being a single category for all of reality.[25] On the other hand, if God and creatures are merely different and not diverse, then there is some real factor common to God and creatures. This undermines God's transcendence. Furthermore, it would mean that God could not be simple, but rather a real composition of common and differentiating factors.

The challenge facing Scotus, then, is to explain how his account of metaphysics can avoid these unwelcome consequences. His response involves many of the distinctive features of his metaphysics: the formal and modal distinctions, the transcendentals, the account of the structure of composite beings. We'll return to the nature of metaphysics by way of conclusion in Section VI, after examining some of the technical aspects of Scotus's metaphysics in the following sections.

II. IDENTITY AND DISTINCTNESS

II.1. Real Distinction and Distinction of Reason

Scotus holds that two items are *really distinct* from one another if and only if they are separable: one can exist without the other, at least by divine power.[26] More precisely, they are said to be "distinct as one thing (*res*) and another" if and only if they are separable. This applies to actually separated things as well as to things and their potentially separated parts, whether the parts be physical or metaphysical. Such a real distinction holds between Socrates and Plato, Socrates and his hand, prime matter and substantial form, items belonging to different categories, and so on; there is no further requirement that the items so distinguished be "things" in a full-blooded sense. Conversely, Scotus maintains that items are *really identical* if and only if they are not really distinct – that is, if and only if neither can exist without the other, even by divine power.[27]

Yet real identity does not entail complete sameness. For, as we shall see, Scotus holds that really identical items can nevertheless have distinct properties – in modern terms, that the Indiscernibility of Identicals fails – in virtue of their being formally or modally distinct. The latter can also be called "real" distinctions in a broad sense, not to be confused with the distinction of one thing from another described in the preceding paragraph. For the formal and the modal distinctions mark out differences that exist independently of any activity on the part of the intellect.[28] On that score, they are to be contrasted with a *distinction of reason*, or conceptual distinction, which is at least partially mind-made: today may be thought of as yesterday's tomorrow or tomorrow's yesterday, for instance, or Venus conceived of as the Morning Star and as the Evening Star. In technical terms, the intellect is a total or a partial cause of the conceptual distinction. Furthermore, there may be some ground in reality for the mind's drawing a conceptual distinction, a ground that may even cause the mind to do so.[29] But even if there is, what makes a distinction conceptual, rather than real in the broad sense, is not whether there is some objective ground in reality for the distinction (which is irrelevant) but whether the distinction is the product of some sort of mental activity. The formal and modal distinctions, however, mark out genuine differences in the world that would be present even if there were no minds at all.

II.2. Formal Distinction

The core intuition behind Scotus's formal distinction is, roughly, that existential inseparability does not entail identity in definition, backed up by the conviction that this is a fact about the way things are rather than how we conceive of them.[30] Since formally distinct items are existentially inseparable, they are really identical, in the sense just defined. Hence, the formal distinction only applies to a single real thing. In Scotus's terminology, it is "less" than a distinction of one thing from another. Now some really identical items may differ in their definitions. More precisely, they may differ in *ratio*, which is a generalization of the strict notion of Aristotelian 'definition' or account: a *ratio*, like a definition, picks out the feature or set

of features that make something to be what it is, although it need not
do so by genus and specific differentia. All definitions are *rationes*
but not conversely: there are items that lack definitions yet do have
a set of features that make them what they are – the highest genera, potencies, the four causes, accidental unities, and so on. Thus
items that are formally distinct have nonidentical definitions or
rationes; that is, the *ratio* of one does not include that of the other. For
example, the psychological faculties of intellect and will are really
identical with the soul but formally distinct from one another, since
what it is to be an intellect does not include the will, and what it is
to be a will does not include the intellect.[31] Furthermore, both real
identity and definitional nonidentity are independent of any activity of the intellect. We discover *rationes* through the intellect but do
not create them.[32] Hence, the distinction between formally distinct
items seems to be present in the world, not even partially caused by
the intellect. It is therefore 'real' in the broad sense.

The formal distinction is central to Scotus's metaphysics. He
holds, for example, that there is a formal distinction between each of
the following (within an individual thing): the genus and specific differentia; the essence and its proper attributes; the faculties of the soul
and the soul itself; the Persons of the Trinity and the divine essence;
the uncontracted common nature and the individual differentia –
and this list is not exhaustive.[33] The presence of formally distinct
items within a thing provides a real basis for our deployment of different concepts regarding that thing, which are thereby anchored in
reality. For, by definition, formally distinct items exhibit different
properties, and these can serve as the real basis for our distinct concepts. Without multiplying the number of things, we can draw finer
distinctions in the world. Yet even if we do not multiply things,
we seem to have multiplied something. What are the items distinguished by the formal distinction? More exactly, to what are we
ontologically committed by using the formal distinction?

Scotus offers a parallel in *Op. Ox.* 4, d. 46, q. 3, n. 3: just as a real distinction in the strict sense distinguishes one thing (*res*) from another,
so too the formal distinction distinguishes one 'thinglet' (*realitas*: the
diminutive of *res*) or 'formality' from another. He elsewhere calls
them "beingnesses," formal objects, intentions, real *rationes*, and
formal *rationes*. The variety of his terminology suggests that Scotus
didn't think a great deal depended on it; after all, formally distinct

items are still really identical. More important are his explicit statements about how to express the formal distinction, since here Scotus does seem concerned precisely with ontological commitment.[34] For example, Scotus carefully distinguishes "A is not formally the same as B" from "A and B are not formally the same" on the grounds that the latter might be taken to imply plurality through its conjunctive subject (n. 2). He likewise rejects "The formality A is distinct from the formality B" since it seems to be committed to the existence of formalities, and indeed to a plurality of them (n.10, 343b); the latter problem is bypassed in "The formality A is formally distinct from the formality B," which involves only formal distinctness and not distinctness *simpliciter* (n. 13). In general, Scotus seems to prefer taking "formally" as a modal operator: "A is not formally B" (n. 4).[35] This formulation minimizes the ontological commitments of the formal distinction, since on its face, it does not require the existence of multiple property bearers within one and the same subject but merely asserts that a particular relation does not hold among two "ways" (A and B) that a thing can be. These ways are real in the broad sense, of course, but need not be understood on the model of things.[36]

Now even if Scotus avoids multiplying entities in things through the formal distinction (a highly contested point), another difficulty remains. Given that the formal distinction is real in the broad sense, must there not then be some degree of complexity in its subject? The formal distinction holds in reality prior to the operation of the intellect. Even if there are not distinct thinglike property bearers in a subject, then, it nevertheless seems as though no thing to which a formal distinction applies can be simple. This would rule out any formal distinction in God.

Scotus argues that the reality of the formal distinction is compatible with God's simplicity. Real composition, for Scotus, is a matter of one item's being in potency to and perfected by the activity of another item: the genus is in potency to the (formally distinct) differentia, for example, which actualizes it as the species.[37] But there is no potency in God at all. God's essence is not in potency to the Persons of the Trinity, nor are the Persons in potency to one another. Hence, the formal distinctions among the Persons and between each Person and God's essence do not introduce any real composition in God, and so divine simplicity can be maintained. Scotus says that the formally distinct elements in God are contained in such a way as to make up a unity (they are contained "unitively"), but not through real composition.[38]

II.3. Modal Distinction

Scotus introduces and describes the modal distinction in *Ord.* 1, d. 8, pars 1, q. 3, nn. 138–40. It is meant to be an even lesser distinction than the formal distinction, but nevertheless real in the broad sense. The core intuition behind Scotus's modal distinction is, roughly, that some natures come in a range of degrees that are inseparably a part of what they are, and that this is a fact about the way things are rather than about how we conceive of them.[39] For instance, take an accidental form that admits of qualitative variation, say "whiteness in the tenth degree of intensity." The degree of intensity of the whiteness is not a differentia of the color: the particular whiteness is the color it is whether it is more or less bright; no formal or essential element in that shade of whiteness is altered by the different amounts of intensity it may have. Instead, the degree of brightness is what Scotus calls an *intrinsic mode* of the given nature, for it spells out how the nature exists: in this case, how intense the whiteness is.

Furthermore, the nature will be inseparable from the degree in which it occurs. While we can conceive whiteness apart from this particular degree of intensity, our concept is not adequate to the reality of the white thing before us, which, after all, actually does have that degree of intensity. Nor can the mode be conceived apart from the nature. It makes no sense to speak of degrees without saying of what they are the degrees. Hence, the intrinsic mode is not formally distinct from its nature, since the mode can only be (adequately) grasped through the *ratio* or definition of the nature.[40] Finally, it is clear that the modal distinction is real in the broad sense, since the nature and its intrinsic mode are really conjoined in the thing, prior to any activity of the intellect; something really has a given degree of brightness whether anyone thinks so or not.

Scotus uses the modal distinction in cases of the intensification and remission of forms (discussed in Section III.2.3), where some qualitative feature admits continuous variation along a given range: the intensity of color, the amount of heat, the strength of desire, and the like. But Scotus's most important metaphysical application of the modal distinction is found in his account of infinite and finite being, to which we now turn.

III. THE STRUCTURE OF REALITY

III.1. Being and the Transcendentals

Being is common to the ten categories and so is not contained under any of them: it is *transcendental* (*Ord.* 1, d. 8, pars 1, q. 3, n. 114). The proper attributes of being are likewise transcendental, for otherwise they could not be proper attributes. Scotus identifies two further kinds of items that are not contained under any category: (1) the "disjunctive attributes"; and (2) pure perfections.

Items included under (1) are coextensive with being and are immediately predicated of it, dividing it by a disjunction of properties, such as "infinite or finite," "necessary or possible," "act or potency," "prior or posterior," and the like in limitless number (*Ord.* 1, d. 38, pars 2, and d. 39, qq. 1–5, n. 13).[41] These are, it seems, primarily logical or conceptual constructions from simpler real attributes; Scotus never gives any sign that he holds there to be a single attribute that has an internal disjunctive structure. Hence, they add nothing to his ontology. Nevertheless, they can be said to divide being completely and thereby qualify as transcendentals.

Scotus understands a pure perfection to be a property that, roughly, it is better to have than not.[42] This formula needs to be made precise in two ways. First, we should not take the contrast implicit in "than not" as pointing to the absence of the perfection – since any positive being is better than mere nonexistence – but rather as compared with any other positive being with which it is incompatible. Second, the perfection must make its possessor better absolutely speaking: wisdom, for instance, makes its possessor better no matter what kind of thing its possessor might be, even if wisdom were contrary to its nature. Dogs cannot be wise and still remain dogs. Yet it would be better for the dog to cease being a dog and to become wise than not. In short, pure perfections are not relative to kinds. Some of their more important properties are as follows: all pure perfections are by definition compossible (*Quodl.* q. 5, n. 20); each pure perfection is irreducibly simple (*Quodl.* q. 1, nn. 8–12) and compatible with infinity (*Quodl.* q. 5, n. 23); they are all equally perfect (*Ord.* 1, d. 8, q. 1)[43]; and no pure perfection is formally unshareable (*incommunicabilis*), an important result for the Trinity (*Quodl.* q. 5, n. 32). They are transcendentals, by definition, since they apply to things regardless of their kind. Unlike the other transcendentals, they are not simply coextensive with being; dogs are beings but not wise. Nor are they simply proper to God alone, since dogs have life as God does, albeit limited life. Rather, their extension may vary.

Since the transcendentals are not contained under any category, they can only be the subject of a science that investigates items outside the categories: metaphysics, which Scotus etymologically explains as "the transcending science, that is, the science of transcendentals" (*In Metaph.* prol., n. 18). This description of metaphysics does not exclude anything, since being is one of the transcendentals, but it gives a particular direction and focus to Scotus's investigations. One salient problem is how the transcendentals are related to "nontranscendentals," namely, the ten categories. Scotus offers the following account[44]: being, "the first of the transcendentals," is quantified into infinite and finite, the latter of which is immediately divided into the ten categories. Now the sense in which being is "quantified" requires some explanation, since it has nothing to do with the category of Quantity. Scotus tells us in *Quodl.* q. 6, n. 18 that there is a transcendental sense of 'quantity' that is more properly called "magnitude," which measures the greatness or intrinsic excellence of what a thing is.[45] (This must be transcendental since greatness is at least in part a function of the pure perfections.) Very roughly, then, magnitude measures excellence among beings or their natures, and this can be of either infinite or some finite degree. The scale of excellence defines a range along which beings can be placed, since their natures exhibit varying degrees of excellence. Quantified being is, in short, an intrinsic mode of being.

Scotus's account of the structure of reality thus has at its foundation a modal distinction between being and its infinite and finite manifestations. Just as a given quality, such as whiteness, can be present in distinct intensive quantities while still remaining whiteness completely, so too can being be present in infinite and finite excellence while still remaining being completely. Being, therefore, appears in two modes: infinite and finite. Finite being divides immediately into the ten categories.

With this claim, Scotus has the first part of his solution to the difficulty posed at the end of Section I.3. (Worries about real composition
are addressed in the conclusion.) For, as we saw in the discussion of
the modal distinction in Section II.3, a modal distinction is less than
a formal distinction, for differences in modes do not affect the formal
content of that of which they are the modes. Hence, modal distinctions cannot function as differentiae and so are not related to their
subjects as to genera. This conclusion seems correct. Different intensities of whiteness are not different in kind, but merely different
in degree. In the present case, Scotus infers that *being* cannot be a
genus, since its distinguishing features are modes rather than differentiae. (Nor is *finite being* a genus above the categories, since there is
no mediating factor for the division.) Being is "above" the categories,
but not in such a way as to be a genus. The univocity of being does
not lead to a single highest genus. Hence, the categories can still be
the highest genera of things; there are just more things than can be
contained under genera – namely, the transcendentals.

III.2. The Categories

Scotus holds that the division of finite being into the ten categories
is immediate and sufficient: that there must be precisely these ten
categories and no others.[46] The distinction is not merely logical, but
"taken from essences themselves" (*In Praed.* q. 11, n. 26). Since there
is no higher genus over the ten categories, however, the only way to
clarify the nature of each category is to consider it independently
of the others and see what its defining characteristics are – to look
at the essences themselves. Scotus follows Aristotle in devoting the
bulk of his attention to the first four categories: Substance, Quantity,
Quality, and Relation. A few words about each are in order.

III.2.1. SUBSTANCE. There must be objects capable of independent existence, Scotus reasons in *In Metaph.* 7, q. 2, n. 24, since otherwise
there would be an infinite regress of purely dependent beings. These
self-sufficient objects, the underlying subjects of predication, are substances. Now substances are beings primarily and *per se* (*Quodl.* q. 3,
n. 13). They are also unities, in a sense to be explored in Section V.3,
and hence *per se* one. More exactly, Scotus holds that a substance is
really identical with its essence though formally distinct from it.[47]

The essential parts that make up a primary substance, namely, matter and form, combine to produce a unified whole. Other features of substance, such as its ability to remain numerically one while receptive of contraries, flow from its existential independence and unity.

These are several of the ways in which substance is distinguished from elements of the remaining nine categories, that is, from accident. Scotus is a realist about accidents. He holds that they have some being of their own that is not simply reducible to the being of the substances in which they naturally are present, and indeed that this was Aristotle's view (*In Metaph.* 7, q. 4, n. 17). Yet from a metaphysical point of view, there seems to be a fundamental distinction between the category of Substance, on the one hand, and the nine accidental categories, on the other hand: the former includes items that are capable of self-sufficient existence, whereas none of the latter do. This division between substances and accidents seems no less immediate than that into ten diverse categories – if anything, it seems more fundamental, since the nine accidental categories could be diversified after the fundamental distinction of substance and accident; it is plausible to take them as subspecies, as kinds of accidents. After all, as one common mediaeval catch-phrase had it, what it is to be an accident is to inhere in something: *esse accidentis est inesse*.

Scotus argues that this line of reasoning badly misconstrues the nature of accidents, and that properly understood, accidents do not essentially involve inherence (*In Metaph.* 7, q. 1). He begins by distinguishing the actual union of an existent accident with its existent subject from the dependence an accident may have of its nature on a substance of its nature. The latter needs proof in a way in which the former does not (n. 9).[48] Furthermore, by "of its nature" Scotus means what is included *per se* in the quidditative concept of an accident, as opposed to whatever might be really identical with it or a necessary concomitant of it (n. 14). Proper attributes, for example, fall outside the strict quidditative definitions of their subjects, as we have seen in Section I.3. They are nevertheless really identical with their subjects.

Once these distinctions have been drawn, Scotus declares that inherence characterizes accidents much the way proper attributes do their subjects: the inherence is really identical with the given accident and a necessary concomitant (barring divine power), but falls outside the essence of the accident properly speaking (n. 15). Otherwise, there would not be a single unified sense of 'being' that applies to substances and to accidents (n. 16); indeed, accidents are beings just as much as substances are even though substances have priority over accidents in a variety of ways (n. 30). Therefore, the contrast between substance and accidents, although real, is not quidditative.

III.2.2. QUANTITY. The category of Quantity is made up of items of which 'more' and 'less' can be predicated, and Aristotle suggests that it is divided into two kinds: (1) discrete quantities, such as numbers and utterances; and (2) continuous quantities, such as time, geometric surfaces, and places.[49] But these claims about Quantity are not sufficient to give it a unitary character. The predicability of 'more' and 'less' of any quantity may be a feature, and even a necessary feature, of quantities, but it cannot be a defining one; the essence of Quantity explains why 'more' and 'less' are predicable, not vice versa. Worse yet, the distinction between (1) and (2) just points up the problem: why think there is a single category at all, instead of the two distinct categories of discrete items and continuous items?

Scotus argues that there is a single feature that unifies Quantity: *homoeomerous divisibility*, that is, divisibility into parts of the same sort.[50] This is more important than *measure*, since all quantities are defined through whether their parts are joined or disjoined, but only discrete quantities immediately have a unit that can be used as a measure. (These remarks do not apply to the transcendental quantity described in Section III.1.) Quantities admit of more and less precisely because they have distinct parts, which allow for comparison. Thus, Quantity is a single unified category.

Homoeomerous divisibility applied to the two species of Quantity yields different results. Discrete quantities have parts that are of the same sort (the parts of numbers are numbers), and they are compared with one another by reference to the unit magnitude they naturally have *qua* discrete. But when applied to continuous quantities, Scotus thinks that homoeomerous divisibility entails a position known as "divisibilism": any continuous quantity is potentially (although not actually) infinitely divisible. For each part of a continuous quantity is itself continuous, and so capable of further division into divisible parts, and so on (*Ord.* 2, d. 2, pars 2, q. 5, nn. 332–53). Scotus is at pains to argue that the infinite divisibility of continuous quantities also has a further consequence, namely, that such quantities are not composed of indivisible elements ("atoms"), although they may consist in them.[51] The distinction may be explained as follows. Scotus allows that continuous quantities may include indivisibles: a line segment, for example, incorporates two indivisibles as its limit points. Furthermore, the potentially infinite divisibility of a continuous quantity suggests that there is a potentially infinite number of such indivisibles existing "in" the quantity. (More precisely, they *potentially* exist in a continuous quantity.) But it is quite another step to say that the continuous quantity is made out of such elements, even if there is a potentially infinite number of them.[52] Hence, although there may be indivisibles in a continuous magnitude, this does not entail that it is composed of them. Scotus provides two reasons to reject the claim. First, it would amount to a category mistake, since then continuous quantities would ultimately be composed of discrete indivisibles; that is, continuous quantities would ultimately turn out to be discrete quantities. Second, Scotus argues that indivisibles such as points, which have literally no extension, cannot be finitely "added up" to produce any finite magnitude – and since only a finite number of such indivisibles are actual, they cannot constitute a continuous quantity (*Lect.* 2, d. 2, pars 2, qq. 5–6, nn. 355–8). The upshot, then, is that continuous quantities may consist in, but not be composed of, indivisibles.

III.2.3. QUALITY. The category of Quality is made up of items having 'like' and 'unlike' predicated of them. The same question that arose for Quantity appears again in Quality, namely, whether there is anything that unifies the category. Aristotle lists four types of qualities: (1) habits and dispositions, and so mental events generally; (2) natural capacities and incapacities; (3) passible qualities and affections, such as bitterness and color; and (4) the shapes and figures of things. Scotus, remarkably, seems not to have made up his mind about the categorical status of this division. In his early work *In Praed.* qq. 30–6, he takes the unusual step of presenting two possible ways of addressing the unity of Quality. First, he proposes that Aristotle is not listing species but simply different "modes" of qualities, that is, accidental differentiae of various sorts of qualities (nn. 35–6).[53] After replying to the several questions that had been raised about Aristotle's list, though, Scotus proposes a second response: that

Aristotle was indeed enumerating the species of Quality and not mere modes, but that he made use of these accidental differentiae because the real differentiae of (1)–(4) are unknown (n. 65). Later, in discussing whether the categories are really distinct, Scotus remarks that two of the divisions of Quality are contained under (1) as a species, although he does not say which two (*In Metaph.* 5, qq. 5–6, n. 113). No simple account of the unity of Quality is forthcoming.

Qualities all admit of the more and the less. Some qualities admit a range of continuous variation, as for instance the brightness of a shade of color, the intensity of a desire, or the degree of temperature. If we think of starting at a given basepoint, the quality may be said to be intensified or remitted over the given range: *intensio et remissio formarum*. Yet if a quality is a simple form, how can it become more or less? Scotus argues that several initially plausible answers to this question have to be rejected. First, we cannot identify the different intensities with different species of the quality, so that different grades of temperature are literally different kinds of temperature, for there is no ready way to identify the atomic differentiae of an infinite number of determinables.[54] In light of Scotus's modal distinction, discussed above, this should seem especially plausible, since two different degrees of heat seem to differ not in kind but in degree, and, as Scotus argued previously, modal differences do not constitute formal differences.

A different strategy tries to explain the underlying metaphysics by appealing to the differential realization of the quality, either because the individual quality participates in its Form to a greater or lesser degree or because the quality is more or less actualized in the individual instance. Scotus rejects this strategy on several grounds, not least of which is that it is nonexplanatory. Differences in qualitative intensity reflect the differing extent to which a quality is somehow realized in a subject, but then these "differing extents" need as much explanation (and the same kind of explanation) as the qualitative variability they were supposed to explain.[55] Therefore, a different approach to the problem of qualitative variation is in order.

Scotus holds that qualities vary in degree by the presence of *parts* of the quality in question. That is, the correct explanation of more or less of a given qualitative intensity is through the presence or absence of homogeneous parts of that quality.[56] The brightness of light is measured in "candlepower" (the amount of light shed by a single candle). To produce a brighter light, add another lit candle, which becomes a new part of the overall light. Furthermore, it is the same sort of part: each part (lit candle) adds exactly the same thing to the whole (the light), but causes a change in the intensive quality of the light (brightness). And as with the brightness of light, so too with other intensive qualities – strength in horsepower, for example. Scotus argues that his theory will even work on more recalcitrant cases. For example, differences in color shades aren't clearly the product of amalgamating more of the same parts of the color; deeper blue doesn't seem to be made by adding more blue-parts (each equally blue as the next) to a given shade. But the model works here as well, Scotus maintains; we are misled by thinking of such parts as spatial parts.[57] The additional blue-parts are not next to the already existent ones, but, as it were, drawn on top of them, and anyone familiar with young children and crayons knows that this does produce a deeper shade of blue. Cases of qualitative variation are therefore reducible to quantitative differences in "parts" of the qualities.

III.2.4. RELATION. Scotus distinguishes beings into *absolute* and *non-absolute*, where the latter "expresses a condition of one thing in respect of another" (*Quodl.* q. 3, n. 12). The distinction serves to set apart items that involve some kind of reference to something else from those that do not. The categories of absolute being are the first three: Substance, Quantity, and Quality. The remaining seven categories, and paradigmatically the category of Relation, are non-absolute in that an item belonging to each depends for its being on something that is neither it nor its subject. However, this distinction does not capture what is unique to the category of Relation; if anything, it suggests that the nonabsolute categories could be amalgamated. Thus Scotus is led to draw another distinction among the nonabsolute categories: each involves a relation in its own fashion, but the relations may be *intrinsically* or *extrinsically* advenient.[58] The sense of this distinction is as follows: the category of Relation is the only category that is completely defined by the "reference to something else" (i.e., the relation) mentioned previously. In the remaining six categories, apart from the intrinsically advenient relation that defines their nature there must be a further extrinsically advenient relation, one that forms a condition for the categorical item to be present (*In Metaph.* 5, qq. 5–6, nn. 93–103). For example, the category of Action includes items such as *heating*, which by its nature involves a relation to something heated. But it is not sufficient for heating to exist that there be something with the active potency to heat, or indeed that there be something with the passive potency to be heated; there must also be an external factor that actualizes the active potency. That which actualizes the active potency is extrinsically related to the action of heating; it is a condition of there being any heating at all – similarly for the category of Passion. The remaining categories require other external circumstances: Place is a distinct kind of relative thing with its foundation in the thing located and the terminus in the place; Time replaces and is replaced by other items of the same sort in succession; Position is a relative thing that exists in the whole or the parts of a substance; State (*habitus*) is a relative thing that inheres in a body that is around or contained in another. Therefore, the category of Relation is uniquely definable as the category including all and only intrinsically advenient relations.

Scotus is a realist about relations: they are accidents that characterize individual subjects (*In Metaph.* 5, q. 11, n. 47), and at least some are really distinct from their subjects and from other accidents.[59] All relations, no matter what kind they are, have the distinctive feature that, although they are in one subject, they are directed "toward" another (nn. 62–3).[60] Suppose, for example, that Socrates is taller than Plato. In this case Socrates has a particular accident, namely, his height, and Plato likewise has his particular height; these are really distinct individual accidents, since they inhere in really distinct individual substances. Each is also really distinct from the substance in which it inheres, since Socrates or Plato could change in quantity and nevertheless remain in existence. Now if Socrates' height is greater than Plato's height, then a particular accident also exists in Socrates, namely, his tallness (relative to Plato). Socrates' height is called the *foundation* of the relation. Scotus argues that in general a relation is not the same as its foundation (n. 50): the inherence of Socrates' particular height in Socrates is a necessary but not sufficient condition for this relation to exist, since Socrates could remain the same height while Plato gradually grew taller than him.[61] Likewise Plato's particular height is necessary but not sufficient, since Socrates could shrink with age. Plato's height is called the *terminus* of the relation, and is what the relation of tallness in Socrates is "toward."[62] The relation itself inheres in Socrates, not in Socrates' height; accidents do not inhere in accidents. Socrates is thus the *subject* of the relation. The relation relates its subject to the thing that is the terminus: tallness is a relation that holds between Socrates and Plato, not between their accidents, although it only exists given the foundation in one and the terminus in the other. Socrates and Plato are what the relation relates.[63]

The relation of tallness in Socrates is itself a particular accident, really distinct from its foundation and its subject, since the latter could exist without the former if Plato were to grow. Now the preceding discussion does not address the ontological question of whether the tallness that inheres in Socrates is correctly analyzed as tallness-toward-Plato that inheres in Socrates – or, in a simpler and perhaps more appealing formulation, whether the relation in Socrates is the particular accident "taller-than-Plato."[64] There are two reasons to hold that it is not. First, if it were "taller-than-Plato," then its proper genus in the category of Relation would not be tallness but rather tallness-toward-Plato, and there would be at least as many species as there are individual cases of tallness. Second, individuals cannot appear in Aristotelian definitions; if we take the individuality of the accident to permit inclusion of the individual as part of the formula of the accident, then the individual will differ in essence from its species, which cannot happen. For these two reasons, then, Scotus concludes that an individual relation does not incorporate an essential reference to the very thing to which it is related. Yet a problem remains: what distinguishes Socrates's being taller than Plato from his being taller than Antisthenes?

This last difficulty is an instance of the more general problem of how accidents are individuated. Scotus clearly holds that relations are individualized: he tells us that "there are as many paternities in the one who is the father as there are filiations in the diverse sons" (*In Metaph.* 5, qq. 12–4, n. 28), to cite one instance among many. Scotus is less forthcoming than one might wish on this point, but an answer in line with his discussion of numerically distinct accidents (*In Metaph.* 5, q. 7) is that an individual relation has a double principle of individuation, namely, through its foundation and through its terminus. The terminus accounts for the directed character an individual relation has without entering into the formula of its essence, any more than its subject does. Hence, the tallness in Socrates is tallness with respect to Plato, but it is not itself a "tallness-toward-Plato":

its feature of being "toward-Plato" belongs to its essence no more than its being in Socrates.

Scotus considers and rejects the view that all relations are somehow merely conceptual or mind dependent, that, in the slogan of the British Idealists, "only thought relates."[65] Socrates is really taller than Plato independent of any mental activity. It is the paradigm of what Scotus calls a *real relation*: a relation for which the real existence of its foundation and terminus are jointly sufficient.[66] Nor should the category of Relation be divided into real relations and merely conceptual relations; as Scotus tartly remarks, "*rose* is not divided into real roses and merely conceptual roses, for they are two modes of being of the same thing" (*In Metaph.* 5, q. 11, n. 42).[67] Instead, Scotus adopts, with qualifications, Aristotle's list of three modes of relations[68]: (1) first-mode relations are numerical relations founded on Quantity, whether they are determinate or not; (2) second-mode relations are between the active and the passive, founded on one of the absolute categories; and (3) third-mode relations are of "the measurable to the measure," which may be founded on any category. The last calls for special comment, since it plays a key role in Scotus's metaphysics.

Three features set third-mode relations apart from first- and second-mode relations. First, as Aristotle remarks, in the case of third-mode relations, the normal ordering of a relation is inverted: something is relationally characterized as "the knowable," for example, because there can be knowledge with regard to it, not conversely. Second, third-mode relations do not entail the real existence of the corresponding co-relations: something may well be knowable without anyone knowing it (the "nonmutuality" condition). Third, as traditionally conceived, the nonmutuality condition suggests that third-mode relations serve as a model of how independent and dependent items are related: the knower is dependent on the knowable for his knowledge, but the knowable is what it is independently of there being any actual knowledge.

The second and third features of third-mode relations, namely, the nonmutuality condition and the dependence condition, are traditionally taken to define third-mode relations. Yet Scotus holds that this is not the case, and that the traditional reading depends on an improper conflation of mutuality (which is a matter of co-relation) and dependence. Rather, Scotus maintains, the dependence that characterizes at least some third-mode relations is of two distinct types (*In Metaph.* 5, q. 11, n. 60). There is dependence in perfection, which I take to be something of the following sort: knowledge must "measure up" to the knowable, in the sense that knowledge is judged to be such in virtue of its accuracy in mirroring the knowable. Second, there is existential dependence: knowledge cannot exist without the knowable, but not conversely. As for nonmutuality, Scotus argues that third-mode relations are mutual, but their relata differ as regards act and potency, unlike the case of first- and second-mode relations (*In Metaph.* 5, qq. 12–14, nn. 100–4). The "nonmutuality" thesis appears to be only a confused way of getting at the act–potency difference. Of course, Scotus does not mean to undermine the genuine dependencies that such relations involve. Mutuality is a matter of the corresponding co-relation (the correlative). This, after all, must somehow be present in order to serve as a denomination for the independent element: the knowable is only knowable *qua* the potential relation it may stand in to a knower. Nor does mutuality entail mutual dependence.

Scotus makes it clear that he holds the co-relation of a third-mode relation to preserve the direction of dependence. Since a relation may be terminated at something absolute, a third-mode co-relation may simply take the entire absolute being, its subject, as the foundation – since the foundation need not be distinct from the relation or, in this instance, the co-relation. When these conditions obtain, the destruction of the co-relation does not produce any change in its foundation, the original relation's terminus. And this is precisely the account Scotus gives of the relation between God the creator and creatures.[69] In short, it is possible for a third-mode co-relation to produce only what has come to be known as a "Cambridge change," a change that takes place entirely in one of the relata without any ontological shift in the other. This suggests a point that Scotus does not make explicitly but which would, I think, be quite to his taste: a third-mode correlative, under the conditions described in this paragraph, is nothing more than an extrinsic denomination of its subject. (God is not essentially a Creator, although we are essentially creatures.) On this interpretation, Scotus can, quite rightly, deny the traditional view that the co-relation of a real third-mode relation is a relation of reason. God really is correctly described as the Creator regardless of whether there are any minds to think so.

Scotus applies his analysis of third-mode relations at many points in his philosophy, perhaps most notably in his technical definitions of intuitive and abstractive cognition (*Quodl.* q. 13, nn. 34–47). But one particularly important application in metaphysics is his analysis of the relation between cause and effect as a form of dependence. Let us now turn to this.

IV. CAUSALITY

IV.1. The Causal Order

Being, as we have seen in Section III.1, is transcendentally divided by disjunctive attributes. One such attribute is the division "prior or posterior": beings may be ordered to one another with respect to some kind of priority or posteriority.[70] Instants of time, for example, fall into a single linear order of "earlier" and "later"; Scotus calls this the "order of duration." Equally, we can rate beings, or perhaps their natures, by how "perfect and noble in essence" they are: this is Scotus's "order of eminence" (*De primo princ.* 1.7).[71] Neither of these instances of priority and posteriority is causal, of course. The items ranked by each are independent of one another with regard to their position in the respective orderings. By contrast, other relations of priority and posteriority involve (essential) dependence, namely, when the prior could be without the posterior, but not conversely (*De primo princ.* 1.8). Accidents depend on substance this way; children likewise depend on their parents in this way, at least for coming into being (although not for their continued existence). Yet Scotus construes dependence as more than just necessary connection, explaining it as follows: "Even if the prior were necessarily to cause the posterior, and hence not be able to be without it, this is not because it requires the posterior for its being, but conversely" (ibid.). There is a distinction to be drawn between (1) what is requisite for the being of *X*, and (2) what follows from postulating the being of *X*, even if it follows from the very nature of *X*.[72] Suppose that *A* is a necessary cause of *B*, and that *B* necessarily causes *C*. If *B* exists, then both *A* and *C* must exist. Yet *A* and *C* are not on a par, since *B* depends on *A* as its cause, but not on *C*. Of course, not all causes are necessary causes, but Scotus holds that there can be dependence even when only necessary causes are involved.

The order of dependence, though, is not identical with the causal order; it is more general. First, there can be dependence where we would not ordinarily speak of causality. A substance is not normally the "cause" of its contingent accidents, nor is a subject the cause of its proper attributes. Second, Scotus specifically introduces a noncausal kind of dependence that plays a key role in his proof of God's existence: his "third division" of the order of dependence (*De primo princ.* 1.11–4), which comes in two varieties. Although noncausal, this dependence relation is induced by causal relations, in particular by the presence of a common cause.

A given cause can have one or several effects, and each of these effects can, in turn, be itself a cause that may have one or several further effects. (These effects-turned-causes can produce their own effects either of themselves or in combination with other partial co-causes, of course.) Thus we have a partial order defined over all the effects of a given cause. Adjacent elements in the partial order are *proximate*, nonadjacent elements *remote*. Now suppose that *A* is the proximate cause of both *B* and *C*, but that *A* cannot cause *C* until it has caused *B*. (It's not that *B* concurs in causing *C*; *A* just has to get *B* out of its system, so to speak, before causing *C*.)[73] In this case, says Scotus, *C* depends on *B*. The relation is not causal, since neither is the cause of the other,[74] although they have a common proximate cause. This is Scotus's first kind of noncausal dependence relation.

For the second, suppose that *A* has the two proximate effects *B* and *C*, but further that *B* causes *D*. In this case *D* is the proximate effect of *B* but the remote effect of *A* (or equally *B* is the proximate cause of *D* and *A* is the remote cause of *D*). Here *C* and *D* have a common cause, namely *A*, although the former is a proximate effect of *A* and the latter a remote effect of *A*. In such a situation, says Scotus, the remote effect depends on the proximate effect of their common cause – that is, *D* depends on *C*. But the relation ship of *C* and *D*, again, is not itself causal, for neither is the cause of the other. This is Scotus's second kind of noncausal dependence relation.

The causal order is therefore a specific kind of dependence, namely, one in which the dependence of the posterior on the prior is direct, having to do with the exercise of powers. This is why causality falls within the province of metaphysics. For the division "to be why another is" (cause) and "to be due to another" (effect) classifies beings independently of anything specifically physical, that is, regardless of change or motion.[75]

Scotus's "fourth division" (De primo princ. 1.15) is the "well-known" classification of the four types of causes and their corresponding effects: formal, final, material, and efficient.[76] Each kind of cause can be given a purely metaphysical interpretation.[77] Furthermore, each produces its own proper result: the formal cause produces what is formed (formatum), the material cause what is made material (materiatum), the final cause its end (finitum), and the efficent cause its effect.[78] These results may coincide in reality, as when the material and formal causes constitute a single thing: for instance, the marble and the shape are combined by the sculptor to produce a statue. The material and final causes are intrinsic, whereas the efficient and final causes are typically extrinsic. In this example, the sculptor is the efficient cause and his payment (say) the final cause.

The example of the sculptor, simple as it is, illustrates an important thesis about causality: multiple causes can act concurrently to produce a given effect.[79] Scotus argues that the four causes not only combine to produce a given effect, but that they are *essentially ordered* in their production of one and the same thing (De primo princ. 2.29–32), a conclusion explored below. Scotus's notion of an "essential order" of causes is fundamental to his metaphysics. Causes of the same kind can form an essential order, too, or they can form only an accidental order. But before we can explore this notion, we need first to distinguish per se from accidental causes.[80] Briefly, a cause is per se if its effect is a per se object of its causal power (as defined in Section I). That is, it brings about the given effect by its very nature. Builders construct houses, and so they are the per se cause of buildings; they may also create traffic congestion by blocking roads, but they are only accidental or incidental causes of traffic congestion. More precisely, accidental causes are not immediately related to the content of the power being exercised in the act of causing a given effect, whereas per se causes are so related.

Scotus holds that an essential order consists in items that are related by a priority ordering in either a causal line or in the orders of eminence or a variety of noncausal dependencies sketched in the first two paragraphs of this section, where essential orders are set apart from accidental orders by three features[81]: (1) the posterior depends *per se* on the prior insofar as the posterior is in its turn a cause; (2) the causality of the prior has a distinct character since it is more perfect or complete; and (3) all members of the series are simultaneous. The key idea at work here is that a cause cannot only cause its effect but can also cause the causality of its effect. Consider the following example. I hold a stick in my hand, and with it I move a stone; the stick has the power to move the stone, since it does so, but it can only exercise that causal power because of my activity. The stick is the proximate cause of the stone's motion, and I am the remote cause of the stone's motion; we could say with equal justice either that the stick moves the stone or that I do. But more important, I am the proximate cause of the stick's causality, since the stick only causes the stone's motion through my exercise of my causal power. The stick might have the power to move the stone (the way a soap bubble, say, never could), but the power is inert until I exercise my powers. Thus, my power to bring about the stick's causal activity is more perfect and complete than the stick's mere power to do so. Furthermore, it is clear that the stick exercises its causality to move the stone only so long as I am exercising my powers; the stick's causality must be concurrent with my exercise of my causality. Hence, they are simultaneous.

The power of Scotus's conception of essential orders may not be immediately evident. I will look at two of the many applications of his theory: the relationship among the four causes, and, in the next subsection, the claim that at least some essential orders must have a first cause.

Scotus holds that the four causes are essentially ordered in their causation of one and the same thing. He argues as follows.[82] The type of order possessed by the four causes is clear from the order exemplified by the end and the efficient cause: the end causes the causality of the efficient cause because the efficient cause only causes (efficiently) in virtue of its pursuit of the end. If the end were not pursued, the efficient cause would not be set into motion. This is an essential ordering, as described previously. Hence, the sort of essential dependence that obtains among the four causes is that of one cause depending on another for its causality. The efficient would not be moved to effecting, unless the end moved it (metaphorically) into action. The efficient depends on the final for its causality.[83]

Now if there is an essential order between the final and the efficient causes, it cannot be a function of noncausal dependence, since the final and the efficient causes do not have a common cause. Rather, it must fall under Scotus's fourth division as a straightforward order among causes. The final cause need not cause the existence of the efficient cause, of course; the payment does not make the sculptor exist. Rather, the final cause (payment) causes the efficient cause (sculptor) to exercise his efficient powers to produce the effect (the statue). Hence, the final cause is prior to the efficient cause, *qua* cause, because the final cause (finally) causes the efficient cause to produce the effect.

The efficient cause, of course, does not finally cause the matter, nor does it finally cause the form. Yet it does efficiently cause the causality of the matter as well as efficiently causing the causality of the form. The sculptor combines the matter and form in such a way as to produce a statue. That is, the efficient cause causes the matter to be informed (in the way that it is), and it causes the form to be "enmattered" (in the way that it is). Hence, the efficient (efficiently) causes the causality of both the matter and the form. This means that the efficient is the common cause of the causality of the matter and the causality of the form (2.32). Furthermore, of these two common effects of the efficient cause, the matter is prior since it possesses some being of its own (see Section V.1); hence, the material cause is prior to the formal cause in Scotus's first variety of noncausal dependence.

Scotus can combine these different sorts of essential ordering together to yield a single unified essential ordering of causes by applying his "transitivity theorem:" if A is prior to B, and B is prior to C, then A is prior to C (*De primo princ.* 2.5). This theorem does not restrict the priorities to the same sort of dependence.[84] Therefore, the final (*qua* final) is prior to the efficient (*qua* efficient) in virtue of final causality; the efficient (*qua* efficient) is the common (efficient) cause of the material (*qua* material) and the formal (*qua* formal), and hence is prior to both in virtue of efficient causality; the material (*qua* material) is the more proximate result of the same common cause, and hence is prior to the formal (*qua* formal). This is the sense in which the four causes can be united in producing one and the same result.

IV.2. The Existence of God

Scotus applies the technical apparatus developed in the preceding subsection in his proof of God's existence.[85] His proof is discussed at length in Chapter 6. Here I will only look at Scotus's application of his analysis of causality in his argument that an infinity of essentially ordered things is impossible, which runs as follows[86]:

> An infinity of things that are essentially ordered is impossible... Proof: The totality of caused things that are essentially ordered is caused, and so it is caused by some cause that is no part of the totality, for then it would be the cause of itself; for the whole totality of dependent things is dependent, and not on anything belonging to that totality.

This dense and intricate argument – call it the "Causal Argument" – is the engine of Scotus's entire proof. It is meant to establish the existence of at least one uncaused cause of the totality or series of caused things that constitute an essential order. Scotus states the Causal Argument in its full generality, without referring to the kind of causality at issue: it works for any order of causes where one generates series of causes. Here he applies it to efficient causality; it will later be applied to finality without any modifications (3.29–30). Once Scotus has used the Causal Argument to deduce the existence of uncaused causes in each distinct causal order – there is a completely different proof for the noncausal order of eminence – he then argues that it must be one and the same item that is the first in each, and from there it is a short step to proving that this one first cause has the relevant divine attributes. The Causal Argument, then, supports the rest of Scotus's proof. But what exactly does it prove?

Scotus takes the Causal Argument to rule out the possibility of an infinity of things that are essentially ordered (for some essential order, that is; hereafter I drop the reminder). Something like this point has traditionally been the weak point of causal arguments for God's existence, since there seems to be no reason why we could not have a series in which any given element always has a proximate prior cause. Yet even before we unpack Scotus's proof, a quick glance shows that he isn't trying to show that between any pair of elements in the series there must be only a finite number of other elements in the series. That point simply isn't addressed. What he does try to show in the Causal Argument is that any ascending series of essentially ordered things must be bounded by something that is simply first with respect to that order. A moment's reflection on the etymology of 'infinite' confirms this point, since *in-finitum* literally meant unbounded. Hence, the Causal Argument is meant to prove that any totality of caused things that are essentially ordered must be bounded, that is, that the series must have some uncaused cause.[87] There is no unbounded totality of essentially ordered things, even if the bound for the totality is infinitely (in the modern cardinal sense) far from any given element of the series where one begins to trace the causal chain.

Scotus begins the Causal Argument with the claim that the totality of caused things that are essentially ordered itself has a cause. He does not offer a proof of this claim, but we can construct one on his behalf. In *De primo princ.* 3.5, Scotus uses the principle that nothing can come into existence unless it is caused (*ex nihilo nihil fit*). But the totality of caused things that are essentially ordered itself comes into being, since otherwise it would not be a totality of such caused things. (Totalities are existing totalities.) Hence, the totality is caused. But if something is caused, then it must have at least one cause. Therefore, the totality has a cause: call it *C*.

Next, Scotus argues that *C*, the cause of the totality, is not part of the totality. For if it were, it would belong to something of which it is the cause, and this is impossible since nothing can be the cause of itself. Yet although *C* is not part of the totality, the totality is essentially ordered to it: by definition, *C* causes the totality, and so is that by which the totality exists and which it requires. Indeed, it should be clear that *C* must be in the series of essential causes that is correlated with the totality. For the totality in question is a totality of things that are caused – a point that is important in understanding the metaphysical character of Scotus's proof, which is to be taken up shortly. The correlated series may include most, if not all, of the things in given totality, since many things will be both caused and in their turn causes, but Scotus's argument does not assume this.

Finally, Scotus reaches the conclusion that *C* must be first in the correlated series of causes: "the whole totality of dependent things is dependent, and not on anything belonging to that totality." For suppose *C* were not first in the correlated series of causes. Then *C* would itself have some cause. But if *C* has a cause, by definition

C is caused. But if *C* is caused, then it must belong to the totality of caused things (which would otherwise not be a totality since it left *C* out). But, by the argument given in the preceding paragraph, this is impossible. Hence, *C* must be first, and the totality is bounded by it. Therefore, given the totality of essentially ordered caused things, there is some cause that is both the cause of the totality and is not itself caused. It is simply first. Thus, there cannot be an unbounded totality of things that are essentially caused: Q. E. D.

The Causal Argument, as reconstructed here, depends on distinguishing the totality of caused things from the correlated series of their causes. Understanding why Scotus begins with the totality of caused things rather than causes directly sheds light on the metaphysical character of his proof. For the Causal Argument is a piece of pure metaphysics: it doesn't include any claims about contingent beings in the world.[88] In *De primo princ.* 3.4–6, in the process of setting up the whole of his proof, Scotus is careful to point out that he is proceeding in terms of the possible rather than the actual. Specifically, he begins with the (metaphysically necessary) premise that some nature is contingent, which is a claim about 'quidditative being' rather than any actual being. Such claims about the possible are necessary, as Scotus says (3.5), and therefore have the modal force needed for metaphysical demonstrations. What is more, they clearly do not involve any change or motion, and hence are not part of physics. The Causal Argument reflects Scotus's commitment to metaphysical investigation by beginning with merely possible effects (namely, causable natures) and deducing the existence of an actual first cause of them, while appealing only to axioms about essential orders of causes.

Apart from reaching his ultimate conclusion that there is a perfect and infinite personal being, creator and goal of all there is, the Causal Argument also illustrates a conception of metaphysics that is typical of Scotus. For in it Scotus explores the nature of being through the ways in which beings are related to one another. It turns out that the causal structure of the world has an underlying order, laid bare by metaphysical inquiry, that shows how different kinds of things depend on one another. In that sense, metaphysics is concerned with all things insofar as they are "attributed to God" (*In Metaph.* 1, q. 1, n. 96).

IV.3. Self-Change

There are causal aspects of the physical world that bear metaphysical investigation, even without reference to God. One example is provided by Scotus's doctrine that self-change is possible – indeed, that it is a widespread feature of the physical world. By "self-change" Scotus has in mind cases of change in which the agent and the patient involved are really identical.[89] In a broad sense, 'change' refers to any case in which nonbeing is prior to being, but for most purposes a strict sense of 'change' was thought to be more useful, captured in the view that change involves "a movement toward form" (*Phys.* 6.5, 235^{b}6–7). Three principles are involved: the subject of the change, which is the persisting substratum; a form φ; and the initial privation of φ in the subject, so that the subject is not φ (but is in potency to φ). A change begins with the subject's being merely in potency to φ and ends with the subject actually informed by φ; the movement "between" these two poles is the change proper, where the subject's potency for φ is progressively actualized.[90] Furthermore, since change essentially involves the actualization of a potency, a fourth factor must be added to this analysis: the cause, or more generally the *principle*, of the potency's actualization. This calls for some comment.

Scotus couches his discussion of change at an abstract level, speaking of principles instead of causes. Now principles stand to causes as genus to species: causes are only one kind of principle (*Metaph.* 5.1, 1013^{a}17). Roughly, insofar as principles are taken as metaphysical constituents of beings, a principle, as a metaphysical constituent of something, is the source of some feature or property the thing possesses. Form and matter are principles of a material substance in this sense, and so too potency and act. Distinctions parallel to those drawn in the case of causation apply to principles as well, for which Scotus coins an artificial vocabulary. The more general version of causation is called "principiation" (*principiatio*), and the activity corresponding to it is called "principiating" (*principiare*). The result of principiative activity is what is "principiated" (parallel to the effect in a case of causation). Yet unlike a strictly causal effect, the result of principiative activity need not be some thing that is distinct: it may be the principiating activity itself, as in the case of potencies generally called "operations" (potencies whose acts are internal to and perfective of the agent: see *Quodl.* q. 13, n. 47). Thus, causal explanation is only one variety of principiative explanation; like causal explanation, a principiative explanation of a particular change will cite some thing as the principle responsible for the change, where the change is the result of principiative activity. For the most part, Scotus will interpret the principles involved in cases of self-change as active or passive potencies.[91]

The actualization of a potency, as described, is a case of change. The existence of the form in the subject depends on principles that are logically, if not temporally, prior, which account for the powers it can exercise, whether active or passive. Scotus argues first that self-change is possible in general, and thereafter considers the reality of self-change in particular cases. His argument for the possibility of self-change, given in *In Metaph.* 9, q. 14, n. 24, is as follows. The primary object of a potency for φ, whether active or passive, must be general. But as we have seen in Section I, whatever is contained under the primary object of a potency must be a *per se* object of that same potency. Now if it is possible for one and the same thing to have an active potency for φ and a passive potency for φ, then one and the same thing can, at least in principle, be the passive *per se* object of its own active causal potency.

Apart from its technical details, the intent of Scotus's argument should be clear: potencies are generally directed toward kinds of individuals, and there is no reason why an individual with a given potency should not fall under the general kind toward which the potency is directed, and so possibly be the recipient of its own causal activity. For such a case to be more than possible, though, a particular kind of causal activity is required. Causation is *univocal* when the induced form is specifically the same as a form contained in the cause, and *equivocal* otherwise.[92] Scotus argues that self-change is only possible in cases of equivocal causality, since for any change to occur the subject must initially be deprived of the form – but, by definition, a univocal cause already possesses the given form, and hence is not deprived of it (*Ord.* 1, d. 3, pars 3, q. 2, n. 514).

According to Scotus, then, self-change is possible when one and the same thing has a form φ that grounds the active causal potency to cause equivocally another form ψ and is also in passive potency to receive ψ. In the language of principles, one and the same thing has an active principle to produce a form it currently lacks and a passive principle of receiving such a form, and these two principles jointly bring about (or "principiate") the result (*In Metaph.* 9, q. 14, nn. 84–5). An example might clarify Scotus's thesis. A stone is informed by the form *heaviness*. Hence, it is active with respect to heaviness, or, in plain English, the stone is actually heavy. Now it is a fact that a stone has the passive principiative potency to being moved downward. Stones can be moved downward, after all! Hence, the stone is in potency to downward motion, and it is passive as regards downward motion. Now suppose that the form *heaviness* produces an active principiative potency in the stone. What might this active principiative potency be a potency for? It seems clear that the heaviness of a body is closely linked to its moving downward. Suppose that the active principiative potency engendered in the stone by its heaviness serves to actualize the stone's passive principiative potency for being moved downward, so that the pair of principiative potencies jointly produce the form *moving downward* in the stone as a result. Hence, the stone is active with respect to moving downward in virtue of its active principiative potency, even if it is not actually moving downward. Therefore, the stone is passively able to be moved downward, and is active with respect to the form *moving downward*. In other words, it is a self-mover.

On Scotus's analysis, there is a full-blooded sense in which it is one and the same thing that changes itself, even though it does so through the operation of internal principles that may be really distinct. It is the sculptor, not his hands or his ability to chisel marble, that is the cause of the statue, even if he can only be the cause through the exercise of his abilities with his hands. So too with active and passive principiative potencies (*In Metaph.* 9, qq. 3–4, nn. 19–20). Whether something has all the requisite principles needed for self-motion is a piece of physics, not metaphysics; it all depends on whether the appropriate principiative modalities are realized appropriately in the subject. For example, an animal's power of locomotion is due to the localization of the relevant potencies in distinct constituent parts of the animal: the soul has the active principiative potency to move the body, and the body has the passive principiative potency to be moved, the combination of which may result in locomotion. Whether it actually does so is not a matter for the metaphysician.

V. PARTICULARS

V.1. Matter

Scotus, notoriously, argues for the existence of prime matter.[93] He begins with Aristotle's account of substantial change, which he says is "more effective than other arguments (even though some reject it)": every natural agent requires something passive on which it acts, which is changed from one opposite to another; but one opposite is not itself changed into the other (whiteness doesn't become blackness); hence, just as in accidental change, there must in substantial generation or corruption be something that remains the same underlying the change from one opposed form to the other – and this is *matter*.[94] Unless there were a preexistent substrate persisting through substantial change, there would literally be no change in the technical sense: one substance would pop into nonbeing and another into being, but there would be no becoming. Substantial "change" would occur only on the model of divine creation or transubstantiation.[95] Scotus concludes that, in any case of substantial change, there must be some matter. What sort of a being is it?

To resolve this question, Scotus draws a distinction between *objective* and *subjective* modal potency.[96] Very roughly, something is in objective modal potency if the whole of it is merely possible, whereas it is in subjective modal potency if the subject already exists although its terminus – what the potency is a potency for (usually some form) – does not. For example, the nonexistent twin brother of Socrates is in objective modal potency, whereas Socrates himself is in subjective modal potency to some accidental change, such as becoming white. Since all cases of change involve a persisting substratum, the substratum must be in subjective modal potency, not objective modal potency. For if it were in objective modal potency, it would not exist but only be possible, "and then simply be a non-being" (*Lect.* 2, d. 12, q. un., n. 32). As we saw in the last paragraph, this is inadequate for substantial change. Furthermore, Scotus argues that matter cannot be simply identified with subjective modal potency, for the matter remains once the subjective modal potency has been actualized (*In Metaph.* 9, qq. 1–2, n. 49). Hence, matter is some positive being in which subjective modal potency resides (q. 5, n. 19).

Scotus therefore rejects the simple alignment of the relation between matter and form with the relation between potency and act. Thus, matter is a being that itself is the "cause and principle" of beings, one that underlies substantial change (*Lect.* 2, d. 12, q. un., n. 29).

Scotus, however, wants to derive a stronger conclusion than this. For he holds that it is one and the same stuff that underlies every substantial change: not only does matter exist, but prime matter exists – that is, matter in potency not just to any form but to all form (*Lect.* 2, d. 12, q. un., n. 37). On the face of it, the inference seems unwarranted. Scotus provides several reasons for it. First, Scotus argues that since God created matter and form immediately (i.e., without any intervening cause) and did not create them together, God could also conserve matter without form. But that just is to admit that prime matter could exist, that it is a being in its own right.[97] Second, Scotus offers a variety of arguments, each trading on the principle that form is not essential to matter in any given combination or composite, and therefore cannot be essential to matter at all.[98] Whether matter is essential to form is another question (discussed in Section V.2). Thus, Scotus concludes, prime matter is a being. Hence, there is a real distinction between matter and form in a composite, and any given composite of matter and form will be a composite of two really distinct items. How the composite can then be a unity requires some delicate argument on Scotus's part. But first we have to consider how many forms can inhere in the matter of something.

V.2. Form

The substantial form of something makes it *what* it is, locating it in the category of Substance. Now the substantial forms of individuals are themselves individual: Scotus argues that if form were instead something abstract, then, first, since matter is all the same kind of thing (namely, prime matter), form would be too; second, created forms such as the human intellective soul, in virtue of their nonmaterial origin, do not have the same essence as matter.[99] Scotus draws the conclusion that substantial forms must be individuals, and indeed individuals with essences distinct from the essence of matter. Forms play two distinct roles in the constitution of material particulars: on the one hand, they inform matter; on the other hand, they are essential parts of the whole composite. But these are not intrinsic features of form, Scotus holds, since we can see that form lacks these "imperfections" in the case of the divine (*Ord.* 1, d. 8, pars 1, q. 4, n. 213). Form can therefore be self-sustaining: it is prior to matter, and prior to the composite as well, since each is in act through the form and not conversely (*In Metaph.* 7, q. 6, n. 9), and thus has some being of its own (n. 12). But if form need not inform matter and has being of its own, then it is possible for a bodily form to exist independently of matter – a conclusion Scotus draws explicitly.[100] As a result, we can sensibly ask about how the substantial form exists in a given concrete individual (*suppositum*). And here, Scotus argues, we can say that although substantial forms are all the same in their nature, one concrete individual may exemplify the nature or essence of the substantial form more perfectly than another (*In Metaph.* 8, qq. 2–3, n. 37), although this admission does not force us to postulate actual degrees among distinct individuals of the same kind (n. 38).

None of these properties of substantial forms, however, settle the question of how many substantial forms a given concrete object may have. (The same thing may be located more exactly in the category of Substance by its different substantial forms.) The answer will vary depending on the kind of object in question, of course, but Scotus clearly argues that in the most complex case – living beings – more than one substantial form must be present. Apart from theological motives, he has two philosophical arguments based on the nature of substantial change for this conclusion.[101]

Scotus's first argument is based on cases of substantial corruption, which indicates that there is a distinction between the animating soul and the "form of the body" (*forma corporeitatis*), where the latter is, roughly, the form that structures the organic body as a whole. He reasons as follows: When a living being dies, its body remains, in the absence of its vivifying soul; hence, the form by which its body is the body it is must differ from its soul (*Op Ox* 4, d. 11, q. 3, n. 54). The body of Socrates before drinking the hemlock and the corpse afterwards are numerically the same and, since by definition death is the separation of the soul from the body, this sameness cannot be explained by appeal to the soul, and so there must be another substantial form, one that preserves the body as the body, before and after death.

This line of reasoning depends on the plausibility of identifying Socrates' corpse with his (previously) living body, to be sure, but the burden of proof is on those who would want to deny this. Scotus offers another reason in support of his claim, though, based on the regularity of substantial corruption. When living things die, they regularly turn into corpses of certain types: dying men are never replaced by moonbeams or elephants, but always by material bodies (corpses) that have a remarkable resemblance to the composite. Nor are living things reduced immediately to the four elements. The corpse, rather, has to undergo a process of decomposition. The explanation, once a plurality of substantial forms is postulated, is obvious and intuitive: the composite has merely lost its "topmost" substantial form; the form of the body remains to account for the identity and resilience of the corpse (n. 38).

The second argument Scotus offers is based on substantial generation, and in particular human generation: if God – and not the parents – provides the soul in generation, the parents seem left with contributing only the matter to their progeny, which seems to underestimate their role. Scotus's solution is to propose that human parents contribute a substantial form, namely, the form of the body, which is further informed by the human soul (*Op. Ox.* 3, d. 2, q. 3, n. 5) contributed by God. However, the matter is not first organized by the form of the body and then by the human soul at different times, but both inform the matter at once (Ibid.). This claim suggests that the form of the body isn't quite "strong" enough to organize the organic body on its own, but needs the concurrent causality of the soul to do so. There is some evidence that this is Scotus's view, for he explains that human corpses decompose because of the weakness of the form of the body (*Op. Ox.* 4, d. 11, q. 3, n. 55).[102]

These arguments furnish grounds for distinguishing the soul from the form of the body in living beings. Scotus rejects any attempt to further split up souls into separate forms (vegetative, sensitive, intellective): the soul and its clusters of powers are not really but only formally distinct from each other, whether in plants, brute animals, or humans, so that one soul is the substantial form of a living being.[103] If we insist that the form of the body can only exercise its causality concurrently with the soul, then Scotus's position begins to look very much like that espoused by defenders of the unicity of substantial form. This similarity is all the more striking in light of a passage in which Scotus remarks that in the natural course of events it is impossible for the same matter to be under two substantial

forms at once.[104] But there are other substantial forms at work besides the form of the body. For Scotus also finds it plausible that
different bodily organs are different in kind through the presence of
distinct substantial forms (n. 46). Otherwise, he reasons, we could
not explain the different local unities found in different organs: the
physical structures of the heart, the lungs, the kidneys, and so on (*In
Metaph.* 7, q. 20, n. 38). Exactly how far Scotus is willing to carry
this line of thought isn't clear, since in the end it would seem to
leave the form of the body with nothing to do, but he clearly thinks
that the form and function of (say) the heart cannot be explained
by the same principles that explain the form and function of the
kidneys. The forms of bodily organs are actual with regard to the
underlying prime matter and potential with regard to the form of
the body, which, it will be remembered, is the form of the body as a
whole.

Scotus rejects the extension of this logic to mixtures of the four
elements (earth, air, fire, water), even in the case of inanimate substances. That is, Scotus denies that we need to postulate substantial
forms of the four elements in mixtures of these elements. His main
argument seems to be that if we really have mixtures, then by definition the forms of the chemical elements do not structure the mixture
or even parts of the mixture: in modern terminology, mixtures do not
merely supervene on their chemical components but are emergent
features (*Lect.* 2, d. 15, q. un., nn. 38–43). Of course, nonmixtures
will preserve the forms of the elements, but in such cases we aren't
tempted to think there are additional substantial forms.

V.3. Composite Substances

For Scotus, then, a particular living being includes prime matter, the
form of the body, local forms of bodily organs, and the soul. Each
of these has some claim to be treated as a being in its own right.
How can all these disparate beings constitute a unified object that
has some claim to be treated as ontologically basic? The answer to
this question is complex, and it will take some delicate handling to
untangle the various strands of Scotus's reply.

Scotus is careful to distinguish the existence (*esse*) that each component element of a particular living being has. For example, the
soul has existence *per se*, and this existence is separate from the

existence of the composite of which the soul is a constituent element, even though when combined with the body the soul has existence through the composite (*In Metaph.* 7, q. 6, nn. 12–3). The point
here is subtle. Scotus is maintaining that although the constituent
elements of a unified whole have their own individual existences,
the whole, nevertheless, may have only one existence, and the existences of the constituent elements may be somehow dependent
on the existence of the whole. In replying to an argument that tries
to infer the uniqueness of substantial form from the fact that the
composite is a single existence, Scotus writes (*Op. Ox.* 4, d. 11, q. 3,
n. 46):

I grant the first claim, that there is only one existence that belongs to one being. But the second proposition, that one existence requires exactly one form,
should be denied. . . . For just as 'being' and 'one' are divided into simple and
composite, so too are 'existence' and 'one existence'. Therefore, existence
that is essentially one is not precisely restricted to simple existence, just
as nothing divided is precisely restricted to one of the divisions that divide
it. In this way there is one existence of the whole composite, which nevertheless includes many partial existences, just as the whole is one being and
nevertheless contains many partial beingnesses. For I know nothing about
this fiction that the existence supervening on the essence is not composite
if the essence is composite. The existence of the whole composite includes
the existence of all the parts in this way, and it includes many partial existences belonging to the many parts or forms, just as the whole being made
up of many forms includes those partial actualities.

The existences of the consituent parts of the composite are not simply added or aggregated; they have instead an essential order to one
another, and overall an essential order to the "topmost" substantial
form that gives existence to the whole composite, as Scotus goes
on to say. In this way the whole composite can be divided into act
and potency, namely, the final "completive" form and the remainder
of the composite. And as with existences, so with the beings themselves: the unity of the composite is to be found in the union of its
constituent elements through an internal essential order. The beings
that are the matter and the form are distinct (*In Metaph.* 8, q. 4, n. 41)
but essentially ordered to one another (nn. 31–3).

Scotus takes the ordering of forms to be pervasive, and the inability of certain forms to be so ordered is a distinctive feature of *per
se* beings. In *Quodl.* q. 9, n. 7, Scotus distinguishes three types of

per se beings: (1) beings existing in isolation, or apart from a subject, (2) beings that neither actually inhere in others nor have any aptitude to so inhere, and (3) beings with ultimate actuality such that they cannot be ordered *per se* to any further act. An example of (1) is whiteness considered apart from any subject. In (2) Scotus seems to be talking about substantial form, which informs its subject *per se* and makes it what it is. But (3) is the crucial sort: these are the beings that are ontologically basic, the fully actual concrete particulars. Being unable to be *per se* ordered to any further act is the mark of the concrete. That is why the individual has a privileged place in Scotus's ontology.

The essential ordering of the constituent parts of a composite substance is a description of the unity of the composite. Note well: it describes the unity but does not explain it, since the principle of the essential ordering has to do with the act–potency relations among these elements, and Scotus thinks that these are given immediately.[105] Scotus is thus well aware of the limits of his account.

The essence of the composite is something distinct from any of its constituent elements: it is a composite of form as such and matter as such. It cannot be identified simply with the substantial form, since that is only one of the constituents of the composite and has its own proper essence and existence, as we have seen. However, the substantial form does give further actuality to the remainder of the elements that make up the composite, and, on this score, it can be called the "partial form" of the composite (*Op. Ox.* 3, d. 2, q. 2, nn. 9–10). It should not be confused with the "form of the whole" (viz. the whole composite), which is "not an informing form" but rather that in virtue of which the composite as a whole has a nature or quiddity.[106] In short, the essence of the composite is something over and above the parts of the composite, not reducible to them. What it is to be this composite (or this kind of composite) is an emergent feature.

The essence of the composite, then, is tightly linked to all the constituent elements of the composite, as they are essentially ordered to one another. Indeed, it seems as though an individual composite can have an essence only if all its constituents are properly aligned. Such seems to be the reasoning underlying Scotus's rejection of any real distinction between essence and existence: "Existence is really the same as essence."[107] The *what* of a thing is that it is put together

that way, which just is what it *is*. Essence and existence are inseparable within the concrete individual.[108] Scotus even suggests that, in
creatures, essence and existence "are like quiddity and its mode," although in God existence is a formal part of the divine essence (*Quodl.*
q. 1, n. 11, addition).

Scotus holds that the essence of a composite in general, as opposed
to an individual composite, is itself composite, since the genus and
differentia that jointly constitute the specific nature of the essence
must be at least formally distinct.[109] On the one hand, if either the
genus or the differentia were taken away, the specific nature would be
destroyed; hence, they are really inseparable. But equally, the genus
and the differentia are formally distinct, since otherwise the differentia could not contribute any formal differentiating feature to the
genus – it would just "repeat" the content of the genus. Furthermore,
since the formal distinction holds *a parte rei*, there must be some
real complexity or composition in any specific nature. Hence, the
quiddity of all creatures must be complex in at least this sense. The
same does not hold of God, however. To see why this should be so,
we need to return to the last question posed at the end of Section 1
to see how Scotus avoids any real commonness between God and the
creature.

VI. CONCLUSION

Recall the problem: if God and creatures are merely different and
not diverse, then there would be some real factor common to God
and creatures, thereby undermining divine transcendence. But it
seemed as though God and creatures were only different, since *being*
is univocal to both.[110] Scotus's response to this difficulty in *Ord.* 1,
d. 8, pars 1, q. 3, has three parts. First, although formal distinctions
may introduce real complexity, they only introduce real composition
when they are combined as genus and differentia. In this case, there
are elements united as potency (genus) and act (differentia), making
up a composite. But unless distinct elements are so related, they will
not produce composition in the relevant sense, and so there need be
no composition introduced by the formal distinction.[111] Second, the
modal distinction between finite and infinite being does not provide
a real basis for composition. The modal distinction reflects a reality with a given intrinsic mode, and there is no conception of the

mode apart from the reality of which it is a mode (see Section II.3).
Hence, the modal degree of being does not point to a real factor different from being itself that could be the foundation of composition
in God. Thus God's simplicity is preserved. Third, the concepts of
a nature with and without its intrinsic mode are related as more or
less perfect concepts of one and the same thing. Applied to the case
at hand, Scotus's claim is that the univocal notion of being is an imperfect concept, although determinable to a perfect concept of either
an infinite reality (God) or finite reality (creatures).[112] Hence, this
notion does not entail a real commonness between God and creatures, since in itself it is only determinable to either. Thus God's
transcendence is preserved.

The complex factors that enter into Scotus's discussion of the nature of metaphysics as an enterprise can serve as a model for the
complexity of the Subtle Doctor's thought. There is still disagreement over many of his doctrines, on points large and small. The
reader is advised to take all surveys of Scotus's metaphysics – even
this one! – with a grain of salt, and to turn to the texts themselves
for more enlightenment.

NOTES

1 See *In Metaph.* 6, q. 1, nn. 55–6, and *In Metaph.* prol., nn. 26–7. See also
   Lect. prol., pars 4, qq. 1–2, and *Ord.* prol., p. 4, qq. 1–2 for the sense
   in which theology can be a science (although a practical rather than a
   speculative science: *Ord.* prol., pars 5, qq. 1–2). God, of course, has such
   perfect knowledge, although Scotus is reluctant to call it "science"
   since God's knowledge is nondiscursive (*In Metaph.* 1, q. 1, n. 135).
2 See *In Metaph.* 6, q. 1, nn. 52–3, nn. 62–3, nn. 73–84. Scotus therefore rejects the traditional claims that mathematics is primarily about
   quantity and physics about the mobile.
3 See especially *In Metaph.* 6, q. 4, nn. 10–2, and *Rep.* 1A prol., q. 3, a. 1
   (text in Wolter 1987). The formula is traditional: see Aristotle, *Metaph.*
   6.1 (1026^{a}30–2). See further Honnefelder 1979 and Boulnois 1988.
4 The immaterial substances are God and angels, but, since angels are
   clearly dependent on God, this alternative is usually given for God
   alone.
5 Scotus's definition is inspired by Aristotle's discussion of "commensu-
   rate subjects" in *Post. An.* 1.4 (73^{b}32–74^{a}3). See *Ord.* 1, d. 3, p. 1, qq. 1–2,
   n. 49. Scotus often talks about primary objects in terms of potencies,

as he does in his introduction of the notion in *Ord*. prol., pars 3, qq. 1–3, n. 142, but the notion is more general. See King 1994, 234–5.

6 In a later annotation to *Ord*. 1, d. 3, p. 1, qq. 1–2, n. 24, Scotus remarks: "The *per se* object is clear from the acts of the potency; the primary object, however, is derived from many *per se* objects, since it is adequate."

7 These claims are equivalent under two generally held assumptions: (1) metaphysics is knowledge attainable in this life, as mentioned in Section I.1; and (2) metaphysics is not subordinate to any other science.

8 See *Lect*. 1, d. 3, pars 1, qq. 1–2; *Ord*. 1, d. 3, pars 1, q. 3; *Quodl*. q. 14, nn. 38–73. Scotus also deals with the issue briefly in *In Metaph*. 2, qq. 2–3, nn. 32–3.

9 See *In Metaph*. 2, qq. 2–3; *Ord*. 1, d. 3, pars 1, q. 3, nn. 185–8; and *Quodl*. q. 14, n. 39.

10 Scotus states a version of this claim with respect to cognitive potencies in *Ord*. 1, d. 3, pars 1, q. 3, n. 118: "Whatever is known *per se* by a cognitive potency either is its primary object or is contained under its primary object."

11 Scotus calls this the "order of perfection" in *Ord*. 1, d. 3, pars 1, qq. 1–2, nn. 95–8. This view, too, has an Aristotelian patrimony (see Morrison 1987) and is a forerunner of the "Great Chain of Being."

12 See *In Metaph*. 1, q. 1, nn. 130–6, and the discussion of essential orders in Section IV.

13 In his *In Praed*. 4.37–8, Scotus holds that 'being' is an analogous notion and thereby logically equivocal; a similar view is, arguably, given at the end of *In Metaph*. 1, q. 1, n. 96 (but see the conclusion of Section IV.2 for an alternative way to read this passage). Scotus defends the univocity of 'being' at length elsewhere: *In De an*. q. 21, nn. 7–8; *In Metaph*. 6, q. 1, nn. 47–8, and q. 4, n. 11; *Lect*. 1, d. 3, pars 1, qq. 1–2, nn. 97–113; *Coll*. 13, nn. 3–5; *Coll*. q. 3 (Harris 1927), nn. 372–3; *Ord*. 1, d. 3, pars 1, qq. 1–2, nn. 26–55, and q. 3, nn. 131–66. The issue is complicated by the fact that Scotus thinks that analogy and univocity may be compatible: see *Ord*. 1, d. 8, pars 1, q. 3, n. 83, and Boulnois 1988.

14 *Ord*. 1, d. 3, pars 1, qq. 1–2, n. 26: "I call that concept 'univocal' which is so unified that its unity is enough for a contradiction in affirming and denying it of the same subject; it also is enough to play the part of a middle term in a syllogism, so that the extreme terms are united as one in the middle so that their unity with one another can be deduced without a fallacy of equivocation." See *In Soph. El*. qq. 15–6 for how analogous terms produce fallacies.

15 See the references in note 13. Scotus's contemporaries called this the "Achilles" of his arguments for univocity (S. Dumont 1998, 308).

16 Substance is knowable in itself, although not by us in our present condition: *In Metaph.* 7, q. 3, n. 16.

17 To be predicated *in quid* of something is to say what the thing is, to describe its essence. Similarly, to be predicated *in quale* is to say how something is, to describe the way it is.

18 *Lect.* 1, d. 3, pars 1, qq. 1–2, nn. 97–104; *Ord.* 1, d. 3, pars 1, q. 3, n. 129.

19 Scotus seems to admit two kinds of ultimate differentia. First, there are the individual differentiae, one for each distinct individual, by which (say) Socrates and Plato are diverse from one another: see *In Metaph.* 7, q. 13, n. 123; *Lect.* 2, d. 3, pars 1, qq. 5–6, n. 172; *Ord.* 2, d. 3, pars 1, qq. 5–6, n. 186. Second, there are the irreducibly simple specific differentiae. Scotus does not say which specific differentiae are irreducibly simple.

20 Scotus gives a similar regress argument in his *In Metaph.* 7, q. 13, n. 121, and q. 17, n. 19.

21 Technically, this is expressed by saying that proper attributes are predicable *per se secundo modo* of their subjects. The notion comes from Aristotle, *Post. An.* 1.4 (73^a37–73^b5).

22 This is an instance of a general theorem: no subject is quidditatively predicable of its proper attributes. Scotus takes the list of proper attributes of being from Aristotle, *Metaph.* 4.2 (1003^b23–36).

23 Scotus writes: "I say that being is the primary object of our intellect, for a double primacy concurs in it, namely, a primacy of commonness and a primacy of virtuality, for anything intelligible *per se* either essentially includes the notion of being or is virtually contained in something that does" (n. 137). He makes the same point in *Quodl.* q. 5, nn. 26–9.

24 Avoiding this conclusion seems to have been the motivation for Aristotle's claim that 'being' is said in many ways that are, at best, only analogous to one another, although perhaps related to a single focal meaning: *Metaph.* 4.2 (1003^a31–1003^b19). Most mediaeval and modern commentators on Aristotle have therefore held that 'being' is not univocal across the categories.

25 Aristotle, *Metaph.* 3.3 (998^b22–27); Porphyry, *Isag.* 2 (Porphyry 1887, 6.5–11; Porphyry 1966, 11.20–12.6).

26 See *Ord.* 2, d. 2, pars 1, q. 2, nn. 92–4, where Scotus adds that two items can be really distinct if they are proportionately analogous to separable things, as in the case of the parts of a definition; I ignore this refinement in what follows. The separability criterion for real distinctness derives from Aristotle, *Top.* 7.1 (152^b34–35); see Chapter 4 for the connection between divine power and possibility.

27 See *Ord.* 2, d. 1, qq. 4–5, nn. 200–2, for Scotus's claim that inseparability is necessary for real identity, and *Quodl.* q. 3, n. 46 for its sufficiency.

28 For example, Scotus writes that the divine perfections are distinct "by an otherness that is neither caused by the intellect nor yet so great as we have in mind when we speak of diverse things (res), but is a lesser real difference, if every difference not caused by the intellect were called 'real' " (In Metaph. 4, q. 2, n. 143).

29 Such a distinction is sometimes called a distinctio rationis a parte rei (a "real conceptual distinction"). If there is no real distinction in the object, but the object nevertheless causes the intellect to conceive it in different ways, Scotus sometimes says there is a virtual or potential distinction in the object; see for instance Lect. 1, d. 2, pars 2, qq. 1–4, n. 271.

30 Scotus discusses the formal distinction ex professo in his Lect. 1, d. 8, pars 1, q. 4, nn. 172–88; Ord. 1, d. 2, pars 2, qq. 1–4, nn. 388–410, and d. 8, pars 1, q. 4, nn. 191–217; and several Parisian lectures, mostly surviving only in student transcriptions (reportationes). These treatments differ in their terminology and, arguably, in the doctrine they present: see Grajewski 1944, Gelber 1974, and Jordan 1984, for further discussion. I'll concentrate on Scotus's presentation in his Ordinatio.

31 See Op. Ox. 2, d. 16, q. un., n. 17.

32 Scotus makes this point explicitly in Ord. 1, d. 8, pars 1, q. 4, n. 193: "Furthermore, the definition indicates not only an aspect that is caused by the mind, but the quiddity of a thing; formal non-identity is therefore ex parte rei." See also d. 25, q. un., n. 10, and In Metaph. 7, q. 13, nn. 90–1.

33 For the genus and specific differentia, see In Metaph. 7, q. 19, nn. 20–1 and n. 43; Lect. 1, d. 8, pars 1, q. 3, nn. 100–5; Ord. 1, d. 8, pars 1, q. 3, nn. 101–7, and 2, d. 3, pars 1, qq. 5–6, nn. 189–90. For the uncontracted common nature and the individual differentia, see Lect. 2, d. 3, pars 1, qq. 5–6, n. 171; Ord. 2, d. 3, pars 1, qq. 5–6, n. 188; and King 1992. It is often said that Scotus postulates a formal distinction between the essence and the existence of something, but there is little textual evidence for this claim: see O'Brien 1964, and Section V.3.

34 Scotus's most extensive analysis of the logic of the formal distinction is in the collatio printed as Quaest. misc. de form. q. 1 (the only authentic part of that collection), also known as the logica Scoti, discussed in what follows.

35 Scotus makes the same point in Ord. 1, d. 2, pars 2, qq. 1–4, n. 404: "Should we then allow that there is some distinction? It is better to use the negative formulation 'This is not formally the same as that' rather than 'These things are formally distinct.' " See also the discussion in Gelber 1974.

36 One drawback to the modal approach is that it seems to license the inference from A's being φ to its subject being φ; if B then has a property ψ incompatible with φ, then the subject in question would have the incompatible properties φ and ψ. Rejecting the inference, however, seems to treat the ways something is as quasi things in their own right, and we are back to the nonmodal versions of the formal distinction. The extent to which Scotus adopts the modal approach, as well as the success of that approach, has been controversial since the fourteenth century.

37 See further the discussion in Sections V.3 and VI.

38 Scotus lists several grades of unity in *Ord.* 1, d. 2, pars 2, qq. 1–4, n. 403. This is a fundamental theme, exploited to good effect, in Cross 1998.

39 The modal distinction seems to be Scotus's generalization of the notion of qualitative variability, discusssed further in Section III.2.3.

40 A nature is separable from any given degree if it allows a range of variation; why do we not have then a real distinction between the nature and its intrinsic mode? For the same reason there is not a real distinction between the uncontracted and the contracted common nature – because *this* particular thing cannot be without its given mode without thereby ceasing to exemplify that intrinsic mode of the nature: see King 1992.

41 See Wolter 1946. Typically one of the disjuncts will properly apply only to God and the other to the rest of creation (e.g., "necessary" to God and "(merely) possible" to any creature); Scotus indicates that in general one ought to be able to conclude the existence of something the more perfect disjunct applies to from the existence of something the less perfect disjunct applies to. Note that some of the disjunctive attributes also carve out relations among creatures: different orders of priority and posteriority, or relations of act and potency, for example.

42 Scotus derives this rough characterization of the pure perfections from Anselm, *Monologion* 5; his gloss on it is found in *Quodl.* q. 5, n. 31.

43 All pure perfections are equally perfect since they are formally infinite, but otherwise they can be ordered. For example, since one must be alive to be wise, life (as a pure perfection) is prior to wisdom (as a pure perfection).

44 See *Lect.* 1, d. 8, pars 1, q. 3, n. 107; *Ord.* 1, d. 8, pars 1, q. 3, n. 113; *Quodl.* q. 5, n. 58.

45 In *Quodl.* q. 5, n. 58, Scotus tells us that magnitude can be used to construct an essential order among natures, presumably in the order of eminence: see Section 4.1.

46 See *In Praed.* q. 11, n. 26, and *In Metaph.* 5, qq. 5–6, n. 81. The last part of this claim may need to be qualified, for in a later addition to the text given in *In Metaph.* 5, qq. 5–6, nn. 73–80, Scotus points out that the arguments used to establish the sufficiency of the division are fallacious.

47 See *In Praed.* q. 15, n. 10; *In Metaph.* 7, q. 7, nn. 22–5, and q. 16, n. 26; *Ord.* 2, d. 3, pars 1, q. 1, n. 32; *Op. Ox.* 3, d. 22, q. un., n. 11.

48 A distinction was traditionally drawn at this point: accidents, it was said, either actually inhere in a subject or have an aptitude to so inhere, and the latter is the defining characteristic of accidentality. Scotus, however, finds that aptitudinal dependence isn't as strong as the essential dependence he has in mind here (n. 10). He sometimes appeals to the notion when less precision is called for (see *In Metaph.* 7, q. 4, n. 17).

49 Aristotle, *Cat.* 6 (4^b20–5^a14) and *Metaph.* 5.13 (1020^a10–11).

50 See *In Praed.* qq. 16–17, nn. 13–16, and *In Metaph.* 5, q. 9, nn. 17–32. Scotus points out in nn. 30–1 of the latter that homoeomerous divisibility is, strictly speaking, the primary proper attribute of Quantity rather than its essence or part of its essence: we can't isolate the essence of Quantity, since it is an immediate division of finite being. See also *In Metaph.* 7, q. 13, n. 98, for the divisibility of particular quantities.

51 Whether Scotus's arguments are successful is another question: see Cross 1998, 118–33.

52 In contemporary mathematics this is the job of a measure function.

53 Scotus proposes the same account in *Op. Ox.* 4, d. 6, q. 10, n. 14, although there again he provides an alternative explanation to the question at hand (what kind of quality the theological virtues are).

54 See *Lect.* 1, d. 17, pars 2, q. 1, nn. 142–3; *Ord.* 1, d. 17, pars 2, q. 1, nn. 202–24, and q. 2, n. 255. Scotus's discussion here is more complex than I have indicated here: see Cross 1998, 173–80.

55 See *Ord.* 1, d. 17, pars 2, qq. 1–2, nn. 241–8 for the first version of the proposal and *Lect.* 1, d. 17, pars 2, q. 3, nn. 188–96 for the second.

56 See *Lect.* 1, d. 17, pars 2, q. 4, nn. 206–39; and *Ord.* 1, d. 17, pars 2, q. 2, n. 249.

57 *Lect.* 1, d. 17, pars 2, q. 4, n. 241, argued for degrees of heat.

58 See *Op. Ox.* 3, d. 1, q. 1, n. 15; 4, d. 6, q. 10, nn. 3–4; 4, d. 13, q. 1, nn. 9–11. Technically, intrinsically advenient relations obtain given their extremes and the foundations; extrinsically advenient relations do not.

59 See Henninger 1989, ch. 5, for Scotus's theory of relations.

60 Scotus argues that a relation is primarily directed only "toward" a single thing (*In Metaph.* 5, q. 11, n. 65) or, in modern terms, that polyadic

relations are reducible to dyadic relations. I'll simply assume that result in the discussion here.

61 See *Lect.* 2, d. 1, q. 5, n. 184, and *Ord.* 2, d. 1, q. 5, nn. 200–4. Scotus offers several other arguments for this conclusion.

62 Scotus points out that a relation can have as its terminus something absolute (*In Metaph.* 5, q. 11, n. 66): it is an artifact of this example that the terminus of Socrates's tallness is an accident inhering in Plato. (This will be important for third-mode relations: see Section III.2.4.)

63 Given a relation, it is a straightforward matter to determine its co-relation: transpose the foundation and the terminus, so that the old terminus is the new foundation and the old foundation the new terminus; there will now be a relation in the subject that has the new foundation. Plato's being shorter than Socrates depends on the same particular accidents of height in each, but this time considered from Plato's point of view, as it were. Co-relations are "simultaneous" with relations in this sense (*In Praed.* q. 27 and *In Metaph.* 5, q. 11, n. 81).

64 This is the standard modern reduction of dyadic relations to monadic predicates: to "end-stop" the relation with its relatum.

65 *Lect.* 2, d. 1, q. 5, nn. 204–9; *In Metaph.* 5, q. 11, nn. 13–21; *Ord.* 2, d. 1, q. 5, nn. 223–7.

66 *Quodl.* q. 6, n. 82. See also *Lect.* 1, d. 31, q. un., n. 6, and *Ord.* 1, d. 31, q. un., n. 6.

67 Scotus's argument for this conclusion depends on his thesis that an object *qua* considered by the intellect has a special ontological status, a lesser kind of being (*esse diminutum*): see n. 44.

68 Aristotle, *Metaph.* 5.15 ($1020^{b}26$–32). Scotus discusses each in *In Metaph.* 5, qq. 12–13. He finds the list clearly incomplete, since there is no obvious way to classify spatial relations, temporal relations, semantic relations, and several others; hence, the three modes are not the species of Relation themselves but rather at most paradigmatic of the genuine species (*In Metaph.* 5, q. 11, nn. 57–9).

69 *Lect.* 2, d. 1, q. 5, nn. 240–2, and *Ord.* 2, d. 1, q. 5, nn. 261–2; Henninger 1989, 78–85.

70 Aristotle gives multiple senses of priority and posteriority in *Cat.* 12 and *Metaph.* 5.11. Scotus argues in *In Praed.* q. 43 and *In Metaph.* 5, q. 8 that they all have the root meaning of "closer to (or farther away from) a source." See Gorman 1993, for a discussion of Scotus's "ontological" senses of priority.

71 Presumably eminence can generate a linear ordering by using magnitude, the transcendental sense of quantity, to rank essences. See Section III.1.

72   The phrase "being of X" is deliberately ambiguous between X's exis-
      tence and X's essence (what it is to be X).

73   The fact that C is therefore produced later in time than B does not
      make it a "remote" effect in Scotus's technical sense, which depends
      on the presence of causal intermediaries.

74   This inference holds only if Scotus rejects so-called sine qua non causal-
      ity. He does: see *Ord.* 1, d. 3, pars 3, q. 2, n. 415.

75   See *In Metaph.* 9, qq. 3–4, n. 16; the same point is made in *In Metaph.*
      1, q. 1, n. 83.

76   Scotus holds there these are all the kinds of causes there are (*Ord.* 1,
      d. 3, pars 3, q. 2, n. 415). In a canceled text that originally made up part
      of n. 414, he cites with approval Averroës's *sufficientia*–proof for the
      four causes presented in his *In Phys.* 2 com. 30–1.

77   *In Metaph.* 9, qq. 3–4, nn. 16–8. The point is evident for the first three,
      but requires some careful handling for the efficient cause. Scotus ar-
      gues that efficient causality only involves "imparting existence" rather
      than the more physical "bringing something about," even if such exis-
      tence can only be imparted through physical means (with the notable
      exception of God's efficient creation of the world out of nothing).

78   *De primo princ.* 1.15. English lacks a term corresponding to Scotus's
      precise *causatum* for what a cause causes; I'll use "effect" in a broad
      sense for this purpose.

79   Scotus discusses concurrent causality in *Ord.* 1, d. 3, pars 3, q. 2,
      nn. 495–6, and *Quodl.* q. 15, nn. 33–5. Causes may concur equally
      or unequally. In the former case, each cause exercises the same sort of
      power, and the two causes operate jointly, as when two people lift a
      table. In the latter case, the causes are essentially ordered to one an-
      other in such a way that the higher cause moves the lower cause and
      the lower cause does not move without the higher cause. (The rela-
      tion between the soul and the form of the body may be like this: see
      Section V.2.) Each of these ways has further subdivisions.

80   A *per se* cause is also called an "essential cause," which can be mis-
      leading: an order of essential causes may not be an essential order of
      causes, as Scotus notes in 2.33 and 3.10; see also *In Metaph.* 2, qq. 4–6,
      n. 80, and 5, q. 8, n. 7. A series of colliding billiard balls, or the series
      of ancestors, are examples of such.

81   *De primo princ.* 3.11; see also *In Metaph.* 2, qq. 4–6, nn. 80–101, and
      8, qq. 2–3, n. 128 for (b).

82   *De primo princ.* 2.25–32; see also *In Metaph.* 5, q. 1, nn. 54–9. Scotus
      gives a special argument for this conclusion in *De primo princ.* 2.30.
      If something can be expected to produce something essentially one,
      and the product flows from a plurality of causes, then the causes are

related to one another as act and potency or possess a unity of order. Then he points out that the four causes are not all related as act and potency (only matter and form are). He then adds that the four causes produce something that is essentially one, namely, the composite (see Section V.3). Therefore, the four causes possess a unity of order in their causing of an effect that is essentially one.

83 Why doesn't the end depend on the efficient for its causality, since without the efficient the final cause could not bring about its result? Because the end initiates the sequence of causes by moving the efficient cause to action. So, although it acts through the efficient cause, the final cause is prior since it initiates the motion. The efficient cause in no way moves the final cause into action.

84 This is slightly inaccurate; one cannot mix eminence and dependence in the transitivity theorem. Proof: Form depends upon matter; hence, matter is prior to form. But form is more eminent than matter; hence, form is prior to matter. If transitivity could cross Scotus's first division, there would be a circle in an essential order. Note that Scotus carefully explicates the transitivity theorem disjunctively in terms of dependence and eminence.

85 We have several versions of this proof. See *Lect.* 1, d. 2, pars 1, qq. 1–2; *In Metaph.* 2, qq. 4–6; *Ord.* 1, d. 2, pars 1, qq. 1–2; *Rep.* 1A, d. 2, qq. 1–4 (text in Wolter and Adams 1982); and the whole of the *De primo principio*. There are also several discussions reported in Scotus's Paris lectures. See Cress 1975 for a survey of the literature to that point. Scotus's proof even has its modern imitators: see Loux 1984.

86 *De primo princ.* 3.12–13: *Infinitas essentialiter ordinatorum est impossibilis . . . tum quia universitas causatorum essentialiter ordinatorum est causata; igitur ab aliqua causa quae nihil est universitatis; tunc enim esset causa sui; tota enim universitas dependentium dependet et a nullo illius universitatis.* The formulation in other versions of the proof is similar.

87 More exactly, the Causal Argument proves that any totality of essentially ordered things is bounded by the first cause in the correlated series of causes, as we shall see in the reconstruction of the proof.

88 Scotus characterizes the whole of the *De primo principio* as metaphysics: see 4.86.

89 Scotus discusses the general possibility of self-change definitively in *In Metaph.* 9, q. 14. He takes up the case of local motion, and in particular the movement of light and heavy bodies, in *Ord.* 2, d. 2, pars 2, q. 6. Quantitative self-change in the case of augmentation and diminution is taken up in *Rep.* 4 , d. 44, q. 1, and in the case of condensation and rarefaction in *Op. Ox.* 4, d. 12, q. 4. Qualitative self-change in the

activity of seeds and semen is taken up in *Op. Ox.* 2, d. 18, q. un., and 3, d. 4, q. un. Self-change in the will is discussed extensively in *In Metaph.* 9, q. 15, and in *Op. Ox.* 2, d. 25, q. un.; self-change in the intellect, *Ord.* 1, d. 3, pars 3, q. 2, nn. 486–94, and 2, d. 3, pars 2, q. 1, as well as *In De an.* q. 13 (this work is considered by some to be spurious). There are frequently parallel discussions in the *Lectura* as well. See King 1994. There is an argument in Sylwanowicz 1996, ch. 6, that Scotus developed the formal distinction from reflections on self-motion.

90 Scotus, like most mediaeval philosophers, took Aristotle's remark that "motion or change" is "the actualization of a potency *qua* potency" (*Phys.* 3.1 [201ª11–12]) as the real definition of change, where the clause "*qua* potency" was understood to refer to all the states of the subject intermediate between each terminus of the change. Cases of change that qualify as motions were more precisely defined in *Phys.* 3.1 (201ª28–29) as "the actualization of the mobile *qua* mobile": the persisting substratum is a substance, and the form in question belongs to one of the categories Quantity, Quality, or Place. Scotus's account applies to self-changers in general, and thereby to the more particular case of self-movers.

91 The distinction between active and passive potencies corresponds roughly to our ordinary modal notions of abilities and capacities, respectively.

92 This is not the same as the distinction between *per se* and accidental causality, since something might of its nature equivocally produce a given effect. There are particular difficulties in the case where the cause "eminently contains" the form of the effect: see *Quodl.* q. 5, nn. 23–4.

93 See *In Metaph.* 7, q. 5, and *Lect.* 2, d. 12, q.un. The subject is also discussed in *Op. Ox.* 2, d. 12, qq. 1–2, but there are textual problems that make this a less reliable source. I will give references, but the following account is based on the first two works.

94 *In Metaph.* 7, q. 5, n. 7, and *Lect.* 2, d. 12, q. un., n. 11 (the quoted remark comes from here); cf. *Op. Ox.* 2, d. 12, q. 1, n. 10. Scotus alludes to the argument in *Ord.* 2, d. 1, qq. 4–5, n. 204. See Aristotle, *Phys.* 1.7 (190ª14–21); *De gen. et corr.* 1.4 (319ᵇ6–320ª7); *Metaph.* 12.1–2 (1069ᵇ3–9); and 12.2–3 (1069ᵇ32–1070ª2).

95 Scotus's argument faces the objection that it effectively turns substantial change into accidental change. To rebut this charge, Scotus argues that substantial unities that are composites of matter and form have a being not merely reducible to that of their constituent metaphysical parts: see Section V.3.

96 *In Metaph.* 7, q. 5, n. 17, and *Lect.* 2, d. 12, q. un., n. 30, for matter, and *In Metaph.* 9, qq. 1–2, nn. 40–8, for the distinction in its own right.

97 See *Op. Ox.* 2, d. 12, q. 2, n. 4, and *Rep.* 2, d. 12, q. 2, n. 6. Hence, Scotus rejects the claim that material beings must be hylemorphic composites.

98 Ibid. Massobrio 1991, 240, and Cross 1998, 23–4, criticize Scotus's move from "not essential in any" to simply "not essential" as fallacious.

99 *Lect.* 2, d. 12, q. un., nn. 56–7. See also the text of *Op. Ox.* 2, d. 12, q. un., given in Stella 1955, 309–10. Scotus makes a similar point in *In Metaph.* 7, q. 16, n. 45. See Wood 1996, for a discussion of Scotus on individual forms.

100 *Rep.* 2, d. 12, q. 2, n. 12: "Hence, since [matter and form] are each an absolute being, I grant that each can exist without the other; but the bodily form is not thereby immaterial, since, despite the fact that it is separate, perfecting matter is nevertheless compatible with it." See *Lect.* 2, d. 12, q. un., n. 55, for Scotus's argument that substantial forms do not have an essential relation to matter. This position gets rid of any need to postulate Bonaventurean "spiritual matter," and indeed Scotus does not postulate it. See Massobrio 1991, ch. 4, on Scotus's repudiation of universal hylemorphism.

101 See also Richard Cross's contribution to this volume, where Scotus's first philosophical argument for the plurality of substantial forms is discussed against its historical and theological context.

102 It's not clear whether for Scotus the soul and the form of the body are equal concurrent causes, much as one man might hold up a heavy weight for a short time but two hold it up indefinitely, or whether the form of the body is essentially ordered to the soul in the exercise of its causality: see Section IV.1 and note 79.

103 See *Ord.* 2, d. 1, q. 6, n. 321; *Op. Ox.* 2, d. 16, q. un., nn. 17–8; *Op. Ox.* 4, d. 11, q. 3, n. 27 and n. 37; *Rep.* 2, d. 3, q. 2, n. 12; and q. 8, n. 8.

104 The passage is *Op. Ox.* 4, d. 10, q. 2, n. 4: *Impossibile est eamdem materiam esse simul sub duabus formis substantialibus.*

105 Scotus explicitly denies that his account provides an explanation: *In Metaph.* 8, q. 4, n. 11 and n. 54; *Lect.* 2, d. 12, q. un., n. 50; *Op. Ox.* 2, d. 12, q. un., n. 16, and 3, d. 2, q. 2, n. 10. See Cross 1995 and 1998. The further inexplicability of act–potency relations is a consequence of the fact that they transcendentally divide being, and hence there is nothing higher in terms of which an explanation could be provided.

106 Ibid. See Cross 1998, 87, as well as his contribution to this volume.

107 *Op. Ox.* 2, d. 16, q. 1, n. 10, where Scotus declares that existence is not related to essence as act to potency. See also *Op. Ox.* 4, d. 13, q. 1,

n. 38: "It is simply false that existence is something different from essence." See further O'Brien 1964, Hoeres 1965, and Wolter 1990a, ch. 12.

108 The problem of the nonactual individual is a difficulty for generalizing this account, but of course nonactual objects don't have essences in the first place: see Boler 1996.

109 *Lect.* 1, d. 8, pars 1, q. 3, nn. 100–5; *Ord.* 1, d. 8, pars 1, q. 3, nn. 101–7, and 2, d. 3, pars 1, qq. 5–6, nn. 189–90; see also *In Metaph.* 7, q. 19, nn. 20–1 and n. 43.

110 The question whether there is a single genus of all things was dealt with at the end of Section III.1. See S. Dumont 1998 for the solution sketched here.

111 See also *Coll.* 36, n. 9, for this point.

112 See Catania 1993.

2 Space and Time

By the end of the thirteenth century, it was clear that Aristotle's physics and cosmology presented claims that were incompatible with God's omnipotence. According to Scotus, "whatever does not evidently include a contradiction and from which a contradiction does not necessarily follow, is possible for God."[1] But many states of affairs, treated as impossible by Aristotle, seemed to involve no contradiction. Already in 1277, Stephen Tempier, Bishop of Paris, had issued his influential condemnation of, among other things, several key claims of Aristotle's physics and cosmology precisely because they implied limitations on God's absolute power.[2] This condemnation did not lead to a wholesale rejection of Aristotelian thought, however. Aristotle had provided the most detailed and powerful conception of the physical universe known to medieval thinkers, and Scotus, like most of his contemporaries, was deeply wedded to this conception in its broad outlines and in a great deal of its detail. But he formed part of a movement, beginning in the late thirteenth century, and gathering momentum in the fourteenth, in which this conception was intensely scrutinized and modified in a number of fundamental respects. Nowhere did Aristotle's thought pose greater problems than in doctrines concerning space and time. Scotus's writings were an important chapter in the reexamination and modification of Aristotelian doctrines on these issues.[3]

I. PLACE

I.1. Place, Whereness, and Position

Scotus has little to say expressly about space. He is far more concerned with *place*.[4] In this he follows Aristotle, who presents theories of time and place in Book 4 of the *Physics* but says little about space, his chief concern being motion (that is, gradual change), and in particular local motion – motion from one place to another.

Scotus uses three fundamental spatial notions: the place (*locus*), whereness (*ubi*), and position (*positio*) of a body. He does not explain these notions in terms of a space distinct from bodies in which bodies are located but, like Aristotle, rejects any such conception of space and instead explains them in terms of relationships of containment or correspondence of parts that obtain between bodies, or, more particularly, the surfaces of bodies.

Thus, Scotus accepts Aristotle's definition of the place of a body as "the first, immobile boundary of the body containing it."[5] This boundary is a two-dimensional surface of the containing body in contact with the contained body that occupies the place. To a body's place corresponds its whereness (*ubi*): "the circumscription of the [contained] body proceeding from its circumscription by a place."[6] The whereness of a body is a relation of *being contained by* that it has to a containing body. It is, Scotus explains, an extrinsically advening relation: the existence of the two bodies does not entail that one is contained by the other; an external cause is required for this.[7] A body has a position provided each of the parts of its surface corresponds to a part of the surface of a containing body, and the whole surface of the body corresponds to the whole surface of the containing body.[8]

The doctrine of God's absolute power distinguishes what can happen in the course of nature from what can happen through the exercise of God's power to do anything short of what involves a contradiction. In the course of nature, each body, with one important exception, must, in virtue of having volume, exist in this or that particular, actual, determinate place equal in size to itself, and have position. And insofar as a body is a natural body, it must exist in a place naturally or violently.[9] The exception to these conditions is the outermost heavenly sphere.[10] Because it has literally nothing beyond it, it is contained by no body and therefore has no place in a strict sense.[11] But Scotus argues that through God's absolute power it is possible that any body whatsoever not satisfy the above conditions, because it is absolutely possible for any body to lack a place.

I.2. The Priority of Body to Place

Scotus notes that, aside from the outermost sphere, Aristotle would deny that a body could exist without a place. Catholics would grant it, however,[12] for, Scotus reasons, if the outermost sphere is contained by no body, then "it includes no contradiction that a body exist without a body containing it [and thus have no place], and therefore, without a whereness."[13] Body is *naturally prior* to place and whereness, which implies, Scotus claims, that for any body B, the state of affairs "B exists and has no place" involves no contradiction and hence is possible for God to bring about. Scotus takes this to be an instance of the more general principle that it is no contradiction for an absolute (that is, nonrelational item) to remain in existence without a relation to what is naturally posterior to it.[14] Yet Scotus grants that a body, if not necessarily in a place, is through its corporeity necessarily able to be in a place.[15]

Scotus presents two thought experiments in which a body exists without a place. First, God could make a stone "although no other placing body existed." Second, he could make a stone "that existed separately from every other body, because he could make it outside the universe."[16] In each case, the stone would not exist in a place. In the first case, Scotus seems to envisage the existence of but a single stone. In the second, he seems to envisage a situation in which the cosmos exists and the bodies within it have places, but the stone exists in some sense outside the cosmos.

I.3. The Existence of a Void

A key doctrine of Aristotle's physics is the denial of the possibility of a void. In a narrow sense a void is a place devoid of body – a concave surface containing no body. More broadly speaking, a void is an empty three-dimensional space devoid of body. According to

Aristotle in *Physics* 4, void in neither sense does or could exist either within or outside the cosmos.[17]

According to Scotus, however, the possibility of at least an intra-cosmic void must be admitted. Such an intracosmic void is possible for God to bring about, although it is not actual and could not be produced through the workings of nature. Thus, God could annihilate the elemental matter contained under the heaven. If he did this, the heaven would not collapse instantly, since such a change must take some time. "Therefore, the concave surface of the heaven can remain in existence and yet not contain any body."[18]

What then are we to make of Aristotle's arguments against a void? Scotus mentions three arguments. The first is that such an empty space would entail the existence of an infinity of places.[19] The text Scotus refers to here is obscure, but Scotus thinks that, however it is interpreted, Aristotle relies on the idea that a void would be an actually dimensioned space and is pointing to the alleged problem that such a space could not be filled by a body, for then two three-dimensional items could spatially coincide, which Aristotle takes to be impossible. Scotus agrees that such an actually dimensioned empty space is impossible. The only actual dimensions that exist are those of a body. Where no body exists, there can be no three-dimensional space. But, according to Scotus, an intracosmic void is not to be conceived of as an actually dimensioned space: "The void posited as possible for God...is not a space having positive dimensions, but here there is only the *possibility* for dimensions of a certain size, together with the lack of any actual dimension."[20] In such a void there would not be anything between the sides – neither a body *nor an empty three-dimensional space* – but there could be a body of a determinate volume.

And yet, Scotus claims, although the sides of such a void would have nothing between them, they would *actually* be distant from one another. We must therefore reject Aristotle's second argument, namely, that items are together if nothing is between them. Instead, we must say that an *actual* distance relation between the sides of an intracosmic void requires only that "a body could be put between them having the same volume as a body that is put between them when the space is actually full." Thus, Scotus holds that although there is not actually something between the sides, there is something between them in "a potential and privative manner": they lack something between them, but something of a determinate volume could exist between them. It is only when no body is *or could be* put between two items that they must be together.[21]

Third, lest it be thought to be a contradiction that two items are actually distant from one another and yet have nothing actually between them, Scotus replies that the case is analogous to that in which there might exist two instants with no time between them. There would, he claims, be an actual distance between these instants, "although there is not a positive time between them ... For there to be a quasi-temporal distance between them, it is enough that a potential or privative time be accepted." The same is true of a void. It would have an *actual* distance relation between the sides, but nothing would actually exist between them.[22]

If an intracosmic void is possible through God's absolute power, what of an extracosmic void? The question of an extracosmic void had been raised in a striking way by the Condemnation of 1277, which had condemned the proposition that "God could not move the cosmos in a straight line, because it would leave behind a void."[23] This suggested that to deny at least the possibility of extracosmic void was heresy.

Scotus did not believe in an actual extracosmic void. He denied that the cosmos was made by God within a preexistent void,[24] and did not think, as some did, that God's immensity required that for God to act on the cosmos he must be present to it in an actual void.[25] But if an extracosmic void is not actual, is it at least possible for God to produce such a void? Henry of Ghent thought so. God could create a body outside and distant from the outermost heaven. Henry emphasizes that he does not mean that such a body would be created in a preexistent void, any more than the cosmos itself was, but rather that the creation of the body would result in a void between the body and the heaven. Henry's description of the nature of this void is akin to Scotus's description of an intracosmic void as involving merely privative potential dimension, an idea Scotus probably drew from Henry. According to Henry, the heaven and the said body would not be distant in the *per se* sense that "there is some positive distance of corporeal dimension between them" but would be distant in what he calls an incidental sense, in that "even though there is not a positive distance between them, still, around or between them there can be something that has in itself a positive dimension through which a distance can be considered between them."[26] Scotus, as we have seen, grants that God could create a stone outside the cosmos but does not expressly say that it would be distant from the cosmos. It is not implausible to think that he meant this, however, having Henry's teaching in mind.[27]

I.4. The Immobility of Place

Another important part of Scotus's reflections on place is his solution to problems posed by the immobility of place, that is, by the facts (1) that a body may move from the place it occupies, and another body may come to occupy the *same* place; and (2) that the same body continues to occupy the *same* place, although the bodies immediately surrounding it change – a boat moored in a river, for example, may continue to occupy the same place despite changes to the water surrounding it. Such phenomena led Aristotle to define place as an *immobile* boundary, for they suggest that place persists, neither being destroyed nor moving upon changes to contained or containing bodies. Yet medieval thinkers saw difficulties in reconciling Aristotle's conception of place with such phenomena.

To see why, we need to understand the difference between numerical sameness and distinctness and specific or type sameness and difference. This distinction may be explained, in contemporary terms, in terms of a distinction between tokens and types. A type has instances; a token is an instance of a type but is not itself a type. The type *human being*, for example, has as tokens Socrates, Plato, and so forth. The type *red* has as tokens this particular redness, that particular redness, and so forth. Similarly, we may distinguish a type of relation – say, *being to the north of* – from tokens of this type, the particular being to the north of that Boston stands in to New York, and the particular being to the north of that San Francisco stands in to Los Angeles, and so forth. Nonidentical tokens of the same type are said to be numerically distinct but specifically the same, that is, the same in type.

Now in the case of relations, we may ask what is required for numerically the same relation to remain in existence. Scotus's answer is that a necessary condition is that the extremes related remain numerically the same. For example, if Fred is next to Mary, the token relation of being next to that Fred bears to Mary, ceases to exist if

Mary relinquishes her position and John comes to occupy it. Now Fred stands in a numerically different (though specifically the same) relation of being next to.

That a numerically distinct extreme implies a numerically distinct relation generates problems concerning the immobility of place. For Aristotle's definition of place as the first, immobile boundary of a *containing* body may suggest that a place is in fact a *relation of containment* holding between a body and what it contains.[28] And this may suggest that the particular place a body occupies is simply a token containment relation between a particular containing body and that contained body. But, if this is so, a change either to the particular container or to the particular content will entail that numerically the same containment relation no longer exists and thus that the place that previously existed no longer exists. Places will not remain in existence as contents and containers change, and this clashes with our everyday conception of place.

Scotus grants that for a place to exist there must be an actual relation of containment.[29] But he leaves open the question of whether places are such relations – as the objections above assume – or rather are bodies as standing in such relations. He claims that we can account for the first type of phenomenon – the sameness of place with changing contents – whichever account we give. If we take a body's place to be the relation of containment that its container stands in to it, we can say that with changes to the contained body the relation of containment is not varied in the subject (in the container), which remains related to the new content *in the same way*.[30] Scotus's point seems to be that although numerically the same place exists only as long as the container and contained remain numerically the same, we may nonetheless say that the same place remains in existence because the same container continues to bear the same *type* of containment relation to the new contents. In effect, in such contexts "the same place" refers not to the numerical sameness of relations but to the sameness of a particular *type* of containment relation.

Alternatively, we may treat a place not as a containment relation but as a body-standing-in-a-containment-relation to a content. We may then say that the numerical difference of the containment relations of numerically the same body to numerically different contents does not entail that there is more than one "body-standing-in-a-containment-relation" any more, Scotus says, than the fact that one

object has many numerically distinct relations of similarity to differing objects entails that that object is many similar objects. Places,
so understood, are counted not by counting the number of numerically distinct containment relations, but by counting the number of
numerically distinct subjects having such relations, and in the case
at issue there remains just numerically one such subject.[31]

The second problem – that of how a body can remain in the same
place as its immediate surroundings change – had occupied the earliest Latin commentators on Aristotle's doctrine of place. Many concluded that an adequate solution must appeal to the permanence of
certain relations involving the whole heaven or its fixed termini –
its poles and the center of the earth. Theories along these lines were
proposed by, among others, Aquinas and Giles of Rome, and before
them, by Grosseteste and Richard Rufus of Cornwall.[32]

Scotus mentions two such theories. Each theory errs, Scotus
thinks, in its claim that, despite the change in a placed object's immediate container, certain key relations remain in existence to guarantee sameness of place. Scotus's presentation of these theories is very
condensed, although they bear resemblances to theories presented
by earlier thinkers such as Aquinas and Giles of Rome.

According to the first theory, the same place continues to exist
because the successive bodies immediately containing a body –
successive bodies of air, for example – all have the *same relation* to
the center and poles of the heaven.[33] But, Scotus objects, each successive container is numerically distinct from the former and must
therefore have numerically distinct accidents, relational and nonrelational. Thus, the successive containers do not stand in the *same*
relations to the poles and center of the heavens but in *numerically
distinct* relations.[34]

The second theory takes the place of a body to be "the boundary
of the whole universe."[35] Scotus perhaps has in mind the theory
of Giles of Rome. According to Giles, although water continuously
flows around a boat moored in a river, the boat is not said to change
place, because "it has the same order in relation to the whole river."
More generally, something whose immediate surroundings changed
would not change place, "because it would have the same order to
the whole universe."[36] By the "whole universe" Giles seems to mean
in particular the outermost sphere. The problem with this, Scotus
thinks, is that the contained object stands in a relation to the whole

universe in virtue of standing in a relation to a particular part of the boundary of the sphere. As the sphere rotates, it will no longer stand in numerically the same relation, for that particular part of the sphere's boundary will have moved away, to be replaced by a numerically distinct part. Thus, the contained object will not retain numerically the same relation to the whole universe.[37]

In these criticisms, Scotus assumes, perhaps unfairly, that these theories refer to the numerical sameness of relations, not specific sameness. Scotus himself proceeds to solve the problem of how the same place can remain in existence, even as the immediate surroundings of a contained body change, by reference to relations that remain specifically, but not numerically, the same.

Scotus starts by assuming that if a body is contained by numerically distinct containers, there are numerically distinct containment relations and the body occupies numerically distinct places.[38] So when the subject (i.e., the container) of a containment relation is moved locally, the original place of the contained object ceases to exist, and the contained object comes to occupy a numerically distinct place. Scotus then introduces the idea of the *ratio* of a place. By this he seems to mean something like the character or nature of the place. He holds that as the immediate surroundings of the placed object change, the numerically distinct places have numerically distinct characters. Yet these characters are nonetheless *equivalent* to one another in respect of local motion. In respect of this equivalence the characters may be said to be the same. Scotus suggests, therefore, that when we say that an object continues to occupy the same place as its immediate surroundings change, this is not because it occupies numerically the same place but because it occupies numerically distinct places whose numerically distinct characters are nonetheless equivalent in respect of local motion.

What is this equivalence? It is for the successive immediate containers of the contained object to have the *same kind* of relation *to the whole universe*. In virtue of this, the numerically distinct places will be indiscernible in respect of local motion: to an observer they would seem to be no more different as places than if there had remained numerically the same place. Scotus's solution therefore is that despite changes to the objects immediately containing it, a contained object will continue to be in the same place provided that the containing objects bear the same *kind* of relation to the whole universe. Sameness of place in this context refers to specific or type sameness of place.

But what is the relation of an object's immediate container to the whole universe? Scotus's use of the expression "the whole universe" strongly suggests that he is presenting a version of one of the kinds of theories he was attacking (in which the same expression is used), but a version in which it is made quite clear that sameness of place refers to the sameness of certain *types* of relation. If this is so, his account of the immobility of place constitutes a useful clarification of, but not a major break from, earlier theories.[39]

II. SPATIAL AND TEMPORAL CONTINUA[40]

II.1. *The Concept of Continuity*

In *Categories* 6 Aristotle distinguishes between discrete quantities – such as number and language – and continuous quantities – such as lines, surfaces, bodies, time, and place. (Aristotle elsewhere also treats motion as continuous.) Aristotle defines *continua* as items whose parts share a common boundary or limit, which lacks extension in the pertinent dimension. For example, adjacent parts of a line share a point as a common boundary; adjacent parts of a period of time share an instant. In *Physics* 6.1 Aristotle repeats this account of continuity and argues that it follows that continua cannot be made up of indivisibles, that is, boundaries lacking extension in the pertinent dimensions – points on a line, surfaces, instants of time, and so forth. Rather, continua are "divisible into divisibles that are always divisible." Indeed, in *De caelo* 1.1 Aristotle defines continuity in terms of infinite divisibility.

Scotus endorsed Aristotle's views on continuity, which formed the mainstream of medieval thought. He agreed that place, time, and motion are continuous and not composed of indivisibles. But he popularized important, non-Aristotelian arguments against the composition of continua out of indivisibles.[41]

II.2. *Successive and Permanent Items*

An important distinction may be drawn between spatial continua, on the one hand, and motion and time, on the other. Following tradition,

Scotus terms the latter "successive items"; the former, "permanent items."[42] A successive item exists in a successive manner. Scotus speaks of it as being made up of "flowing parts." It does not, and cannot, exist as a whole at any instant of time, but its existence is precisely a matter of one part succeeding another. Such an item, therefore, may be said to have temporal parts. Time and motion are of this nature. Permanent items, on the other hand – a body, for example – exist as a whole at any instant of time at which they exist. Scotus argues that it is possible for such items, unlike successive items, to exist as a whole for only an instant.[43]

Despite this important difference between successive and permanent items, Scotus agrees with Aristotle that there is an important similarity between successive and permanent continua: "Either all of [spatial magnitude, time, and motion] are composed of indivisibles and are divisible into indivisibles, or none."[44] Call this the Correspondence Thesis (CT). CT means that if one type of continuum is not composed of indivisibles, this will be true of all types.

II.3. Indivisibilism

According to Indivisibilism, continua are composed of indivisible items as their ultimate parts. Thus, Indivisibilism not only asserts that there are indivisibles *in* continua but claims that they are literally *parts* of continua. Indivisibilism may take a number of forms, depending on the answers given to the following questions: (1) How many indivisibles are in a continuum? (2) How are indivisibles in a continuum ordered? (3) What is the nature of indivisibles? Scotus's critique of Indivisibilism is unfortunately marred by a failure to specify clearly the form of Indivisibilism he has in mind, but in general he appears to be concerned to attack a form of Indivisibilism according to which continua are composed of indivisibles that are entirely lacking in magnitude in the pertinent dimension or dimensions and that are ordered *immediately* with respect to one another. By saying that two indivisibles are immediate to one another, Scotus means at least that there is not between them an item of the kind they may form boundaries of, nor another indivisible. Thus, two immediate points on a line would have no line segment or point between them. Let us call any such doctrine a form of Immediate Indivisibilism (II). We may note that it is unclear whether Scotus is concerned with a form of II that takes indivisibles as in some manner right next to each other, or rather with a form of II that takes them to involve some kind of gap between them.[45] Moreover, it is often unclear whether he is concerned with a form of II that takes continua to contain a finite number of indivisibles, or a form that takes them to contain an infinite number. The arguments Scotus mentions in favor of II, and his arguments against it, sometimes suggest differing versions of II.

Indivisibilism may take forms other than II. Some forms take indivisibles to have magnitude but nonetheless hold them to be incapable of division. Scotus does consider an Indivisibilism of this sort. He describes such indivisibles as *minima* and, following Aristotle, denies that continua can be composed of *minima*.[46] Indivisibles might also be ordered in ways II does not envisage. One possibility is to hold that indivisibles are densely ordered – having the structure of the rational numbers – such that between any two indivisibles is another.[47] Another, not recognized by any medieval thinker, is to take indivisibles not only as densely ordered but also as ordered continuously in the sense defined by Dedekind, that is, as having the structure of the real numbers.[48] Furthermore, some medieval thinkers held that different-sized continua contain different-sized infinities of indivisibles.[49] Scotus considers none of these possibilities.

II.4. Scotus's Criticisms of Arguments for Indivisibilism

Scotus mentions two arguments in support of II when considering the question of whether an angel can move with a continuous motion.[50] He notes that if motion were discrete, a negative answer would have to be given to this question. But Scotus holds that motion is continuous, and he is concerned to reject the view that motion is composed of indivisibles – boundaries of phases of the motion – for he takes it that this would imply the discreteness of motion and, given CT, of other continua.

The first argument for Indivisibilism that he considers is that the infinite divisibility of continua entails that it is possible that a continuum has been infinitely divided up. This implies the existence of indivisibles into which the continuum is able to have been divided up. And this, in turn, implies that such indivisibles are parts of continua.[51] We may note that even if this argument does not obviously imply that indivisibles are ordered immediately, it does seem to imply that they are infinite in number.

The argument obviously can be attacked at various points, but Scotus focuses on the claim that the fact that a continuum is infinitely divisible entails that it is possible for it to have been infinitely divided up. This inference, Scotus claims, is simply fallacious. It is true that continua are infinitely divisible, but infinite divisibility – the possibility for a process of division to go on without end – does not entail that such a process is able to have been completed: quite the contrary! In this Scotus is repeating a point Aristotle had already made, but unlike Aristotle, Scotus provides a detailed and sophisticated account of the logic of statements concerning infinite divisibility.[52]

The second argument raises a problem about the existence of successive items. If only an indivisible of a successive item is real, it seems we cannot account for the existence of that successive item except in terms of one indivisible of it being immediately followed by another, and this seems to imply that time and motion are composed of indivisibles.[53] Scotus, I shall suggest, agrees that only an indivisible of time (or motion) exists, but rejects Indivisibilism. This argument therefore raises a pressing difficulty for him. I return to it in the discussion of time.[54]

II.5. Scotus's Arguments Against Indivisibilism

A number of Scotus's arguments against Indivisibilism are standard arguments drawn from Book 6 of Aristotle's *Physics*.[55] But Scotus thinks that two even more effective arguments of a geometric nature may be made against Indivisibilism. "In general," he notes, "all of Book 10 of Euclid refutes the composition of a line out of points [and thus, granted CT, Indivisibilism in general]. For [if lines were composed out of points], there would be no irrational or surd line at all."[56] These arguments defy brief summary. One, stemming from Algazel and popularized by Roger Bacon,[57] aims to show that if Indivisibilism were true, the diagonal of a square would have to be commensurable, indeed equal, with the sides. Another, also stemming from Algazel, aims to show that two concentric circles would have to be of the same size. In each case, Scotus's strategy is to show that if Indivisibilism were true, the sides and the diagonal, and the circles, would have to be composed of the same number of points; and this, he holds, would imply sameness of size, since "it is impossible that two unequal items be composed of parts that are equal in magnitude and multitude."[58] In these arguments, we may note, Scotus assumes that points are immediate to one another and, therefore, fails to undermine forms of Indivisibilism other than II.

II.6. The Nature of Indivisibles

Because Scotus rejects Indivisibilism, he denies that indivisibles exist as either actual or potential *parts* of continua. But he thinks that indivisibles do exist actually as actual boundaries of continua – as the endpoints of a line, for example – and potentially as potential boundaries – as a potential point of the division of a line, for example. But what is the nature of such items? According to one view Scotus mentions, such boundaries are not absolute or positive entities. To say that an indivisible of a successive item[59] exists, for example, is simply to say that there is a lack of continuous succession. According to this view, indivisibles are purely privative items.[60] Such a "nonentitist" conception of indivisibles, as it is now termed, suggests that reference to indivisibles may be paraphrased away in terms of references to divisible items alone. William of Ockham and other fourteenth-century nominalists were to develop an approach along these lines.[61]

Nonentitism is attractive because to treat indivisibles as absolute entities raises difficult problems. Scotus notes that if indivisibles are absolute entities, it would seem that God could separate an indivisible from a continuum. We also face the problem of explaining how an indivisible and the continuum it bounds form a unified entity. Moreover, it seems that before a line is actually divided, there is but a single point in the middle of it. But when it is divided, two points exist in actuality. So now a point exists that did not exist before, and it does not seem to have come into existence through a process of generation. How then did it come into existence?[62]

Scotus does not respond to these arguments but thinks that there are several other arguments that show that nonentitism must be rejected.[63] According to Scotus, indivisibles as absolute items are needed to explain generation. Nonentitism contradicts Aristotle's claim that "the nature of a line is from points."[64] Nonentitism will have to treat lines, surfaces, and bodies as mere privations, or will have to hold that the only dimension is body. And if surfaces are privations, then, according to nonentitism, points will be privations of privations, and, in addition, many sensible qualities will have no subject in which to inhere – colors will have no surface to inhere in, for example.

III. TIME

In his discussions of time, as of place, Scotus confronts certain key assumptions of Aristotelian physics with the theologian's richer set of possibilities.[65] Scotus is concerned, in particular, with the relation between time and motion. Aristotle had denied generally the possibility of time without motion, and in particular the possibility of time without the motion of heaven. But Scotus wishes to claim that there can be time – in a sense to be explained – without the motion of the heavens and, indeed, without any motion at all. Scotus's writings also raise issues that have deeply concerned twentieth-century metaphysics of time. Such twentieth-century thinkers as McTaggart, Russell, and Broad helped to clarify and bring to philosophers' attention questions concerning the ontological status of past, present, and future and the flow of time. Is there an objective flow of time, or is the sense we have of the flow of time simply a psychological phenomenon? Are the categories of past, present, and future ontologically significant, telling us something about what is part of reality and what is not? Earlier philosophers grappled with these issues but often did so in ways that made it unclear just how to interpret their remarks. Scotus is no exception. He has many things to say that suggest a stance on these issues, but it is often unclear exactly what his view is.

III.1. The Ontological Status of Past, Present, and Future

According to some philosophers, the distinctions of past, present, and future have no more ontological significance than do the distinctions of here and there. This position is usually defended by appeal to the idea that terms like "past," "present," and "future," and the tenses of verbs, have a purely indexical function. By this it is meant, for example, that the informational content of an utterance of "*X* is present" is simply the fact that *X* is simultaneous with that very utterance. The content of an utterance of "*X* is past/future" is simply the fact that *X* is earlier/later than that utterance. The present, according to this view, has no special ontological status. In fact, we should hold that all times and their contents are on an equal ontological footing, all being equally real. It is difficult to express this view, however, since "are equally real" involves a use of the present-tensed verb "is," and thus seems to mean "are presently real," which has the incorrect suggestion that they are all equally present. A metaphysically perspicuous language would therefore do well to employ tenseless verbs, as is done in mathematics. Thus, the claim that all times and their contents are equally real might be put as the view that whatever *exists* at a time (including the time itself) *is* real, where the italics indicate tenseless uses of the verbs.[66]

Against this view has been opposed a doctrine now termed "Presentism." It is the view that only what is present is real. By this it is not meant that only what is present is presently real, as if the past or future might be real, just not real *and present*. Rather, it is denied that it is intelligible to speak of what is not present as being real in any sense. The concept of the real just is the concept of the present.[67] The notions of past, present, and future are therefore invested with ontological force, the present expressing reality; past and future, modes of unreality. This view requires rejection of the view that the adjectives "past," "present," and "future" and the tenses of verbs have a purely indexical function.

In at least one text – *Lectura* 1, d. 39, q. 5 – Scotus may plausibly be interpreted as adopting a form of Presentism.[68] His form of Presentism is limited, however, in that it concerns only the reality of *temporal* items – that is, successive items and items susceptible of change. In regard to such entities, all that is real of them is what is present. Scotus accepts that there are some non-temporal items,[69] and these do not fall within the scope of his version of Presentism.

That Scotus adopts a form of Presentism in *Lectura* 1, d. 39, q. 5, is suggested in his attack on the Thomistic account of how God knows future contingents.[70] According to Scotus, the Thomists hold that "all things are present to God in eternity in respect of their actual existence." They are not successively present to God, as the whole stream is successively present to a stick fixed amidst it. Rather, "the whole of time and anything successive in time is present to eternity." An item's being present to God, we must note, is not to be confused with its being temporally present (as opposed to past or future). For the Thomists' view is precisely that items that are past and future are also present to God, although they are not temporally present.

In support of this view, some Thomists appeal to God's immensity. His immensity, they claim, requires that all places be present to him, and therefore should also require that all of time be present to him. Scotus disputes this. God's immensity requires only that *actually existing* places be present to God, not that merely potentially existing places be present to God. So neither does his immensity require that the future be present to God, for the future is merely potential, no more a part of reality to be present to God than a merely potential place. Furthermore, if all future things were present to God in respect of their actual existence, God could not newly cause anything. What is related to God as present to him in respect of its actual existence is related to God as caused, not as yet to be caused. So if a future contingent is present to God in respect of its actual existence, God will only cause the future contingent if he causes the same thing twice over.

These criticisms assume the unreality of the future but do not seem to presuppose the unreality of the past. It turns out, however, that Scotus is in fact working with the assumption that both the past and future are unreal. For he later summarizes his position to be that "there is nothing of time but an instant. Therefore, although [time] flows continuously, it will not simultaneously be a whole in respect of eternity... Therefore, nothing is present to eternity but a 'now' of time."[71] The claim that there is nothing of time but an instant, if it is to ground an attack on the Thomistic conception of divine knowledge, cannot simply mean that all that is *present* of time is an instant. For this leaves open the possibility that the future and past are real, only not present, and thus are fit objects for God's eternal vision, which extends to all that is real. Rather, Scotus means that all that is real of time is an instant – the present instant.

And yet Scotus also holds that *time flows continuously*. He therefore implies that this is compatible with the doctrine that all that is real of time is the present instant. But, as I mentioned in the last section, there is an argument to show that if all that is real of time is an instant, in order that time itself be real, time must be discrete, composed of instants ordered immediately to one another, which is a view Scotus rejects.

The argument is that for there to be time is for there to be an indivisible of it in existence, for all there is of time is an instant. But if this is so, then the successiveness of time can only be accounted for if this instant is immediately followed by another instant. If it were not so followed, then since for there to be time is simply for an indivisible of it to exist, there would not be time once an instant passed away. To account for the reality of time, therefore, we must hold that one instant is immediately followed by another.[72] To Scotus, however, this amounts to the erroneous view that time is discrete and composed of indivisibles.

Now Scotus agrees with the assumption that all there is of time is an instant – the view he had proposed in *Lectura* 1, d. 39, q. 5. Does it really follow, however, that to secure the existence of time we must take it to be composed of immediately ordered instants? Scotus thinks not. The argument errs in supposing that the being of time consists in the existence of an indivisible of time. To his opponent's claim that "there is only time when there is an indivisible," Scotus replies that "if this were the case, time would never have being except the being of an indivisible. But its being is in flowing."[73] Scotus's point, if I understand it, is that in a strict sense it is wrong to say that there *is* time at an instant, if by this we mean that time as a whole exists at an instant. For time, being a successive item, is the kind of thing that cannot exist as a whole at an instant. In general, when we say that a successive item exists, we cannot mean that it exists as a whole at a given point of time. A motion, for example, does not exist as a whole at an instant, for at an instant there is not even a part of the motion, but simply an indivisible boundary of its phases. Does it follow then that motion does not exist, if all there is of motion is an indivisible? No, for what it is for motion "to exist" or to "have being" is simply for it *to be occurring*. In fact, since Scotus takes motion to be a flow of form,[74] for motion to exist is for a form to be flowing. Similarly, what it is for time, another successive item, to exist or to have being is for it to be flowing. The phenomenon of flow cannot be captured if we limit our attention to a single instant. Rather, for time to be flowing entails that the present instant will fall away and be succeeded by something. But

succeeded by precisely what? Will we not have to take the instant as
being immediately succeeded by another instant? Scotus thinks not.
Although all there is of time or motion is an indivisible instant, this
indivisible will not be followed immediately by another indivisible,
but by a flowing *part* of time or of form. According to this view, the
structure of time and motion is the same as that of a line. One point
is not immediate to another; immediate to a point is a *part* of a line.
The point forms an extrinsic boundary of that part; the part itself
that is immediate to the point has no initial point, for between any
point of that part and the bounding point will be yet another point.[75]
The same relation holds between instants and indivisibles of motion
and stretches of time and motion, respectively.[76]

III.2. Objective Time Flow

Scotus's reply to the argument that time is composed of indivisibles
refers to the idea of flow. But what does this reference to flow amount
to? One might claim that it simply refers to the fact that time, like
a line, is continuous and not discrete. As a line, as it were, "flows"
from endpoint to endpoint, so too do time and motion. But something
more than this may be meant. Scotus's pervasive use of the notion
of flow in reference to time and motion, although not in reference to
spatial continua, suggests that the concept of flow indicates something more than mere continuity. This must certainly be the case
if Scotus endorses Presentism. For in numerous places Scotus holds
that an instant "suddenly passes away" (*raptim transit*).[77] Thus, the
present instant has but a fleeting existence. What is present at once
becomes past, and this marks an objective feature of temporal reality.
This passage of what is present into the past is precisely what pro-
ponents of the flow of time have in mind, and so, given Presentism,
Scotus appears to hold that time is characterized by objective flow.

Perhaps the chief reason for thinking that Scotus may not endorse
such a conception of objective time flow is to be found in his forceful
rejection of the idea of a flowing 'now'. For one of the ways in which
one might try to envisage objective time flow is in terms of a 'now'
that somehow flows, as it were, along the time line, its being at a
given position rendering that position and its contents present.

The idea of a flowing 'now' is suggested in the *Physics*, where
Aristotle likens the 'now' to a body being carried over a spatial

magnitude. Although the body changes in the predicates true of it (in its "being"), the self-same body (the same body "in substance") remains in existence.[78] So, Aristotle might be thought to suggest, the self-same 'now' flows, successively being characterized by different predicates. Scotus himself thinks that this is a misinterpretation of Aristotle, but there is little doubt that some of Scotus's contemporaries did adopt a conception of a flowing 'now'. In his *Questions on the Metaphysics*, Scotus provides long quotations from William of La Mare's account of time. In considering the question of whether the 'now' of the *aevum* (the mode of duration angels have) is the same as the 'now' of time, William argues that this is not impossible, holding that as a line "flows" from a simple, intrinsically unchangeable point, so the 'now' "causes time by its flow" and as such "is changeable and variable in its being [i.e., its characteristics]," even though in its essence it is unchanging and stands still (and as such is the *aevum*). It appears to be this conception of a 'now' that causes time by its flow that Scotus is concerned to attack.[79]

The idea of a flowing now is also suggested by a problem Aristotle had mentioned of accounting for the generation and corruption of 'nows'.[80] If the self-same 'now' does not flow, it might be thought that there is a plurality of successive 'nows', one 'now' being corrupted and another being generated. But when might a 'now' be generated or corrupted? Not at itself, for it exists then. Nor at a now immediate to itself, for Aristotle (and Scotus) deny that 'nows', or indivisibles in general, are immediate to one another. Nor at a now that is not immediate, for then the same now would continue to exist at the intermediate 'nows', which is absurd. Scotus thinks that this argument is sophistical. It errs in supposing that the existence and nonexistence of a 'now' must be a matter of generation and corruption. 'Nows' are neither generated nor corrupted, and yet it does not follow that once they exist they cannot go out of existence. In fact, it is characteristic of nows, or instants, to exist and not exist without generation and corruption. To this view, which Aristotle had proposed, Scotus adds a logical analysis of the beginning and ceasing of a 'now' or instant. To say that a 'now' or instant ceases is to say that it exists and does not exist afterwards; to say that it begins is to say that it exists but did not exist beforehand.[81]

The fact that 'nows' are not generated or corrupted, therefore, does not require us to posit a single flowing 'now'. And Aristotle had

already given arguments against a single flowing 'now'. A period of
time is a continuum, and must therefore be bounded by two really
distinct limits. These limits are instants of time, and therefore are
really distinct 'nows'. Moreover, if the same 'now' continued to exist,
this would entail the simultaneity of all items in time, since any
two items simultaneous with the same item are simultaneous with
each other, and every item in time would be simultaneous with the
flowing 'now'. These arguments, we may note, all rest in part on the
assumption that an instant is a 'now' – a point a defender of a flowing
'now' might wish to dispute.

Is Scotus's rejection of a flowing 'now' intended to be a rejection of
the idea that time flows? As tempting as it might be to think so,[82] I
suggest that this is not Scotus's intent. He instead is particularly concerned to reject the flowing 'now' because it characterizes the flow of
time in terms of the motion of an indivisible, and this, Scotus thinks,
implies that time is composed of indivisibles. Thus, Scotus asks:

How could an indivisible now itself flow according to different beings (which
necessarily would be indivisibles) without its whole flow being composed
of indivisibles? For the Philosopher aims to prove in Book 6 of the *Physics*
that an indivisible cannot move, for then its motion would be composed
of indivisibles. For it would traverse something less than or equal to itself,
before it traversed something greater. Therefore, time would be composed
of indivisibles, which is contrary to the Philosopher.[83]

And in support of this interpretation of Scotus's rejection of the flowing 'now', we may note that in place of a conception of time as composed of indivisibles, Scotus proposes an account that nonetheless
retains the notion of flow. "When an indivisible falls away," he tells
us, "a continuous flowing part, not an indivisible, succeeds it."[84] If
the rejection of a flowing 'now' was motivated fundamentally by a
rejection of the idea that time objectively flows, it would be odd to
replace it with talk of flowing parts.

III.3. Time and Motion

Perhaps Scotus's most radical modification of Aristotle's physical
theory concerned the relation between time and motion or gradual
change. Although many philosophers have been quite prepared to
grant, against Aristotle, the possibility of extra- or intracosmic void,

very few have been prepared to dispute Aristotle's rejection of the possibility of time without motion. And yet Scotus thinks that it is possible for there to be time in a certain sense in the total absence of motion.

According to Aristotle, time is a number of motion in respect of before and after. Scotus more often describes time as a measure of motion.[85] In any event, they agree that time is in some sense relative to motion or, as Aristotle puts it, "some aspect of motion." In fact, Aristotle argued in *Physics* 4.11 that the temporal ordering of items as before and after and the continuity of time derive from the logically prior continuity and before–after ordering of motion, and this in turn from the continuity and a before–after ordering of the magnitude over which motion occurs.

Scotus agrees with Aristotle that motion itself has continuity and a before–after ordering that is logically prior to that of time. In fact, he seems to hold that when we speak of the continuity of time and temporal priority, we are not speaking of a continuity and priority over and above those of motion. Rather, our reference to time adds, over and above these, simply the idea of a universal measure of motion. For there to be time is simply for there to be motion functioning as such a measure.[86] This universal measure of motion will be, as it were, a cosmic clock,[87] and such a clock, like any clock, will be a certain periodic motion. Scotus follows Aristotle and holds that this periodic motion must be absolutely uniform and the fastest of all motions. According to Aristotle, only circular motion could satisfy the regularity condition, and only the circular motion of the outermost sphere could satisfy the speed condition. Time therefore requires the occurrence of the first motion, the diurnal circular motion of the outermost sphere. Should we therefore identify time outright with this first motion? Scotus notes difficulties in general in identifying time with motion,[88] but this does not mean that time cannot be an attribute of motion in some way, and in fact Scotus concludes that time is an attribute of the first motion.

If time is an attribute of the first motion, however, it seems to follow that were the first motion not to occur, there would be no time – not, at least, unless another cosmic clock were possible, and Scotus envisages no such possibility. Thus, Scotus is led to conclude that were the first motion not to occur, "the feature of a measure in respect of every other motion would be found in no motion, and therefore time would not exist in the way in which it is now posited to be an attribute of the first motion."[89]

This remark suggests, however, that in such a case time might exist in some other way. Now unlike Aristotle and Averroës, Scotus and his fellow theologians believed not only that it was possible that the first motion not occur and yet other motions occur, but also that this actually was and will be the case. The Bible recounts miracles in which the heavens stood still but motion went on (for example, Joshua 10:13), and although the heavens will come to a standstill, some motion will continue to occur, if for no other reason than that this is required by the eternal torment of the reprobate.[90] Some theologians also believed that before the heavens started to turn, there had existed another kind of motion, be it bodily or spiritual in nature.[91]

Now it is surely plausible to think that if any motion whatsoever occurs, there is time. If, like Scotus, we think of time as an attribute of the first motion, what are we to say about such cases in which there is motion without the first motion? Two responses suggest themselves. One is to hold that time in the sense of a measure of motion is only one kind of time, and that time in another, nonmetrical sense might exist in the absence of a cosmic clock. The other is to retain the idea that time as such is a measure of motion, but to hold that there can in some sense be time as a measure even in the absence of the first motion. An example of the former course is provided by Grosseteste, who held that by time may simply be meant the nonmetrical conception of a "space of intervals that passes from future expectation, through the present, into the past." Time in this sense "would have had to exist even without the constellations, if any motion, bodily or spiritual, had preceded the condition of the luminaries."[92] But Scotus took the second course. He retained a tight link between the notion of time and the notion of a cosmic clock, and concluded that when there is motion without the first motion, there is what he calls *potential* time – a potential measure of motion. Indeed, Scotus goes further and envisages the possibility of such potential time in the absence of any motion whatsoever.

The idea that in the total absence of motion there may be potential time relies on Aristotle's view that rest is measured by time, and on the view, not shared by Aristotle, that it is absolutely possible for items to be in a state of genuine rest in the total absence of motion.

Such, Scotus notes, could be the state of the bodies of the blessed. With no other objects in motion, they could be in a state of genuine rest, in that they could exist without motion but nonetheless be naturally capable of motion. But if an object is in a state of genuine rest, Scotus reasons, there must be a sense in which there is time, for rest, no less than motion, is measured by time. We measure a particular rest by reference to the time a motion would have taken had it occurred instead of the rest. And since such a motion is itself measured by reference to the motion of the cosmic clock, we may say that in general motion and rest are measured by the motion of a cosmic clock. If there were genuine rest in the absence of all motion, there would be no cosmic clock, and yet this rest would have to take some time.[93]

The time this total rest would take is potential time. Actual time requires the actual operation of a cosmic clock – the actual occurrence of the first motion. Although there would not be actual time in a state of total rest, there would be potential time in a way analogous to that in which there would be potential dimension in an intracosmic void. Just as the sides of an intracosmic void would be *actually* distant from one another, so in a case of total rest, instants bounding that state of rest would be *actually distant* from one another in a quasi-temporal way (that is, as if they were in time). But just as the sides of the void would have no actual dimension between them, so neither would such instants have actual time between them. When we speak of potential time and dimension in such cases, we are referring, respectively, to the possibility of the occurrence of the first motion between the instants in question and the possibility of the existence of a body of determinate volume between the sides of the void.[94]

The doctrine of potential time also applies, as I mentioned, to the case in which some motion occurs without the motion of the heaven: "When the heaven stands still, Peter will be able to walk after the Resurrection, and yet that walking is not considered to be in any time other than our common, continuous time. And yet it exists, while the first motion of the heaven does not exist."[95] Scotus does not mean here that Peter's walking is in our *actual* time but instead that we *consider or think of* his walking as if it were in our time because we have in mind the counterfactual supposition that if the first motion were occurring then, so much actual time would elapse.

The doctrines of potential time and potential dimension mark a major shift from the Aristotelian tradition, for they allow for the possibility of items that lack dimension or time between them but are no less actually separated from one another than are items separated by actual dimension or time – a possibility Aristotle would certainly have denied. But we must realize that in each case the doctrine was dictated in part by Scotus's acceptance of key Aristotelian claims, notably the impossibility of actual dimension without body and of actual time without motion.

NOTES

1   *Ord.* 4, d. 10, q. 2, n. 11.
2   On the Condemnation, see Grant 1979.
3   Scotus's discussions of these issues are typically embedded within elaborate theological discussions. Of particular importance are *Ord.* and *Lect.* 2, d. 2, qq. 1–2, where Scotus considers time and place while discussing the duration, place, and motion of angels. See also *Ord.* 4, d. 10, q. 2, and 4, d. 48, q. 16, where Scotus discusses, respectively, whether the same body can be in two places at once and whether two bodies can be in the same place at once. Space constraints prevented consideration of these two issues in this chapter. (The interested reader will find a brief discussion of them in Cross 1998, 200–1. This book is essential reading on Scotus's physical theory and contains detailed accounts of all the issues treated in this chapter as well as much else.) *Ord.* 4, d. 48, q. 2 is an important discussion of the relation of time to the motion of the heavens. Scotus expressly discusses place at some length in the important eleventh Quodlibetal Question.
4   On Scotus's views on place, see Duhem 1913–59 (a convenient English translation, which contains all the pertinent material on Scotus on space and time, is found in Ariew 1985); Cross 1998, ch. 11; Lang 1983; and Harris 1927, 2:122–9.
5   See Aristotle, *Phys.* 4.4 (212^{a}201); Scotus, *Ord.* 2, d. 2, pars 2, qq. 1–2, n. 219. Aristotle's definition aims to capture the idea that the place of a body must not be a part of the body but must contain it, must be neither greater nor smaller than the body contained, must be separable from the contained body, and must be distinguishable in respect of up and down. Aristotle argues that only the immobile surface of the containing body in contact with a body can meet all these conditions. In the *Categories* (4^{b}2–25), however, Aristotle proposes a different account of place that treats a body's place as in effect a three-dimensional extension. Medieval

thinkers viewed this as a vulgar conception of place and usually followed the *Physics*, where Aristotle expressly rejects such a conception of
place.

6 Scotus takes the definition of "whereness" from the twelfth-century
Liber sex principiorum, falsely attributed to Gilbertus Porretanus. See
Quodl. 11.1, n. 1. In the *Categories*, Aristotle implicitly distinguishes
place and whereness by treating place under the category of quantity but
assigning a distinct category of "whereness." This led to the development of the distinction between a body's place and its whereness. See
Grant 1976.

7 *Quodl.* 11.4, n. 34. More specifically, Scotus holds that an extrinsically
advening relation "does not necessarily accompany the foundation, even
when the term is posited." The foundation is the feature of the item
standing in the relation (i.e., of the subject) that founds the relation – an
object's color, for example, serves to found a similarity relation of it to
objects of the same color. An object's corporeity founds its being contained by another body. In the case of extrinsically advening relations,
such as *being contained by*, the existence of the foundation and term
(that to which the relation is) does not entail that the relation holds between the relata. An external cause is also required to bring them into
the relation with one another.

8 *Ord.* 4, d. 10, q. 1, n. 14.

9 *Ord.* 2, d. 2, pars 2, qq. 1–2, nn. 216–7; *Lect.* 2, d. 2, pars 2, qq. 1–2,
nn. 191–2.

10 For an overview of medieval cosmological doctrines, see Grant 1978.

11 If it has no place, how then can it have a local motion (i.e., motion
from place to place)? Medieval thinkers offered a number of solutions
to this problem. According to Scotus, "if the first heaven is moved, it is
moved as placing, not as being placed, for it now places the contained
body differently than it placed it before. But it is itself not placed in
a different way, because it is not placed at all. This is what Averroës
means when he says that 'the heaven is in a place through its center,'
because for it to be in a place is for it to place a placeable item fixed in
a place" (*Quodl.* 11.1, n. 12).

12 *Ord.* 2, d. 2, pars 2, qq. 1–2, nn. 230–31; *Lect.* 2, d. 2, pars 2, qq. 1–2,
nn. 223–4.

13 *Quodl.* 11.1, n. 4.

14 *Quodl.* 11.1, n. 4. As Cross points out (Cross 1998, 204–5), if Scotus
means here simply that for any absolute item A, and any naturally posterior item B to which A is related, it is possible for A not to be related
to B, this will not entail that it is possible for A to have no relations at
all to such items as B. To draw this conclusion would involve a fallacy

along the lines of the following: For any color, it is possible that an object not have that color; therefore, it is possible that an item have no color at all.

15 *Quodl.* 11.1, n. 10.

16 *Ord.* 2, d. 2, pars 2, qq. 1–2, n. 231; *Lect.* 2, d. 2, pars 2, qq. 1–2, n. 224.

17 For Aristotle's and medieval discussions of the void, see Grant 1981.

18 *Quodl.* 11.2, n. 17.

19 See *Phys.* 4.4 (211^b20-3).

20 *Quodl.* 11.2, n. 21.

21 *Quodl.* 11.2, n. 22.

22 *Quodl.* 11.2, n. 24.

23 For the influence of the condemnation of this proposition, see Grant 1979, 226–32.

24 *Ord.* 1, d. 37, q. un., n. 9.

25 For such arguments, see Grant 1981, 144–7.

26 *Quodlibet* 13.3 (Henry of Ghent 1979–, 18:16–7).

27 The alternative would be to take Scotus's reference to the stone's being "outside" the cosmos to be a way of making the point that the stone would bear no spatial or quasi-spatial relations to the cosmos.

28 The reader should bear in mind that here and in what follows the relation of containment is a relation of the *containing* body to the contained body. The contained body instead stands in the relation of being contained (its whereness).

29 *Quodl.* 11.3, n. 28.

30 *Quodl.* 11.3, n. 28.

31 *Quodl.* 11.3, n. 28.

32 For Aquinas and Giles, see Duhem 1913–59, ch. 4. For Grosseteste, see Dales 1963, 80–2. For Rufus's views on place as they contrast with Roger Bacon's, see Wood 1997a, 239–46.

33 *Ord.* 2, d. 2, pars 2, qq. 1–2, n. 221; *Lect.* 2, d. 2, pars 2, qq. 1–2, n. 198.

34 *Ord.* 2, d. 2, pars 2, qq. 1–2, n. 222. See also *Lect.* 2, d. 2, pars 2, qq. 1–2, nn. 200–1.

35 *Ord.* 2, d. 2, pars 2, qq. 1–2, n. 223; *Lect.* 2, d. 2, pars 2, qq. 1–2, n. 199.

36 *Sent.* 1.37.2.1.1 (quoted in Vatican 7: 163, note F). Richard Rufus proposes a similar theory. See Wood 1997a, 242, n. 72.

37 *Ord.* 2, d. 2, pars 2, qq. 1–2, n. 223; *Lect.* 2, d. 2, pars 2, qq. 1–2, n. 202.

38 Scotus presents his account of the immobility of place in *Ord.* 2, d. 2, pars 2, qq. 1–2, nn. 224–9, and *Lect.* 2, d. 2, pars 2, qq. 1–2, nn. 204–6.

39 Alternatively, Richard Cross has suggested (Cross 1998, 210) that "the (specific) identity of a place is determined not by its relation to any immobile reference point, but by its relation to the whole universe: that

is, presumably, to the whole framework of other (immobile) places," the "identity of a place" being "established merely by its location within this whole."

40 Cross 1998, ch. 7, provides an excellent, detailed discussion of the issues considered in this section.

41 For medieval accounts of continuity, see Murdoch 1982.

42 See *Quodl.* 12.1, n. 7.

43 See *Quodl.* 12.3, n. 18.

44 Aristotle, *Phys.* 6.1 (231^b18–20) (Barnes's translation).

45 Cross 1998, 118, suggests that Scotus has the latter in mind.

46 I omit discussion of *minima* here. On this issue, see Cross 1998, 127–33.

47 Bradwardine ascribes this view to Grosseteste in *De continuo*. See Murdoch 1982, 578, n. 42.

48 A lucid explanation of Dedekind's theory of continuity is given in Waismann 1959, 198–204.

49 This was Grosseteste's view in *De luce* (Bauer 1912, 53–4).

50 Murdoch 1982, 576, notes that this question formed an important motivation for fourteenth-century discussions of continuity.

51 *Ord.* 2, d. 2, pars 2, q. 5, n. 288; *Lect.* 2, d. 2, pars 2, qq. 5–6, n. 263.

52 See *Ord.* 2, d. 2, pars 2, q. 5, nn. 354–75; *Lect.* 2, d. 2, pars 2, qq. 5–6, nn. 360–73.

53 *Ord.* 2, d. 2, pars 2, q. 5, n. 289; *Lect.* 2, d. 2, pars 2, qq. 5–6, n. 264.

54 See Sections III.1 and III.2 in this chapter.

55 *Ord.* 2, d. 2, pars 2, q. 5, nn. 316–9; *Lect.* 2, d. 2, pars 2, qq. 5–6, n. 348. For the arguments of *Phys.* 6, see White 1992, ch. 1.

56 *Ord.* 2, d. 2, pars 2, q. 5, n. 331. The geometrical arguments are presented in nn. 320–30. These arguments are translated by John Murdoch in Grant 1974, 316–17, and discussed in Cross 1998, ch. 7.

57 See Muckle 1933, 12–13, and Thijssen 1984.

58 *Ord.* 2, d. 2, pars 2, q. 5, n. 321.

59 That is, an instant of time or an indivisible of motion, a so-called *mutatum esse* – the boundary between two phases of the motion.

60 *Ord.* 2, d. 2, pars 2, q. 5, n. 376.

61 For Ockham's theory, see Stump 1982.

62 For these arguments, see *Ord.* 2, d. 2, pars 2, q. 5, nn. 377–79.

63 See *Ord.* 2, d. 2, pars 2, q. 5, nn. 380–5.

64 *Post. An.* 1.4 (73^a34–7).

65 For Scotus's views on time, Duhem in Ariew 1985, 295–9, remains important. Harris in Harris 1927 bases his account of Scotus's views on time almost wholly on the unauthentic *De rerum principio*, now attributed to Vital Du Four, and is followed in this by Dolnikowski 1995, 67–71. Cross 1997a and 1998, chs.12–13, provide the most detailed and

sophisticated account, although one that diverges in a number of important respects from the account I give. Craig 1988, 129–33, provides a brief account in substantial agreement with much of what I present in this section.

66 See, for example, Smart 1963, ch. 7.

67 The most notable recent exponent of this view is Arthur Prior in Prior 1970, 245–8. According to Prior, to conceive of the past and future as real, just not present, is on par with thinking of what is merely possible as real, just not actual.

68 *Lect.* 1, d. 39, is translated with a running commentary in Vos Jaczn, Veldhuis, Looman-Graaskamp 1994. Cross 1998, 245 (see also Cross 1997a), takes the adherence to Presentism in this text to be "atypical."

69 Namely, an item in which there cannot be a flow of form and in which there cannot be such a flow in anything that naturally accompanies the item. See *Ord.* 2, d. 2, pars 1, q. 4, nn. 171–2.

70 Parallel material may be found in *Ord.* 1, d. 39, but since this text was interpolated into the *Ordinatio* by a later editor it must be used as a source for Scotus's doctrines with some caution.

71 *Lect.* 1, d. 39, qq. 1–5, n. 85.

72 *Ord.* 2, d. 2, pars 2, q. 5, n. 289; *Lect.* 2, d. 2, pars 2, qq. 5–6, n. 264.

73 See *Lect.* 2, d. 2, pars 2, qq. 5–6, nn. 374–9. In the *Ordinatio* Scotus simply replies that "when that [indivisible] falls away, a continuous flowing part and not an indivisible succeeds it. Nor does anything immediately [succeed it], except in the sense in which a continuum is immediate to an indivisible" (*Ord.* 2, d. 2, pars 2, q. 5, n. 387).

74 *Ord.* 2, d. 2, pars 1, q. 4, nn. 171–2. On motion as a *fluxus formae*, see Maier 1982.

75 For further discussion of the sense in which a line segment may be said to be immediate to a point, see Cross 1998, 136–7.

76 If we assume Presentism, however, as I think Scotus does, there is a significant disanalogy between the cases of time and a line. For the whole of a line is actual, and therefore there is little difficulty in the idea that a point is followed by a line segment. But according to Presentism only the present instant and its contents are actual. How then can the present instant be immediately followed by a part of time, something that necessarily lasts longer than an instant and of which nothing is ever actual but an instant, which itself is not a part of time?

77 For example, *Ord.* 2, d. 2, pars 1, q. 1, n. 55.

78 *Phys.* 4.10 (218^{a}8–11).

79 *In Metaph.* 5, q. 10, n. 23. It is far from clear that Scotus's quotation of William's view should be taken as an endorsement of it, and that Scotus therefore adopted different views in the *Metaphysics* and

Sentences commentaries. The bulk of 5, q. 10, including the passage introducing the idea of a flowing 'now', consists of direct quotation from William and opens with the words "there is another opinion about the unity of time and the *aevum*, one that is more subtle, and, I believe, more true." The first person "I" here is William.

80 *Phys.* 4.10 (218^a8–21).

81 *Ord.* 2, d. 2, pars 1, q. 1, n. 56. For Scotus's account of beginning and ceasing, see Cross 1998, 221–6.

82 Cross 1998, 242–51, appears to adopt this interpretation.

83 *Ord.* 2, d. 2, pars 1, q. 2, n. 99; *Lect.* 2, d. 2, pars 1, q. 2, n. 91. Presumably the indivisibles that would make up the flow of time would not themselves be identical with the single flowing 'now' itself. As Cross notes (Cross 1998, 251–3), this argument seems to be inconsistent with Scotus's claim that an angel, which is an indivisible, could move with a continous motion. See especially *Ord.* 2, d. 2, pars 2, q. 5, nn. 412–27, and *Lect.* 2, d. 2, pars 2, qq. 5–6, nn. 396–419, where Scotus responds to Aristotelian arguments against the continuous motion of indivisibles.

84 *Ord.* 2, d. 2, pars 2, q. 5, n. 387.

85 Whether these two definitions amount to the same thing is a matter of scholarly disagreement. Some scholars think that by "number" Aristotle means a unit of the duration of motion – say, an hour – and in this sense time clearly is a measure of motion. An alternative interpretation is to hold that by the numbering of motion Aristotle has in mind not the assignment of a numerical value of its duration but rather the counting of one motion as distinct from another, or perhaps the counting of 'nows' bounding phases of motion. On this issue see Sorabji 1983, ch. 7.

86 *Ord.* 4, d. 48, q. 2. If time is an attribute of the first motion, this raises the question of in what sense time can measure the first motion itself. Scotus's view is that "if the first motion is measured by time, this is either because motion is taken to be something other than time ... or, if time is taken to be the same as motion, that motion can measure itself – not indeed in a primary way, but in respect of a part that is known as it measures the whole. As Aristotle says in Book 4 of the *Physics*, 'time measures motion itself by marking out a certain motion, which will later measure the whole motion, in the way the length of a cubit [measures] by marking out some magnitude which measures the whole'" (*Ord.* 2, d. 2, pars 1, q. 3, n. 140).

87 The concept of measurement, as it is used in this context, is not psychological. It is true that we say that *a person* measures something by using a clock. Measurement in this sense requires the existence of minds, a point that led many medieval thinkers to hold that the idea of time as

a measure implies that time is in at least some respects a psychological phenomenon. But when Scotus speaks of time as a measure of motion, he is simply referring to the existence of something having the features required of a cosmic clock, whether or not anyone uses that clock to measure motion, and he gives no indication that he thinks of time as even partly psychological.

88 *Ord.* 2, d. 2, pars 1, q. 2, n. 111; *Lect.* 2, d. 2, pars 1, q. 3, nn. 109–11. He notes that motion, unlike time, may be faster and slower, the same motion taking up more or less time. But it is far from clear that this could be true of the first motion, in reference to which time is measured. For this motion to be able to go, say, twice as fast, would seem to imply an absolute duration independent of all motion, and there is no indication that Scotus endorses any such view. Perhaps a realization on Scotus's part that the arguments against identifying time with motion in general may not apply to an identification of it with the first motion was responsible for Scotus's refusal to deny outright that time is identical with the first motion.

89 *Ord.* 4, d. 48, q. 2.

90 In *Ord.* 4, d. 48, q. 2, Scotus expressly refers to Joshua 10:13 and Augustine's *Confessions* 11.

91 For example, Alexander of Hales, *Summa theologica*, 1.1.2.4.2 (Alexander of Hales 1924–48, 1:108).

92 *Hexaemeron*, 5.12.2 (Robert Grosseteste 1982, 172)

93 *Quodl.* 11.2, n. 23.

94 *Quodl.* 11.4, n. 24.

95 *Ord.* 2, d. 2, pars 2, q. 7, n. 502.

3 Universals and Individuation

Both present-day historians of philosophy and those working in the past two centuries have considered the thought of Duns Scotus regarding the philosophical problems of universals and individuation as laying the groundwork for much of the philosophical speculation of the fourteenth and fifteenth centuries. Their judgment is well founded, being based on numerous texts in writers such as William of Ockham, Adam Wodeham, Walter Burley, and a host of others whose starting points in discussing both universals and individuation were often the views of Duns Scotus. Furthermore, as the problem of justifying and delimiting the range of natural knowledge became more and more central to philosophical as well as theological investigation, the influence of Duns Scotus on the two problems under discussion continued to grow. Realists as late as the sixteenth and seventeenth centuries looked to Scotus's works for supporting arguments and conceptual tools whereby to salvage their claims that universals exist outside the mind, whereas the conceptualists and nominalists of later centuries often began their critique of contemporary opponents by pointing out the weaknesses in Scotus's theories. The historical importance of Scotus's thought on the subjects being considered here is then clear enough. But the systematic value of his solutions to the problems of universals and individuation should not be overlooked. Several contemporary philosophers working in the areas of metaphysics and epistemology appeal to distinctions bearing striking resemblances to those advanced by Scotus and his followers, especially regarding the problem of individuation.

Yet to understand Scotus's outlook on the problems of universals and individuation requires that we enter to some extent into the history and progress of these problems as they were treated by Scotus's predecessors and contemporaries; for Scotus, as we shall see, is quite engaged in considering, modifying, and rejecting their views when arriving at his own solutions. Nor is this surprising, since medieval thought, to a degree that we find remarkable, is based upon reading a range of classic, authoritative texts (auctoritates) that discuss various philosophical and theological themes and upon rendering an account of one's own ideas in response to such texts. In the case of the problems of universals and individuation, the classic texts were, by the time of the Subtle Doctor, Porphyry's Isagoge; Avicenna's De prima philosophia, Logica, and De anima; Aristotle's Metaphysics and De anima; and the commentaries of Averroës upon the latter. Of these sources for philosophical reflection, the most important for Scotus's discussion of the problem of universals are the writings of Avicenna, whereas the most important for his views on individuation are the Aristotelian writings as these were interpreted not only by Averroës but also by more recent writers such as Thomas Aquinas, Godfrey of Fontaines, and Henry of Ghent.

If we turn to our own experience to discover the basis for the philosophical theories we are about to consider, we may say that the problem of universals amounts to examining the question of whether the kinds that we grasp intellectually and talk about in both everyday and technical discourse are really found in the concrete, individual things that we perceive around us, and if so, how. The problem of individuation is just the converse of that of universals.[1] We need to explain the features or status we ascribe to individuals precisely taken as such, in contradistinction to kinds, by appealing to some principle, cause, or entity that renders them individuals or in some way accounts for the status they have as individuals. Of course, this way of stating the problem of individuation presumes that the question regarding universals was answered affirmatively and that there is some need to develop an account of individuals as opposed to kinds that invokes ontological features, rather than simply stating that universals are solely in the mind and focusing attention on the logical and epistemological aspects of universals. Indeed, although we shall begin the account of Scotus's theory of universals by tracing its background in Avicenna, much of Scotus's discussion in both the Ordinatio and the Quaestiones on Aristotle's Metaphysics is devoted to allaying the suspicion that a simpler ontology would suffice to explain the world as revealed to us in experience, thought, and language – a suspicion already found in some of Scotus's Oxford Franciscan colleagues such as William Ware and soon to become even more widespread and systematic in its expression within the thought of William of Ockham.[2]

Hence, the place to begin our treatment is with Scotus's theory of universals and his efforts to defend and elaborate the ontology for a moderate realism akin to, though by no means the same as, that found in Aquinas,[3] while critiquing competing accounts of universals found in such extreme realists as Roger Bacon and dispelling the specter of a reduced ontology with its allied conceptualism. Once the realism of Scotus is sketched, we shall turn to his views on individuation, which are even more embroiled in controversies with his contemporaries, and see the extent to which his own solution of the problem of individuation is determined by the matrix of his convictions regarding the preeminent status of individuals and his own commitment to the reality of common natures. Finally, we shall offer some reflections on the place Scotus's theories occupy in the medieval philosophical tradition.

I. UNIVERSALS

I.1. Avicenna

For the most part, the thought of thirteenth-century Scholastics regarding universals was dominated by the outlook of Avicenna, the renowned Islamic philosopher whose writings were translated into Latin in the second half of the twelfth century. Working in an Aristotelian tradition that Tweedale has identified as Aphrodisian,[4] Avicenna attempted to distinguish the nature as such – the content of the universal concept, if you will – from the universality that the nature has in the mind, and both of these, in turn, from the nature as found in a particular individual possessing that nature. Typical of the texts expressing the distinction is the following, taken from Avicenna's *Logica*:

Animal in itself is a certain thing and the same whether it is an object of sense or understood in the soul. In itself, however, it is neither universal nor singular. For if it were in itself universal in such a way that animality as such (*ex hoc quod est animalitas*) were universal, then it would necessarily be the case that no animal is singular, but rather every animal would be universal.

If, however, animal as such were singular, it would be impossible for there to be more than one, singular animal, namely, the very one to which animality belonged as such, and it would be impossible for any other singular item to be animal. Animal in itself, moreover, is a certain object understood in the mind... and, in accord with this, what is understood to be animal is animal only. If, however, in addition to this, animal is understood to be universal or singular or something else, now something else over and above animal is understood which befalls animality.[5]

Here the essence or nature of animal is being analyzed from the viewpoint of logical predications. The argument is that universality in the sense of predicability of many is not what animal is essentially and necessarily. Were that so, then every instance of animal would have to be predicable of many, and so my dog Seamus could not be properly called an animal, since the animality found in him does not bear the property of being predicable of many. Alternatively, if the notion of singularity, impredicability of many, were included in the very concept of animal, then there would be only one animal and presumably as many genera and species as there are individuals. Since neither of these alternatives appears correct, Avicenna contends that 'animal' just in itself is bereft of either universality in the sense of predicability of many or singularity in the sense of impredicability of many. What the status is, precisely, of animal just in itself is unclear, however, since it has been described as "a certain thing" earlier in the passage, yet also being "a certain object understood in the mind."

Turning to his *De prima philosophia*, we find Avicenna initially characterizing the nature in itself more by what it is not than by what it is. Horseness (*equinitas*) is only horseness. It is not one, nor is it many; it does not exist among sensibles – in fact, it is none of these of itself either actually or potentially. Community, too, accrues to the nature extrinsically, since it is deemed common just insofar as many things agree in its definition, whereas singularity accrues to it extrinsically as well just insofar as the nature is found in an individual substance with its particular properties and concrete accidents.[6] The nature seems, then, to be entirely neutral to either extramental or intramental existence, since existence and its concomitant numerical unity are outside the nature as such.[7]

But does this mean that the nature or quiddity does not exist or that the Avicennian nature is just a Platonic Form under a different guise? Not at all. Avicenna recognizes that the nature always exists either in the mind or in extramental reality,[8] and, although he does allow an existence to the nature at the level of supersensible reality in the mind of God and the Intelligences,[9] such an existence is not at all like that of mind-independent Platonic Forms.

Still, the ontological status of the nature in itself remains ambiguous. From the various descriptions given it, the nature seems to be an ontological component, and we get a view of it something like this:

> Nature + spatiotemporal accidents = individual substance
> Nature + the mind's universality = universal notion.

That is to say, the nature seems to be a constituent (and the more important one, since it characterizes the items in question) of the concrete, individual item of a kind and of the thought predicable of many whereby we attend to items of that kind. Indeed, there is at least one text, often appealed to by Scholastic readers of Avicenna, wherein he describes the nature not simply as a component or constituent but also as one that is prior by nature to either the individual thing or the universal notion:

But animal as common and animal as individual, and animal taken relative to the potential to be common or proper or relative to being in these sensible things or understood in the soul, are animal and something else besides, not animal merely considered in itself. It is obvious, moreover, that when there is animal and something else that is not animal, animal is then in this item a part as it were, and man is similar in this regard. Animal, however, may be considered *per se*, although it exists with something else, for its essence exists with something else. Therefore, its essence belongs to it [alone] *per se*, but being together with something other than itself is something that befalls the essence or something that accompanies its nature, just as [we find in] this animality or this humanity. Accordingly, this consideration is prior in being both to the animal which is individual on account of its accidents and to the universal which is in these sensible things and intelligible, just as the simple is prior to the composite and the part is prior to the whole. From this being (*esse*), it is neither genus nor species nor individual nor one nor many, but [rather] from this being (*esse*) it is just animal and just man.[10]

The nature here is identified as prior both in consideration and in being (*esse*). From the priority it has in being, Avicenna can account for its relationship to the items it constitutes as analogous to the relationship found between a part and its whole and yet also imply that it is prior even in the resulting composite to the other constituents. The being the nature has is not what makes it be universal; rather its being universal follows upon its being found in sensibles and being received into an intellect. Nor is its being the source of the individual item of a kind taken as individual, since the individuality of the individual item arises from the accidents that accompany the nature in extramental reality rather than from the nature as such.

On balance, then, we are left in the Avicennian portrayal of essence or nature with the following intriguing, if unsatisfactory, picture. Essences may be considered in themselves and as such enjoy some kind of being (esse) in their own right,[11] although they lack any unity as such. Essences are also found in sensible things outside the mind and in thoughts within the mind. Under these aspects,[12] the essences are accompanied by conditions that are extraneous to their nature, and hence they may legitimately be considered apart from these accompanying features, since the essences are prior by nature to the wholes that they help to constitute.

Among the puzzling claims involved in this picture of essence is the claim that natures or essences have being but no unity.[13] The commonplace Scholastic doctrine of the coextensive transcendental properties of being would seem to be irreconcilable with this Avicennian doctrine of essence. A related puzzle is how the nature has a being (esse) that would be equally and fully realized both outside the mind and within. In other words, if the nature is found both in and outside the mind, it must have an extraordinary ontological status, one that is self-effacing in the extreme. Solutions to these puzzling features of Avicenna's thought were attempted before Scotus, but in Scotus's thought efforts to cope with the difficulties raised by these puzzles lead directly to his doctrines of the common nature and its minor unity.

I.2. Scotus

In several texts, Scotus distinguishes a logical treatment of universals from a metaphysical one. Although, as Marmo has shown,[14] the logical treatment of universals cannot be entirely disentangled from the metaphysical one, since Scotus's interpretation of the properly logical treatment is intimately connected with his own ontology, distinguishing between the logical and metaphysical approaches to universals will nonetheless prove helpful to clarifying what Scotus thought was at stake in his own theory of universals. A text that throws some light on the distinction between logical and metaphysical aspects of universals may be found in Scotus's *Quaestiones* on Porphyry's *Isagoge*:

Sometimes [the term universal] is understood in reference to the subject, namely the thing of first intention to which the universal intention is applied, and in this sense the universal is the first object of the intellect. At other times, [universal] is understood in reference to the form, that is, the thing of second intention caused by the intellect and applicable to things of first intention, and it is in this sense that the logician speaks properly of the universal. In a third way, universal is understood in reference to the aggregate of subject and form, and that is a being incidentally since it combines diverse natures ... and in this sense it does not belong to the consideration of any philosophical study.... Henceforth, we shall only speak in this work of universal taken in the second sense.[15]

A universal in the second sense applies to an intention or notion of the intellect, such as the concept 'man', which fully verifies the definition of universal stated by Aristotle.[16] According to Scotus, the intellect forms the logical intention of universal when it perceives that the nature of man is both found in many individuals and predicable of many individuals and attributes the second intention of species to that sort of concept.[17] By a similar process, the other Porphyrian predicables (genus, difference, property, and accident) are identified and, while they themselves are types of universals picking out distinct first-order concepts, they are also in the genus of universal as the logical *genus generalissimum*.[18] Universal in the first sense is what Scotus identifies in the logical writings and elsewhere as that-which-is (*quod quid est*), a technical term for concrete essence; the universal as *quod quid est* is a feature of being and not a logical intention since, as intelligible, it moves the intellect to activity.[19] Yet a universal, more precisely speaking, is not the content of that-which-is but rather the mode under which such an essence is understood.[20]

When Scotus proposes a theory of universals, accordingly, he is discussing universals in the first sense described in the preceding paragraph. In the text cited, he is interested, naturally enough, in the epistemological role essences play in the formation of first-order

concepts, since he needs to sketch in that background to describe
the domain of logic, which deals with second intentions. But in his
theological commentaries and his *Quaestiones* on Aristotle's *Metaphysics* he treats universals in terms of their ontological status and
directly in relation to the sorts of issues we saw earlier in Avicenna.
The *Lectura* (2, d. 3, pars 1, q. 1), the *Ordinatio* (2, d. 3, pars 1, q. 1),
and the *Quaestiones* on the *Metaphysics* (7, q. 13) all have texts
on universals occurring in the context of Scotus's treatment of the
problem of individuation and the issue of whether natures in
the Avicennian sense are singular of themselves. Let us begin with
these texts before turning to one of Scotus's *ex professo* treatments
of the problem of universals in the *Quaestiones* (7, q. 18).

What is characteristic of the first group of texts referred to is the
trouble Scotus takes to establish that the nature as such is not singular of itself, doubtless owing to the suggestion by William Ware
and others that natures are actually singular in their own right and
that only universality needs explaining. Scotus presents two main
arguments for the thesis that natures are not singular of themselves,
though his proofs of some of the premises of these main arguments
are much more numerous. First, Scotus argues that, if the nature
when presented as an object to the intellect is actually singular,
then the intellect is fundamentally misunderstanding the nature presented in the object, since it is "understanding" it in a manner opposed to the way the nature actually is. For the nature is always apprehended by the intellect as universal, not as singular. Second, Scotus
contends that anything that has its proper and adequate unity in the
form of a real unity less than numerical unity cannot be one through
numerical unity. The nature, even as it is found in this stone, has
its own adequate, proper, and real unity that is less than numerical
unity. Hence, the nature even as found in this stone has a lesser, or
minor, unity proper to itself.[21]

The first argument seems incontestable, and Scotus does little to
buttress its claims. The second argument, however, is much less secure because the minor premise seems less than obvious, namely,
that the nature even as found in the particular individual has a real
but less than numerical unity. To prove the minor premise of the
second argument, Scotus suggests that there is only one alternative
to allowing some kind of less than numerical unity to the nature,
namely, to say that there is no real unity at all less than numerical
unity, and this alternative is simply unacceptable. Precisely why it is

unacceptable Scotus shows through seven arguments, three of which are noteworthy. First, and perhaps most important, if all real unity is numerical unity, then all genuine diversity is numerical diversity, since unity and diversity are correlatively opposed features of being. What this entails, in turn, is that specific and generic unities are to that extent without any extramental foundation, and hence the concepts binding items of a species or genus together owe their content to the mind alone; they are *figmenta* or *fictiones*.[22] Second, real opposition, such as contrariety, requires distinct, real extremes that would function as such even in the absence of human understanding. Yet there must be unity to each of the extremes that is not merely numerical, since otherwise we would have to say that this white object is the opposite of that black thing, and this would mean that there are as many fundamental contrarieties as individuals opposed.[23] Third, even the senses have a kind of unity in their object that is not merely numerical, since the object of the sense is not the singular as such but rather the singular as bearing the formal feature that the sense power detects.[24]

Having argued for a real unity and identity for the nature distinct from, though less than, numerical unity and identity, Scotus must now address the question of how he conceives the nature's ontological status. He does so by first suggesting a gloss for Avicenna's famous dictum that "horseness is just horseness". The claim of Avicenna that the nature in its own right is neither one nor many, neither universal nor particular, should be understood to mean simply that the nature is not one numerically nor many numerically nor actually universal nor particular of itself.[25] The gloss placed on Avicenna's words opens up the possibility of attributing to the nature the minor unity that Scotus thinks the nature must be said to possess to explain the repeatable character of the nature in individual supposits, that is, in concrete subsisting ontological subjects, and the causal role played by the nature in informing the intellect. Moreover, this gloss will allow Scotus to introduce a distinction between universality and community quite foreign to the thought of the Islamic philosopher.

Here, then, is how Scotus describes the nature's status in the succeeding paragraphs of the *Ordinatio*:

For although [the nature] never exists without one of these [being numerically one or many, being universal or particular], nonetheless it is not any of these but is naturally prior to them all. And, in accord with this natural priority, that-which-is (*quod quid est*) is the *per se* object of the intellect, is considered *per se* as such by the metaphysician, and is expressed through a definition.... Not only, however, is the nature indifferent to being in the intellect and in the particular (and thereby to universal being and particular, or singular, being), but also, when it first has being in the intellect, it does not have universality in its own right. For although it is understood under universality as under a mode of understanding, universality is not part of its primary concept.... Therefore, the first act of understanding is of the nature precisely without any concomitant understanding of the mode.... And just as in accord with the being it has when first in the intellect the nature is not universal of itself..., so too in extra-mental reality, when the nature is found with singularity, the nature is not determined of itself to singularity, but is prior naturally to the cause (*ratio*) contracting it to singularity; and insofar as it is naturally prior to the cause contracting it, it is not repugnant to it to exist without that [particular contracting cause]. And just as the object in its first presence and 'universality' in the intellect has truly intelligible being (*esse intelligibile*), so too in reality the nature has, according to its entity, true real being outside the soul and in accord with that entity it has a proportional unity that is indifferent to singularity in such a way that it is not repugnant to that unity to be of itself placed together with any given unity of singularity.[26]

Like Avicenna, Scotus thinks that the nature never exists apart from concrete things outside the mind or thoughts in the mind and that there is, nonetheless, a natural priority enjoyed by the nature with respect to either manifestation of the nature, within the mind or without. But there the similarities to the doctrine of Avicenna stop. First, the nature is so lacking in determination to singularity that the nature could of itself be conjoined to a principle of singularity other than a given one. Clearly, this means that the nature enjoys a level of ontological priority and identity that it retains even in the singular item outside the mind, where it is in its contracted state. Next, the nature has a real being outside the mind precisely because it has its own entity that naturally enters into the constitution of the singular item outside the mind. Third, because the nature has its own entity, it has its own unity, and it is this minor unity that is sufficiently indifferent to allow the nature of itself to be found, in principle, with any given individuating principle. As Scotus states elsewhere, a lesser, or minor, unity is compatible with a greater unity.[27]

What we have in Scotus's ontology of universals, accordingly, is the doctrine of a *common* nature, not that of Avicenna's *neutral* nature; in this doctrine, the community of the nature is described negatively ("the nature is not of itself this"), yet that description points to a positive feature. Scotus stresses the community of the nature in a paragraph summarizing his views:

To confirm the opinion [stated], it is clear that community and singularity are not related to the nature, as being in the intellect and true being outside the soul are. For community belongs to the nature apart from the intellect and likewise too does singularity, and community belongs to the nature in its own right, whereas singularity belongs to the nature through something in the thing that contracts the nature. But universality does not belong to a thing in its own right. And that is why I grant that we should seek the cause of universality, but no cause of community should be sought apart from the nature. And once the community within the nature is posited in accord with its proper entity and unity, we must necessarily seek a cause of singularity to add something to that nature to which it belongs.[28]

The notion of community expressed in this text bears directly on the claim by Scotus in the previous text that the nature is not, properly speaking, universal when it is first present in the intellect. Indeed, the following statements are intimately related, though not identical, ways of describing the status of the nature: (1) the nature has a minor unity and entity of its own; (2) the nature is not of itself this, that is, its unity is a kind of community; (3) the nature of itself could be found together with a distinct individuating principle without contradiction (or repugnance); and (4) the nature is not actually universal when first present in the intellect. Since entity and unity are related as transcendental notions, they are, in keeping with standard Scholastic views, concomitant, and the nature enjoys a unity that is proportional to its entity. What that unity and entity amount to is that the nature has an identity that is real but sufficiently indeterminate to be able to be repeated in a number of supposits in the world, yet sufficiently rich in content to be able to be received into a cognitive faculty without losing its identity as a nature and thereby failing to have its proper effect in cognitive activity. In other words, the nature and its identity are what make individual substances in the world be the same in kind and what cause the mind to become aware of that kind when the nature is received in the intellect. As

regards the concretely existing subject or individual substance in
the world, the nature is an ontologically prior, yet determinable element that stands in need of actualization and determination; that is
why a further source must be sought to explain the singularity characteristic of individual substances. With respect to the intellectual
faculty, the nature's presence in the soul provides only the content
of the universal notion, not the predication of many, and that is why
its community stands in need of further indetermination for true
universality.[29]

Scotus's position might at first glance seem to be a return to the
realism, albeit expressed in Avicennian language, characteristic of
the twelfth-century opponents of Abelard.[30] Actually, this is not at
all the case. First, the community of the common nature is not at
all universality in the robust sense; in fact, Scotus sharply distinguishes full universality from the universality that he sometimes
uses as a synonym for community.[31] This becomes abundantly clear
from the noetic role that Scotus assigns to the nature in another
one of his main texts on universals, the *Quaestiones* on Aristotle's
Metaphysics 7, q. 18. The nature, owing to the fact that it is not of
itself this, is not repugnant to being said of many as well as being
found in many, the two necessary and jointly sufficient conditions
for complete universality. Upon its first presence in the intellect,
the nature moves the mind to the activity of understanding (*intel-
lectio*) and only then, when the nature is actually considered with
reference to many supposits outside the mind, are both aspects of
universality realized through the mental activity of predication. The
nature, accordingly, may be said to be the remote subject of the universal predication or in remote potency to the universal in its full
realization, which is in the mind.[32]

Second, Scotus intends his own views to be a corrective, in part, for
the more extreme realism of some earlier Oxford Franciscans. In the
same question, after noting that the Platonic view is by no means
shown to be incoherent by Aristotle but is rejected rather on the
grounds of its being unnecessary, Scotus outlines two extreme views
that employ Aristotelian principles. One is the extreme realism associated with Roger Bacon (among others)[33] in the generation of Oxford
Franciscans prior to Scotus. This view locates universals primarily
in things and only secondarily in the mind; universal things are predicated of particular things on this score.[34] The opposing view locates

the universal primarily in the mind and only secondarily, if at all, in things; this view is associated with Peter John Olivi's writings.[35] Scotus strives to carve out a position intermediate between the two extremes. In response to the second extreme position, Scotus uses reasoning similar to that seen above in regard to the view that the nature is singular of itself. In response to the first extreme position, he argues that one of its main tenets is false, namely, that a universal thing is predicated of particular things. What is predicated is a universal intention or notion, not a thing, albeit the basis for predication is an isomorphic feature of a thing, namely its nature.[36]

II. INDIVIDUATION

Although the precise degree to which Scotus is indebted to earlier discussions of individuation at Oxford and Paris has been subject to some recent scholarly disagreement,[37] the general historical context of Scotus's theory of individuation is clear enough. Much attention had been given to the problem of individuation in theological and philosophical works during the course of the thirteenth century; indeed, the problem had become a central occupation of theologians in the final decades of that century, ever since the Aristotelian (and perhaps the Thomistic) theory of individuation had been officially condemned by Etienne Tempier, the bishop of Paris, in 1277.[38] What may be said of this attention is that it led to a plethora of opinions: individuation was explained by appealing to the collection of accidents found in a subject,[39] the quantity that the subject possesses,[40] the matter that in part constitutes the subject,[41] the actual existence (*esse*) of the subject,[42] the relation that the subject bore to the agent that produced it,[43] or, finally, nothing positive, but simply the nonidentity of a thing with the species to which it belonged in respect of the species' divisibility and the nonidentity of a thing with other things of the same species.[44] As we have seen apropos of Scotus's discussion of universals, even the need for a principle of individuation had been questioned in the late thirteenth-century literature. By the early fourteenth century, what this bewildering variety of opinions seemed to cry out for was a critical systematic treatment to assess the merits of each view.

In several of his works, but most especially in the *Quaestiones* on Aristotle's *Metaphysics*, Scotus provides a schema that allows

for ready comparison and measured evaluation of these various positions.[45] Although adumbrations of Scotus's approach to laying out
the problem may be seen in some form in the writings of Henry of
Ghent and Peter John Olivi,[46] the Subtle Doctor's detailed organization of the various positions deriving from a strict disjunction is
a masterpiece of analysis. In seeking the principle of individuation,
we must postulate, Scotus claims, either a positive principle or a
negative principle. If the principle is positive, it must register as an
element of the Aristotelian ontology: it must either be a substantial
principle, such as form or matter, or an accidental principle, such as
quantity, quality, relation, or actual existence.

Turning to the notion of individuality and drawing upon Gracia's
framework for analyzing philosophical outlooks on individuality, we
may quickly perceive what is characteristic of Scotus's approach.
Philosophers have described individuality in terms of impredicability (Colleen cannot be said of something else), identity (Colleen is
the same now as before, even though she was formerly pale and now
is rosy-cheeked; in fact, she is so much the self-same that she could
not, in principle, be identified with anything else), divisiveness (the
ability of Colleen to divide up a larger group or species, i.e., human),
distinction (the nonidentity of this individual, Colleen, with any
other in her species, e.g., Paula), and indivisibility (noninstantiability
or unrepeatability, i.e., Colleen cannot recur – she is unique).[47]

Of these five salient features of individuality, Scotus points to
the last as being the most important and basic; in this, indeed, we
may say that his emphasis differs from that of many of his contemporaries. For example, in a particularly awkward moment of his
debate with William Peter Godinus, the Thomist with whom he debated the question whether matter is the principle of individuation,
Scotus expresses his attitude toward individuality this way:

Against this [i.e., Godinus's] position: the singularity about which we are
asking in this discussion is being a something *per se* one among other beings
(*aliquid per se unum in entibus*) to which it is repugnant to be divided into
subjective parts; of this repugnance there can only be a single cause.[48]

The phrase "to which it is repugnant to be divided into subjective
parts" is meant to express the idea of noninstantiability: Paula may
be divided into integral parts, such as her heart or lungs/her body
and soul, but not into subjective parts, that is, parts each of which is

an instance of the thing divided – the way, by contrast, the species human may be divided into Socrates and Plato. In Scotus's view of individuation, instantiability is contradictory with the notion of individuality as such.

II.1. Scotus's Criticism of Alternative Positions

Given Scotus's emphasis on noninstantiability as the most fundamental of the features of individuality and his equally telling emphasis on individuality as an ontological perfection, we should not be surprised to see Scotus reject any effort to locate the source of individuality in negation, the position associated with Henry of Ghent. However unfair to Henry's actual position Scotus's analysis may be,[49] the Subtle Doctor always construes Henry's theory as one invoking two negations to explain how natures are rendered individual: one whereby the thing that is individual is not divisible in the manner that the species is; another whereby the individual item is made nonidentical to any other member of the same species. Scotus's line of criticism is quite predictable. The negations Henry proposes, taken as logical expressions, simply describe aspects of an individual's individuality; they do not uncover what makes individuals have those features. If the negations, however, are meant as ontological principles, they must be positive, or be meant to point to something positive, since the numerical unity they are trying to explain is a positive feature of things. Scotus metes out similar treatment to any effort to avoid the problem of explaining individuality by claiming, as perhaps did Peter of Auvergne early in his career,[50] that the nature is only one through the mind which supplies 'singular' as a logical intention just as the mind supplies its counterpart 'universal'.

Eliminating any negative principle of individuation, Scotus considers the range of opinions on the side of a positive principle. Here the opinions facing him have very distinguished names allied with them. The opinion of Thomas Aquinas, though subject to differing interpretations, was generally considered to fall under the rubric of the "official" Aristotelian position that matter is the principle of individuation. Godfrey of Fontaines, the illustrious disciple and critic of Henry of Ghent, was thought to hold that quantity is the principle of individuation, though in the view of Wippel this construal does not do full justice to Godfrey's thought, since he postulated form as the principle in addition to quantity; form is the principle of individuation and quantity the source of numerical multiplicity within a species of physical substances.[51] The view that actual existence (*esse*) is the source of indviduation also had adherents, including Giles of Rome early in his career.[52] Finally, the theory that what makes things individual is just their relation to the First Agent, God, was a thesis proposed by Roger Marston.

What is common to all these theories, in Scotus's view, is that they all appeal to something accidental in order to explain the individuation of substances.[53] (Scotus focuses on the individuation of substances, believing that the individuation of accidents is to be explained with reference to the substances in which they inhere.) According to Scotus, four considerations (*quadruplex via*) compel the conclusion that each of these solutions to the problem of individuation is flawed: the notion of substance as *per se* being, the ontological priority of substance to accident, the nature of numerical unity, and the integrity of each categorical order.

Substance, in the sense of first substance, is *per se* being in the primary and truest sense; it is also the source of activity and operation as well as the ultimate subject of predication. If this is so, any combination or aggregation of substance and accident is itself a being *per accidens*, not a *per se* being. Consequently, the aggregation of any accident, even quantity, and the substance cannot explain what makes that substance as primary and *per se* being to be that individual being. The accident is outside, so to speak, the range of substance as *per se* being.[54]

Closely related to this consideration is Scotus's second one: the priority of substance to accident. Substance is prior to accident by a priority of nature; therefore, this substance, as substance, is prior by nature to this accident. Yet if this is the case, this accident (say, this quantity) cannot make the substance upon which it depends to be this because on that showing the ontologically posterior is prior by nature to the ontologically prior, which is impossible.[55]

The third consideration springs from Scotus's own emphasis on individuality as noninstantiability, what Scotus often calls *singularitas*. If to be a singular individual entity is to be noninstantiable and the entity in question is a substance, then, short of a substantial change, the entity in question will remain 'this' and not become 'not-this' no matter what reconfiguration of accidents it suffers. Yet the accidents that belong to a given substance vary throughout the duration of that substance, sometimes drastically. If that is so, then should the varying accidents be the ones adduced as the cause of individuation, such as the dimensive quantity, the substance will become 'not-this' without any substantial change being involved, contrary to the notion of what it means to be numerically one or singular in the case of substance.[56]

The fourth and final consideration is drawn from the idea that each of the categorical or predicamental orders should be complete without any confusion with the members of another order, regardless of the interrelation of the categorical orders. To take an example, we should be able to move from 'quantity' to 'continuous quantity' to 'line' to 'this line' without adverting to the category of quality or any other category. If, however, we take the category of substance and try to complete the categorical descent, we can only, on the basis of these explanations of individuation, arrive at the species, say 'human being'; we cannot arrive at 'this human being' without adverting to an accidental category because, on the strength of these theories of individuation, it is something outside the order of substance that yields 'this human being' from 'human being'.[57]

What may strike the reader as questionable and even objectionable about Scotus's criticisms is that he lumps together the materialist theory of individuation under the heading of an accidentalist account, whereas matter is clearly a substantial principle in the Aristotelian ontology, and much the same point could be made about actual existence, since it is one of the two principles constituting a being (ens), that is, a substance, in Thomistic metaphysics. The first of these points may be addressed by noting that Scotus is dealing with a particular version of the materialist thesis, one that appeals to the accident of dimensive quantity to explain how prime matter, of itself indeterminate, has the structure of parts of the same sort and hence becomes signate matter.[58] Drawing upon material in Aquinas's early writings,[59] Thomists at Scotus's time were quite explicit on this point. To cite just one example, William Peter Godinus argued that the source of numerical plurality is ultimately matter insofar as it possesses the capacity for many forms of the same species; but the proximate principle that reduces this capacity to act, so that a given individual of a species may be produced, is quantity, which gives matter extension.[60] Accordingly, there seems to be a legitimate foundation – textual, historical, and systematic – for Scotus's claim that the materialist theory of individuation appeals to the accident of quantity in describing how matter functions as individuating principle. As to the potential objection that *esse* is misconstrued as an accidental principle, one needs to bear in mind that Thomas Aquinas himself describes it as an accidental principle on several occasions.[61]

After his general line of criticism against accidentalist accounts, Scotus raises objections to each of the particular ways of explaining individuation mentioned. Since space does not allow for anything more than a summary treatment of these, I shall only mention the more important ones. Against the quantity thesis, Scotus reasons that the quantity is either *terminata* (quantity with definite and distinctive dimensions) or *interminata* (quantity with indefinite and generic dimensions). If the latter, the quantity precedes and succeeds the given physical individual; hence, it cannot be what accounts for the uniqueness of the individual. Alternatively, if the quantity is *terminata*, such definite dimensions are the expression of the substantial form of the individual and depend upon it for their entity, not the converse.[62] Regarding the materialist thesis on individuation, one of Scotus's favorite criticisms is that matter, as a principle of potentiality, is ill-suited to function as the source of determination and actuality for the individual thing. For positing matter as the principle of individuation seems to entail locating the source of the greatest unity (*unitas maxima*) and actuality in a principle that is ordinarily the source of multiplicity and potentiality.[63] Two of Scotus's chief criticisms of the *esse* theory of individuation are that (1) although the theory is correct to seek a source of actuality as the principle of individuation, *esse* would seem to lack the characteristic of determination also required in the individuating principle, since *esse* receives its determination from the essence it actuates;[64] and (2) if *esse* functions as the principle of individuation, nothing can, properly speaking, be individual if it does not actually exist, since it lacks precisely what constitutes it as individual. The latter claim would seem to rule out possible individuals and would call into question the possibility of God's knowing individuals prior to their actual existence. As to the theory that individuals are such thanks to the relation they have to the Agent who produces them, Scotus points out that substance is absolute and prior to any relation; hence, it cannot be made 'this' by a relation.[65]

We should now pause to see what we have learned from Scotus's criticism of alternative solutions to the problem of individuation. First, in seeking to explain the individuation of substances, Scotus wishes to discover what principle would account for the most telling feature of their individuality as he conceives it, noninstantiability. Second, Scotus faults the theses we have been considering for failing in various ways to come to grips with the depth of the problem of individuation in the case of substances, since in each case an appeal is made to the order of accident as the ultimate ground of substantial individuation. Third, we know by implication what we are looking for in a principle of individuation through reflecting on the strengths and weaknesses of the alternative positions. We are searching for a principle that is a positive element in the individual thing that must have the following characteristics: the principle must be in the substantial order (to avoid the flaw of appealing to accidental being); it must be a principle of actuality (failure to appeal to such a principle is what is mistaken in the materialist theory, whereas positing such a principle is the virtue of the *esse* theory); it must be a principle of determination (failure to add this feature is what mars the *esse* theory); and, finally, it must be individual of itself, not needing further individuation in turn (this is the virtue of the quantitativists' account, since quantity, as the source of parcels, is individual of itself).

II.2. Scotus's Own Solution

In many ways we have already arrived at Scotus's own position, since what he proposes as the principle of individuation is a principle that is, in the main, a theoretical construct fitting the requirements just mentioned as being desirable in a principle of individuation. But some elaboration is, nonetheless, needed to explain precisely the full implications of his position.

A preliminary point must be made about the terminology that Scotus uses to describe his principle. In the early *Lectura*, Scotus's preferred term for describing his own principle of individuation is *realitas positiva* (positive reality); this is continued in the later *Ordinatio*, with *entitas positiva* (positive entity) also making a frequent appearance. In only a single instance does Scotus adduce the language of form to describe his individuating principle in the Oxford theological writings: at *Ordinatio* 2, d. 3, pars 1, qq. 5–6, n. 180, he uses the terminology of *ultima realitas formae* (ultimate reality of the form). Yet he consistently employs the language of form in his description of the individuating principle in the later *Quaestiones: forma individualis* (individual form), *ultimus gradus formae* (ultimate grade of the form), and *haeceitas* ('thisness') are the terms used in Book 7, q. 13.[66] What are we to make of such a shift in terminology? Is there a shift in doctrine corresponding to the change in terminology? The position we shall assume here is that there is not a change in doctrine but only a change in emphasis and expression, although there is certainly room for disagreement; those interested should consult Dumont's excellent article for documentation of the terminological shift.[67]

What we regularly find in Scotus's texts are direct arguments for his principle of individuation and then a series of analogies to explain what he means by the principle he calls *forma individualis/ultimus gradus formae/entitas positiva/haeceitas*. In the interest of space, only one of the direct arguments will be mentioned. Just as unity in general follows upon being, so a given unity follows upon some type of being. Everyone, Scotus avows, recognizes that there is individual unity, implicitly at least acknowledging that such unity consists in the individual thing's noninstantiability. Yet if there is individual unity, there must be some positive being corresponding to it to provide the ontological foundation for such unity. Such positive being cannot be that of the specific nature, since the formal unity of the nature is quite different from that of the individual inasmuch as the formal unity of the specific nature is indeterminate and open to multiple instantiations, whereas the unity of the individual thing is precisely a unity that is not in any way open to multiple instantiations. Therefore, there must be an individual entity that functions as the ontological fundament of individual unity.[68]

Having reasoned to the existence of such an entity, Scotus is at pains to describe what it is. According to the very terms of the theory he proposes, the positive entity that is the ultimate source of the individual thing's unity cannot be an object of scientific knowledge, since it cannot be something of which we can form a quidditative concept, that is, a concept that could be essentially predicable of many. If individual entity prompted our intellects in the present life, it would be indicative of what the individual is as such in contradistinction to any and all other individuals, real or possible.[69] Since we lack any direct acquaintance with the positive entitative principle that functions as the source of individuation, Scotus must explain what it is analogically by reference to what we know better and must focus on how it functions, since we are at least acquainted with the unity of which this entity is the cause.

Scotus compares the determining role of the individuating principle, as he conceives it, to a specific difference's interrelation to other items on the Porphyrian tree: the specific difference may be compared with what is below it, what is above it, and what is adjacent to it on the Porphyrian tree. If the specific difference is viewed in reference to what is below it, namely the specific nature, the specific nature determined or informed by the specific difference is such that it is no longer open to multiplicity at the specific level; it is determined to be that species and no other. Likewise, the individual difference determines the individual in such a way that it is no longer open to further numerical multiplicity but is determined to be this individual and no other: that is, it is noninstantiable. If the specific difference is viewed in reference to what is above it, we may say that it contracts the genus to the species, as act relative to the potency represented by the genus.[70] So, too, we may say that the individual difference functions in like fashion with respect to the specific nature, yet with an important and noteworthy qualification. In the case of the specific difference and the genus a formal determination is added to a formal determination, but in the case of the individual difference a form is not added to a form; rather, the addition is from the very reality of the form itself – the individual entity is the ultimate expression of the thing's form – and the resulting composite is not constituted in quidditative being but in what Scotus calls material being or contracted being.[71] Finally, if we compare the specific difference with the items adjacent to it on the Porphyrian tree, namely other specific differences, we may say that every ultimate specific difference, while simultaneously giving the items in the species a certain distinguishing feature and constituting the items in the species in the being they have, is nonetheless diverse from other differences. Consequently, when we ask what is common to rational and irrational as they divide animal, the proper response, if we wish to avoid an infinite regress, is that they share in nothing but are simply diverse. Likewise, the individual differences are primarily and simply diverse, although the individuals constituted by those differences are items sharing the same specific nature, just as the items in the different species share in the genus despite the fact that they are each constituted in their respective species by differences that are primarily diverse.[72]

Two problems arise immediately regarding Scotus's account of individuals. First, how are the common nature and the individual difference distinct in the individual thing? Second, how can the nature as contracted retain its minor unity, which is indifferent to being just this, when it is contracted to being just this through individual difference? Are we not saying that the nature has two contradictory properties, minor unity and numerical unity? Scotus's reply to the first problem is that the common nature and the individuating difference are formally distinct while they are really identical.[73] What this means is that, to the extent that the two principles could be given logical descriptions, the common nature would not be included in the description of the individual difference and vice versa, yet they both are constitutive parts of one thing. The second problem, which King has well labeled "Ockham's problem,"[74] is a bit more thorny. Scotus suggests in the *Ordinatio* and elsewhere that, although the nature as contracted is one in number, it is only denominatively so; that is, just as Socrates may be called white, but not properly 'whiteness', though it is through the form of whiteness that Socrates is white, so too the nature may be said to be numerically one because the subject in which it is found is numerically one, but only improperly so, since it enjoys its own minor unity in its own right. In the *Quaestiones* on the *Metaphysics*, he supplements the appeal to denominative predication through the doctrine of unitive containment. Humanity does not include the individual difference of Socrates, nor does Socrateity include humanity essentially. Socrates, however, unitively contains both human nature and Socrateity, and they are both essential to him.[75]

III. CONCLUDING REMARKS

In the final analysis, Scotus's views on universals and individuation connect to some of the more wide-ranging and central themes of his metaphysical thought such as the formal distinction and the doctrine of unitive containment. But they also show the extent to which Scotus is committed both to the reality of common natures and the ultimate importance of individuals. Most of the tension in his theories stems from the strength of his desire to locate a place for commonness and uniqueness in the texture of individual substances.

Viewed in a more historical perspective, Scotus's efforts to articulate minimal ontological foundations for moderate realism can be seen as an attempt to forestall the tendency toward conceptualism latent in Henry of Ghent's intentional distinction by undercutting the plausibility of the simplified ontology of individuals suggested by William Ware. Whether all the metaphysical elements called upon to establish this minimal foundation are judged to be warranted will doubtless be subject to differing philosophical evaluations; but that Scotus, at least, believed that anything less would undermine the possibility of Aristotelian science is beyond question. On the problem of individuation, Scotus brings to fulfillment one approach outlined much earlier by Bonaventure.[76] In order to locate his principle of individuation within the framework of the received Aristotelian ontology, Scotus characterized his individuating principle as formal but by distinguishing two types of forms: quidditative forms capable of multiple instantiation and individual, unique forms that function as sources of actuality but are incommunicable. Scotus's theory of individuation seems, accordingly, to support the general observation that the framework of the Aristotelian ontology provided Scholastic authors no ready solution to the problem of individuation and that the more outstanding among them only resolved the problem by creatively adding elements of their own devising to the received Aristotelian ontology.

NOTES

1   For remarkably comprehensive overviews of the problem of individuation, see Gracia 1988, 17–63, and 1994, 1–20.
2   William Ware, *Quaestiones in Sententias* 2, d. 9, q. 3 (Vienna, f. 117va); Roger Marston, *Quodlibeta quatuor* 2, q. 30 (Roger Marston 1994, 297); and Duns Scotus, *In Metaph.* 7, q. 13, n. 53. For Ockham's account, see *Summa Logicae* 1, c. 15–17.
3   For some apt observations on the similarities between Scotus's and Aquinas's views, see Wolter 1990c.

4   Tweedale 1993, especially 81–9.
5   *Logica tertia* pars (Avicenna 1508, f. 12ra).
6   *Liber de philosophia prima sive scientia divina* V. 1 (Avicenna 1977/80, 228–9).
7   Numerical unity is the unity that belongs to an individual substance taken as such, that is 'Socrates' and 'teacher of Plato' both designate the same historical personage who died in 399 B.C.E. and was one in number. Numerical unity is contrasted by Scholastic authors with specific unity (the unity of Plato and Socrates in the species human), generic unity (the unity of Socrates and his dog in the genus animal), and analogical unity (the unity found in proportional pairings, i.e., color is to white as mammal is to human). The classical authoritative text for medieval discussions of unity is Aristotle, *Metaph.* 5.6 (1016^{b}33–1017^{a}3).

Although my remarks here should be taken as bearing exclusively upon *Avicenna Latinus*, since I have no facility in Arabic, Marmura 1988 and 1992 have proved useful in coping with the difficult Latin texts. I would like to thank my colleague, Dr. Thérèse-Anne Druart, for her assistance in providing me with bibliographical information regarding Avicenna.

8   *De prima philos.* V. 1 (Avicenna 1977/80, 234).
9   *Logica*, pars tertia (Avicenna 1508, f. 12va).
10 *De prima philos.* V. 1 (Avicenna 1977/80, 233–4).
11 *De prima philos.* I. 5 (Avicenna 1977/80, 34 5).
12 *Logica*, pars 1, c. 1 (Avicenna 1508, f. 2rb).
13 The problem that the Avicennian natures posed for Scholastic authors has been well described by Owens 1957, 4.
14 Marmo 1989. Marmo's comprehensive and thorough analysis provides a corrective to an earlier article by Daniel A. Dahlstrom (Dahlstrom 1980). Dahlstrom was one of the first to draw modern scholarly attention to the significance of Scotus's distinction between logical and metaphysical features of universals.
15 *In Porph.* q. 4 proemium.
16 Aristotle, *Peri herm.* 1.7 (17^{a}39–40); *Post. an.* 1.4 (73^{b}26–7).
17 *In Porph.* q. 9, n. 17.
18 *In Porph.* q. 7, nn. 24–6.
19 *In Porph.* q. 4, n. 6.
20 *In Porph.* q. 5, n. 4.
21 *Lect.* 2, d. 3, pars 1, q. 1, nn. 8–9; *Ord.* 2, d. 3, pars 1, q. 1, nn. 7–8; *In Metaph.* 7, q. 13, n. 61.
22 *Lect.* 2, d. 3, pars 1, q. 1, n. 26; *Ord.* 2, d. 3, pars 1, q. 1, n. 23; *In Metaph.* 7, q. 13, n. 65. De Libera 1996, 333, suggests that this line of argumentation is appropriated by Scotus from *sophismata* literature.

23 *Ord.* 2, d. 3, pars 1, q. 1, n. 19.

24 *Ord.* 2, d. 3, pars 1, q. 1, nn. 20–2. A protracted discussion of the unity of the sense object may be found in *In Metaph.* 1, q. 6, nn. 7–63.

25 *Ord.* 2, d. 3, pars 1, q. 1, n. 31.

26 *Ord.* 2, d. 3, pars 1, q. 1, nn. 32–4.

27 *In Metaph.* 7, q. 13, n. 61.

28 *Ord.* 2, d. 3, pars 1, q. 1, n. 42. Boulnois 1992 rightly emphasizes, in light of this text, the importance of community for Scotus's doctrine of universals.

29 On the stages of ideogenesis in Scotus, see R. Dumont 1965.

30 For the view that Scotus's position is tantamount to a conceptualism of universals with a realism of community and hence not properly realist or conceptualist, see Boulnois 1992, 3; 28–33.

31 *Ord.* 2, d. 3, pars 1, q. 1, n. 38.

32 Scotus, *In Metaph.* 7, q. 18, n. 41, n. 44, and n. 48. For a more extended discussion of the relationship between the nature and moments in the intellective process, see the introduction to Sondag 1993, 48–72, and Sondag 1996. The broader significance of Scotus's discussion of the nature as a partial cause of intellection may be seen in de Muralt 1991, 112–18.

33 See Sharp 1930, 182–3, for Peckham's position.

34 See Maloney 1985; Roger Bacon, *Quaestiones supra libros Primae Philosophiae Aristotelis* (Roger Bacon 1905–40, 7:241–5); *Communia naturalium*, I p. 2 d. 3 c. 4 (Roger Bacon 1905–40, 2:204).

35 Peter John Olivi, *Sent.* 2, q. 13 (Peter John Olivi 1922, 4:253).

36 *In Metaph.* 7, q. 18, n. 43.

37 That Richard Rufus's thought is the predominant influence on Scotus is the position of Wood 1996. That the immediate background is to be found in the writings of Scotus's Parisian master, Gonsalvus Hispanus, is the claim advanced by Sondag 1997.

38 Hissette 1977, 1982, maintains that Aquinas was not a principal target. This interpretation of the condemnation has been challenged by Wippel 1977 and 1981, 381–2.

39 The view traditionally was ascribed to Boethius but was held with some variations up through the thirteenth century. See Boethius, *In Isagoge Porphryrii editio secunda* lib. III (CSEL 48, 235; PL 64, 114); and *De Trinitate* c. 1 (PL 64, 1249). Boethius's view here is traceable to Porphyry, and it is perhaps from Porphyry that the wording of a "collection" of accidents is taken. See Porphyry, *Liber praedicabilium* cap. "De specie" (AL I.6, 13–14; ed. Busse 7.21–23); cf. Hamesse 1974, 300. On the popularity of this view and its subsequent development in medieval philosophy,

see Gracia 1988, 108–111. That the view was by no means abandoned altogether by the end of the thirteenth and the beginning of the fourteenth centuries may be gathered from the fact that Scotus's contemporary John Quidort devotes time to this view also in his disputed question on individuation in 1304–5. See the text of Quidort in Müller 1974, especially 343.

40 Thomas Aquinas, *Sent.* 4, d. 12, q. 1, a. 1, qc. 3 in corp. and ad 3 (ed. Parmen. VII 655a 1); *ST.* 1.50.2 in corp.; 3.77.2 in corp. (XII 196b); *SCG* 2.50 arg. 1 (XIII 383a); 4.65 (XV 209b); Giles of Rome, *Quodl.* 1, q. 11 in corp. (ed. Venice 1502, f. 7ra–b); Godfrey of Fontaines, *Quodl.* 7, q. 5 in corp. (Godfrey of Fontaines 1904–37, 3:328); *Quodl.* 6, q. 16 in corp. (Godfrey of Fontaines 1904–37, 3:259); Thomas de Sutton, *Quodl.* I q. 21 in corp. (Thomas of Sutton 1969, 140–3, 146).

41 Aristotle, *Metaph.* 7, t. 28 (AL 25:137; 7.8, 1034ᵃ 4–8). The chief text in Aquinas for this theory is the early *De ente et essentia* c. 2 (ed. Leonina 371a–b), but see also Thomas, *Sent.* 4, d. 11, q. 1, a. 3, qc. 1 in corp. (ed. Parmen. VII 634b); d. 12, q. 1, a. 1, qc. 3 ad 3 (655a); *ST* 1.7.3 in corp. (IV 75b); 3.77.2 in corp. (XII 196b); *SCG* 2.75 arg. 1 (XIII 473a); 2.83 arg. 20 (XIII 523b); 2.93 arg. 2 (XIII 563a); 3.65 arg. 3 (XIV 183b); 4.63 (XV 201ab); Giles of Rome, *Quodl.* 1, q. 11 in corp. (f. 7rab); Godfrey of Fontaines, *Quodl.* 7, q. 5 in corp. (Godfrey of Fontaines 1904–37, 3:324).

42 Roger Bacon, *Communia naturalium* c. 9 (Roger Bacon 1905–40, 2:99); Petrus de Falco, *Quaest. ordinariae* q. 8 in corp. (Petrus Falcus 1968, 1:311).

43 Roger Marston, *Quodl.* I q. 3 (Roger Marston 1994, 13); *Quodl.* II q. 30 (Roger Marston 1994, 295); *De anima* q. 2 (Roger Marston 1932, 233); cf. James of Viterbo, *Quodl.* I q. 21 (James of Viterbo 1968, 223).

44 Henry of Ghent, *Summa* a. 39 q. 3 ad 2 (Henry of Ghent 1979, 1:246 Q–S).

45 For the structure of Scotus's texts discussing individuation, see S. Dumont 1995, 1: 200–1, and Noone 1995, 1: 393–4.

46 Henry of Ghent, *Quodl.* II, q. 8 (Henry of Ghent 1979, 6:54–5); Peter John Olivi, *II Sent.* q. 12 (Peter John Olivi 1922, 212–3).

47 For a useful description of these different features of individuality, see Gracia 1994, 9–13.

48 Stroick 1974, 596. Corrections to defective readings have been supplied by consulting the sole manuscript (Erfurt, Bibliotheca Amploniana, MS F 369).

49 S. Brown 1994, 205–6.

50 Peter of Auvergne, *Metaph.* VII q. 25 in O'Donnell 1955, 173.

51 Wippel 1994.

52 Giles of Rome, *I Sent.* d. 36 princ. 1 q. 1 (Ed. Venice, 1521, f. 185v N); Nash 1950–1.

53 *In Metaph.* 7, q. 13, n. 20: "Istud autem quod videtur commune omnibus, aut saltem tribus primis opinionibus de individuatione, 'per accidens formaliter', potest improbari quadruplici via satis rationabili."

54 *In Metaph.* 7, q. 13, n. 21.

55 *In Metaph.* 7, q. 13, n. 24.

56 *In Metaph.* 7, q. 13, n. 27.

57 *In Metaph.* 7, q. 13, nn. 28–30.

58 "Primae duae viae patent quod ponunt accidens formaliter individuare. Tertia etiam communiter ponitur includere secundam, quia differentia in materia absolute secundum rationem potentialitatis distinguit genera physica, ex fine X. Ergo illa, quae distinguit individua, est differentia partium eiusdem rationis, quarum una est extra aliam, et aliam formam recipit. Sed ista diversitas ponitur in materia esse per quantitatem. Quarta etiam ponit accidens, si illud 'esse' ponitur accidens."

   In Metaph. 7, q. 13, n. 19.

59 Thomas Aquinas, *Sent.* 4, d. 12, a. 1, q. 1 ad tertium (Thomas Aquinas 1929, 503): "Et ideo primum individuationis principium est materia, qua acquiritur esse in actu cuilibet tali formae, sive substantiali sive accidentiali. Et secundarium principium individuationis est dimensio, quia ex ipsa habet materia quod dividatur."

60 Scotus/Godinus in Stroick 1974, 589: "Nam licet prima radix et causa dictae pluralitatis sit natura ipsius materiae, inquantum apta nata est habere plures habilitates ad formas eiusdem rationis, tamen ad hoc quod haec potentia reducatur in actum, oportet materiam esse cum quodam alio, scilicet quantitate, ut extensa est. Ex divisione enim quantitatis sequitur divisio omnis extensi." John of Paris distinguishes the roles of matter and quantity as the principle of individuation and the principle of multiplication: Jean de Paris (Quidort), O.P., *Commentarie sur les Sentences: Reportation, livre II*, Studia Anselmiana, fasc. LII, ed. Jean-Pierre Müller (Rome: Herder 'Orbis Catholicus', 1964), q. 15 (d. 3, q. 3), resp., 67–8: "Quia aliud est principium individuationis et aliud principium multiplicationis individuorum sub una specie, quia hoc habet fieri per quantitatem materiam dividentem per partes."

61 See Owens 1958; on the need of *esse* to be limited, and hence determined, by essence, see Wippel 1998.

62 *In Metaph.* 7, q. 13, n. 33.

63 Godinus/Scotus in Stroick 1974, 588: "... quod non est per se hoc, habet causam suae distinctionis; ex quo sequitur, quod non est causa prima

distinctionis. Sed materia non est se ipsa haec, nam si sit, non posset esse communis multis, ergo etc."

64 *In Metaph.* 7, q. 13, n. 48:

"Contra quartam viam: quod solummodo aliunde determinatur, non est ultimum determinans. Esse non determinatur in diversis generibus et speciebus nisi per determinationem essentiarum quarum est esse; alioquin dabimus ipsi esse proprias differentias et species et genera praeter illa quae sunt quiditatis."

For a study of Scotus's critique of the existentialist theory of individuation, see O. Brown 1979.

65 *In Metaph.* 7, q. 13, n. 50.

66 For the dating of the *Metaphysics,* see the Introduction to *Opera Philosophica* III–IV (Bonaventure 3:xlii–xlvi).

67 See S. Dumont 1995.

68 *Ord.* 2, d. 3, pars 1, qq. 5–6, n. 169.

69 *In Metaph.* 7, q. 15, nn. 14–17.

70 The language of contraction used by Scotus seems to be traditional by Scotus's time; it may date as far back as Bacon. See *Quaestiones super libros primae philosophiae Aristotelis* (Roger Bacon 1905–40, 11:226–39), and Hackett 1994.

71 *Ord.* 2, d. 3, qq. 5–6, n. 182.

72 For this whole paragraph, see *Ord.* 2, d. 3, pars 1, qq. 5–6, nn. 176–86, and *In Metaph.* 7, q. 13, nn. 115–64. This point is well brought out by Gracia 1996, 246–7.

73 *Ord.* 2, d. 3, pars 1, qq. 5–6, n. 188.

74 King 1992, 51. King suggests that the relationship between the nature and the contracted nature is that of a reality compared to its intrinsic mode.

75 *In Metaph.* 7, q. 13, n. 131:

"In Socrate enim, non solum prius secundum considerationem intellectus sed secundum ordinem naturalem perfectionum unitive contentorum, prius est animal quam homo, et homo quam hic homo... sicut tamen in aliis unitive contentis non est separatio realis, nec etiam possibilis, sic natura... numquam separatur ab illa perfectione unitive secum contenta vel ab illo gradu in quo accipitur differentia individualis. Cum etiam numquam fiat in rerum natura nisi sub determinato gradu, quia ille gradus, cum quo ponitur, est secum unitive contentus."

n. 138:

"natura non continet unitive illum gradum, sed compositum ex natura et illo gradu."

76 Bonaventure, *Sent.* 2, d. 3, pars 1, a. 2, q. 3 (Quaracchi: Collegium S. Bonaventurae, 1885), 109b:

> "Quaelibet istarum positionum aliquid habet, quod homini non multum intelligenti rationabiliter videri poterit improbabile. Quomodo enim materia, quae omnibus est communis, erit principale principium et causa distinctionis, valde difficile est videre. Rursus, quomodo forma sit tota et praecipua causa numeralis distinctionis, valde est difficile capere, cum omnis forma creata, quantum est de sui natura, nata sit habere aliam similem, sicut et ipse Philosophus dicit etiam in sole et luna esse."

4 Duns Scotus's Modal Theory

Recent interest in John Duns Scotus's modal theory derives largely from the suggestion that Scotus was the first in the Middle Ages, and perhaps the first ever, to employ a synchronic conception of modality, one that allowed for alternative possibilities at a given time, and from the debate about whether Scotus introduced a notion of logical possibility divorced from any question of what powers there are. These issues interact in the question of whether Scotus had any analogue of the notion of possible world in either the Leibnizian or the late twentieth-century sense. Late medieval interest in Scotus's modal theory derived largely from its role in his account of divine and human freedom and from the debate about whether possibility itself depended in any way upon God. This discussion attempts to shed some light on these issues and to locate them in the context of the issues in the theory of modality with which Scotus and his contemporaries were themselves concerned.

It would be desirable in an essay of this kind to present a picture of the development of Scotus's thought about modality, but in the current state of scholarship that is not possible. Despite nearly a century of work by the Scotus Commission and by a number of very able scholars outside it, our understanding of the textual tradition of Scotus's works remains radically incomplete. In such a situation any hypothesis about the development of Scotus's modal theory must be highly speculative. In what follows I will not attempt to trace such a development but will attempt to limn the modal theory with which Scotus seems to have been working at the end of his (unfortunately short) life. To that end I concentrate on works which, while not unproblematic, are now widely agreed to be authentic, and to be, at least for the most part, mature. They are the *Questions on the*

Metaphysics, the *Lectura* on the *Sentences* of Peter Lombard, the *Ordinatio* on the *Sentences* of Peter Lombard, the Paris *Reportatio* on the *Sentences* of Peter Lombard, and the *Tractatus De Primo Principio*.

That said, it does seem quite possible that Scotus did not have at the beginning of his philosophical production some crucial elements of the modal theory that he held in his latest work. If the *Octo Questiones* printed in the Wadding edition of Scotus's *Opera Omnia* is authentic, then it is noteworthy that there is no hint in it of the doctrine Scotus adopts in other works – that "A is B at t" and "A can be not-B at t" are sometimes true together at t. Instead, in Question 8 Scotus argues explicitly that a future-tensed sentence like "You will be pale in A" (Tu eris albus in A) has two readings.[1] On one it "signifies it now to be thus *in re* that you will be in pale in time A." On the other it signifies now that you will be pale then. Scotus understands the first but not the second reading to commit one to there being something about the present state of affairs that serves as truthmaker for the sentence and so understands the first reading to be making a stronger claim than the second. On the first, stronger reading Scotus takes the sentence "You will be pale in A" to be determinately false and, so understood, to be inconsistent with "You can be not going to be pale in A" (Possis [in A] esse non albus). On the second, weaker reading of "You will be pale in A" it is, he says, "indeterminately true or false," and on that second reading it is consistent with "you can be not going to be pale in A." He claims that the first pair are no more consistent than the pair "You are pale now" and "You are able not to be pale now." Scotus's use of the analogy with the present-tensed case here strongly suggests that he does not yet have in mind his own (later?) doctrine of the contingency of the present, since on that doctrine the present-tensed pair is consistent.[2]

I. THE CONTINGENCY OF THE PRESENT

The doctrine that I am calling the contingency of the present and that others have called the synchronic picture of modality is clearly present in the discussion of foreknowledge and future contingents in Book 1, d. 39 of Scotus's *Lectura*.[3] Scotus there argues that God knows the future and predestines it but that much of it is,

nevertheless, contingent. Scotus accepts the necessity of the past.[4]
He denies the same necessity to the present. The key to his position
is the claim that God's activity all takes place in a single indivisible "moment" or *nunc* that never "passes into the past" (transit in
praeteritum), and that God's willing, like our own, is the exercise of
a rational power – that is, a power for opposites – that includes the
"nonevident" power for the contrary at time *t* of whatever it is actually choosing at time *t*. Positing this "nonevident power" is a bold
move on Scotus's part because the tradition to which he is heir takes
more or less for granted a view like that presented in a treatise on
obligations sometimes attributed to William of Sherwood and with
which Scotus was familiar.[5] The treatise has it that

again, a false contingent about the present instant having been posited, it,
namely the present instant, should be denied to be. Which is proved thus.
Let *a* be a name of the present instant (a name, I say, which is discrete, not
common). Since, therefore, that you are at Rome is now false, it is impossible
that now, or in *a*, it be true, for it cannot be made true except through a
motion or a sudden change. It cannot be made true through a motion because
there is no motion in an instant, nor through a sudden change because if
there were a sudden change to truth in *a* then it would be a truth in *a* –
because when there is a sudden change there is a terminus of the sudden
change. Thus it is impossible for this falsehood to be made true in *a*. So,
therefore this is true: '*a* is not'. Therefore, if the falsehood is posited, it is
necessary to deny that *a* is, and this is what the rule says.[6]

To see what this text asserts – and what Scotus is denying in his assertion of the contingency of the present – it is useful to consider the
text in the context of Aristotle's discussion of the relation between
potentiality and change.

Aristotle distinguishes several different senses in which items can
be ordered as prior and posterior. One of the most familiar and most
important is the prior and posterior in time. In his *Physics* Aristotle
defines time as the measure of change (*kinesis*) with respect to prior
and posterior and defines change as the actualization of a potentiality
as such. This picture ties the ordering of items as prior and posterior
in time directly to the potency–act relationship. In a given change
potency is prior to act in time. Aristotle also distinguishes several
different senses of 'possible' in one of which something is possible
just in case there is a potency to bring it about. If we marry these two
notions we produce a picture according to which to bring about what

is possible but not actual requires the actualization of a potentiality, which in turn takes time. We could encapsulate the picture in the principle

> A) If X is A then X can be ~A if and only if it can change from being A to being ~A

and the observation that the result of a change is always later than the beginning of the change. It is this picture that underlies the rule enunciated in the Sherwood (?) *Obligationes*.

Principle A and the associated doctrine that time is the measure of change pose serious difficulties for any attempt to suggest that a being acting outside time (God, for example) can do anything other than it does. They also raise difficulties for the suggestion that a being acting at a time can do anything other than it actually does at that time. Both of these sets of difficulties become acute if we also suppose that a being acts freely only if it can do other than it does. This complex of worries was focused by an example first formulated, as far as I am aware, by Grosseteste, and taken over by Scotus in his *Lectura*. Consider a rational creature – an angel, for example – that exists only for an instant during which it is, let us suppose, loving God. The question posed is whether it could be loving God freely.

The argument that the angel could not be loving God freely is that for it to do so it has to have a power to do otherwise, say, to hate God. But, the argument continues, there is no power to hate God if it is impossible to actualize that power; and it is impossible (at least for a being that acts in time) to actualize a power if that power could not be actualized at any time. The angel in question exists only for an instant and can't actualize its supposed power when it does not exist, so if it has the power to hate God, it can actualize this power at the very instant it exists. Aristotle's most general definition of the possible is that which, when posited, doesn't entail an impossibility. Suppose then that we posit that the angel hates God at the very instant it exists and see what follows.

We have already hypothesized that the angel is loving God, and we didn't take back that supposition, so we have now supposed that the angel is loving God and that the angel is hating God – and that is a contradiction. It seems that if we are to suppose that the angel that is loving God can, nonetheless, hate God for that same instant, we have to suppose that the angel cannot be doing what it in fact is doing at the very moment it is doing it. That is what Principle A rules out.

Scotus sees this argument clearly and is moved to modify the principle that being other than you actually are requires change. His way of doing this is to take up a device used by thirteenth-century physicists to treat problems of the continuum and then extended to problems in theology – the device of *signa* or instants of nature. This device is grounded in another of Aristotle's senses of prior and posterior – what he calls priority and posteriority according to nature or substance. In the late Aristotelian tradition this idea was extended in various ways, and in the debates recorded, for example, in Averroës' *Tahafut al-Tahafut* and Maimonides' *Guide* we find an exploration of the idea that in creation the creator need not be temporally prior but only naturally prior to the created. In his *De primo principio* Scotus himself elaborates the notion in this way:

I understand "prior" here in the same sense as did Aristotle when in the fifth book of the *Metaphysics*, [relying] on the testimony of Plato, he shows that the prior according to nature and essence is what may be (*contingit*) without the posterior but not conversely. And this I understand thus: that although the prior may cause the posterior necessarily and therefore not be able to be without it, this, however, is not because it needs the posterior to be (*ad suum esse*). Rather the converse, because even if the posterior is held not to be, nonetheless the prior will be without a contradiction. But it is not so conversely because the posterior needs the prior, which need we can call 'dependence', so that we may say that every posterior depends essentially on a prior and not conversely, even though the posterior sometimes follows it [the prior] necessarily. Prior and posterior can be said according to substance and species, as they are said by others, but for precise speech are called prior and posterior according to dependence.[7]

Aristotle introduced natural priority in modal terms, but Scotus here explains it in terms of what can be posited without contradiction and explicitly claims that there can be necessary relationships (the posterior sometimes following the prior necessarily) that it would not be contradictory to deny. This sense of 'prior' takes on new significance in light of Scotus's *Propositio Famosa* – a claim to the effect that[8]

> PF) The order among concepts is the order there would be among the significata of the concepts if these could exist separated from each other.

The *Propositio Famosa* enables Scotus to give a more fine-grained account of natural priority than we find earlier in the tradition and to employ in articulating it a number of logical devices. The result is that we cannot only meaningfully order two items with respect to each other as naturally prior or posterior but we can induce larger orderings that share many of the properties of time. In particular we can sometimes induce orderings of nature in which we can meaningfully speak of items as naturally prior, naturally posterior, or at the same point. Once we have this much, we can introduce the idea of an instant of nature as a way of talking about the items that are at the same point in the natural ordering.

To see this more clearly it might help to reflect a little on how an instant of nature might be constituted. Once one is open to the thought that there are types of causation that are not changes, it does not seem so farfetched to suppose that not all causal relations (largely understood) involve succession in time. For Scotus the productive relations within the Trinity serve as obvious cases in which no temporal succession is involved, and the creation of the world (and with it motion and so time) is another. Even in natural philosophy the picture of light's being propagated instantaneously through a diaphanous medium by the sun, a hypothesis certainly compatible with the empirical data available to Scotus, served as a case of a causal process in which the effect and the cause were coincident in time and in which, despite the temporal coincidence, there is a clear sense in which emission of light by the sun is prior to its reception on the earth. Now if one holds, as Scotus did, that in the relevant sense a power must be prior to its actualization (see *In Metaph.* 9, q. 14, for example) and one accepts the *Propositio Famosa*, one could generalize these examples to produce a partial ordering of instants of nature. A is naturally prior to B if and only if mention of A is required in giving an explanation of B. We can now give a sufficient condition for the distinctness of two instants of nature n1 and n2. They are distinct just in case something indexed to n1 is naturally prior to or naturally posterior to something indexed to n2. We shall return to this partial ordering when we discuss Scotus's modal ideas in his proof of the existence of God.[9]

In the context of the angel existing only for a single temporal instant, Scotus treats an instant of time as divisible into a sequence of instants of nature. The present instant can, at a minimum, be regarded as a pair of instants of nature ordered as before and after in nature. The prior is that in which the angel has both the power to love God and the power to hate God, and the posterior is that in which the angel has actualized the power to love God. These are prior and posterior in nature because the power to love God is naturally prior to its actualization. Since "in" the instant of time there is an instant of nature (namely the prior of the two) at which the angel has the power to hate God, we can say that the angel has the power to hate God at that instant of time (and could, relative to that "prior" instant of nature, actualize it at the posterior instant of nature), and thus the angel is now free.[10]

Scotus thinks that it is because of this ordering of nature within the present instant of time that we can speak of the present as being only contingently the way it is. It is as if the past and future met in the present instant with the prior instant of nature belonging to the past (as its endpoint) and the posterior one to the future (as its beginning).[11] So, as we might by now expect, Scotus's response to Principle A and the rule of *Obligatio* embodying it is to reject them both.[12]

Scotus argues that the present is contingent, but he insists that it is determinate and, in at least one explicit discussion of the matter, he insists that, unlike the future, it is actual.[13] In so distinguishing determination from necessitation he is part of an early fourteenth-century movement that reshaped the terms of the discussion of future contingents. As we shall see in Section III, the distinction between determination and necessitation plays a role in his discussion of how the will can be inferior to another cause in an essential order and still be free.

The contingency of the present, or more precisely the contingency of what has not "passed into the past," is a notion that Scotus employs widely. In the human case he uses it to explain what it is for a human will to be free at a time t: a human will is free at t just in case it has at t the power to do at t other than what it is doing at t. In the divine case Scotus relies on this notion to explain how there can be contingency in the world at all. He argues that since divine causal cooperation is required for everything, and since God is immutable, if God's activity were not contingent "while" it is happening, nothing would be contingent. There can be no doubt that Scotus does think that at the present moment things could be other than they are. This contrasts sharply with views like Ockham's or Holkot's that at least purport to accept Principle A. Nevertheless, for Scotus, the alternatives to the present at the present are exactly the actualizations of the potentialities there are at present. Unless there are the same potentialities at every time, what is possible will vary from time to time, and so time and modality will not yet have completely separated.

Moreover, although he rejects the necessity of the present, Scotus thinks that the past is necessary. For example in his *Lectura* 1, d. 40, q. un., he considers the objection that

what passes into the past (*transit in praeteritum*) is necessary – as the Philosopher wishes in Book 6 of the *Ethics*, approving the saying of someone who says that "this alone is God not able to make, that what is past is not past."

He replies:

To the first argument, when it is argued that that which passes into the past is necessary, it is conceded. And when it is argued that this one's being predestined passes into the past, it should be said that it is false. For if our will were always to have the same volition in the same immobile instant, its volition would not be past but always in act. And thus it is of the divine will, which is always the same.... Hence [with respect to] what is said in the past tense – that God has predestined – there the 'has predestined' joins (*copulat*) the now of eternity as it coexists with a now in the past.[14]

This is a bit gnomic but seems to say both that there is no past for God – whose act is like an eternal present – and that although that act has coexisted with our past, it does not share the necessity of our past. On the other hand the passage also seems to say that what is genuinely past really is necessary. If what is genuinely past is what is past for us, this raises a very delicate issue of whether what is in our past is really necessary or not. I know of nowhere where Scotus himself faces this issue clearly.

In Chapter 4 of *De primo principio* Scotus argues from the premise that something causes contingently to the conclusion that the First Cause is an agent endowed with a will (DP 4.15).[15] He then argues from the premise that the First Agent is endowed with a will to the conclusion that the First Cause causes contingently whatever it causes (DP 4.23). He has already argued in Chapter 3 that every cause except the first causes only insofar as its causing is itself caused by the activity of the first cause. Since the human will is a cause in the relevant sense, it follows that it too causes only insofar as its causing is caused by God. This obviously raises the specter of determinism, and Scotus apparently thinks that he banishes this specter by showing that the First Cause causes contingently and that the human will is a rational power (that is, a power that is not of its nature determined to a particular effect in given circumstances). Is he justified in thinking this?

II. POSSIBILITY AND THE EXISTENCE OF GOD

To answer this difficult question we must first look more closely at the structure of the first part of Scotus's proof of the existence (and infinity) of God, which Scotus presents in his *Ordinatio* and develops at greater length in *De primo principio*. The two presentations overlap considerably, and in what follows I will focus on the more detailed version in *De primo principio*.

Scotus begins Chapter 1 of *De primo principio* by introducing the notion of essential order. The term, he says, is equivocal and includes both orders of items according to (pure) perfection and orders of items according to dependence – a notion that, as we saw in the previous section, Scotus immediately associates with natural priority. He then proceeds to identify four "direct" orders of dependence, one corresponding to each of the four Aristotelian causes, and two orders that relate items indirectly – through their mutual relations to some third item. He argues that this classification of orders of dependence is complete. In the second chapter Scotus argues that the various types of dependence are so ordered that if an item depends on something else in any of the orders, both it and what it depends on depend in turn on something in the order of efficient causes and on something in the order of final causes. In the third chapter he argues that there necessarily is a unique nature that is prior to all others in the order of efficient causes, the order of final causes, and the order of eminence. The proof itself focuses on the order of efficient causes.

Possibility enters the proof at the very beginning because Scotus begins with the premise that

> P) Some nature is contingent; therefore, it is possible for it
> to be after not being (DP3.5).
> From this he immediately infers

    C1) Some nature can produce (DP 3.4), and then presents a
    subargument to the conclusion that
    C2) Some nature is simply first, that is, it is neither causable
    nor does it cause in virtue of something else (DP 3.7).

In many ways the core of the proof is in this subargument. It is
there that Scotus argues that, although a sequence of causes ordered
accidentally could be infinite in extent, a sequence of causes essentially ordered could not. The key to this argument is Scotus's account
of the distinction between an essentially (or *per se*) ordered and an
accidentally ordered causal sequence.

The terminology of essentially or *per se* versus accidentally ordered causal sequences at once brings to mind Aristotle's distinction
between *per se* and accidental causes but, as Scotus himself emphasizes (DP 3.10), it is crucial to his argument not to conflate an essentially or *per se* ordered sequence with a sequence of *per se* causes. In
the causal sequence child – parent – grandparent – great-grandparent,
and so on, each link in the causal chain is one of a *per se* cause to
its effect, but this sequence is Scotus's paradigm of one that is accidentally, not essentially, ordered. Instead of focusing on the intrinsic
character of the causes at work, we should, Scotus advises, focus on
the role they play in the causal process. A sequence of causes essentially ordered is one all of whose members operate to produce a
single effect of a single *per se* cause. Scotus himself characterizes a
sequence of causes essentially ordered this way:

Per se or essentially ordered causes differ from accidentally ordered causes in
three ways. The first difference is that in *per se* [ordered causes] the second,
insofar as it causes, depends on the first. In accidentally [ordered causes] this
is not so, although [the second] may depend [on the first] in being or in some
other way. The second [difference] is that in things ordered *per se* there is
causality of another *ratio* and order. In accidentally [ordered causes] it is not
so. This [difference] follows from the first, for no cause depends essentially
in causing on another cause of the same *ratio*, because in causation one of
a single *ratio* suffices. A third [difference] follows – that all causes ordered
per se are necessarily required at the same time for causing [the effect];
otherwise some causality *per se* to the effect would be lacking. Accidentally
ordered [causes] are not required [to act] at the same time.[16]

Although the most obvious distinctive mark of an essentially ordered sequence is the third – that all its members act at once – Scotus

claims that this is a consequence of a deeper difference. This difference is that a posterior member of the sequence depends on those prior insofar as it causes (*inquantum causat*) rather than for its existence. A prior cause in an essentially ordered sequence does not cause a posterior cause but causes (in a sense of 'cause' with a different *ratio*) the causal activity of the posterior cause. To understand this dark doctrine we must look to what Scotus takes to be another consequence of it – that, since to produce a given effect one *per se* efficient cause is enough, we should understand the prior members of the sequence to exercise a different kind of causality, one of "a different *ratio* and order (*ordo*)" (DPP 3.11). We are not to understand the prior members of a sequence essentially ordered to a given effect to act as partial causes of the effect combining with the usual efficient cause to yield the total efficient cause of the effect. Scotus is happy to think that the total efficient cause of an effect is just what we thought it was; the efficient causes prior to it in the essential order play a very different role.

There is much here that is still mysterious, but I think we can see already that to think of God's relation to an event like an act of the human will as that of a cause of the event of the same kind as the will itself is to mistake Scotus's picture radically. God does not cause the act of will in the sense that the will does. God is not total or partial, final or efficient or formal cause of the will's act. God causes the will's causing of its act. Exactly what this means is far from clear. I suggest that at least this much is true: God causes it to be the case that what the will does is a causing of its act.

From this perspective we can see both why Scotus thinks that were God's act to be past, what it is causally connected with would be necessary, and why, given that God's act is still contingent, the act of the will is free. Were God's act to be past it would already be the case, and so necessarily be the case, that what the will is doing is producing that act. Given that it is still contingent whether what the will is doing is producing that act, it is in the power of the will to not be producing that act.[17]

The conclusion of this stage of the argument is just that some nature is uncausable and were it to exercise causality would do so independently. To get to

> C4) Some simply first cause exists in act and some nature actually existing is thus a cause

we need an argument of a different kind. Scotus argues that since a simply first nature cannot be caused, then either it exists *a se* or it is impossible. If it were possible but did not exist, he suggests, then it would have to come into existence; and, he seems to assume, coming into existence requires a cause. C2 shows that it is possible. Hence it exists *a se*. Here we have Scotus assuming that

> **Principle S**: what does not exist but can exist can be caused to exist (DP3.19).

Scotus strengthens his result in

> C5) Uncausable being is necessarily of itself (DP 3.21).

Here the argument is that if something that does exist can not-exist then something privately or positively incompossible with it can exist – where A is privatively incompossible with B if A entails a lack of something B requires to exist. Scotus argues that anything privately or positively incompossible with an uncausable being would itself have to be uncausable and so, if it could exist, would itself exist by C4. But then we would have two actually existing incompossibles. That is impossible, so there cannot be anything incompossible with the First uncausable Being.

It is striking how far this modal framework is from one in which we consider possible situations unconnected with one another by relations of causality and their ilk. A twenty-first-century theorist might suggest that there is nothing absurd about the idea of there being in some possible situation the uncausable being X although X failed to be in the actual situation. We do not need to look for factors that account for X's being in one and not the other – these facts are primitive. For example, let X be that nothing whatever exists. Nothing in our current modal theory shows that to be impossible, and we might consistently suppose X possible and at the same time suppose that in another possible world (perhaps this one) there is another uncausable being, which many are prepared to call God. Scotus reasons otherwise. What exists exists in every situation in which its causal requirements are met and nothing preventing it exists. Hence, if something does not exist but could, then there is a privative or positive cause of its nonexistence.

III. NECESSITY AND FREEDOM

Scotus claims that the contingency of God's causal activity with respect to creatures is a necessary condition for human freedom. A number of writers have suggested that human acts are nonetheless necessary relative to God's act and hence, even if contingent absolutely speaking, are necessary in the sense required by the usual understanding of determinism.[18] It was suggested in the last section that this line of argument mistakes God's causal activity as a higher-order cause for efficient causing in the usual sense. It is now time to treat this issue more fully.

In *De primo principio* 4.18 Scotus distinguishes between a sense of 'contingent' that is opposed to the necessary or sempiternal and another in which something is contingent only if "its opposite was able to be at the very time that it [the thing in question] was." In this sense something is contingent only if it is *contingently caused* when it is caused. It is this second sense of 'contingent' that is relevant to discussion of freedom of the will.

Scotus is anxious to safeguard the freedom of both the human and the divine will. In several places, including Chapter 4, Conclusion 4 of *De primo principio*, he argues that it is characteristic of a will to cause contingently, and that it is necessary for anything to will that the first cause be a will and cause contingently. As we have already seen, Scotus thinks that such contingent causation requires that we posit in the will a nonevident power for opposites.

This does not entail that all acts of will are contingent. Scotus argues, notably in *Questiones Quodlibetales* q. 16, that the acts by which God loves himself and by which the Father and the Son spirate the Holy Spirit are acts of will and are simply necessary.[19] He claims that this is because the divine will is infinite and hence "is related to the supremely lovable object in the most perfect way that a will can relate to it. But this would not be the case unless the divine will loved this object necessarily and adequately."[20] We conclude then that loving an object necessarily is a more perfect way of loving it than loving it contingently. Scotus goes on in the second article of question 16 to claim that liberty is an intrinsic condition of a will as such and so must be compatible with the most perfect way of exercising the will. Since, as has already been claimed in the case of God's love of himself, the most perfect way for a will to act is necessarily, it follows that acting necessarily is compatible with liberty.

Of course it does not follow from this that every sense of 'necessity' or every way of acting necessarily is compatible with liberty. Scotus is particularly concerned to distinguish freely acting necessarily from naturally acting necessarily. These involve, he suggests, two ways in which a thing can be more or less determined. He writes:

To the claim, then, that a natural principle cannot be more determined than a necessary principle, I say: Although the necessary be most determined in the sense that it excludes any indetermination as regards an alternative, nevertheless one necessary thing may in some way be more determined than another. That fire be hot or the heavens be round is determined by the cause which produced simultaneously the being of the heavens and its shape. A weight, on the other hand, is determined to descend. Still, it does not receive from its progenitor the act of descending, but only that principle that naturally causes it to descend. But if the caused will necessarily wills anything, it is not determined by its cause to will such in the way the weight is determined to descend. All it receives from the cause is a principle by which it determines itself to this volition.[21]

What seems to be under discussion here are three ways in which a thing might come to have a property necessarily. It might be directly caused to have the feature necessarily, caused to have a nature in virtue of which it has the feature necessarily, or caused to be such that it can freely cause itself to have the feature necessarily. Scotus evidently thinks that something that comes to have a feature necessarily in one of the first two ways is in some sense more determined than something that comes to have the feature necessarily in the third way. He thinks this even though in all three cases it is impossible that the feature be absent.

What is it, then, to freely cause oneself to have a feature necessarily, as contrasted with being caused naturally to have the feature necessarily? Scotus explains it using nested counterfactuals:

Every natural agent either is first in an absolute sense or, if not, it will be naturally determined to act by some prior agent. Now the will can never be an agent that is first in an absolute sense. But neither can it be naturally determined by a higher agent, for it is active in such a way that it determines itself to action in the sense that if the will wills something necessarily, for example A, this volition of A would not be caused naturally by that which causes the will even if the will itself were caused naturally, but once the first act by which the will is caused be given, if the will were left to itself and could have or not have this volition contingently, it would still determine itself to this volition.[22]

We have here a thought experiment conducted under two suppositions. Consider the case of a will that causes itself to have a volition necessarily. First, suppose that the will itself is caused – even caused naturally – but that the natural cause of the will does nothing further by way of eliciting an act of the will. Second, suppose that the feature we are considering to be brought about necessarily by the will is not necessarily present. Still, Scotus claims, that feature would *be* present because the will would itself bring the feature about. This contrasts with the case of a natural agent. If we suppose that a natural agent exists but that nothing is acting on it, then if the feature were not there necessarily it would not be there at all. In other contexts Scotus speaks of the necessity of an act freely willed as a necessity that is consequent upon the will's choice, whereas the necessity of something naturally produced either precedes or accompanies the agent's activity.

In what sense of 'necessarily' could a will cause itself to will necessarily? Scotus argues that it is in the sense in which *necessitas* is *firmitas* – steadfastness of will. He makes this clear in *Quodl.* q. 16, where, in speaking of the kind of necessity that perfects an action he identifies it with *firmitas*. Such *firmitas* rules out mutability but does not rule out the nonevident power for opposites.[23]

But is this enough? Suppose we grant that the human will has the nonevident power for opposites, that God has it too, and that God causes contingently whatever God causes. If we also grant, as Scotus's proof for the existence of God requires, that God is a higher-order cause with respect to the human will's production of its effect, and grant, as Scotus explicitly requires, that God knows the future by knowing his own choices, can we avoid the conclusion that God's choices so determine the choices of every human will that a twenty-first-century philosopher would say the choices of the human will are necessitated?

According to Scotus a will is a self-mover and, in particular, one that is not determined by nature to one rather than another of a pair of contradictories. Scotus claims that we experience that we could have not willed or willed the contrary of what we in fact did will.[24] When we do act rather than not, or act in one way rather than another, there is no cause of such a choice other than that "the will is the will," as he likes to put it. This indeterminacy in the will is not because of a lack of actuality in the will but because of a superabundant sufficiency derived from a lack of limitation of actuality (*superabundantis sufficientiae quae est ex illimitatione actualitatis*). Things that are indeterminate in this second way are able to determine themselves, and that is what the will does.[25]

All of this, and especially the last, suggest that the will is not acted upon, strictly speaking, by anything else, but this must be reconciled with the claim that the human will is, after all, a creature and so, in its activity, essentially ordered to God as a higher-order cause. As was stressed in the last section, higher-order essentially ordered causes are typically not causes of the effects to which they are ordered. They are, rather, causes of the causing of those effects by the causes that do cause them. Hence, while God causes any given human will, God does not cause the willing of that will. Instead God causes it to be the case that the willing of that will is a production of what it does produce. Scotus seems to think that the only efficient cause of a willing is the will that does it. God is not another, partial, efficient cause of that willing. Nonetheless, it is the case that, were God not to act, the human will would not suffice to produce its act. It is also the case that God's acting as a higher-order cause of the will's willing of A is not compossible with the human will's not willing A. Moreover, it is the case that God's willing is not causally dependent on the acts of the human will. In this context, how it is possible that a human act be free?

This problem is most acute for the blessed in heaven because Scotus claims that in some sense of 'cannot,' they cannot sin. Yet Scotus also insists that they retain their wills and their freedom – from which it seems proper to infer that they retain the nonevident power for opposites. So they have a power – and a possibility of acting – that they necessarily will not exercise.

Scotus's resolution of this aporia relies on his distinction of *firmitas* from other types of necessity. God ensures *firmitas* to the blessed in heaven, and so while they retain the power to refrain from loving God and so *can* refrain, they steadfastly (and in that sense necessarily) exercise their power to love God. How does God ensure *firmitas* to the blessed? Scotus does not say.[26]

IV. LOGICAL POSSIBILITY

So far I have written as though for Scotus what is possible is just what there is a power to bring about. But that there is some significant difference between them seems clear in the light of passages like *Ordinatio* 1, d. 7, q. 1, n. 27. There he writes:

> I respond to the question therefore in the first place by distinguishing 'potency'.
>
> For in one way a potency which is said to be a mode of composition made by an intellect is called 'logical'. And this indicates the non-repugnance of terms of which the Philosopher in *Metaphysics* V, ch. "De Potentia," says "that is possible of which the contrary is not true of necessity." . . .
>
> If before the creation of the world not only had the world not been but, *per impossibile*, God had not been, but [God] had begun to be *a se*, and then had been able to create the world, [then] if there had been an intellect before the world composing this: 'the world will be', this would have been possible because its terms are not repugnant.

One of the oldest debates among interpreters of Scotus is over the nature and significance of this *potentia logica*. The debate seems to have reached its classical form in the seventeenth century, when Johannes Poncius interpreted Scotus as holding that whatever is possible is possible of itself apart from any power to realize it, and Bartolomeus Mastrius defended the view that possibilities depend upon God for their very possibility. In this form it has reappeared in twentieth-century discussion.[27]

There are in fact several issues here. There is first whether the existence of a *potentia logica*, that is, of a nonrepugnance among terms, is sufficient for possibility apart from any "real" power to realize the state of affairs in question. A second issue is whether that *potentia logica* itself does or does not presuppose or involve any real power. Then there is the question of whether there is a real power corresponding to every *potentia logica* and the question of the relationship between this issue and the proofs of the existence of God that Scotus offers both in his *Ordinatio* and in the *De primo principio*.

Scotus characterizes the notion of logical possibility in terms of a (*non*) *repugnantia terminorum* but appears to take the notion of a *repugnantia terminorum* itself as primitive. He never attempts to characterize it in other terms and to elucidate it provides only examples and special cases. Explicit contradictions are a special case of *repugnantia*, but they cannot be the only case, because Scotus admits impossibilities that cannot be shown to be so in an *obligatio* under impossible *positio*, and any explicit contradiction could be so shown. One might guess that the notion of *repugnantia* extends at least to cases of contraries (like 'red' and 'green'), where there seems to be something that we might now characterize as a semantic tension, even if we have no good theory of exactly what the tension consists in. But what of other cases? The doctrine of the Incarnation, as Scotus understood it, requires that the same *suppositum* could be both God and human, and so it cannot be that there is a *repugnantia* in the conjunction "Christ is God and Christ is human"; and while Scotus never says so, his account of the Incarnation seems compatible with the assumption by the Word of other natures besides human nature. Perhaps there is no *repugnantia* in ascribing any group of substantial predicates to the same *suppositum*. What then of the cases sometimes discussed in late-twentieth-century philosophy under the heading of a posteriori necessary truths – cases in which the nature of something is discovered empirically and it is then suggested that it would be impossible that that thing not have that nature – as it would be impossible that gold not have the atomic number 79? Scotus apparently counts the denial of a part of the real definition of a species and the denial of a *proprium* of a species as cases of *repugnantia*. Given the isomorphism between metaphysical structure and conceptual structure expressed in the *Propositio Famosa*, it would seem that he would think anything there is to be discovered about the metaphysical structure of things is reflected in the divine idea of it and so is reflected in an adequate concept of it. If this is right, then the distinction between semantic incompatibility and metaphysical incompatibility vanishes, and with it the distinction between logical necessity and metaphysical necessity found in some late-twentieth-century modal theories. Thus, Scotus's *potentia logica* could be identified with logical possibility in a late-twentieth-century sense only with reservation.

As we have seen already, for Scotus an affirmative predication asserts a unification of some kind between the subject and predicate. Since a unification certainly requires a nonrepugnance, for Scotus the truth of any affirmative categorical sentence whatever involves a nonrepugnance among terms. The claim that the muskox is an ungulate is true only if there is no repugnance of 'muskox' and 'ungulate'. In many cases the truth of an affirmative categorical sentence requires more. In any case the truth of the sentence requires the sentence, and since the sentence is some kind of being, no sentence exists apart from every real power, and so none, no matter what its modal status, is true apart from every real power.

But this hardly gets to the root of the issue between those who think that Scotus regards a *potentia logica* as sufficient for possibility and those who deny it. Within 40 years of Scotus's death, Jean Buridan was carefully formulating a distinction between the possibility of things' being as a sentence describes and the possible truth of the sentence itself. The latter requires that the sentence exist in the situation it describes, but the former does not – and seems in general not to require the existence of any sentence at all. Surely we can ask whether, even if nothing, not even God, existed, it would still be possible that God or the world exists.

Both in the seventeenth century and in our own time there have been scholars who read the passage last quoted as evidence that the possibility of "The world will be" did not depend on the existence of that sentence or on any real power. After all, the situation we are to consider is one in which nothing yet exists. True, we then consider an intellect that composes a sentence, but there is at least the suggestion that the possibility of the sentence is in some sense there when the sentence is composed and does not depend upon its composition. One might suggest that the example is tortuous precisely because Scotus is somewhat obscurely anticipating Buridan's distinction between the possible and the possibly true and wants us to evaluate not the truth of the sentence but the possibility that the world will be in the counterfactual situation in which nothing whatever exists.

This is, I think, a plausible reading of the passage, but it is not an unproblematic reading. The passage is immensely complicated. First, it involves iterated reasoning under an impossible assumption – and reasoning under an impossible assumption is something that for Scotus is a technical matter – one to which we shall return below. Second, the passage involves some rather complicated interaction of modality and tense. Suppose we draw a distinction like Buridan's. Then, Scotus seems to suggest, for the possibility that the world will be we require that God had begun to be *a se* and had then been able to create the world. It seems to be the natural reading of this that while the possibility that the world will be doesn't depend on anything actual, it does depend on something that, by hypothesis, *will be* actual and will *then* have a power to create the world. This is, no doubt, a rather unusual foundation for a possibility, but it does seem to suggest that possibilities do after all require a categorical foundation – even if not a present-tensed one. What we seem to be told here is that it *is* possible that the world will be because there *will be* a God with the power to create it. This seems rather far from the thought that *all* that possibilities require is a nonrepugnance of terms.

Consider on the other hand what is required for the possible truth of the sentence "The world will be." At a first approximation we require the sentence. Hence, we require its terms so that relations of repugnance or nonrepugnance might exist between them. But although we have talked amiably about the terms of spoken sentences and of mental sentences indifferently, it is pretty clear that Scotus thinks it is among the terms of mental sentences that relations of repugnance hold in the first instance. These terms are concepts; and concepts, as the *Propositio Famosa* teaches us, mirror the metaphysical structure of what is conceived. Relations among concepts mirror relations among essences.

Consider now this passage from *Ordinatio* 1, d. 43:

So it is in the [case] being considered: 'not being something' is in man and in chimera from eternity. But the affirmation which is 'being something' is not repugnant to man – instead the negation inheres [in man] solely on account of the negation [which is] of the cause not being present. It is repugnant to chimera, however, because there is no cause which could cause its 'being something'. And the reason why it is repugnant to chimera and not to man is that this is this and that is that. And this is so whichever intellect is conceiving, since whatever is repugnant to something formally in itself is repugnant to it, and what is not formally repugnant in itself is not repugnant to it as was said. Nor should we imagine (*fingendum*) that it is not repugnant to man because [a man] is a being in potency and it is repugnant to chimera because [a chimera] is not a being in potency. Indeed, it is more the converse: because ['being something'] is not repugnant to man, [man] is possible by a logical potency, and because it is repugnant to chimera, [chimera] is impossible in the opposite [manner]. And this is so, even positing the omnipotence of God, which is with regard to everything possible (as long as it is other than God). Nevertheless, that logical possibility could stand absolutely by its nature, even if *per impossibile* there was no omnipotence with regard to it.

If we consider this text in the light of our discussion of *Ordinatio* I, d. 7, q. I, n. 27, a natural reading of it is that (to take Scotus's example) the concept of 'chimera' is internally incoherent in the sense that the metaphysical constituents out of which the common nature of chimera would be composed (the *notae*) simply cannot be combined, and that is why there is a further repugnance between 'chimera' and 'being something'. But this repugnance presupposes that 'chimera' is itself a complex term in which several *notae* are combined. A chimera is perhaps an animal with the head of a lion, the body of a goat, and the tail of a serpent. These *notae* are themselves complex and could be analyzed in the same way. On Scotus's view, we eventually reach simple *notae*. Suppose we ask then whether all simple *notae* are possible – and further, whether they are possible of themselves. Scotus adds:

This, therefore, is the process there: just as God in his intellect produces a possible in possible being, so also he formally produces two entities (each in possible being). And those products themselves are formally incompossible, so that they could not simultaneously be one [thing], nor could there be a third [composed of them]. This incompossibility which they have they have formally by themselves, and "principiatively" from him who produced them in some mode. And from their incompossibility there follows the incompossibility of the whole fictional construct (*figmenti*) that includes them. And its incompossibility with respect to any agent whatever [follows] from the impossibility of the construct in itself and the incompossibility of its parts.[28]

There are several things to be noted about this passage. First, the process begins with a natural divine production *in esse possibili*. These possibilia are naturally and *ex se* either compossible or not. The compossible ones can be combined to produce complexes with *esse possibile*. When these primitives are naturally repugnant they cannot be so combined. The very idea of a primitive *ens impossibile* is nonsense on Scotus's view. As he puts it in the same chapter:

And from this it is apparent that the imagining of those seeking the impossibility of some things as if [the impossibility] were in some one thing, is false – as if something one – whether an intelligible being or whatever [other] kind – were formally impossible in itself, in the way in which God is formally necessary being in himself. . . . Rather, everything that is unqualifiedly nothing includes in itself the essences (*rationes*) of many.[29]

So it seems that for Scotus impossibility is a fundamentally relational idea. We can intelligibly speak of it only when we are dealing with several *notae*. Similarly, we can only ask whether *notae* are consistent when we are dealing with more than one. Thus, in the typical cases the question of whether some possible is possible of itself reduces to the question of the status of a relation among its metaphysical constituents: Are they related of themselves, and in what sense does that relation presuppose its relata?

I suggested above that the simple *notae* are in one sense possible – they aren't internally incoherent and can be combined to produce natures that are compatible with being something, that is, could exist. But they are not possible in the sense that they could exist by themselves, and in their case the question of whether they have their possibility of themselves seems especially odd. Their having any status at all depends on God *principiative*. But since their being possible is simply their lacking a relation of repugnance to themselves, why not say that they are possible *formaliter* of themselves? Here the debate over whether the possibles are possible of themselves seems to have lost its point.

We have seen that, whatever he makes of it, Scotus introduces a *potentia*, the *potentia logica*, corresponding to the nonrepugnance of terms. What has not yet been stressed is that he introduces this precisely to correspond to what he understands to be one of Aristotle's senses of 'possible'. Let us look a little more closely at the context. He writes

in response to the question therefore in the first place by distinguishing 'potency'. For in one way a potency that is said to be a mode of composition made by an intellect is called 'logical'. And this indicates the non-repugnance of terms, of which the Philosopher in *Metaphysics* V, ch. "De Potentia," says "that is possible of which the contrary is not true of necessity."[30]

Scotus contrasts this potency with the potency that "is said to be divided against act," which is not found in God, and the "real potency" that is said to be "a principle of acting and being acted on." He makes it clear in *In Metaph.* 9, qq. 1–2 that this is for him a fundamental division of potency, and his introduction there of *potentia geometrica* to correspond to the possibility of mathematical claims suggests that he thinks there should be a kind of potency – real or metaphorical – corresponding to each sense of 'possible'.

The connection between possibility and power is made tighter for Scotus by his claim that there is a real power corresponding to every logical power. From a medieval theologian this claim is not surprising, closely connected as it obviously is with such claims as that God can bring about whatever does not include a contradiction, but it raises the complex issue of whether it is part of the very conception of a logical power that there *be* a real power that can realize it. Is it even part of that conception that there *can be* a real power to realize it?

Scotus's proof of the existence of God is, he says himself, a proof in the quidditative order. We learn something about the nature of a contingent being when we see how it depends upon a first efficient cause. Scotus intends his argument to be a demonstration and so not to require any contingent premises. The argument proceeds from the necessary premise that some being can exist to the conclusion that God must exist. Hence, if it is a demonstration, it rules out as impossible any situation in which a being can exist and God even could fail to exist. This is precisely the kind of situation to which Scotus appeals in the passage from *Ordinatio* 1, d. 7, quoted two paragraphs earlier. So it is already clear that the situation there described is impossible. How then are we to reason in it?

Thirteenth- and fourteenth-century theorists worked out rather elaborate accounts of reasoning from an impossible premise and enshrined them in the theory of impossible *positio.* Central to Scotus's understanding of the theory (which he clearly knew very well) is the thought that from an impossible assumption or *positio* one can reason only using what he calls natural or essential consequences and not using accidental consequences or ones that hold only through an extrinsic middle. That is, one can reason from an impossible assumption to any conclusion that is contained in the understanding (*de per se intellectu*) of the assumption, but not to one which is not.[31]

If all of this is correct, then in the thought experiment of Book 1, d. 7, Scotus is inviting us to consider a situation in which there is no world and there is no God but in which it is nonetheless still possible that the world will be. But, as his proof of the existence of God shows, a situation in which it is possible that the world will be is one in which God in fact will be – and, since the world depends essentially upon God, that God will be follows by essential consequences from the claim that it is possible that the world will be. Hence, while Scotus does not have to include in his description of the situation of the thought experiment that God is, he does have to include that God will be. Since God is uncausable, God will be *a se*.

Of course, Scotus thinks that it is impossible that God does not exist but will. Indeed, Scotus's proof for the existence of God itself involves a subargument to the effect that if God does not exist, it is impossible that God come to exist. But that is irrelevant here. The entire thought experiment is carried on under impossible assumptions, and what is crucial is not whether an assumption is impossible but whether it follows formally from the claim that it is possible that the world will exist. Scotus's argument that if God did not exist God could not exist depends on the claim that if (*per impossibile*) God did not exist, it would be because something existed privatively or positively incompossible with his existence. But it would be remarkable if the proof that such an incompossibile could not cease to exist (and hence that God could not come into existence *a se*) were contained in our understanding of what it is for it to be possible that the world will be – and so remarkable if it followed formally from such an assumption. Scotus apparently does not think it does and so thinks he can, without formal contradiction, assume both that the world is possible and that God does not exist. What he cannot assume without formal contradiction is that the world is possible and God will not exist.

Although a natural (perhaps the most natural) reading of *Ordinatio* 1, d. 7, this interpretation is strained as a reading of a very slightly different passage in *In Metaph*. There Scotus writes:

The logical power...is some mode of composition made by an intellect caused by a relation of the terms of that composition, namely because they are not repugnant. And although commonly there may correspond to it *in re* some real power, yet this is not *per se* of the *ratio* of this power. And thus it would have been possible for the world to be going to be before its creation if there had been then an intellect forming this composition "the world will be," granted that then there would not have been a passive power for the being of the world, nor even, having posited this *per impossibile*, an active power, as long, however, as without contradiction there could be going to be an active power for this.[32]

Here Scotus seems to require, not that the active power that could bring the world into existence be going to be but merely that, without contradiction, it be able to be going to be.

We are now in very deep water indeed. If we take the *Ordinatio/ De primo principio* proof of the existence of God to trace out a chain of natural or essential consequences from the premise that some contingent thing is possible to the conclusion that God exists necessarily, then even if we grant the impossible *positio* that God does not exist, we will be able to derive his existence from the *propositum* that it is possible that the world will exist. On the other hand, if we take seriously the suggestion here in *In Metaph.* 9, q. 1, that the bare possibility that the world will exist requires formally only the bare possibility that there be an active power to make it, then we seem forced to deny that the *Ordinatio/De primo principio* proof could proceed by natural or essential consequences. Since the proof explicitly has it that God lies at the top of every essential order that proceeds from a contingent thing, we must then conclude that it is the step from the possible existence to the actual existence of God that does not proceed by natural or essential consequences. But that is to say that someone who granted that the existence of God is possible but insisted that God does not actually exist could not be shown the error of his ways in a fashion that he would have to accept on pain of irrationality. And if that be so, then what does Scotus think his proof accomplishes?

However we resolve this conundrum, we can now, I think, answer some of the questions with which this section began. Scotus thinks that to say that some sentence is possibly true is formally merely to assert a nonrepugnance of its terms. This is the burden of the very last sentence of the preceding quotation from *Ord.* 1, d. 7. Thus, when we claim that "the world will be" is possibly true, we are not formally asserting anything about a power to bring the world about. But Scotus thinks that the issue of the nonrepugnance of terms has presuppositions. Since it is a question about terms, we must presuppose that there are the terms, and so that there is an intellect

that thinks the terms and that thinks the *notae*, the objective corre-
lates of those terms. Moreover, the nonrepugnance of terms entails
by a natural consequence at least that there *can be* an active power
that could realize the situation the sentence described. Whether the
nonrepugnance of terms naturally entails more – that at least there
will be such an active power – is an issue on which our central texts
seem unclear. Perhaps it is one about which Scotus himself was un-
easy or on which he changed his mind.

V. POSSIBLE WORLDS

Some scholars have noticed in Scotus an anticipation of the
Leibnizian notion of a possible world. Scotus does not use the term
"possible world" or any equivalent, but support for the idea that he
has the concept comes from at least two places. First, as we have
just seen, Scotus has as a basic notion in his modal picture that of
a nonepugnant collection of *notae*. Second, he claims that having
thought the *notae*, the divine intellect naturally and in a single instant of nature considers all nonrepugnant combinations of them.
Some of these combinations are such that it would be repugnant for
their elements not to be so combined. These correspond to necessary propositions. Others are such that it is not repugnant for their
elements either to be so combined or not. These correspond to contingent propositions. The divine intellect presents these contingent
propositions to the divine will as not yet having a truth value, and the
divine will then (in a second instant of nature) contingently determines each to be true or be false. The divine will thus contingently
determines a maximal consistent collection of contingent propositions to be true. Such a maximal consistent collection of propositions is a description of (or, on some views, is) what both Leibniz
and twentieth-century modal theorists would call a possible world.
Assuming that the divine intellect considers the collections of these
propositions and not just the propositions themselves (and given the
entailment relations among contingent propositions it is hard to see
how it could be otherwise), we have the idea that the divine intellect
surveys all the possible worlds and the divine will chooses among
them.

This picture is certainly Scotus's, and a very good case can be
made that it lies behind Leibniz's own.[33] There are, nevertheless,

significant differences between Scotus's view and at least some more recent theories. First, there is no analogue in Scotus of the way in which Leibnizian possible objects mirror their whole universe. Scotus explicitly argues that God could not know the truth of contingent propositions simply by examining the divine ideas. If he could, Scotus claims, it would be because the connections that ground contingent truths would be "built into" the ideas themselves, and then there would be no contingent truths.[34] This is, of course, a famous crux for Leibniz scholarship – how can "Caesar will cross the Rubicon" be contingent if *crossing the Rubicon* is part of the concept of Caesar? Scotus's anticipatory answer is that it cannot, and so the divine idea of Caesar does not include such *notae*.

This difference is connected with a deeper (and wider) one. Modern modal theorists work with the notion of *truth in a world*. For example, possibility will be explained in terms of truth in some possible world. Scotus has the notions of truth and of logical possibility, but he does not work with the notion of truth "in" (or "of") some collection of divine ideas or some collection of propositions that God has not willed to make true. For Scotus, propositions that are logically possibly true are not logically possibly true because they belong to some collection of propositions. They are, rather, logically possibly true because their terms are not repugnant, and they are compossible with other propositions because their terms are not repugnant. Again, propositions that are really possibly true are not really possibly true because of their copresence with other propositions in a maximal collection but because there is a real power for realizing them. Thus, although one can find the ingredients in Scotus's picture for talking about possible worlds, the notion would do little or no work within that picture itself. There the basic notions are those of power (*potentia*) and repugnance (*repugnantia*).

VI. CONCLUSION

That Duns Scotus is a pivotal figure in the history of modal theory seems beyond doubt. Although apparently not the first to claim that the present is as contingent as the future, he argued for and employed the thesis with such verve that the doctrine became associated with him. His successors further developed it so that by the middle of the fourteenth century there had emerged, perhaps for the first time, a view that modality has no essential connection with time. Scotus articulated a notion of logical possibility as the nonrepugnance of terms and claimed that there is a real power corresponding to every logical possibility. Later thinkers took this equivalence to show that the only necessities were those expressible by sentences whose negations were formally inconsistent. For Scotus the theory of the will was central to both his theology and his ethics, and for him modal theory was central to his theory of the will. His focus on the power for opposites as the defining characteristic of a will and his effort to articulate this conception in his discussions of future contingents, foreknowledge, predestination, and the confirmation of the blessed has set much of the agenda in dealing with these issues right to the present day.

A pivot can face in more than one direction, and so it is with Scotus. While his picture led easily to the divorce of time and modality, he himself never completely divorced the two, retaining a significant distinction between the modal status of the past and that of the future and the use of notions of priority and posteriority modeled on temporal relations in his account of the contingency of the present. While his account of logical possibility suggests how possibilities could be completely independent of both intellects and real powers, he himself never completely divorced these either, always discussing even logical possibilities in a framework in which intellects and real powers are in the background. And while there are in his thought the ingredients for the accounts of modality in terms of quantification over possible worlds that we find in Leibniz and in theories developed in the second half of the twentieth century, Scotus founded his own modal picture on the notions of *repugnantia* and *potentia*. The Janus-faced character of Scotus's modal thought makes him especially important today both for the historian of modality – for whom he both sums up a tradition and begins one – and for the modal metaphysician concerned to look beyond modal theory to discover what possibility and its ilk really are – or could be.

NOTES

1   The discussion in this paragraph is based on the text of the *Octo Quaestiones* (= *In Periherm.* II, q. 8) found in Wadding 1:221–3.

2   The entire discussion in q. 8 is remarkable not only for the divergence from the doctrine in Scotus's theological works but for the introduction

of the values "indeterminately true" and "indeterminately false," which are distinguished not only from determinately true and false but from true and false *simpliciter*. Scotus, if it is he, goes on to argue that the inference from a determinately true sentence to one indeterminately true is not valid, but he does not develop the logic further. For additional discussion see Normore 1993. I there took a stronger stand against the authenticity of the *Octo Quaestiones* and a weaker stand for the text's rejection of the inference from an indeteterminate truth to a truth than I now think warranted.

3 The terminology of "synchronic picture" is taken from Simo Knuuttila. See Knuuttila 1993 and the references therein. There is an important difference between Knuuttila's way of posing this issue and my own. As he conceives it, one has a synchronic conception if one thinks that it is possible that p at t and it is possible that not-p at t *for any time t* that accords with the tense of the verb of p. I do not think that there is any significant body of medieval opinion that would have denied this for *future* times. As I see matters, the debate is about whether it is possible that p at t and it is possible that not-p at t when p is *present*-tensed and t is a name for the *present* time; thus, I prefer to talk about the contingency of the present. Marilyn Adams has pointed out to me that my own terminology is not unproblematic, suggesting as it does that the contrast is with a view that present-tensed *sentences* are, if true, necessarily true. I think that all of those medieval figures who maintain that the present is not contingent in my sense are fully aware that most present-tensed *sentences* become false as things change and so are not necessarily true. Exactly how to state their view (other than as the view that it is not the case that it is possible that p at t and it is possible that not-p at t when p is present-tensed and t is a name for the present) and, in particular, how to state it in the language of their own tense and modal logics is an issue to which I hope to return elsewhere. In this connection, see *De primo princ.* 4.18.

4 See, for example, *Lect.* 1, d. 40, q. un., where he writes "Ad primum argumentum, quando arguitur quod illud quod transit in praeteritum est necessarium, – conceditur."

5 It is possible that the novelty of this move has been somewhat exaggerated. Stephen Dumont and others have shown that Henry of Ghent advances a doctrine very like Scotus's claim about the nonevident power of the will in his *Quodlibet* 10, q. 10. Dumont has pointed out that he applies it to problems about the vacuum in *Quodlibet* 13, and Susan Brouwer, Stephen Dumont, and Tim Noone that he applies it to the Immaculate Conception in *Quodlibet* 15, q. 13. There are related suggestions in Peter John Olivi's Sentence Commentary. Henrik Lagerlund has recently argued that Richard Campsall rejects the necessity of the

present in his *Questiones super Librum Priorum Analeticorum*, dated at least before 1308. See Lagerlund 1999, 91–6.

6   William of Sherwood? *Obligationes*, cod. Paris Nat. Lat. 16617, f. 56 v. Quoted at Vatican 17:498, note 2.

7   *De primo princ.* 1.8 in Wolter 1966, 4.

8   This is not one of Scotus's formulations. One of the ways he puts it himself is "qualis ordo realis esset aliqua, si essent distincta realiter, talis est ordo illorum secundum rationem, ubi sunt distincta secundum rationem" (*Rep.* prol., q. 1, a. 4, n. 39.)

9   We can connect the notion of an instant of nature to the idea of *obligatio* by the following, again very speculative, idea: n1 is distinct from n2 if for some claim A indexed to n1 and some claim B indexed to n2, were "A and ~B" to be taken as *positum* in an *obligatio* under impossible *positio* it could be maintained. Thus, a single instant of nature could be treated as just the collection of claims that could not be distinguished in impossible *positio*. For criticism of my approach to this, see Martin 1999, ch. 7.

10 In fact Scotus thinks that the power to hate God in this context just is the same power as the power to love God because both just are the will, which is a rational power in his sense.

11 This metaphor may seem less farfetched if one considers that the device of instants of nature may be indebted to thirteenth-century efforts to understand how – although between any two points in the geometrical line there are others – if one divides a line AC into two segments AB and BC so as to leave nothing out one obtains segments both of which have termini. This seemed to some to require that the endpoint of AB has been in the same place in the line as the beginning point of BC. I think that Stephen Dumont and others have noted this connection but am unsure whether they agree with me about the direction of influence.

12 This he does baldly, saying merely, "This rule is denied. Indeed the art of *obligatio* is well treated by that master without this rule. Hence it does not depend on the truth of this rule."

13 For the claim that according to Aristotle the present is determinate and that the future is not, and Scotus's apparent acceptance of it, see *Lect.* 1, d. 39, qq. 1–5, n. 69. For Scotus's rejection of the claim that the future *is* actual, see *Lect.* 1, d. 39, qq. 1–5, n. 28 and n. 85. Richard Cross has argued that this does not represent Scotus's considered opinion: see Cross 1998, 244, and the work referenced there. I do not share Cross's view.

14 *Lect.* 1, d. 40, q. un., n. 9.

15 Because especially frequent reference to the text of *De primo principio* is necessary in this section I will refer to it within the body of the text as DP followed by the paragraph number in Wolter 1966.

16 *De primo principio* 3.11 (Wolter 1996, 47). I have used my own, excessively literal, translation.

17 The notion of higher-order causality involved here is closely connected with issues about instrumental and secondary causation. If I act on very specific authority from you to perform a certain act, it is I who act, but I would not be able to act were your grant of authority not simultaneously in effect. You do not cause my act, partially or totally, but your grant of authority does play an explanatory role in accounting for how what I do accomplishes its effect.

18 Notably Douglas Langston in Langston 1986.

19 *Quodl.* q. 16, n. 5. On this see Frank 1982a and Wolter 1972.

20 *Quodl.* q. 16, n. 6 (Alluntis and Wolter 1975, 370–1).

21 *Quodl.* q. 16, n. 16 (Alluntis and Wolter 1975, 385, ¶ 44).

22 *Quodl.* q. 16, n. 15 (Alluntis and Wolter 1975, 384, ¶ 43).

23 This point is owed to William A. Frank, who discovered that the oldest manuscripts of the *Questiones Quodlibetales* make the point that *firmitas in agendo est perfectionis* in a place where the printed editions, by substituting *libertas in agendo est perfectionis*, had blurred it. See Frank 1982b and the discussion in Allunits and Wolter 1975, 14–16.

24 See *In Metaph.* 9, q. 15: "Experitur enim qui vult se posse non velle sive nolle, iuxta quod de libertate voluntaris alibi diffusius habetur." See also *Lect.* 1, d. 39, qq. 1–5.

25 Cf. Wolter 1986, 152.

26 As the expert reader may have noticed, I have not repeated here the claim made in earlier work that Scotus is a "modal monist." For some of the reasons why, see Peter King, ch. 1 in this volume.

27 Cf. Mondadori 2000.

28 *Ordinatio* 1, d. 43, n. 18.

29 Ibid.

30 *Ordinatio* 1, d. 7, q. 1, n. 27.

31 He develops his account in Book 1, d. 11, of his commentaries on the *Sentences* of Peter Lombard, where the issue under discussion is the *Filioque* doctrine that separates the Latins and the Greeks. The issue is whether the Holy Spirit proceeds from both the Father and the Son, as the Latins hold, or from the Father alone, as the Greeks hold. Both sides hold that their view is a necessary truth. One issue that comes up in Latin discussions is whether the Greek view has the consequence that the Holy Spirit cannot be distinguished from the Son. To explore this they must reason from the (impossible as they think) premise that the Holy Spirit does not proceed from the Son. One view (sometimes attributed to John of Berwick) held that such reasoning could not be carried out because to suppose the premise was to consider a contradictory

situation and so one in which the rules of logic themselves fail. Scotus is of a different mind. In his *Ordinatio* he writes, "The question is posed so that it may be inquired what is the primary thing distinguishing the Son from the Holy Spirit – whether it is filiation or only active spiration – because if it is filiation, then however much active spiration is set aside (*circumscripta*) *per impossibile*, the ground for the distinction will still remain" (*Ordinatio* 1, d. 11, q. 2, n. 28). For a pathbreaking and much more thorough discussion of Scotus's account of natural and essential consequence than is possible here, see Martin 1999, ch. 7.

32 *In Metaph.* 9, q. 1, n. 3. I thank Rega Wood for showing me the corrected version of this text before its publication.

33 Some of that case is made in Langston 1986.

34 Scotus writes, "Secundo, quia ideae repraesentantes terminos simplices non repraesentant complexiones nisi quatenus termini includunt veritatem complexionum, sed termini contingentium non includunt veritatem complexionis factae de illis, quia tunc esset illa complexio necessaria." *Lectura* 1, d. 39, a. 1, q. 1, in corp.

5   Duns Scotus's Philosophy of Language

Unlike many thirteenth- and fourteenth-century authors, Scotus never wrote a grammar or logic handbook. Nor did he compose a treatise dealing explicitly with the grammatical and semantic issues that were eagerly debated at his time – for instance a treatise about the famous "properties of terms" or the "modes of signifying." The only work concerning grammar and semantics, entitled *Tractatus de modis significandi sive Grammatica speculativa*, that was attributed to him until the beginning of the twentieth century, proved to be inauthentic; it was written by his contemporary Thomas of Erfurt, a leading representative of the school of the "modistae."[1] Given such an apparent lack of writings dedicated to grammatical and semantic problems, one may have the impression that Scotus was not particularly interested in linguistic analysis and that he should be regarded as a theologian, metaphysician, and moral philosopher, but not as a philosopher of language.

Yet such an impression would be quite misleading. Although Scotus never wrote a grammar or logic handbook, he had a keen interest in linguistic theory. This interest is most obvious in his commentaries on the *Isagoge*, on the *Categories*, and on *Peri hermeneias*.[2] In these early writings, Scotus does not confine himself to paraphrasing Aristotle's and Porphyry's view. He rather uses their opinion as a starting point for a thorough discussion of fundamental issues in philosophical semantics – a discussion that allows him to critically examine various linguistic theories of his contemporaries and to develop his own theory. Such a discussion can also be found in some parts of his later works, especially in his metaphysical and theological writings. For he holds the view that one cannot deal with metaphysical and theological questions unless one has a clear understanding of the questions themselves. But in order to have such an understanding, one often needs to analyze the semantic function of the words used in the phrasing of the questions. For instance, one cannot answer the theological question of how the puzzling statement "God begot God" ("Deus genuit Deum") is to be understood, if one does not know the semantic function of the word 'God' in this statement. But one can hardly know the semantic function in this particular case, if one has no insight into the semantics of terms. That is why Scotus first presents a detailed analysis of the semantics of terms before he tackles the theological problem of God's self-generation.[3] This example shows that it would scarcely be adequate to look for linguistic analysis only in those works that are explicitly labeled as writings dealing with language. Linguistic analysis (Scotus calls it the analysis of "the logic of a question"[4]) can also be found in works that appear at first glance to be purely theological or metaphysical.[5]

If one takes into account all the works in which Scotus provides an analysis of language (from the early commentaries on Aristotle's logical writings to the later *Ordinatio* and *Lectura*), one can see that he chose at least two approaches to language. Using modern terminology, one may characterize these approaches by saying that he was concerned both with philosophy of language and with linguistic philosophy.[6] That is, on the one hand he was concerned with philosophy of language by making language the *subject* of philosophical investigations. This concern led him to give a detailed account of the semantics of terms and sentences. He discussed extensively the questions of how various types of terms can have a signification and how their signification affects the truth value of a sentence. On the other hand, he was also concerned with linguistic philosophy by making linguistic analysis the *method* of philosophical investigations. This second concern led him to tackle metaphysical and theological problems by analyzing the linguistic expressions used in the phrasing of these problems. In this chapter, I first look at some crucial elements of Scotus's philosophy of language (Sections I–III). Then I examine two areas in which he was primarily concerned with linguistic philosophy (Sections IV and V). Finally, I assess the significance and the function that both philosophy of language and linguistic philosophy have in the entire project of Scotus's philosophy (Section VI).

I. WORDS, INTELLIGIBLE SPECIES, AND THINGS

Every theory of language has to deal with a fundamental question: How is it to be explained that spoken and written words are not merely strings of sound and ink spots but linguistic signs – signs that may be used to refer to things in the world? In their answers to this question, most medieval authors appealed to a semantic model that Aristotle had sketched in the first chapter of *Peri hermeneias*.[7] Spoken or written words function as linguistic signs, they said, because they are connected to "affections of the soul" (*passiones animae*), which are, in turn, connected to things in the world. It is indeed this connection that makes them more than mere strings of sound or ink spots.

In giving such an answer, the medieval Aristotelians (including Scotus) clearly chose a mentalistic approach to language. What makes a relation between words and things possible, they claimed, is neither a mere set of conventional linguistic rules, nor the use of words in language games, but the presence of something mental: the "affections of the soul." Yet such a claim raised at least two serious questions that were eagerly debated in the late thirteenth century.[8] First, many authors asked what kind of entities the "affections" are. Are they simply mental acts, mental images, or another kind of entities that somehow reside in the intellect? Second, how is the connection between words, "affections," and things in the world to be understood? Given that the connection makes it possible that words be linguistic signs, it must be some kind of semantic relation. But what are the relata of this relation? Do the words stand as signs for the "affections of the soul" or for the things in the world?

Scotus is well aware of the importance of these questions and treats them extensively in his questions on *Peri hermeneias*.[9] He thinks that the first problem can be most easily explained if one realizes that the "affections of the soul" are the product of a cognitive process that starts with the sensory perception of things in the world. The "affections" are exactly those mental entities that make the perceived things cognitively present to us. Using the standard terminology of his time, Scotus calls them "intelligible species" (*species intelligibiles*). Let me illustrate the status and the function of these species by means of an example.[10] When I have a sensory perception of a tree, I first receive a kind of sensory image (*phantasma*) from the tree. This image enables me to visualize the tree with all the individual features I have perceived, that is, with a certain color, shape, size, and so forth. On the basis of this sensory image my intellect then abstracts the intelligible species, which makes nothing but the nature of the tree cognitively present to me. This species is not simply a passing imprint of the tree in my intellect. It is rather a cognitive entity that may be stored and that enables me to grasp the nature of the tree even when the originally perceived tree is no longer present.

Given such an understanding of the "affections of the soul," the second problem can be rephrased as follows: What do words (primarily spoken words, secondarily written ones) stand for as signs? Do they signify intelligible species in the intellect or things in the world? Scotus remarks that this question had given rise to a great controversy among his contemporaries.[11] In their attempts to answer this question, they developed two semantic models. According to the first model (let us call it the "direct signification model"), words directly signify things in the world. The presence of the intelligible species is nothing but a necessary condition for the existence of this semantic relation. Thus, a word like 'tree' directly signifies individual trees in the forest, not the cognitive entity I have formed by perceiving a tree and abstracting its nature. According to the second model (let us call it the "indirect signification model") words signify things in the world only indirectly, namely, insofar as they are mediated by the intelligible species. The immediate objects signified by words are nothing but these species. Thus, the word 'tree' signifies the cognitive entity in my intellect that enables me to grasp the nature of a tree. It signifies trees in the forest only insofar as they are made present to me by means of this cognitive entity.

Both models seem to have some plausibility at first glance, but both turn out to be insufficient if they are examined more closely, as Scotus is quick to point out. With the first model, it may be possible to explain the signification of such simple words as 'tree' or 'human being'. For in using these words, we do indeed intend to signify trees in the forest and living human beings, not just some cognitive entities in our intellect. But the model looks less convincing in more complicated cases. How should we explain the signification of words such as 'Caesar' or 'chimera'? Since there is neither an actually existing Caesar nor an actually living chimera, one would have to say that these words do not signify anything because there is no appropriate significate in the world. But such an explanation is hardly convincing. Even if there is no actually existing significate (in modern terminology: no object of reference), these words can signify something, namely, our concept or mental representation of Caesar and of a chimera.

In order to resolve this problem, one may turn to the second model. For according to this model, one can easily explain the signification of 'Caesar' and 'chimera'. These words simply signify our intelligible species of Caesar and chimera, one may say, no matter whether there is an actually living Caesar or an actually existing chimera in the world – signification does not require the actual existence of extramental things. Yet the second model looks less promising in the context of the simpler cases mentioned before, for words such as 'tree' and 'human being' would have a relation of direct signification with nothing but cognitive entities in our intellect. With such a statement one would have to give up the basic thesis of semantic realism, namely, that there is an *immediate* link between linguistic signs and things in the world. Further, one would have to concede that two speakers uttering the word 'tree' signify two different entities because each speaker would use this word to signify the intelligible species existing in his or her own intellect. Each speaker would somehow have a private object of signification. Finally, one would hardly be able to explain predicative sentences, for in these sentences, say in 'A human being is running', one would only make a predication with regard to a cognitive entity. But it is obviously a human being made of flesh and blood, not a cognitive entity, that is running. Therefore, the subject term 'human being' of which we are predicating 'is running' cannot simply signify the intelligible species of a human being.

These and similar reasons lead Scotus to the conclusion that both the direct and the indirect signification model are deficient, if they are presented in a crude form.[12] On his view, we are not able to explain the signification of words if we assume they must signify either extramental, individual things or else mere cognitive entities existing in the intellect. So how can we successfully explain their signification? Scotus presents a sophisticated answer to this question by distinguishing two ways of looking at the intelligible species.[13] On the one hand, we can consider them with respect to their ontological status. Looked at in this way, they are nothing but accidents of the intellect, that is, mere mental entities existing in a particular subject. As such, they are private mental entities, for every intellect has its own accidents. On the other hand, intelligible species can also be considered with respect to their function. Looked at in this second way, they are signs that immediately refer to the signified things. As such signs, they are immediately linked to things in the world, no matter in what intellect they exist. Two species existing in two different intellects may be linked to one and the same extramental thing.

Let me illustrate this important distinction with a modern example. When we look at the photographs taken on our last vacation, we may look at them under a *material* aspect and ask, What are they made of? The answer to this question is clear. They are nothing but pieces of paper with a certain physicochemical structure, and they are all alike because they all have the same structure. But this way of looking at them is of interest only to a photographer concerned with the quality of the paper. When we show our photographs to our friends, we look at them under a *representational* aspect and ask, What do they depict? The answer to this second question is equally clear. They depict various items – children playing on the beach, dogs, monuments, and so forth – and they are thus immediately linked to things in the world. Looked at under the representational aspect, some photographs may be alike because they depict the same things in the same way, while others may be different because they depict the same things in different ways or because they depict completely different things.

It is on these lines that one may understand Scotus's explanation of the intelligible species. If we look at them under a material aspect, we may say that they are nothing but accidents of the intellect; they are somehow made of "mental stuff." Looked at under this aspect, they are qualitatively identical (they are all made of the same kind of "mental stuff") but numerically distinct (every intellect has its own "mental stuff"). However, we can also look at the species under a representational aspect. Looked at in this second way, they have a certain representational content (they "depict" something), and they may be alike or different, depending on their content. It is exactly the representational content that is of crucial importance for Scotus. He claims that we need to focus on this content if we intend to explain the signification of a word. Three things are to be clearly distinguished in such an explanation:[14] (a) the intelligible species considered under its material aspect, (b) the very same species considered under its representational aspect, and (c) the extramental, individual thing. What a word signifies is (b). Thus, a word like 'tree' signifies the representational content of a species, that is, what is cognitively present to us when we think about a tree. But this word does not signify the species considered merely as a thing made of "mental stuff."

This is quite a sophisticated solution to the signification problem.[15] It avoids at the same time the problems the direct and the indirect signification model were confronted with. Against the first model, Scotus claims that words do not simply signify extramental things. Otherwise, they would lose their signification as soon as there is no appropriate extramental thing. To maintain such a position (as it was indeed maintained by Roger Bacon)[16] is absurd on his view. Even words like 'Caesar' or 'chimera' do have a signification, because there is an appropriate representational content for them. That is, there is something cognitively present to us when we think about Caesar or a chimera. Signifying this representational content does *not* require the actual existence of Caesar or of a chimera. At the same time, Scotus also opposes the second model, emphasizing that words do not signify intelligible species considered as mere accidents existing in the speaker's intellect. Otherwise, one would have to concede that two persons uttering the word 'tree' signify two distinct things, because each observer has his own accident in his intellect. Such a consequence would be as absurd as the consequence following from the first model, Scotus claims. In his opinion, these two persons signify the same representational content. That is, when they utter the word 'tree', they have the same thing cognitively present to them. Having two distinct representational vehicles does *not* prevent them from having the same representational content.

So far, Scotus seems to have found a safe way between Scylla and Charybdis, avoiding the snares of both the direct and the indirect models of signification (at least when presented in their crudest form). But one may have the impression that he is falling into the trap of another sea monster, so to speak, namely, that of semantic representationalism. It seems that he is committing himself to the view that all our words *immediately* signify is representational contents, and that we have only a mediated semantic access to things in the world. He seems to come quite close to the position defended by a number of early modern philosophers (for example, Locke or the authors of the Port-Royal Logic), namely, that our words do not signify anything but the representations or ideas in our mind – representations that are clearly distinct from extramental things.[17]

Although it is tempting to ascribe such a position to Scotus, it would be quite misleading to call him a semantic representationalist. If one carefully examines his explanation of the representational content, it turns out that he does not characterize it like the early modern representationalists but instead says that it is the 'nature' or the 'essence' of a thing (*natura, essentia, ratio rei*, or *quod quid erat esse rei*).[18] In certain passages, he also calls it the "thing insofar as it is understood" (*res ut concipitur vel intelligitur*), contrasting it with the "thing insofar as it exists" (*res ut existit*).[19] In using this terminology, Scotus makes it clear that the representational content is not a special entity (an early modern "idea") that is completely distinct from the extramental thing. The representational content is rather the nature of a thing – the very same nature that can also be present outside the intellect. Thus, when someone has an intelligible species of a tree, the representational content of this species is the very same nature that is also present in the material trees in the forest. There are not two different entities in this case, one inside the intellect and one outside, but two ways of being of one and the same nature.

Lurking behind this important thesis is a metaphysical theory that is only hinted at in Scotus's early writings but became very important in his later works: the theory of common nature.[20] According to this theory, which was inspired by Avicenna, the nature of a thing can be considered in three ways, namely (1) in itself; (2) insofar as it is present in an individual, material thing; and (3) insofar as it is conceived of and present in the intellect. The important thing is that it is *one and the same nature* that can be considered in these three ways; there are not three different types of nature. That is why Scotus can say that it is one and the same nature that may be looked at and signified either insofar as it is the content of a species, or insofar as it is present in a material thing. Let me illustrate this crucial point with the photograph example mentioned before. When we look at a photograph and say, "This is the Eiffel Tower!," we do, in some sense, look at a thing that is completely different from the Eiffel Tower in Paris. For what we look at is nothing but a depiction of the Eiffel Tower on a piece of paper, which clearly differs from the iron construction in Paris. But in another sense, we look at and speak about the same thing, namely, the nature of the Eiffel Tower that is present to us on the photograph. This nature has, so to speak, two ways of being, one on the piece of paper (the depicted way of being) and one in the iron construction (the material way of being).

If we understand Scotus's distinction between the *res ut concipitur* and the *res ut existit* in this way, it becomes clear that he is not committing himself to semantic representationalism. What a word signifies is not some distinct representational entity, but the nature of a thing that has (or may have) two ways of being. That is why Scotus can claim that a word signifies the content of an intelligible species without thereby giving up the crucial thesis that there is an immediate link between words and things in the world. In making this claim, he simply commits himself to the view that a word signifies the nature of a thing, present in a species as its representational content. This is not a unique view in the late medieval context. It can also be found in other thirteenth-century authors, for instance in Thomas Aquinas and Siger of Brabant, who stressed the point that a word does not signify an existing, extramental thing, but the nature of a thing.[21]

Although Scotus's view is certainly not unique when compared with the positions defended by his contemporaries, it is far from being an innocent mainstream view. First of all, it presupposes a metaphysical theory according to which the nature of a thing, taken in itself, is "indifferent" to being present in an individual, material thing or in an intelligible species. It is exactly this theory that was rejected by later authors (for example, by Ockham) who attacked the metaphysical foundations of Scotus's semantics: his explanation of signification collapses as soon as one gives up the thesis that one and the same nature may be instantiated in different places.[22]

Second, Scotus's view is problematic as far as the signification of singular terms is concerned. For a term like 'Caesar' or 'Socrates' does not seem to signify a common nature (be it present in something extramental or in an intelligible species), but some individual possessing that nature. How can Scotus cope with this problem? He tries to resolve it by introducing a distinction between (a) the nature as such that is predicable of many individuals and is signified by a general term, and (b) the nature that is individuated and signified by a singular term. Thus, in a sentence like "Caesar is a human being" the predicate term 'human being', a general term, signifies the human nature predicable of this or that individual human (technically speaking, the *natura ut dicibilis de pluribus*), whereas the subject term 'Caesar', a singular term, signifies the nature insofar as it is individuated in Caesar (the *natura ut haec*), or simply Caesar.[23] The important point is that both general and singular terms signify the nature to be found in extramental reality. That is why Scotus's position does not have the awkward consequence that all we are able to signify are spooky representational things in the mind and that we are, to use Richard Rorty's expression, somehow imprisoned in the "inner arena" of our mind.[24]

While holding the view that the nature of a thing can be signified in different ways and that it can have different ways of being, Scotus hastens to add that it does not always need to have all possible ways of being. In particular, the nature does not always need to have the way of being in an actually existing, extramental thing. For instance, after Caesar's death his nature ceased to be individuated in an actually living human being. Nevertheless, his nature can still have the way of being in a thought: it can still be the content of an intelligible species. For that reason, 'Caesar' can still signify Caesar (to be precise: Caesar's *natura ut haec*) even when there is no actually existing Caesar. Every word (be it a singular or a general term) can signify a nature, Scotus claims, whether this nature has actual, extramental existence or not.[25] This claim has an important consequence for an issue that was subject to heated debates in the thirteenth century. A number of logicians (for example, Siger of Brabant, Simon of Faversham, and Roger Bacon) asked whether sentences such as "Man is an animal" or "Caesar is a man" are still true when no man and no Caesar actually exists.[26] Should we not say that their truth value depends on the *actual* existence of at least one thing signified by the subject term? No, Scotus replies, thus rejecting the position taken by Roger Bacon.[27] The truth value of a sentence only depends on the semantic relation between its terms and a nature (or several natures), whether or not this nature has actual existence in an extramental thing. Thus, "Man is an animal" or the tautological sentence "Man is a man" is true even if there is no actually living human being in the world, because the subject term "man" still signifies the nature of man, belonging to the genus animal. This answer shows that Scotus's semantics is closely connected to his metaphysics. It is by appealing to his account of common nature, a crucial element of his theory of signification, that he tries to resolve the semantic puzzle of sentences about nonexisting things.

II. CONCRETE AND ABSTRACT TERMS

In his questions on *Peri hermeneias*, Scotus confines himself to analyzing the semantic function of concrete singular terms (for example, 'Caesar') and concrete general terms (for example, 'human being'). But these terms are not the only ones to be examined in developing a comprehensive semantics of terms. There are also abstract terms (for example, 'humanity', 'whiteness') that need to be explained. What do these terms signify: the same thing as their corresponding concrete terms or some special entities? The medievals were well aware of the importance of this question, which is, of course, motivated by ontological concerns. For in answering this question, an author has to make clear what his ontological commitments are. That is, he has to spell out what type or types of entities he is willing to admit as the relata in various relations of signification.

Medieval authors had a keen interest in both abstract essential terms (for example, 'humanity') and abstract accidental terms (for example, 'whiteness').[28] In the late thirteenth century, many philosophers (Boethius of Dacia, Peter of Auvergne, Radulphus Brito, Simon of Faversham, and others) developed a particular interest in the semantic function of abstract accidental terms.[29] How are these terms related to concrete accidental terms, they asked, and how are they to be understood when they are used as predicate terms in sentences? At first sight, one may be inclined to reply that abstract and concrete accidental terms, for instance 'whiteness' and 'white', signify the same thing, namely the color white (an accident, ontologically speaking) that inheres in a subject. But such a simple reply turns out to be deficient for at least two reasons. First, it is clear that only 'white' signifies the color insofar as it inheres in a subject, say in Socrates or in some other individual. 'Whiteness', however, seems to signify the color in itself, without there being any relation with a subject. Second, the two terms cannot be substituted for each other in a sentence, as a simple example makes evident. The sentence "Socrates is white" is grammatically correct and true given the state of affairs that Socrates is white. The sentence "Socrates is whiteness," however, is grammatically incorrect and cannot be ascribed a truth value. Given such nonsubstitutability, the two terms can hardly have exactly the same semantic function.

How then are the significations of 'white' and 'whiteness' to be explained? Scotus answers this question by introducing a distinction that is of crucial importance for his semantics, namely, the distinction between the signification of a term and its way of signifying (*modus significandi*).[30] He claims that the two terms have the same signification because they stand as signs for the same object, namely, for the essence or the nature of the color white. Admittedly, this nature is only a dependent one (it can exist only insofar as it is in a subject), and in that respect it differs from the independent nature of a subject, say of Socrates. Nevertheless, the color white has a distinct nature, not to be confused with the nature of the subject in which it inheres, and is therefore a distinct object of signification. While having the same signification, 'white' and 'whiteness' have two different ways of signifying. For these two terms signify the nature of the color white under two different aspects. 'Whiteness' signifies the nature without taking into account its inherence in this or that subject; it signifies the nature on its own, so to speak (*sub propria ratione*). The concrete term 'white', on the other hand, signifies the nature of the color insofar as it is in a subject, that is, insofar as it "informs" the subject with a certain quality (*inquantum informat subjectum*). Given these two different ways of signifying, the abstract term cannot simply be substituted for the concrete one in a sentence. One term can be substituted for another in a sentence *salva veritate* only if the two terms have the same signification *and* the same way of signifying.

There are several interesting points in this account of the semantic function of concrete and abstract accidental terms. First of all, it is clear that Scotus is consistent in his explanation of signification. Not only as far as terms such as 'Caesar' and 'human being' are concerned does he hold the view that they signify the nature of a thing. He holds the same view with respect to terms such as 'white' and 'whiteness'. Every term (at least every categorematic term[31]) primarily signifies a certain nature; it signifies neither a mere cognitive entity in the intellect nor an actually existing thing. That is why the sentence "Whiteness is a color" is true regardless of this or that white patch in the world. For 'whiteness' does not primarily signify this or that white patch but the nature of the color white.

Second, Scotus's account turns out to be interesting if it is compared with the rival theories that were known and defended in his time.[32] Unlike Avicenna, he does not hold the view that 'white' signifies some kind of aggregate, namely, the complex entity consisting of a concrete subject and the color white. He stresses the point that 'white' (as well as 'whiteness') has its distinct object of signification. This point has, of course, an important consequence for the theory of predication. Given that the predicate term in a sentence like "Socrates is white" has its distinct object of signification, there are *two* objects to be taken into account – two objects that are linked to each other by a relation of inherence. Therefore, this sentence must be explained by means of the "inherence theory of predication."[33] It is true if and only if the object signified by the predicate term (the accidental feature of being white) inheres in the object signified by the subject term (Socrates).

But Scotus does not only distance himself from Avicenna's view. He also rejects the opinion defended by Siger of Brabant and Siger of Courtrai according to which a term such as 'white' signifies both a subject and the accident, though each of them under its own aspect. On his view, a single term cannot signify two things at once. It can only signify one thing under a certain aspect. It is a complex expression compounded of several terms that is able to signify two or more things.

Finally, Scotus's explanation of concrete and abstract accidental terms is also of interest because it shows that he was strongly influenced by the theory of the modes of signifying (*modi significandi*) that was used by many of his contemporaries. This does not amount to saying that he was a member of the school of the "modistae," who took the modes of signifying to be the cornerstone of their theory. Scotus does not defend the thesis, lying at the core of the system of the "modistae," that there is a strict correspondence between the modes of signifying, the modes of understanding, and the modes of being. Nor does he use the modes of signifying as a starting point for a general theory of grammatical construction, as was typical for the "modistae."[34] One should be careful in evaluating Scotus's theory: not every medieval author talking about modes of signifying is a modist.[35]

Although Scotus can hardly be called a modist, his use of the theory of modes of signifying should not be overlooked. It shows that he does not confine himself to explaining the classical semantic triangle in sketching a semantic theory. That is, he does not simply look at the various relations between words, concepts (or intelligible species), and things. An analysis of these relations only reveals what the signification of words is. But a comprehensive semantic theory also has to look at the various ways in which words signify. Only by taking into account these ways of signifying can a semantic theory explain why different words may signify different aspects of one and the same thing, or why one and the same word may signify the same aspect in different things. It is by using a theory of modes of signifying that one is able to make clear why there is not just a one-to-one correspondence between words and things.

III. TERMS OF FIRST AND SECOND INTENTION

If one were confining a semantic analysis to terms such as 'human being' and 'white', one would limit the scope of philosophical investigations to the class of those linguistic expressions which immediately signify a thing or nature that can be found in extramental reality. In standard medieval terminology, these expressions were called "terms of first intention." However, besides these terms there are also linguistic expressions that signify items that are in some way based on extramental reality but exist primarily in the intellect. Classical examples for such terms, usually called "terms of second intention," are 'species' and 'genus'. These terms gave rise to a number of questions and were eagerly discussed in the later Middle Ages.[36] Many philosophers asked, do these terms signify mere concepts existing in the intellect, or features that can also be found in extramental reality? And do we acquire these terms simply by abstracting them from terms of first intention, or by looking at and comparing features of extramental things? Thirteenth- and fourteenth-century authors asked these questions not just because of their profound interest in semantics and ontology but also owing to a specific interest arising from their logical studies. For according to a classical definition of logic, stemming from Avicenna, logic is the science that deals with second intentions.[37] Given this definition, medieval logicians who tried to delineate their field of research were naturally led to ask what second intentions and terms signifying such intentions are. Scotus is no exception in that respect. Although he does not accept Avicenna's definition (Scotus defines logic as the science dealing with syllogisms),[38] he is well aware of the influential theory of second intentions and discusses it at length in his logical writings.[39]

Scotus tackles the problem of second intentions by analyzing different ways of conceiving of things in the world.[40] First of all, these things can be conceived of insofar as they have *esse materiale*, that is, insofar as they have concrete, material existence. Thus, we may conceive of a person standing in front of us as a living human being made of flesh and blood and endowed with a number of individual features. Second, things in the world can also be conceived of insofar as they have *esse quidditativum*, that is, insofar as they have a certain essence or nature. Considered in this second way, the person standing in front of us may be conceived of simply as a human being, regardless of all her individual features. As such, she can be conceived of when she is no longer standing in front of us or even when she is dead; conceiving of the essence does not presuppose actual, material presence. If a thing is conceived of in this second way, we are able to predicate the so-called essential predicates. That is, we are able to form predicative sentences such as "A human being is mortal" or "A human being is endowed with reason." For in grasping the nature of a thing, we always grasp its essential features. But, third, a thing can also be conceived of insofar as we compare its nature with the nature present in other things and insofar as we focus just on the relation between the natures known to us. Scotus calls this third type of conceiving the grasping of a thing insofar as it has *esse cognitum*, and he claims that this act enables us to form second intentions. Illustrating this type of conceiving with the example of the person, we may say that we are not only able to grasp the nature of the person standing in front of us but are also capable of comparing her nature with the nature we have grasped in other persons as well as with the natures in dogs, cats, and so forth. In doing so, we become aware that the same nature, though in individualized form, can be found in all human beings and that, consequently, human beings must be distinguished from dogs and cats. Thus, we are able to form the second intention *species* and to come up with a term for this intention, which may be used in a predicative sentence such as "Human being is a species." At the same time we also realize that the natures of human beings, dogs, and cats, though different in many respects, must have something in common because they are all natures of living things. This enables us to form the second intention *genus* and to come up with a term for this intention, which may be used in a predicative sentence such as "Animal is a genus."

Scotus does not spell out all the steps of the cognitive process that is required to form second intentions. He confines himself to remarking that such intentions are the product of a process of "compounding and dividing," that is, of putting together and separating different natures.[41] With this statement he emphasizes the fact that second intentions cannot be abstracted from one single nature. For instance, one cannot come up with the second intention *species* simply by grasping the nature of human being. One also needs to put this nature in relation to other natures (of dogs, cats, and so forth) and to evaluate the similarities and dissimilarities between this specific nature and other natures. Given such a relation between different natures, second intentions may also be called "relations of reason."[42] Unfortunately, Scotus does not give a detailed account of these relations. Nor does he explain why we are able to form the hierarchically ordered second intentions *species* and *genus* when we establish a relation between different natures. Does our intellect have an inbuilt capacity to come up with just these second intentions, which are two of the five famous predicables,[43] when it compares different types of natures? And does our intellect always know how to establish a correct relation between the natures grasped in reality? Does it, for instance, always know that the nature of whales is to be related to that of other mammals and not to that of fish?

Scotus does not tackle these thorny problems, presumably because he takes it for granted that our intellect is, at least in principle, able to establish the right kind of relation between different natures, thus coming up with the right kind of intentions. In any case, he holds the view that our intellect is able to form the right kind of second intentions by grasping and comparing natures. Second intentions are not things or features that can be immediately found in extramental reality (only the feature of being human or being a dog can be immediately found in reality, not the second intention *species*), nor are they things existing in a Platonic realm of ideas. They are rather products of the intellect. Such an account of second intentions has, of course, an immediate consequence for the explanation of terms of second intention. These terms signify neither things to be immediately found in extramental reality nor Platonic entities. They rather signify products of the intellect: concepts formed on the basis of the grasping and comparing of natures. Given such a basis, Scotus emphasizes that terms of second intention rely upon something to be found in reality. Unlike terms for fictitious entities, they do not signify something that is simply contrived by the intellect. Indeed, Scotus claims that they signify concepts that are caused by real things, but he hastens to add that they are only "occasionally" or "materially" caused by these things; they are always "effectively" caused by the intellect.[44] Let me illustrate this important point with the example mentioned before. When we grasp the natures of human beings, dogs, cats, and so forth and compare them, thus coming up with the second intentions *species* and *genus*, these intentions are not entirely caused by the human beings, dogs, and cats we have seen in reality. They are not some sort of imprint that material things, endowed with a certain nature, automatically make on our intellect. Such things are only an "occasional" cause for the production of second intentions, because they only provide an occasion for our intellect to perform acts of comparison and to come up with the appropriate second intentions. It is always the intellect that is the efficient cause for second intentions.

This is an important point not just for Scotus's theory of cognition (in various contexts he emphasizes that cognition is not simply a passive process but a process that requires an active, causally efficient intellect)[45] but also for his semantics. He does not subscribe to a semantic theory according to which all our signifying terms perfectly correspond to things or features of things in reality. On his view, there cannot be a simple one-to-one correspondence between terms and things in reality because our intellect is an active power – a power that produces concepts that are based on things in reality but that do not simply mirror these things. The terms signifying such concepts have to be taken into account as well as the terms that immediately signify things in reality.

IV. NAMING AND UNDERSTANDING

Scotus's discussions of the semantic problems considered so far are to a large extent motivated by his interest in philosophy of language. Of course, this interest often goes along with a keen interest in ontology and epistemology. For the semantic question of how words can signify things is closely linked to the ontological question of what things or types of things there are to be signified, and to the epistemological question of how these things may become known to us. Yet it is primarily an interest in philosophy of language that leads Scotus to ask all these questions: he intends to gain a better insight into the function of terms and sentences.

In his metaphysical and theological writings, Scotus often pursues other interests when he raises semantic questions. There he primarily intends to have a better insight into the structure of the world and its relation to God, the creator. But to gain such an insight, it is often necessary to tackle semantic problems. For a discussion of metaphysical and theological questions often presupposes a semantic analysis of the words used in the phrasing of these questions, or an examination of the general semantic framework in which the questions are raised. This is most evident in the case of a question that was eagerly debated in the thirteenth century, namely, whether we can use names for God. At first glance, there seems to be an easy answer to this question. "Of course," someone may respond, "we can use names, as the examples 'JHWE', 'God', and so on show, and we can even use these names in predications, for instance, when we say 'God is almighty'!" Yet such a response is hardly convincing, as many Scholastic theologians remarked. Referring to our limited cognitive capacities, they pointed out that we do not know God's essence. Nor do we fully understand all the divine attributes. Therefore, we cannot have a distinct concept of God that would characterize him accurately. So how can we name God, if we do not understand him and if we are not able to characterize him accurately? Do we not simply pretend to name him by uttering certain words without successfully naming him?

Taking his cue from Henry of Ghent, Scotus tries to answer these questions by looking at the general semantic issues lurking in the background of the theological debate.[46] He emphasizes that we cannot know whether it is possible to name God unless we know how it is *in principle* possible to name something or someone. For that reason, we first need to ask how a speaker can name a thing, and how this linguistic act is related to his or her understanding of that thing. The specific theological question can be answered only when the more general semantic question has been examined.

Scotus reports that many philosophers and theologians examine this general question with the assumption we can name a thing only insofar as we have an understanding of it, and that they even go so far as to claim that we are able to name a thing only to the same extent as we are able to understand it: as it is understood, it is named (*sicut intelligitur, sic et nominatur*).[47] In his opinion, it is exactly this assumption that is groundless and misleading, and not just when it is used in theological debates. He illustrates this point with the simple case of our understanding of a stone. In a normal perceptual situation, we understand such a thing only insofar as it is present to us with several accidents, that is, with a certain color, shape, size, and so forth. Unless we have gone through a process of abstraction, we do not understand the "naked" substance of the stone. We rather have an understanding of the concrete material thing with all the perceived accidents. Nevertheless, we are able to use the word 'stone' that names just the substance and not all the accidents that go along with it. Thus, we can name a substance *without* having a precise understanding of it; naming and understanding do not simply match each other.

This example shows, according to Scotus, that one should be careful in claiming that we can name only what we perfectly understand. In some cases we do indeed name what we perfectly and distinctly understand. But there are also other cases that need to be taken into account. Scotus draws a list of four different types of naming.[48]

1. In a very basic case, one can name something without having any understanding, not even an understanding of the fact that one is uttering a word endowed with a signification. This is the case when a person is simply uttering a string of sounds that happens to be a word unknown to the speaker or when a parrot repeats the sound "human" after hearing it.
2. In a more complex case, a person can name something when he knows that a word is endowed with a signification but does not know its signification. This happens when a person

who does not know English utters "human," a string of sounds he has been told is a word in English.

3. In a still more complex case, someone can name something if an understanding of the thing intended to be named exists but the understanding is based on a vague concept. This is the case when someone uttering the word "human" has a concept of 'human being' but one that is rather inexact and does not take into account the specific difference between human beings and other animals.

4. Finally, a person can name something when he has a perfect understanding of the thing to be named, that is, an understanding that relies upon a precise concept. This happens when someone who is in possession of the most accurate concept of "human being" utters the word "human."

Obviously, there is some kind of progress in these four types of naming. Starting with the most imperfect type of naming, one can improve one's linguistic and conceptual skills until the most perfect type is finally reached. But the existence of these different types of naming demonstrates the error of believing that someone is able to name something only if he or she has a perfect understanding of that thing. This would amount to reducing all cases of naming to instances of Type 4. Such a bold reduction would be quite wrong, as Scotus points out, because there are many cases in which we name something without having a perfect understanding. The case of naming God is just one example: we utter divine names while having only a vague concept of God. This is an instance of Type 3. Although our concept may be imperfect in many respects and not appropriate for God's essence, we *do* have a concept. And given such a concept, the divine names we are uttering are more than mere strings of sounds. (We are not simply parrots who mechanically reproduce sounds they have heard. Nor are we speakers who always utter names of a foreign language without understanding them.) The names we are uttering are real names endowed with a semantic function, and they enable us to signify God.

This explanation is of considerable interest, not just because of its theological aspects (it is a crucial point in Scotus's theology that humans do have a concept of God), but also because of its consequences for a semantic theory. First of all, the four types of naming Scotus mentions make clear that he does not subscribe to a semantic theory that holds that the use of language always depends on successful understanding. Language is not a system of signs we use only *after* we have acquired a perfect understanding of the things we intend to signify. In some cases, we use linguistic signs while having little understanding; in other cases we use them while having a more developed or even a perfect understanding. It would be erroneous to assume that we use them only when we have fully activated our cognitive capacities, which are limited, after all. If someone wants to know how humans use names and other linguistic signs, he or she should look at a large variety of cases. There is not just one kind of use humans make of names, as those philosophers assume who think that naming always presupposes a perfect understanding.

Scotus's explanation is also interesting because it shows that he does not confine himself to the traditional mentalistic approach to language discussed in Section I of this chapter. That is, he does not only endorse the view that names and other spoken words need to be linked to something in the mind – intelligible species, concepts, understandings, or whatever mental items there may be – so that they have a signification. Scotus also takes into account the intentionalist approach to language.[49] He stresses the point that the speaker's intention should not be overlooked in an evaluation of the semantic function of words. For in many cases, the understanding linked to the spoken word may be incomplete or vague, but the speaker nevertheless successfully signifies a certain thing. This is due to the speaker's intention, which somehow picks out an object in the world, although the speaker may not be able to grasp the nature of that object perfectly. It is to a considerable extent the speaker's intention, not just his or her concept or understanding, that makes it possible that words "hook onto the world." And a speaker can have such an intention while having only a poor understanding of the objects in the world; a speaker's intention is not just derivative of his or her understanding.[50]

This is an important point that has some striking similarities with a point that has been stressed by recent philosophers of language. Let me illustrate it with an example that became well known in recent debates.[51] When a person utters the word 'gold' and intends to signify – in modern terminology: to refer to – the shiny, hard piece of metal in view, the speaker is able to refer successfully to this piece of metal no matter how confused his or her understanding of it may be. This person may have a layperson's or an alchemist's understanding of gold and may give a very incomplete, a befuddled, or even a wrong description of gold. This does not matter. What matters for a successful reference to gold is this person's intention to pick out just the piece of metal in view. An imperfect understanding and an imperfect or a wrong definite description of gold do *not* prevent the speaker from referring to gold. Referring is largely independent of successfully understanding and describing. What matters for reference is the speaker's intention and the causal chain linking him or her to the thing being named.

V. SIGNIFICATION AND FALLACIES

Scotus applies the method of linguistic analysis to metaphysical and theological problems not only when he intends to show that these problems are instances of a general semantic problem and that they need to be discussed within the framework of a general semantic theory but also when he examines the linguistic expressions used in the phrasing of the problems. A clear example for such a use can be found in his discussion of the statement "God begot God" ("Deus genuit Deum"). This enigmatic statement is structurally very similar to the semantic puzzles (*sophismata*) that were to become famous in the fourteenth and fifteenth centuries.[52] The statement looks as if it could be answered both positively and negatively. For on the one hand, it is true within the context of a Trinitarian theology that there are three divine persons and that God the Father begot the Son. On the other hand, it is false that God somehow begot another God; there is just one God, even if there are three divine persons. So what truth value does the statement have?

Scotus provides an answer to this question by scrutinizing the semantic function of the words used in this statement.[53] He remarks that one may understand the words 'God' and 'begot' in such a way that the statement means either (a) that God begot himself (Deus genuit se Deum), or (b) that God begot another God (Deus genuit alium Deum). Yet both ways of understanding would be false on his view. Against (a), he argues that such an understanding is inadmissible because it relies upon a fallacy of the figure of the expression (*fallacia figurae dictionis*). Assuming that his readers are familiar with this fallacy, he gives no further explanation. But it may be explained as follows. According to Aristotle, there is such a fallacy when someone signifies two things that are different in some respect in the same way – for instance when one signifies two animals, a male and a female one, both as males or both as females.[54] Such a signification is inadmissible because a decisive qualitative difference between the two items that are signified is not taken into account. Now in the case of "God begot God" one becomes a victim of such a fallacy if one assumes that the subject and predicate term signify two things *in the same way* and that this statement simply expresses some kind of divine self-generation. In making such an assumption, one overlooks the fact that there is a qualitative difference between the items signified by the subject and predicate term and that, consequently, they cannot be signified in the same way. For the subject term signifies God insofar as he is the Father, whereas the predicate term signifies him insofar as he is the Son: the two divine persons, manifesting two different aspects of God, are signified *in different ways*.

Given that understanding (a) proves to be false, one may turn to (b). But this understanding would be equally false, as Scotus emphatically states. For if one were to accept this understanding and claim that God created some divine being that is really distinct from himself, one would again become victim of a fallacy, this time of the fallacy of the accident (*fallacia accidentis*). According to the classical definition, there is such a fallacy when one fails to distinguish between a subject and its accidents and thinks that the same thing can be said of the subject as may be said of one of its accidents.[55] In particular, such a fallacy arises when one makes statements of the form "*x* is different from *y*" and thinks that the same thing can be said to be different from the subject *x* itself as can be said to be different from one of the accidents of *x*. Now let us look at the statement "God begot God." According to understanding (b), this statement implies "The begetting God is different from the begotten God," which is to be taken in the sense of "The begetting God is really distinct from the begotten God." But if one takes it in that sense, one commits the fallacy of the accident. For one is only allowed to say that God when considered with respect to the accidental feature of begetting is different from God when considered with respect to the accidental feature of being begotten. The expression 'is different from' only applies to God's accidental features, not to God as a subject.

That is why it would be wrong to say that God, considered as a subject, is really distinct from God, considered as another subject. (Compare: "John, considered as the father of Peter, is different from John, considered as the son of Michael." This statement is correct as long as it is understood as a statement about the difference between two features of John. But it would be incorrect if it were understood in the crude sense of "John, considered as one subject, is different from John, considered as another subject.")

Given that both understandings rely upon a fallacy, neither of them can be accepted.[56] So how is "God begot God" to be understood? Scotus suggests that it should be taken in the sense of "God begot the same God" (Deus genuit eundem), where "the same" means "numerically the same" but not "qualitatively the same." That is, the statement should be understood in the sense of "God having one quality (that is, being the begetting Father) begot the same God having another quality (that is, being the begotten Son)." Only if the statement is taken in this sense does it turn out to be both meaningful and true.

Besides its significance for Trinitarian theology, this explanation is also important for Scotus's semantic theory. It reveals a point that has already turned out to be crucial in his explanation of abstract and concrete accidental terms: an account of the semantic function of terms should not only provide an answer to the question of *what* they signify but also an answer to the further, equally important question of *how* they signify. For one and the same term may signify the same thing in different ways, depending on the context in which this term is used. Thus, 'God' can signify the divine being in different ways (as God the Father, as the Son, etc.), depending on its relation to other terms in a statement. According to Scotus, one cannot account for either the semantic function of this term, or the meaning and truth value of statements in which it is used, if one neglects its ways of signifying. This approach to semantic problems shows that it is above all by making use of the key concept of the ways of signifying (not so much of the theory of supposition) that Scotus tries to provide an answer to semantic questions arising within a theological context.[57]

Lastly, Scotus's discussion of the statement "God begot God" is also of particular interest because it clearly shows that he chooses a linguistic approach to the theological question at stake. He tries to answer this question neither by simply appealing to authority nor by introducing controversial theological assumptions. He rather looks at the words 'God' and 'begot' in the context of the statement in question and asks how these words ought to be understood so that one does not fall into the trap of a fallacy. This method allows him to reject possible interpretations of the statement not so much on theological as on linguistic grounds. In his opinion, some interpretations can be ruled out because they rely upon an incomplete or deficient understanding of the statement itself. If one intends to replace these faulty interpretations by more convincing ones, a more accurate understanding of the statement and all the words used in it is necessary. Given that the statement in question has all the characteristic features of a *sophisma*, one may say that Scotus does theology, at least in some contexts, "the sophismatic way": he approaches theological problems by analyzing the semantic puzzles involved in the formulation of these problems.[58]

VI. CONCLUSIONS

An analysis of the passages in which Scotus discusses semantic questions shows that the first impression a reader may have when briefly looking at his writings is not necessarily correct. Although it may seem that Scotus was not interested in linguistic analysis, given the lack of any *Summa grammaticae* or *logicae*, a detailed examination of his writings, including those that appear to be purely theological or metaphysical, reveals that he had a profound interest in such an analysis. It is an interest both in philosophy of language, where language is the proper subject of philosophical investigations, and in linguistic philosophy, where semantic analysis is the method used in philosophical (as well as theological) discussions.

Taking into consideration the large variety and richness of semantic analyses in his works, one may finally ask how original these analyses are and what function they have in the entire project of Scotus's philosophy. Given the lack of detailed and comprehensive studies (there is not one single book on Scotus's semantics), it would be incautious to give a definite answer to these questions. At the moment, one can only give some hints that need to be further elaborated in future research. As far as Scotus's originality is concerned, one needs to evaluate his works within the historical context and to compare his solutions to various semantic problems with the solutions given by his immediate predecessors and contemporaries, such as Roger Bacon, Thomas Aquinas, Siger of Brabant, Boethius of Dacia, Radulphus Brito, and Simon of Faversham. Only a detailed comparison will show how much of an innovator Scotus was and to what extent he repeated well-known positions and continued the semantic discussions prominent in his time. Considering the issues presented in this chapter, one can hardly call Scotus an original author if an original author is taken to be someone who creates new problems or who comes up with surprisingly new solutions to traditional problems. All the problems discussed by Scotus are problems that were well known in the late thirteenth century and extensively treated by his contemporaries. And most of the solutions Scotus presents to these problems are solutions that can also be found in other authors. For instance, the distinction between two ways of looking at the intelligible species – a distinction of crucial importance for Scotus's explanation of the signification of terms – was made before him by Albert the Great and Thomas Aquinas.[59] The explanation of the significate of a general term as the nature of a thing, not the actually existing thing, was already given by Siger of Brabant.[60] And Scotus's account of the signification of concrete accidental terms is very similar to that defended by Boethius of Dacia.[61] Given these parallels and obvious influences, Scotus should be seen as an author who made extensive use of the various sources available to him, rather than as an author who created new problems or new solutions.

Note also that Scotus did not yet apply the method of "metalinguistic analysis"[62] to problems in natural philosophy, ethics, or other philosophical disciplines. That is, he did not discuss questions like What is time?, What is quantity?, or What is virtue? by providing a linguistic analysis of the terms 'time', 'quantity', and 'virtue'. Nor did he develop special analytical tools that would have enabled him to tackle problems concerning the use of these terms in propositional contexts. Such an approach to philosophical problems – an approach that makes linguistic analysis the cornerstone of every philosophical analysis – can be found only two or three decades later in authors such as Ockham and Buridan. Seen from the point of view of these fourteenth-century philosophers, Scotus is a traditional author who confines linguistic analysis to a fairly restricted number of problems.

Yet a philosopher can be original not just in creating new problems, new solutions, or new types of analysis, but also in sharply analyzing traditional problems and in evaluating old solutions and criticizing, improving, or rejecting them. Seen from that perspective, Scotus is highly original. He uses all his *subtilitas* to scrutinize various semantic positions, to point out their strengths and weaknesses, and to modify them in such a way as to make them powerful enough to provide satisfactory solutions to complex problems. This is most evident in his detailed discussion of the two traditional models explaining the signification of words (the direct and the indirect signification model) but also in his meticulous analysis of semantic puzzles (for example, the statement "God begot God"). In these and other contexts his originality may be less obvious in his results than in the rich and subtle arguments used to attain these results.

But what place and function does semantic analysis have within the general framework of Scotus's philosophy? There is a simple and a more complex answer to this question. Choosing the simple way, one may say that semantic analysis was an indispensable instrument for Scotus – an instrument that permitted him to formulate traditional problems in a more precise way and to analyze these problems with better tools.[63] Semantic analysis allowed him to detect all sorts of ambiguities, fallacies, and other traps into which an author who is not aware of fine-grained but important semantic distinctions may easily fall. A close examination of the semantic function of terms and sentences enabled him to be better armed in the metaphysical and theological battles of his time. But of course all warriors in these battles were armed to their teeth because all of them had a thorough training in grammar and logic. Semantic analysis was a sine qua non for every philosopher and theologian trained in a late thirteenth-century university.

But semantic analysis was not just an instrument for Scotus. It was also an integral part of his philosophical investigations. This leads me to the second, more involved answer. If one looks at various contexts in which Scotus discusses semantic problems, one can see that these discussions are part of his entire philosophical project – in many cases even an essential part that is closely linked to other parts. This is manifest, for instance, in his examination of the question concerning the signification of words. Such an examination has not only an instrumental value; it does not only enable him to introduce some subtle distinctions that prove to be useful in further discussions. It is rather part of an all-embracing philosophical project that intends to elucidate what types of things there are in the world and how humans can establish a relation to these things when using language. Given such a project, it is not surprising that Scotus's semantic discussions are interwoven with ontological, psychological, and epistemological ones. For in explaining the signification of terms, he not only distinguishes various types of terms but also appeals to the metaphysical theory of common nature, to the psychological theory of intelligible species, and to an epistemological theory of abstraction. It is by putting together pieces of various theories, including those stemming from a semantic theory, that he attempts to explain how words and sentences can "hook onto the world." Thus, semantic analysis is more than an instrument helpful for further philosophical analysis. It is *in itself* philosophical analysis because it deals with the problem of how humans can establish a relation with things in the world by using language, one of the most basic problems in philosophy that cannot be dispensed with.

NOTES

1   In his "Habilitationsschrift" *Die Kategorien- und Bedeutungslehre des Duns Scotus* (first published in 1916) Martin Heidegger still ascribed this work to Scotus. He was corrected in 1922 by M. Grabmann, who successfully identified Thomas of Erfurt as the real author.

2   Scotus's students were well aware of the importance of these commentaries. Antonius Andreas, a Spanish Scotist of the first generation, reports that he tried to compile the main elements of these commentaries in one single book, thus creating a handbook in Scotist logic and semantics. See Sagüéz Azcona 1968, esp. 4.

3   See *Ord.* 1, d. 4, pars 1, q. un. (Vatican 4:1–2, Appendix A, 381–384); *Lect.* 1, d. 4, q. un.

4   For instance, in *Ord.* 1, d. 5, pars 1, q. un.

5   Scotus's logico-semantic approach to metaphysical and theological questions is, of course, not exceptional in the later Middle Ages. It is rather the standard approach, chosen by many of his contemporaries, as the contributions in Marmo 1997 show.

6   I borrow this terminological distinction from Searle 1969, 4.

7   See *Peri herm.* 1 (16^a3–8). It is, of course, a highly controversial question whether Aristotle does indeed present a semantic model in this very short passage. According to Norman Kretzmann, there is "not even a sketch of a general theory of meaning" in this text; see Kretzmann

1974, 5. For a comprehensive interpretation of the crucial passage, see Weidemann 1994, 133–53.

8 On the main positions and the terminology used in this debate, see Pinborg 1971 and Ashworth 1991.

9 He wrote two sets of questions on this authoritative text. I will use both, referring to them as *"In Periherm.* I" and *"In Periherm.* II". Since the critical edition of this text is still in preparation, my references apply to the Wadding edition.

10 I confine myself to sketching the most basic elements of the species theory. For a detailed account, see Spruit 1994, vol. 1, and Perler 1996.

11 See *Ord.* 1, d. 27, qq. 1–3, and *Lect.* 1, d. 27, qq. 1–3, where he alludes to a "magna altercatio." In his earlier works he speaks more modestly about "two ways" that were chosen to answer this question. See *In Periherm.* II, q. 1. Note that it is only in the earlier works that he speaks about intelligible species. In the later ones he uses the expression *conceptus.*

12 He concludes his first commentary with the remark that the indirect signification thesis is more plausible "according to the authorities" (i.e., Aristotle and Boethius), whereas the direct signification thesis is more plausible "according to the arguments" (*In Periherm.* I, 1, q. 2). At the end of his second commentary, he states that "neither way is absolutely necessary" (*In Periherm.* II, q. 1).

13 See *In Periherm.* I, 1, q. 2, and II, q. 1. Note, however, that Scotus was not the first author in the medieval context who drew this distinction. It can already be found in Albert the Great, *In Sent.* 1, d. 37, a. 27 (26: 273), and in Thomas Aquinas, *In Sent.* 2, d. 17, q. 2, a. 1, ad 3 (429). (I am grateful to Giorgio Pini for bringing these passages to my attention.)

14 See *In Periherm.* I, 1, q. 2, and II, q.1.

15 Note, however, that Scotus does not intend to give a definite solution. Neither in the first nor in the second *Commentary on Perihermeneias* does he present a *determinatio quaestionis.* He rather evaluates the two standard solutions and tries to improve them by adding further distinctions – in particular the crucial distinction between the two aspects of an intelligible species.

16 See his *Compendium studii theologiae,* ch. 2, in Roger Bacon 1988, 64–72.

17 See *An Essay Concerning Human Understanding,* bk. III, ch. 2, in Locke 1975, 405. Note, however, that the characterization of Locke's position as "semantic representationalism" or "idealism" has been partly revised by recent commentators. See, for instance, Guyer 1994.

18 See *In Periherm.* I, 1, q. 2; 1, q. 5; and II, q. 1.

19 See *In Periherm.* I, 1, q. 2, and II, q. 1.

20 On this development, see Sondag 1996. On the place and function of common nature in Scotus's metaphysics, see Wolter 1990d and Timothy B. Noone, ch. 3 in this volume. Note, however, that in his commentaries on *Peri herm.* Scotus does not yet use the technical term *natura communis*. He speaks in a more neutral way about the *natura* or *essentia* of a thing (see note 18). Thus, it may be that in these early writings he is still following Thomas Aquinas and Siger of Brabant, who also speak about the *natura* as the significate of a word, without appealing to the complex theory of common nature. For textual arguments in favor of such an interpretation, see Pini 1999 and 2001.

21 See Thomas Aquinas 1989, 11; Siger of Brabant 1974, 63.

22 In Ockham's opinion, there is no common nature that may be the content of a thought. Therefore, a word cannot signify such a common nature; it immediately signifies things in the world. See his *Summa Logicae* I, ch. 1, in William Ockham 1974, 8.

23 See *In Periherm.* I, 1, q. 8.

24 See Rorty 1979. With his metaphor of the "inner arena" Rorty does not intend to characterize Scotus's position but that of early modern representationalists.

25 This is possible because a term has a "univocal signification"; see *In Periherm.* I, 1, q. 5, and II, q. 2.

26 See the collection of texts dealing with this question in de Libera 1991a. See also Siger of Brabant 1974, 43–66; Zimmermann 1967.

27 See *In Periherm.* I, 1, qq. 7–8. For a detailed account of Scotus's arguments, see Schneider 1996. An analysis of the opposite opinion is provided by de Libera 1991b.

28 This interest was largely inspired by two passages in the *Categories*: (a) the passage in the first chapter ($1^a12–15$) in which Aristotle deals with *paronyma* (Latin: *denominativa*), that is, with terms derived from other terms (one of Aristotle's examples is 'brave' derived from 'bravery'); (b) the passage in the fifth chapter ($3^b10–24$) in which Aristotle discusses the relation between primary and secondary substances.

29 A thorough discussion of their approaches to this problem is provided by Ebbesen 1988.

30 See *In Praed.* q. 8.

31 A categorematic term (e.g., 'white', 'Socrates', 'runs'), opposed to a syncategorematic term (e.g., 'if', 'and'), is a term that has a signification by itself, regardless of its combination with other terms, and that can be used as a subject term or a predicate term in a sentence. On this terminology, which has its origin in Priscian's *Institutiones grammaticae*, see Kretzmann 1982.

32 A list of the four main theories popular in the thirteenth century is provided by Ebbesen 1988, 118.

33 For a discussion of this theory, which is usually contrasted with the "identity theory," see Malcolm 1979.

34 On the core theses of the "modistae," see Pinborg 1982 and Rosier 1983.

35 Irene Rosier has convincingly shown that the expression *modus signif-icandi* was used in different contexts by different authors (among them Albert the Great and Thomas Aquinas), not just by the Parisian masters usually called "modistae"; see Rosier 1995a.

36 On the origin and development of these debates, see Knudsen 1982.

37 See Avicenna, *Liber de philosophia prima sive scientia divina* I, ch. 2, in Avicenna 1977/80, 10. On the reception of this influential passage in the Latin Middle Ages, see Maierù 1987.

38 See *In Porph.* q. 3.

39 He also discusses it to some extent in his later *Ordinatio* and *Lectura*. For a detailed comparison of the earlier and the later works, see Pini 1997, ch. 2. I confine myself to presenting the main elements of Scotus's view, which can be found both in his earlier and in his later works.

40 See *In Porph.* q. 11.

41 See *Ord.* 1, d. 23, q. un., and *Lect.* 1, d. 23, q. un.

42 In *Ord.* 1, d. 23, q. un., Scotus claims that "omnis intentio secunda est relatio rationis, non quaecumque, sed pertinens ad extremum actus intellectus componentis et dividentis...".

43 The five predicables, introduced by Porphyry in his influential *Isagoge* and thoroughly discussed throughout the Middle Ages, are genus, species, differentia, *proprium*, and accident. Scotus discusses them in detail in his *In Porph.* For an overview, see Henry 1982.

44 See *In Porph.* q. 3 and q. 4; *In Praed.* q. 3.

45 See, for instance, his extensive discussion "De imagine" (*Ord.* 1, d. 3, pars 3, q. 2) in which he argues that intelligible species are not just caused by extramental things or by phantasms but to a considerable extent by the intellect. There cannot be intelligible species without there being an *activo* intellect.

46 On Scotus's background, see Rosier 1995b. An analysis of Scotus's reaction to the various views of his contemporaries is provided by Boulnois 1995.

47 See *Ord.* 1, d. 22, q. un.; *Lect.* 1, d. 22, q. un.

48 See *Ord.* 1, d. 22, q. un., Appendix A (Vatican 5: 390–1).

49 Scotus is, of course, not the only author in the thirteenth century who became aware of the importance of this approach. It can also be found

in other authors (e.g., Roger Bacon, Pseudo-Kilwardby), as Rosier 1994 has shown.

50 Scotus makes this clear in *Ord.* 1, d. 22, q. un., Appendix A (Vatican 5: 392), where he states: "quod autem intendimus significare sub propria ratione, nec tamen illud sic intelligimus, hoc nominamus..." He adds that we name such a thing only imperfectly. Yet what is important is that we *do* name it.

51 See Putnam 1975, 227.

52 Note, however, that Scotus himself does not call it a *sophisma* when he introduces it in *Ord.* 1, d. 4, pars 1, q. un. On the *sophismata* in the technical sense, which were already discussed by Scotus's contemporaries (e.g., Boethius of Dacia), see Read 1993.

53 See *Ord.* 1, d. 4, pars 1, q. un., Appendix A (Vatican 4: 382–3).

54 See *Soph. El.* 1.4 (166^{b}10–14). On the reception of the *Soph. El.* in the Middle Ages and on the importance of the analysis of fallacies, see Ebbesen 1981.

55 See *Soph. El.* 1.5 (166^{b}28–36).

56 In *Ord.* 1, d. 4, pars 1, q. un., Appendix A (Vatican 4: 382) Scotus concludes: "Et quando dicitur 'aut se Deum, aut alium Deum', nullum do, sed dico quod nec se, nec alium."

57 This becomes apparent if one compares his approach with that chosen by later authors, such as William of Ockham and Walter Chatton, who discussed the statement "God begot God" by making extensive use of the supposition theory. For a detailed analysis, see S. Brown 1993. However, this does not amount to saying that Scotus completely ignores or neglects the supposition theory. He occasionally refers to it, as Marmo 1989, especially 170–4, has shown.

58 For a general description of the "sophismatic way," see Ebbesen 1991.

59 See note 13.

60 See note 20.

61 See Ebbesen 1988, 120–9.

62 I borrow this term from Murdoch 1981.

63 Scotus himself alludes to this instrumental function by explaining that logic (of which semantics is a part) should always be taken as *logica docens*, that is, as a discipline that teaches the methods and rules of formal thinking, and as *logica utens*, that is, as a discipline used in argumentative discourse; see *In Porph.* q. 1. It is above all when taken in the second way that logic is an instrument to be used in other disciplines.

6   Duns Scotus on Natural Theology

Scotus's natural theology has the following distinctive claims:

1. That we can reason demonstratively to the necessary existence and nature of God from what is actually so but not from imagined situations or from conceivability-to-us; rather, only from the possibility logically required for what we know actually to be so.
2. That there is a univocal transcendental notion of being.
3. That there are disjunctive transcendental notions that apply exclusively to everything, like 'contingent/necessary', and such that the inferior cannot have a case unless the superior does.
4. That an a priori demonstration of the existence of God is impossible because there is nothing explanatorily prior to the divine being; thus, reasoning must be a posteriori from the real dependences among things we perceive to the possibility of an absolutely First Being (The First Principle).
5. That such a being cannot be possible without existing necessarily.
6. That the First Being (God) is simple, omni-intelligent, free (spontaneous), omnipotent, and positively infinite.[1]
7. That there is a formal distinction, which is more than a distinction within our concepts or definitions, among the divine attributes.

He makes that first point obvious throughout his several treatments, that one cannot reliably reason from conceptual consistency *for us* to the *real* and formal possibility or necessity of something; one must reason only to those necessities that are conditions of the possibility of what is known to be actual. The schema of the reasoning is, in a word, that "only the existence of God can make an effect even possible."[2] Thus, it is explicitly incorrect to classify him along with St. Anselm, Descartes, and Leibniz, among those who reason a priori to the being of God.[3]

Scotus characteristically and deftly argues by *indirect proof*. He supposes the opposite of his intended conclusion and deduces a contradiction between that supposition and certain self-evident or previously proved propositions, thus getting his own conclusion by using the principle that whatever entails the denial of what is already known to be so is false and its opposite true:[4] "si negatur negatio, ponitur affirmatio."[5] He also uses the argument form " if 'p' is not necessary, then 'not-p' is possible." And he uses the general rule "if possibly P, and not contingently P, then necessarily P" as well as the rule that whatever is possible is necessarily possible.[6]

Although Scotus is bold, direct, and logically explicit about demonstrating the existence of God, he retrenches on some claims in natural theology that others had thought demonstrable: he says the power of God to produce whatever is possible is demonstrable, but not the divine power to do so immediately, without any secondary causes; and he says the immortality of the human soul cannot be demonstrated. He rejects[7] the usual deduction of particular divine perfections, like love or wisdom, from the mere fact that God has all pure perfections, saying each requires an additional experiential basis to assure us that the attribute *is* a pure perfection; for parallel reasons he rejects St. Anselm's proof as well. He thinks only probable (likely but persuasive) reasons can be given that time will end, that the world was created "in time" (though demonstrably created *ex nihilo*[8]), and that the created cosmos will somehow endure beyond the end of time.

Two other distinctive positions are (1) that we name the divine attributes univocally, that is, in the same sense, as the pure perfections found in creatures, such as being, life, intelligence, freedom, and love; such perfections, as mentioned, are not just conceptually distinct from one another in God but are formally distinct "on the part of the thing" from one another. And he says (2) that freedom of choice, both divine and human, is marked by spontaneity; it is the *ability* to choose that *alone* explains the election to act one way or

another, not any prior reason or any merit in the objects; and in that
lies the explanation of how there is anything contingent at all. This
chapter addresses the key parts of the argument for the existence of
God and some aspects of the discussion of the divine nature, ending
with a brief comment about human immortality.

I. DUNS SCOTUS'S CONCEPTION
OF NATURAL THEOLOGY

Scotus takes up what we call natural theology within "the science
of metaphysics" in accord with Aristotle's practice in his *Metaphysics*: the inquiry into the first principles of being, which accounts
for the title of Scotus's book.[9] The science of metaphysics "considers the transcendentals as such,"[10] among which are disjunctive
attributes such as "necessary-or-possible,"[11] and among those disjunctive transcendentals is the one that Scotus uses to begin his
proof for the existence of God, by "the more fruitful source of *essential order*,"[12] among efficient and final causes and orderings of
eminence.

The fact that natural theology falls within metaphysics does not
deter Scotus from being guided by what he already knows by faith –
from Scripture and the faith of the Church. He is explicit about that,
even in the restrictively philosophical work *De primo principio*, addressing God, as did St. Anselm in his *Proslogion*, at the outset of
that philosophical inquiry. Scotus says, "You are truly what it means
to be, you are the whole of what it means to exist. This, if it is possible for me, I should like to know by way of demonstration. Help me
then, O Lord, as I investigate *how much our natural reason can learn*
about that true being which you are if we begin with the being that
you have predicated of yourself."[13] He is guided by faith, in what to
look for and where: to look for "what he [your servant] holds with
faith most certain, that you are *the most eminent, the first efficient
cause, and the last end*,"[14] and "where": among the things that begin
to be. But notice that Scotus is also guided by philosophy in his understanding of the Scripture and his Faith, as is indicated in the three distinctly philosophical concepts – eminence, efficiency and finality –
of his inquiry and prayer. Scotus does not premise revelation in his
metaphysical arguments; still, what he knows by faith prompts him

toward demonstrating certain conclusions and suggests certain questions and conceptions.[15]

I.1. Limitations of Scope

Because Scotus treats natural theology as the part of metaphysics concerned with the existence and nature of the First Principle of Being, his explicit scope is much narrower than his words "how much our natural reason can learn about the nature of the being you are" will permit. Related topics, like the temporal beginning of the world, divine providence, governance and foreknowledge, the immortality of the human soul, whether there can be life after death, human freedom, the possibility and scope of miracles, the possibility of divine action in history, the conditions of possibility for various mysteries such as the Trinity and Incarnation, the problem of evil, and the end of the world are usually considered to be within the capacity of unaided reason and to be part of the subject nowadays. And indeed, Scotus treated most of them and did so philosophically, but in (revealed) theological contexts.

II. ON THE UNIVOCAL TRANSCENDENTAL CONCEPT OF BEING

There is a universal, all-encompassing, univocal concept, 'being', with which we can think of anything. Scotus considers such a conception a necessity for a demonstration of God's existence and, indeed, for a coherent science of metaphysics. A concept is univocal if it cannot be affirmed and denied to fit the same thing without a contradiction; and if univocal, it can function as the middle term of a demonstration without equivocation. A concept is transcendental just in case it has no superior genus and it applies to anything, no matter what. In addition to such transcendental terms as 'being', 'one', and 'true', there are also universal, logically exclusive, contrast-dependent disjunctions, such as 'necessary/contingent', 'causable/uncausable', 'finite/infinite', and 'perfect/imperfect' that are subject to a 'law of the disjunctive transcendentals', namely, that it is impossible that there be a case of the inferior without there being a case of the superior. The proof of that law seems, however, to be cognitively a consequence of a proof of the existence of a divine being rather than a premise for it.

We can ask, beginning with what exists contingently, "whether among actual things there is one that is infinite." So Scotus's conception has to present anything there is to the understanding,[16] regardless of its manner of being. Another way he puts the idea is that only a transcendental, univocal notion of being allows a person, uncertain whether a first principle is finite or infinite, to inquire, without circularity of thinking, whether there is such a thing.

For if some empirical predicates are not also univocally applied to whatever we are inquiring about, then "a disconcerting consequence ensues; namely, that from the proper notion of anything found in creatures nothing at all can be inferred about God." He seems to think that Aquinas could not have known that 'being' applies to God by analogy of proper proportionality, where the meaning of the term is captured by the *modus essendi* of its referent, unless he first knew through some neutral notion of 'being' that God exists. For Scotus also holds that God exists in a manner ontologically only analogous to contingent things, but conceptually we have a univocal notion that embraces the ontological diversity of intrinsic modes of being, that is, both the infinite and the finite.

The *Theoremata*, probably a late work (maybe not directly Scotus's, and maybe not reliably in the order we have it,[17] or even more than a collection of drafts), might seem, and was so thought,[18] to repudiate his project in natural theology by affirming opposed positions.[19] But he was not refuting or retracting his other work – rather, he was dislodging the contrary, Latin Averroist position by deducing absurdities that would result if the notion of 'being' were restricted to the domain of Aristotle's categories. His opponents' assumption that 'being' immediately divides into the ten categories, rather than into universal, contrast-dependent[20] disjunctions like 'infinite/finite' and 'necessary/contingent', leads to contradictions and anomalies. In Theorem 9, Proposition 5 he writes, "No concept common *per se* will be the same between the created and uncreated." There will be no univocal transcendental notion of 'being' or of anything else. Among the absurd outcomes is that "it cannot be proved that something numerically the same is or was first among efficient causes" (Theorem 16, Prop. 3, n. 2). Basically he is saying, "look where saying you are reasoning with a narrowly categorical notion of being will lead you."[21]

III. THE PROOF OF THE EXISTENCE OF A FIRST EXPLANATORY BEING

Scotus offers an original line of argument for the existence of a divine being, using considerations that originate with Avicenna (ca. 1000). For Avicenna made clear that if it is possible that a divine being exists, it *must* exist, and that nothing else exists on account of what it is. He reasoned, neo-Platonically, that the divine being emanates, necessarily, all contingent being. Scotus adapted that reasoning to his a posteriori framework and refined the notion of contingency to include not only not existing on account of what it is but also that even while existing such a thing *still* might not exist. So Scotus deduces the *possibility* of a divine being (a First Cause and Eminent Being) from the causation we perceive. His key innovations are (1) to convert the inquiry about the causation of contingent beings (ones that exist but might not have), into an explicit[22] discussion of *essentially ordered* series and (2) to reach the intermediate conclusion that it is *possible* for there to be a First Being, so as to conclude by deducing that the *possibility* of such a being requires its *necessary being*. So he does not end with the existence of such a being as a hypothetical necessity for the contingent effects but as a necessary being on its own (*ens a se*).

He presents his arguments at least three times, in somewhat varying versions.[23] They vary as he reached for a transparent expression of the insights and one that does not rely on inferences from conceivability-to-us to formal possibility. As a result, commentators have diverged in explaining and appraising the arguments and have offered some inventive suggestions.[24] But overall there seems to be a consensus that the issue of whether there can be an infinite regress is pivotal.[25] So we treat that at length.

He does *not* rely upon St. Anselm's argument, even after he gives it a "coloration" that he approves,[26] because without a posteriori arguments we would not be in a position of unaided natural certainty, by recognition, that such a conception, "a being than which a greater cannot be [consistently] conceived," *is* consistent. He sees that consistency to a human is not sufficient for the formal possibility of the thing.[27] (This is, historically, a very important point that was missed from seventeenth- through twentieth-century philosophy.) So the possibility of a First Being has to be demonstrated a posteriori as one of the necessary conditions for what is actually so.

Some reminders are as follows:

1. What is formally possible[28] is what can be, nonrepugnantly to being-as-such. Everything formally possible is necessarily formally possible, for compatibility with being-as-such is not made or caused. Nor is that a semantic, conceptual, or other mind-dependent relation. The "terms" of propositions that he has in mind are realities presented to *us* conceptually, even where what we think of is a combination that is impossible. Possibility is not a semantic condition but is, as it turns out later in his metaphysics, nonrepugnance *in esse intelligibili* to being-as-such.

2. Some philosophers may be tempted to understand Scotus anachronistically as if he thinks of modalities semantically, as is fashionable nowadays.[29] There is a superficial similarity because the axioms and theorems, considered entirely syntactically, are like the system S-5. But his modalities, even as logical, are propositional operators (adverbials modifying propositions), not quantifiers. And his propositions cannot be understood extensionally, or metalinguistically, as having truth conditions mapped onto domains of worlds of propositions or sentences, or even of *abstracta* (cf. the "individual essences" of Plantinga). In fact, his syllogistic logic cannot be interpreted as first-order quantification at all and still express his propositions about real natures and active natural principles.

3. For him the explanatory order is from the real modalities of things to the modalities of propositions, whereas recent logicians talk as if necessity were a feature of sentences or statements in relation to arrays of truth values and as if we could analyze real necessity into an array of propositional or sentential truths "in all possible worlds."

4. Scotus's modal principles are derived from the metaphysical relationships of things considered modally, *de re*.[30] However, modalities *de re* are understood nowadays to be shorthand

for sentential modalities; not so for Scotus. 'Being necessarily human' is a *real* condition of Socrates, that his humanity is essential to him. That cannot be reductively analyzed as an arrangement of propositional truths. And God's necessary being is a manner of divine being, not a feature of some propositions about God.

5. To say it is possible that something can make something is either to say there is something that is apt or able to make another thing or to say there *can* be, compatibly with being-as-such, such a maker. And there are two senses of the first sort of assertion as well: that some particular existing thing is able (actively or dispositionally) to do something or that things of some particular *sort* are able to do something, as in "it is possible for women to bear children" and "penguins cannot fly but can swim." In such cases, we are talking about real possibility, real impossibility, and real necessity located in common natures of things that exist. That is what Scotus is talking about – the *sorts*, the natures of things.

To repeat, conceptual consistency-to-us (seeming to be consistent) is no assurance of real possibility, or, a fortiori, of formal possibility. And natural causes are really necessary for the actions of things (no babies without parents), yet such effects can, in principle, be produced in other ways as well. And something can be really impossible, say, for lack of an agent able to do it (flying cockroaches, or airplanes up to a while ago) and yet be formally possible. And something may be formally impossible even though some persons think it to be really possible, as the Islamic occasionalists thought God had made the world without natural active principles, and some philosophers think *we* might have existed with all our experiences when no actual physical world existed at all.

Scotus argues in terms of the *sorts* of things (the natures, or natural kinds). Common natures are the relevant effects in the essential order of causes, and common natures are the relevant subjects of real necessity and possibility as well.[31] And, "if . . . understood in terms of the natures [rather than individuals], the quiddity and the possibility, then the conclusions follow from necessary premises."[32] Nevertheless, the real, not the formal, possibility, say of airplanes, is caused, because the real nature, in *esse essentiae*, is caused; it is produced by things of the further natures (humans, metals, designs, etc.) on which it depends. There did not have to be "things able to see" any more than there had to be "glowing mice" or "fireflies." And the ones there are depend on further sorts, for example, "birds able to see" or "mammals able to see," and so forth. That is the kind of production Scotus is concerned with, production where one sort of thing depends in being and in action on the natural action of another sort of thing. Thus, the existence of what we start out to explain, say a newborn chick, depends on its sort (*swallow*) and then upon things of further sorts that have to be all at once. So we get to the question of whether "natures-producing-natures" spirals up to a first or not. Scotus reasons both that it must, and that it ends at a certain sort of thing: something that exists by nature.

Note also some of the recently recounted criticisms of Scotus's arguments: that he needs to show all of nature is essentially ordered, that there appears to be a supposed and cognitively circular principle of sufficient reason, that he skips whether there can be uncaused contingent being, that his reliance on modal logic presupposes the existence of God, and that the elimination of an infinite regress is not really decisive. (Ockham thought the reasoning would be more obvious in the case of conserving causes.[33])

IV. THE ARGUMENT

Scotus asks whether among the things that actually exist there is one that is infinite in act. Immediately he asks a subquestion: "whether among beings *which can produce an effect*, there is one that is *simply first*."[34] And he promises that if there is, he can show there is an infinite being.

He reasons that (1) some things *can* be produced (*effectibile*) because some *are* produced. So, (2) there can be something productive (*effectiva*), that is, something of a sort naturally disposed and able to produce things, say, *swallow*, or *fertile female frog*. Now, given that there is such a thing, that there *can* be such a thing is *formally* necessary (absolutely, unconditionally necessary).[35] The same will hold, then, for each further premise and for the conclusion as well: because each is a necessary condition for the former.

The productive sort, say, *swallow*, is either itself caused to be, and its producing caused to happen, by something of a prior sort (such as genetically organized carbon molecules) or not. If not by another, but on account of itself, then we already have what we seek: an unproduced producer. But suppose that the producing sort, say, *swallow*, depends on another producing sort, via things of the sort, not only for its being but for its producing, as when a pencil makes a mark, for its marking is caused, too, by a moving person. Does that essentially ordered regress end? Does it all spiral up to a first productive sort of thing that can depend on nothing? It seems that it must.

Objector: Suppose that the dependence goes on forever, each sort of thing being of a different kind (nature) from its effect, but each "inside and hanging onto" a prior real nature of a different kind, without end. Scotus calls such a series "infinite," by which he means "nonterminating." It would be like the regression from a chick to "being a chicken," which depends on "being vitally organized carbon molecules," which together depends on "being particularly organized atoms," and so on, to further and further conditions, but without end. And if this series were nonterminating, it would be nonterminable.

Scotus thinks a nonterminable regress is formally impossible. He deploys two lines of argument to block that option. First he argues that a nonterminating regress of essentially ordered causes, where all the causing has to be continuous right through to the last effect, and each successive effect is of a different sort from the prior, as in our "pencil marking" example, is inconsistent. Secondly, a nonterminating regress of that sort is not formally necessary because its denial is not *in*consistent.[36] So in the first case, there *cannot be* such a thing, and in the second, there *need not* be such a thing. And so in either case *an unproduced producing cause (of a suitable sort) is known to be really possible.* For, if the negation of a proposition is either impossible or not necessary, the affirmative is possible.[37] So the heart of the reasoning is to reject the nonterminating regress (the "infinite series").

IV.1. As to the Inconsistency of a Nonending Regress

Scotus does not offer a taxonomy of ordered natural kinds, and so we have to speculate about examples. Further, he is not committed at the outset to saying that all of nature belongs to a single such order.

Rather, he relies upon *some* actual cases only. For if it is impossible that every regress of essentially ordered causes is infinite (unending), then a terminating one is possible. But that is possible only if a certain sort of thing actually exists, a First Being. And the sort of thing that actually exists will logically prevent there from being any nonterminating regresses of essentially ordered causes at all, because it will be the explanation of all contingent being. So the universal order in nature is a consequence and outcome of the proof, not a premise of it.

Consider some cases. For aspirin to help a headache, chemical reactions are required, and those require certain sorts of, and arrangements of, molecules (molecular natures: acetylsalicylic acid). For that, a certain molecular structure is required along with molecular bonding, and for that a certain atomic organization is required, and so on. All of these requirements have to be actual and causing, "all at once," "all the way down" for the aspirin to work. The "all at once" can be physical and so time-bound by the light constant and the medium, and there can even be quantum gaps between cause and effect; the nested causes must still be operating all together. Thus, Ockham's doubts about whether "simultaneity" of all the causes is demonstrably satisfied are obviated.[38]

Someone who says, "still, maybe such a line does not twist up to a first" is committed to a contradiction. For this person has to say that at *every* stage a sufficient condition is absent and one is never reached by stepwise regression; so one is *always absent*. And at the same time, he has to postulate the final effect, and, so, that there *is* a sufficient condition for it. That is explicitly contradictory.

A sentence with an infinite number of "if, if, if, if . . ."clauses cannot be made complete by adding more; so too with a phrase inside brackets, inside brackets, repeating without end, never coming to an assertion. Thus, supplying an infinite number of necessary conditions is not enough, by itself, to supply a sufficient condition.[39] Consequently, supposing *only* the regression, each member necessary but none sufficient, contradicts the actuality of the effect, for which a sufficient condition is manifestly present. *That* is Scotus's insight.

An objection that such reasoning is a "fallacy of composition"[40] is mistaken. One is not attributing some feature to the series as a whole solely on the basis of features of the members, but contrasting something *always missing* in each and every member of the series with *something present* in the final effect: a sufficient condition for being. Another illustration: the predicate "unexplained" applies in regression to every member of the series, whereas its *negation* is by supposition present in the granted effect. Where could "explained" come from? It could not, at all. A logical analogue is that the modal operator of a whole conjunction, no matter how long, even infinite, is the weakest operator of any conjunct.

The objection that Scotus did not establish that an infinite regress of essentially ordered causes is impossible has been around at least since Ockham raised it, and it gets repeated in the literature now. Perhaps Scotus did not articulate his reasoning transparently enough. But the substance of the argument is implicit in the text, needing only examples, as illustrated in the preceding paragraphs. And the objection is merely conclusional, without any basis in fact. Besides, Scotus could also point out that if such a nonending series *per impossibile*[41] could happen, it would, nevertheless, be formally causable, whether caused or not. (And that would contradict the supposition that a nonterminating regress of essentially ordered causes could be nonterminable). For conjoining anything at all to the contingent effect would still give a contingent conjunction. And the contingent, as such, is causable.[42] So, even on such a supposition, a first uncausable cause would still be possible, and thus actual, given the reasoning presented in this subsection. As a result, the supposition of a nonterminating regress of essentially ordered causes is impossible (inconsistent).

IV.2. As to the Nonnecessity of any Unending Essentially Ordered Regress

Scotus has in mind that there actually are such regresses, although obvious ones, like pencil marks, terminate at members belonging to a series of accidentally ordered causes, like people. (But he has a response to that as well: that such additional series are themselves essentially ordered, through their forms, in a series that must terminate.) For instance, a mark is caused by a pencil whose marking is caused, both in act and in ability, by a writer's gesture caused by his moving his hand, caused by his acting freely, which he can do on account of what he is. His 'being' is accidentally dependent on generation from his parents, but his causation originates from him, as from an uncaused cause of acting. So there *can* be a terminating essentially ordered series of causes. That shows that an essentially ordered series of efficient causes does not *have* to be nonterminating. So the universal proposition "every essentially ordered series of causes is nonterminating" is demonstrably false – indeed, found to be inconsistent a posteriori.[43]

The objector may rejoin, "But I am talking about the whole cosmos: that may regress infinitely." Scotus's proper reply, which we make for him, is, "that is a *petitio*, because there is no other case, and whether that regress is infinite is exactly what is in dispute." Besides, we know that an essentially ordered series of efficient natures that terminates in a first uncaused production is possible. So, because such a terminating regress, to a cause of all contingent being, is possible (known a posteriori, too), a nonterminating regress is impossible.

Thus, to make clear that a regress has to end, he supposes first that it does not end and shows that a contradiction follows. Then he supposes that it need not end and shows that the possibility of a First Being follows from that, too; but the possibility of a First Being excludes any possibility of a nonterminating essentially ordered regress.[44] Therefore, a First Efficient Nature is possible on either supposition; thus, an unending regress is impossible.

IV.3. The Necessary Being of the First Efficient Cause

Scotus could have stopped at concluding that there is a first actual producer of all essentially dependent effects because there cannot be an infinite regress. That would be sufficiently obvious, he says: "contingens, sed manifesta." But he wants a stronger conclusion: that there has to be a first unproducible producer of such actual effects; that it is both really necessary[45] and formally necessary to be. Indeed he wants to establish its necessary being as an intrinsic mode of the being (see Section V.12, "Infinity"). That way, he can establish the causal ground for any contingent being at all.[46] So he takes two more steps: that an unproduced first producer is unproducible, and that an unproducible producer has necessary being.

His "second conclusion"[47] is that if a thing can exist unproduced and have causal power to produce whatever is producible, it has to be uncausable. (It would be contradictory to say something could cause itself to be). And his "third conclusion" is that, if it is possible, it exists necessarily. For whatever is really possible is either causable (such that there can be something that is able to cause it) or exists *a se*. But whatever exists that is uncausable must then exist necessarily.

Does Scotus premise a principle of sufficient reason? No,[48] he does not premise even a weak principle of explicability. For his reasoning here is that what *can* exist necessarily, *must* do so, whereas what is causable need not exist and might not have existed at all. Thus, the First Being is uncausable. His earlier claim that there is something producible (*effectibile*) is made a posteriori from known singulars and not from a general principle of explicability. And so a producible actual thing is either producible by itself, from nothing or by another, exclusive options.[49] He eliminates the first two as incompatible with production and proceeds to the question of the regress, as discussed in the preceding subsection.

Still, the inquiry, as part of metaphysics, does suppose that being is explicable, but that is by presupposition (entailment as a necessary condition) and not as something cognitively prerequisite for the steps of the existence argument, which starts from something that is actually caused and is either first or from something causable. Instead, it is from the actuality of the First Being that we can deduce that every contingent being is causable.[50]

Suppose an objector says, "but maybe something could, formally, come into being *without* a cause, say a nonterminating series of ascending causes that does not 'top out'." This objection misses Scotus's point; his argument is based on the actual causation we know (say, a produced chick). His argument is not based on denying the objector's speculation; rather, it reaches such a denial only *after* its conclusion is established. So he can get to his conclusion without asserting such a general principle of causation.[51]

IV.4. About the Ways of Finality and Eminence

Scotus says that in the case of both finality and eminence the reasoning to a First Being parallels that from effective production (efficient causation). The arguments that there cannot be an infinite regress are the same as those expressed in Sections IV.1–2; and the starting point is the same: the production of some effect, say, a bird. But the fulcrum for each is different. In the order of finality, the principle is that a produced thing is aimed at something else, usually its sort, and sorts are aimed at other sorts, and so, *finibilis*, "orderable to another" (as in the food chain, ecosystems, and bodily organs). But a dependent order of natures, each ordered to another required for it, all together, has to twist up to a first, not orderable to anything else;[52] and besides, the first efficient being cannot be orderable to another because it is unproducible.[53]

Similarly, anything essentially dependent on another sort of thing is less eminent than it. But a first being cannot bc ordered to something more eminent. So a first being is not surpassable in eminence, and hence, is most eminent. That there are some things "more eminent than others" is evident from the fact that a cause of causes of a different nature has to contain the capacity of the latter by eminence (or virtually), for it is, *ex hypothesi*, of a different nature than the latter. Since there are such causes, the decisive question is whether such an order can be nonterminating. And Scotus's answer is that it cannot, for that would be contradictory to other truths, as was shown in the case of efficient causes.

The Finality and Eminence arguments have the same internal structure. For being ordered to an end and being excelled are both aliorelative, and thus, either order must end in a first that is not ordered to anything else, or the ordering is nonterminating. But then the double argument, that a nonterminating regress is impossible, applies to the latter supposition; and so, in either case, a First Being is possible, but if possible, it exists necessarily. Thus, everything in the three argument lines seems to rest on the impossibility of an infinite regress of essentially ordered causes.

But we think we have shown that Scotus's reasoning on that point is more formidable than some of his near contemporaries thought and tighter than many recent commentators have supposed. In fact, he seems to have displayed that postulating a nonterminating series of nested causing *natures* contradicts the supposition that there is an actually produced contingent thing of such a final nature.

IV.5. Embedded Argument

Perhaps the arguments are still not elementary and obvious enough. And perhaps one might wonder how much, beyond the superficial structure of argument, rests on the then unchallenged (except for discussions of future contingents) idea that all well-formed propositions are either true or false (bifurcation), and so, on whether indirect proof is valid. And even more, maybe too much rests on the principle that whatever is possible is necessarily possible, which may not follow even from the supposition of a creating necessary being.[54] Still, too much is usually expected from medieval demonstrations because of myths about how such arguments were understood and intended. For such reasoning is by no means presuppositionless, or intended to be. No one ever pretended that one argument all by itself will eliminate all possible oppositions to its conclusion without any reliance on a larger logical and metaphysical background. Such an idealization does not have any historical cases at all, not even in Euclidean geometry. Indeed, Scotus's demonstration is embedded in a nest of wider assumptions. And Scotus does not claim otherwise.

However, little of his realism about common natures and real kinds and possibilities, his "active-principle" notion of causation, his commitment to real forms (like programs in things),[55] his understanding of real natures as active dispositions, his notions of individuation, of the certainty of perceptual knowledge, and the like, is explicitly mentioned or used until after the necessary existence of the First Being has been concluded. Yet it is obvious that the proof depends on there being real common natures, known to us, and upon absolute (formal) possibilities and necessities and various unchallenged principles of logic as well as active causal principles in nature.

So evaluation of his demonstration has to be against objections coherent with his backgrounding assumptions and not put against the wavering demands of competing philosophies in general, for instance, critical idealist theories (Kant), or nominalist views of kinds (say, Quine), or purely sentential views of possibility and necessity, each of which would deny some key element of his presuppositions. And certainly one cannot read his modal logic as an instance of any version of quantified modal logic to be found prominently today; the resemblance is, as we remarked, only superficial.

Scotus's argument has to be evaluated nowadays, not as to how effective it is at changing convictions (for it was not intended for changing convictions about the conclusion even then, but as to how effective it was at eliminating all other options) but as to how excellent his craftsmanship is at deriving his conclusions against his general background. That is how we appraise arguments generally. Beyond that, for those who share the broad realism and cognitive confidence of Scotus, the argument may still, as it were, "put a lock" on the conclusion that there is a divine, infinite being, or, at the least, be "probative,"[56] that is, highly likely and persuasive – which is about the best we get in philosophy for anything beyond a mere technicality.[57]

We think the wonderments at the end of Section III do not bite; the really interesting difficulties are over (1) whether anything really is contingent, and (2) whether we can reduce to contradiction the speculation that the cosmos as a whole is an unexplained and inexplicable phenomenon. If Scotus is right that the latter is a contradiction (and it would have to be if God is possible), and that the former is evident, then making his reasoning decisive against its background seems to be a matter of fine-tuning. Disagreements would have to shift to disputes about elements of the background, that is, to a quite different part of general metaphysics and of natural philosophy and logic.

To summarize, then, tracking *Ord.* 1, d. 2, qq. 1–2, n. 43: something is produced, so something is of a sort that is producible; that sort itself is either producible or not. If it is, then there is either an interminable regress of producers (of caused sorts) for it, all of which act together (like the embedded natural bodily organs, cells, molecular, atomic, subatomic, etc., energy-particle systems . . .), or there is a First Producing Sort. An unending regress is inconsistent with the being of the actual and producible effect.[58] So a First Being (nature), able to produce others, but itself unproducible, is possible; therefore, it exists. For such a thing cannot be *merely* possible because (1) the original effect would not exist and (2) such a thing would not be unproducible.[59] But if existing, it is necessarily existing, for the supposition that that sort of thing is possible but not existing leads to a contradiction.

V. THE NATURE OF THE FIRST PRINCIPLE OF BEING

Scotus determines the intrinsic attributes of the First Being by figuring out, a posteriori, what features a thing must have in order to produce the effects we perceive. He explicitly renounces deduction a priori of the attributes from the idea that God has all pure perfections, mainly because of the uncertainty whether particular predicates are genuinely consistent and genuinely each "better than any denominative characteristic incompatible with it."[60] The "absolute," nondenominative divine attributes include necessity, uniqueness, simplicity, intelligence and omniscience, freedom, omnipotence, creation, and infinity. The order of reasoning in each case is structurally the same: an indirect proof deriving an inconsistency between the denial of the attribute in question and something already known to be true.[61] We next sketch some of his derivations and indicate his distinctive interpretations of the attributes.

V.1. Necessity

Necessity follows from primacy. "Nothing can be non-existent unless something either positively or privatively incompatible with it *can* exist."[62] And "nothing can be positively or privatively incompatible with a being that exists of itself and is uncaused."[63] Therefore, it cannot *not* exist. A "largest natural number" is positively inconsistent with "there is a successor by one to every natural number" (positively incompatible), but, of course, such a thing is not possible; and "being a human mother" is privatively incompatible with "being a male human" by some preventing cause.[64] An indirect proof (a destructive dilemma) is as follows: (1) suppose there could exist something logically incompatible with the First Being; an absurdity follows: that "two incompatible entities will coexist, or rather neither will because each will cancel the other."[65] Instead, (2) suppose something could prevent the First Being from existing. That, too, is inconsistent because the uncausable would have to be causable (preventable). As a result, a First Efficient Cause cannot be a contingent thing. Thus, it must be something that exists necessarily.

V.2. Unicity and Uniqueness

The first being in each explanatory order (efficient and final causation, and priority by eminence) must exist necessarily, by application of the same reasoning to each. But is the first in each order the same being as that which is first in the others?[66] Scotus reasons as follows: If there were several, they would each be necessary by one common feature, by one nature; so there could not be a plurality of first beings. For any feature by which one might be supposed to differ from the others cannot be a feature an *a se* thing has as such and thus must be either an additional contingent feature or an additional necessary feature. Again an indirect proof (a destructive dilemma) is offered. Suppose (1) the difference is contingent; then the being is a composite and causable – a contradiction with its being First. Suppose (2) that differences are necessary to each; then each lacks some essential feature that some thing, one of the others, has on account of being necessary, and so, is not necessary: another contradiction with what has been established. Thus, on any relevant supposition, a contradiction results from denying that the First Beings in the distinct orders are one and the same being.

V.3. The First Principle Has All Pure Perfections[67]

A pure perfection requires no limitation on the part of the thing to have it and excludes no other positive feature that requires no limitation: for example, "to live," "to be," and "to understand." As a result, all pure perfections are compatible with one another, and thus there can be a thing that has all such perfections on account of what it is. But if there can be such a thing, there must be. Still, what can be concluded from that, as to particular attributes, is limited by the unreliability of our mere conceptions to ensure possibility.

V.4. Simplicity

Scotus agreed with other theologians that God's unconditional actuality rules out his having parts, composition of act and potency, or any real distinction as to substance.[68] But he argues that there can still be real difference without real distinction among God's attributes.[69] For among things distinct in conception, there are some that, though inseparably realized in God's case, are separately definable and separately realized among finite things, like the attributes of rationality, goodness, and wisdom. Moreover, the tendencies of the prudent man are distinct from those of the intelligent man, even when they coincide. So the attributes cannot be *only* conceptually and definitionally distinct.

Moreover, the *unity* of the infinite being is more than that of mere simplicity (lack of composition); Scotus says, "simplicity is simply a perfection," but "it does not follow that every simple creature is more perfect than those not simple."[70] In addition, "actuality is simply a perfection," and "actuality is simply more perfect than simplicity."[71] The infinite being has the unity of "complete actuality." The degree of a being's actuality matters more than its simplicity to its perfection and unity. The necessarily first, being *a se*, maximizes actuality: it is all that it could be.

For this and other purposes in metaphysics and theology, Scotus reasoned that there is often a difference in reality that is not great enough to amount to a real distinction but is greater than a merely conceptual–definitional distinction; it is, rather, "a formal distinction on the part of the thing" (*distinctio formalis a parte rei*). For instance, he thought there are features that really differ and are sometimes separately realizable (like wisdom and justice) even though actual inseparably in the unity of one being, the way the intuitive and the deductive intelligence might belong to a single person. Such formally distinct items are (1) separately knowable (at least one without the other, differing in definition where definition is appropriate); (2) their difference is real independently of our thought;[72] (3) none can, in a given thing "exist on its own" independently of the other(s); and (4) each is "perfectly the same" as its related items in the same being, so that even an omnipotent being cannot remove such copresent items from one another. The diverse divine attributes are in that way formally distinct, yet really the same in being. So, too, are the human nature and the individuation of Socrates.

Scotus thinks a contradiction would result if we regarded the divine perfections as no more than distinct through our conceptions, because "if infinite wisdom were infinite goodness, then wisdom in common, formally would be goodness in common."[73] They could not, then, occur separately as they do: so "wisdom in the thing is not formally goodness in the thing."[74] Thus, there must be a distinction in reality, but less than the distinction of separable elements or elements related as potentiality to act (real distinction). Note that he uses the following argument form: what entails the false, is false.

V.5. Analogy of Meaning vs. Univocity

What then of the meanings of the words we use to describe God, like "wise," "loving," "intelligent," and "living"? Do they mean the same things as when applied to creatures? Thomas Aquinas says no: as to the verbal definitions, the *res significata*, yes, they are the same; but as to the *modus significandi*, no.[75] For the thing signified, the meaning, follows the definitions of our words, but the manner of attribution (*modus significandi*) is contracted from the *modus essendi* (the manner of being) of what is referred to (God, or creature).[76] That is the analogy of proper proportionality, like the contextual capture when you say "the paper *turned red* with spilled ink," "his face *turned red* with embarrassment," and "the sky *turned red* with the dawn"; the signification, the verbal meaning, "*turned red,*" is the same, but the manner, the *modus significandi*, differs according to the different ways the reddening happens. So, Aquinas said, it is with God and creatures; and thus, there is no univocation of positive predicates, only analogy (relatedness of meaning).

Scotus rejects that idea. The mode of being of the referent is not part of the meaning of the words. Indeed, the intrinsic modes of being of creatures and God differ (see Section V.12, "Infinity"), but that does not affect the words; he says, "infinity does not destroy the formal nature of that to which it is added."[77] Scotus thinks the differences of mode of signification that do track the different modes of being of what we are talking about are *not* part of the conceptions (the meanings) of what we predicate but are extralinguistic – "modes of referring," as we might call the differences now. So theirs is a difference in philosophy of language that overflows into natural theology (though the order of suggestion might be the reverse). For Scotus sameness of definition is enough for sameness of meaning. Thus, the divine perfections are univocally predicated of creatures and God.

V.6. Intelligence

The intelligence of the First Being does not derive from some prior explanatory trait: "Intellectuality is the primary nature of intelligent being, constituting it in such being, and nothing exists in the thing essentially prior to that, by which this can be shown of it."[78] So it has to be established a posteriori, as a condition of the free agency required for the production of something contingent by a being that is necessary. The First Being is "a *per se* agent,"[79] that is, an agent on account of itself – nothing else moves it to action. But "every *per se* cause acts because of an end."[80] Yet this agent cannot act for an end naturally determined, because the effect is contingent, whereas the agent acts necessarily. It must act by choice. But such an agent does not act "because of an end it naturally chooses, or wants without cognition."[81] So it has to be intelligent.

V.7. The Extent of Divine Knowledge

Scotus accords with theologians generally in saying God knows whatever can be known: "To be able to know actually and distinctly each and every other thing that can be known is something that pertains to the perfection of knowledge."[82] But he is more expansive than some (for instance, Aquinas as we interpret him) about what can be known antecedently to any divine election. For example, he holds that the entire realm of possibility is determined by the divine self-understanding, with no possibility dependent on the divine will, and includes all unrealized possibilities and unelected choices as well as uncreated natures and individuals in all their particularity. So he takes quite literally Augustine's claim (De Civ. Dei 15) that God has proper ideas of all that is or might have been made.

The basic argumentation for such a realm of divine omniscience is that it is a necessary condition for the free creation of all contingent being. As we said, freedom in the cause is required for contingency in the effects of a necessary being. But knowledge of possibilities is required for free choice, with the extent of the knowledge being the whole of what is possible, both the necessary and the contingent. Yet the only way a divine being could have such knowledge, logically antecedently to creation, is by knowing itself directly and completely. Thus, Scotus takes without exception that God "knows everything intelligible actually and distinctly"[83] by nature and antecedently to any election.

That differs fundamentally from Aquinas,[84] who, on our account, thinks the possibilities, particularly the natural kinds, the regularities of nature, and the individuation of things are not fully determinate from the divine self-knowledge but are created along with the things[85] and the individuals, and there are no empty natures or merely possible individuals, even in divine conception (in Scotus's esse intelligibile of haecceities[86]). So what there might have been, instead of what is, including how some actual things might have acted, is indeterminate, apart from divine elections, and unknowable. Scotus disagrees.[87]

He thinks God has from eternity a complete idea (concept) of each creature, say Adam, that includes everything Adam does, might have done, had happen, and so on, but not with the effect that every feature of the creature is essential to it (as Leibniz later thought). No. Scotus holds very emphatically that humans, even when they act one way freely, are still, in the very act, actively able to choose the opposite. (It is like a pianist who, even while striking one key, is able to strike a different one.) Yet there is nothing knowable about creatures that God does not know through himself from eternity. In brief, the difference we attribute to Scotus and Aquinas is that Scotus thinks all possibility, down to the smallest detail, has determinate content from the divine self-knowledge logically antecedently to any creation.

V.8. Multiplicity of Divine Ideas?

Aquinas had denied any real multiplicity of divine ideas by saying the ideas are denominated (counted) by us from the multiplicity of the objects created and are at most virtually (as the less perfect is contained in the more perfect) distinct in God. Furthermore, for him, there is a difference between ideas of things that are made[88] and ideas for things that might have been made but never are made.[89] Scotus says there is real multiplicity among formally distinct divine ideas and does not make a distinction between eternal ideas for things that are made and those that are not because even individuals are eternally known as possible: "the singular is *per se* intelligible as far as it itself goes."[90]

That discards Aquinas's idea that material individuation is consequent on matter with determinate quantity, and so individuation is not, as such, anything intelligible and not, as such, anything before creation. Scotus says that whatever can be made, "whether in another, or an absolute being, or a relation" is an object "that can be known distinctly by the divine intellect."[91] Why? "Since another intellect can know this being distinctly, and it can be an object distinctly knowable by a created intellect."[92] Otherwise, something knowable would not be known as possible, prior to divine willing, by God. So "every such positive being has a distinct idea." Hence, while for Aquinas it might be indeterminate without a divine choice whether there might have been humans with plastic intestines, star-sized tomatoes, or electrons that think, for Scotus that has to be eternally determinate.

Some differences between Scotus and Aquinas about features of the divine knowledge can be traced to their divergent views about universals and natures. Scotus says the common nature, say, 'humanity', has true "real being outside the soul; that is, the common nature has the being proper to it independently of any operation of an intellect."[93] He discards Aquinas's position that the common nature has no reality of its own apart from the understanding where it is abstracted from particulars in which it is wholly individuated. Instead, for Scotus, common natures are *in re* explanatorily (naturally) prior to individual being and have the created status, *esse essentiae*, as conditions of the real possibility of the things that come to be; they are knowable as common natures by both humans and God, abstracted from particulars by humans, and in eternal understanding (*esse intelligibile*) by God.

V.9. Instants

To escape confusion about the apparent multiplicity of stages of divine knowledge, Scotus used the metaphor of instants, succession without separation or interval, to indicate how the diverse knowledge of the essences of all creatures, actual and possible, and divine reflexive awareness of what is known, and divine awareness of the divine knowing itself, can all exist at once, though ordered, in one perfect being who knows by nature only its own being.[94] The divine knowing is something ontologically simple but logically complex. The "instants" are phases of logical order, not phases of experience or events. They are like "exploding" drawings of one machine, "there all at once" but distinct by internal contrast dependence and "natural order." The order of such "instants" is the order of logical priority that he calls natural priority.[95] In some cases, where he uses the same metaphor, for instance, for the relationship of common nature to individuation, the order of natural priority is an order of explanatory priority as well, and in some cases, that order is one of real posteriority, as with creation.

Creation is, from the divine standpoint, eternal.[96] Time is a dimension of the created world; all time is of the world, for all change is in creatures. Similarly, a (nonautobiographical) novel has its own internal time but no real connection to the (temporal) activity of its author. Even more obviously, musical time is internal to musical compositions and can be transported with them, and has at most conventional relationships to cosmic time. (You can play "Three Blind Mice" one note per millennium, just as long as the intervals remain harmonically and rhythmically proportional – there is no time relationship of the progressing notes to the being of the composer.) Thus, for the First Being to understand its time-bound and contingent creatures is as much eternal and without succession as is its own being; the condition of being known is successive in the creatures. (See the discussion of divine freedom, Section V.11.)

V.10. Omnipotence

The power to cause some contingent being (known a posteriori) has to be the power to cause any contingent being whatever, since only one being can have such power and all contingent being is causable. That power is called omnipotence, "that active power or potency whose scope extends to anything whatever that can be created."[97] The First Being, the ultimate cause of all contingent things, has to be omnipotent, that is, able to cause whatever is possible and not necessary.[98] Furthermore, unlike any other thing, whatever is consistently conceivable to God is really possible because of the perfection of divine knowledge. It is the power to bring about whatever is not repugnant to being-as-such. Scotus says, "it can be concluded naturally that it [the First Being] is omnipotent."[99]

Creation requires the ability to make "an immediate effect,"[100] that is, something that does not require a prior effect. Otherwise, God would be unable to cause anything, since "if between that caused effect and God there is another more immediate effect, and before that another, there will be a progress to infinity in *per se* ordered causes, and consequently absolutely nothing would be able to cause."[101] But it does not follow from that that God can create just anything immediately.

Scotus distinguishes two senses of "omnipotence." In one sense, an agent is omnipotent "which can do anything possible either with mediation or immediately, and in this way omnipotence is an active power primarily of efficiency."[102] This can be derived from the requirement that the divine being be free (spontaneous; see Section V.11), in order for there to be any contingent thing at all, and omnipotent in that such power has to extend to whatever is possible. And since this requires that the First Being cause something immediately, it is natural to ask whether the omnipotent being can cause directly everything it can cause through secondary causes. He calls that "omnipotence proper, as Catholics understand the term."[103] That mode of almighty power cannot be demonstrated,[104] though it is revealed in the Faith. There is a reason for this, namely, that in general, "in the order of superior and inferior causes, this does not follow, since even if the sun had in itself causality more eminent than a cow or any other animal has, still it is not conceded that the sun can immediately generate the cow."[105] So the general principle that the higher cause, acting though secondary causes, can directly produce its effects without such causes is not true. Thus, there is no known premise from which to conclude that the First Being can do immediately whatever it can do through secondary causes.

Now the impossible is not made to be so by the divine will but by the repugnance of things that are possible one by one, *in esse intelligibili*, to combine to "make one thing,"[106] like the head of a man and the body of a lion. Those items do not so combine in the divine understanding but only in the human imagination. So if "thinking electrons" are impossible, granting that each part is possible, the combination harbors an inconsistency (or a de facto repugnance) that may not be conceptually accessible to us but is to God. So God is not to be considered unable to produce such things, but such things, although the parts are possible, cannot make a whole and, so, cannot be. (Aquinas holds the same view, *ST* I.25.3: the impossible is not a limitation on God's power but what cannot be at all.) Notice, the impossible with content is directly a product of human imagination (a figment: *fingere*).[107] Thus, apart from imagining creatures, there are no impossibilities with content at all.

It cannot be demonstrated either that the world is in fact created without a beginning in time or that there is a beginning in time. For both are within the power of God. Because some effect has to be immediate for there to be any contingent being, time is not required for divine effects. So it is possible that there is no beginning of time within creation: "novelty can be in the divine production because of the novelty in the thing produced, although there is no novelty in the producing thing."[108] But God can also produce temporally ordered effects with a temporal beginning that has no temporal relation to God at all. So the Christian belief that the world had a beginning in time is not in conflict with any demonstrable truth but cannot itself be demonstrated.

Next, some points have to be distinguished to avoid contradictions. Obviously, an omnipotent being cannot solely cause something whose very description involves a secondary cause, for example, "an oration by Cicero." But the same sort of thing, a "Ciceronian oration" described by its qualities and not by its particular causes, can indeed be produced directly. But what of the actions we ascribe to creatures, which Muslim Occasionalists think are caused directly and only by God? Scotus wants to dislodge that while leaving open the Christian understanding of divine direct power. So he distinguishes between direct divine causation that preempts the natural consequence of a creature disposed to cause such effects – which God can do by intervening – and what he wants to exclude: divine causation that eliminates the dispositions, the ability, of creatures to cause such effects. For the latter is the Muslim Occasionalists' view: that no creatures perform any transitive actions of their own at all; all events are directly caused by God but in the manner that displays what we regard as natural order,[109] so that nothing naturally produces anything at all; thus, there are no active principles in nature[110] and "no being has any natural action of its own. . . . They have no essences of their own."[111] Scotus says that is not possible, for the outcome would contradict the evident fact that there are active secondary causes. The divine omnipotence not only includes the power to intervene in the created order but also the power to have acted entirely outside the created order: "So I say that God can not only act other than is ordered in particular cases, but otherwise than the universal order, or even the laws of justice."[112] Thus, things that are impossible and even inaccessible from the created order lie within the absolute power of God.

V.11. The Freedom of the First Being

Now one cannot prove by a demonstration from something cognitively prior that things exist contingently: contingency in things "can be proved. . . neither by something more evident, nor *a priori*."[113]

But one need not prove it either because it is obvious that things perceived do not exist on account of what they are and thus might not have been at all.[114] From that beginning, Scotus concludes that the First Being does not by nature, as Avicenna thought, necessitate other things (by emanation); thus, it must cause contingently, and so, freely.[115] A contradiction would follow from supposing that the First Being exists necessarily and causes by nature (as Avicenna proposed), yet what it causes is contingent. For that would cancel the contingency of things[116] and reduce them to necessities.

The contingency of the effects cannot originate with First Being's intellect, since "anything it [the intellect] knows before the act of the will, it knows necessarily and naturally, so that there is no contingency in relation to opposites here."[117] Thus, the First Being has to have a power to operate that is distinct from its intellect, namely, the power of free will. For "the first distinction of active power is according to the different ways of eliciting an operation," and if the active power is not "determined *ex se*," then "it . . . can perform this act, or the opposite act, and so act or not act,"[118] which is freedom.

In a word, for there to be contingent being, there must be a being that exists *a se* and acts freely.[119] There are three focal features of free will for Scotus: (1) the power to choose is neutral to the outcomes, which, for God, are absolute possibilities; (2) the will remains able to choose the contrary while actually in the choice of the opposite; and (3) there is no explanation of the choosing except the ability, as such, to do so.

1. Neutrality: the divine intellect "understands it [any such complex] as neutral."[120] The neutrality is not impeded by the divine immutability (unchangeability) because neutrality and preserved ability to do the opposite do not require an ability to change what you do. "The divine will can only have one single volition"; but the First Being's will "can be related to opposite objects" in the immutable act of its single volition.[121] Scotus says, "the divine will, of which its being operational precedes its being productive, can also will and not-will something, and . . . can produce and not-produce something at the same moment of eternity. . . . The potency is not temporally before the act, neither is the potency with the act, but the potency is prior by nature with regard to the

act."[122] He explains that a "potency is only logical, when the terms are possible in such a way that they are not repugnant to one another, but can be united, even though there is no possibility in reality."[123] For example, it was true that there can be a world even "before there was a world," but the possibility of a world before there was a world was merely logical, since "there was no factual reality which corresponded to the terms."[124]

2. The will's remaining able to choose the opposite at the very moment of choosing as it does is a key idea for Scotus. About the contingent in general, he says, "by 'contingent' I do not mean something that is not necessary or which was not always in existence, but something whose opposite could have occurred at the time this actually did."[125] Just as the occurrence of an event does not render the opposite impossible, so the choice of an act does not render the opposite impossible. On the contrary, it remains possible. So the person, able to do the opposite, remains able to do the opposite, just as one lifting his arm is still actively able not to, though, of course, not able to do both at once. There is no further explanation of a free election beyond the ability to make it: "Just as there is no reason why this being has this mode of being except that it is that sort of thing, so also there is no reason why this agent has this mode of action (i.e., free, though necessary) except that it is this sort of active principle."[126] And the only explanation of an individual choice is in the ability to make it.

   Now this is very important to his natural theology because the whole explanatory pattern would collapse if there were some further explanation to be sought, say, in some reason or understanding, for the divine elections. Scotus's unique answer is that the explanation of the elections by freedom of will is in what the will is just as the explanation of why a thing is a fish is in its form.

3. A free action is spontaneous: it originates entirely from the ability to do it. He gave as an example of a free election one's simply stopping consideration of the other alternatives.[127] Free election is from the ability of the agent, undetermined, and from its form, within the range of its ability, unexplained

by any other factor at all, whether reason, motive, justification, or aim. In a free act, the will is the total cause of the action: "nothing other than the will is the total cause of volition in the will."[128]

Free action is entirely from the will (*voluntas*).[129] It is an ability that, although within the agent's understanding, is not determined by what is understood; it does not have an explanation from outside it. Nor is free choice a consequence of other features, like absence of obstacles, a possible object, a sufficient reason for so acting, and so forth. Freedom is spontaneity of acting from the ability, alone, to do so. (One can see why Scotus thinks divine grace confers freedom in the most important sense, as Augustine thought (*De libero arbitrio*), because it restores to the sinful person the ability "to act rightly," or as Anselm called it, "the ability to keep uprightness of the will for its own sake.") What we call the "spontaneity" element of free will contrasts markedly with the "activity in accord with the predominant understood good" (Aristotelian) notion of freedom that seems more prominent in Aquinas and leaves his explanatory order of divine action incomplete.

Scotus distinguishes features in what Aquinas acknowledged as necessity of will by separating necessity of nature from necessity of inevitability from perfection. Scotus says there is a necessity of inevitability from the perfection of the divine willing power,[130] but "there is no necessity of nature involved" in divine self-love, acting rightly, living, and so forth. For "necessity of nature" is definitionally opposed to "acting freely": "the will *per se* is never an active principle that acts naturally"[131]; "it can no more be naturally active than nature, as other than will, can be freely active." It is not that the beatified's loving God is not inevitable or that God's acting rightly is not inevitable; in both cases there *is* the ability to act otherwise, but the willing is inevitable because of the perfection of the agent and not because of its natural order that takes away election.[132]

However, there seems to be a philosophical "loose end" as to whether it *is* immediately evident that free will is "spontaneity" of action explained only by the ability so to act. For that would leave an irresolvable dispute with an Aristotelian. Scotus says free action

cannot be explained, as an ability, from some prior element of the being, any more than intelligence is. Is it self-evident that we humans
have that ability? It is obvious, however, that such an ability must
be attributed to God in order to avoid a regress in searching for "sufficient reasons" to account for divine free choice. The "loose end"
issue concerns where philosophy "bottoms out" in first principles.
Could one, perhaps, reason that such spontaneity is an analyzable
precondition of the empirically obvious suitability of human action
for moral praise and blame, reinforced by the failure of other theories
to explain wrongdoing as a result either of ignorance or weakness?
Not that the latter is cognitively prior, as something that must be
known first, but rather, prior in the order of our cognitive experience
by which we are sure spontaneity is a necessary condition?

V.12. Infinity

Scotus considers "infinite being" the most proper (suitable or fitting)
characterization of the divine being:[133] it stands to 'being' as 'intense
whiteness' stands to 'white', not as a kind but as a mode. He says,
"infinite is not a quasi-attribute or property of 'being' or of that of
which it is predicated," but rather "it signifies an intrinsic mode of
that entity."[134] For "if an entity is finite or infinite, it is not so by
reason of something incidental to itself, but because it has its own
intrinsic degree of finite or infinite perfection, respectively."[135] "As
'being' virtually includes the 'good' and the 'true,' so 'infinite being' includes the 'infinitely good', 'the infinitely true', and all pure
perfections under the aspect of infinity."[136] The divine infinity is
manifested from intensively infinite creative power. Note we say
"manifested," not "constituted," for infinity is a mode of being, not
a sort of power. The First Being's power "would be [intensively] infinite, because...it has power enough to produce an infinite number
all at once, and the more one can produce simultaneously, the greater
the power in intensity."[137] Why? That is because the higher cause
virtually contains, in its being, all that is actual in any essentially
dependent cause. For "the full causal power that each thing may have
in itself, the First Being possesses even more perfectly than if it were
formally present."[138] For "where each of the things in question needs
some perfection proper to itself," the more things that can be produced, the greater the perfection of the producer.[139] Infinity is not,

however, just the extent of the power but the positive mode of being required for such power. "We, nevertheless, understand infinity negatively."[140] And "even where the nature of the effect was such as to make its simultaneous existence in an infinite number impossible," it would still follow that the primary agent is infinite in power, "provided that, so far as the causal power of the agent is concerned, it could produce simultaneously an infinite multitude."[141] Among the five reasons why God is infinite in being given in *De primo principio* (4.48–63), Scotus concludes by observing that whatever is possibly infinite is actually infinite (4.63). And he says that, although it cannot be proved a priori that 'being' and 'infinity' are compatible, this is deducible from both omniscience and omnipotence.[142]

VI. IMMORTALITY OF THE SOUL

Scotus holds that we cannot know naturally, and a fortiori cannot demonstrate, that the human soul is immortal, and even less that there will be a resurrection of the dead. He acknowledges that understanding requires activity that cannot be performed by a bodily organ, and that such activity is naturally human. For "intellection properly speaking is a knowledge which transcends all sense knowledge," since intellection is not limited to a certain kind of sensible like colored things; but any cognitive act with an organ would be so limited.[143] We know from experience that we "possess some knowledge of an object under an aspect it could not have as an object of sense knowledge," as for instance when "we experience in ourselves that we know the actual universal."[144]

Nevertheless, it does not follow, as Aristotle apparently thought and Aquinas claimed, from our understanding's not employing a bodily organ, as sight does, that the soul, whose power it is, is immortal. It only follows that the intellect is "incapable of dissolution in the same sense that an organic power is corruptible."[145] But, still, the soul may cease to exist not by separation of organic parts but simply because, as could occur with angels, "its existence is succeeded by the opposite of existence."[146] Because its operation is "proper to the composite as a whole," that is, it is the human as a whole human who understands, and this composite is perishable, then "its operative principle [the intellectual soul] is also perishable."[147] Besides, Scotus is as definite as Aquinas on this: the soul is not the person but the form of a person. The person is the incommunicable *suppositum* of the rational nature and for that is required the haecceity (the final individuation). So we cannot demonstrate that persons will survive death. He does not discuss, nor does Aquinas, whether by natural faith in the order of nature we could be rationally certain of personal survival.

A fortiori, it follows that we cannot naturally know that there will be, or even can be, a resurrection of the dead. For "the soul, so far as its own being is concerned, is equally perfect whether it is separated from or joined to a body."[148] So there is no natural necessity for the soul to be embodied once it has come to be. It may have a disposition to be the proper form of a body, yet even if that disposition were "forever suspended," "nothing unnatural" would be implied, since no imperfection in its existence would be implied.[149] Since the First Being contingently and freely elects to create, we cannot demonstrate that God will resurrect human beings or that he will not create individuated human souls for the entire course of their existence without bodies at all.

VII. PARTING THOUGHTS ON SCOTUS'S NATURAL THEOLOGY

If one is realistic, not simplistic, about what a demonstration amounts to and what a medieval Aristotelian intended, namely, a deduction from surely known premises, which for Scotus are also necessary, to equally certain conclusions, one recognizes there are no demonstrations without background presuppositions. Scotus's include logical commitments (for example, to bifurcation and to iterative modalities[150]), metaphysical ones (to forms, real common natures, active causal principles), and epistemological ones (as to the role of self-evidence and demonstration, probable reasoning, and the like). Given that, Scotus does as well showing the existence of a First Explanatory Being as any philosopher has ever done on any substantive point. He also displays masterly craftsmanship on many aspects of the divine nature – particularly in his originality about what divine freedom involves and how it terminates the explanatory inquiry without begging any question.

We emphasized the a posteriori character of Scotus's reasoning because his constant talk of possibility and necessity might lead our contemporaries to regard him as an a priorist about God's existence. It may confuse things to regard Scotus as one advocating "modal arguments" for the existence of God as such arguments were understood in the late twentieth century, for those, like Plantinga's and Malcolm's, are a priori arguments, that is, arguments that do not depend on premises from experience.[151] Scotus's argumentation about both the existence and the nature of God is grounded in our experiences of the production, function, and eminence of things that might not have been at all. Moreover, his notions of modality are not semantic ones but are rooted in the capacities of being and do not rest on a quantificational logic that is extensional in the way first-order quantification is nowadays.

Nevertheless, there seem to be two central points that need further support than he provides: (1) that there are active causal principles in nature, like forms and efficient causes, as well as some things essentially ordered by finality and by eminence; and (2) that anything at all exists contingently – the very point on which he departs from Avicenna. He regards both as indemonstrable because there is nothing explanatorily prior to either. So they may have to be argued by refutation internally of the opponents. (He did that sort of thing in Theoremata.) But there may also be features that, from general experience, can be used to dislodge error about those points.

The first, that there are active principles in nature, is outright denied by many major philosophers since the seventeenth century, as we pointed out; but that, of course, is no reason to doubt Scotus, especially since their reasons are flimsy and conflict with the accomplishments of the very physical sciences they revere. Still, refutation of common opinion on such points does not have to be deductive; it can be by better explanations in natural science than the others can offer, and in that respect his argumentation should be supplemented for our time.

And the second principle, that there are contingent things, is pretty much enthusiastically affirmed by recent philosophers (though notably not by David Lewis), but on the even flimsier ground that everything might have happened by chance or for no reason at all. Scotus was quite impatient with silliness. But it is such an important metaphysical matter, involving the key rejection of Avicenna in favor of a central Christian commitment to creation (that perceived things might not have existed at all), that it needs some philosophical justification. Even allowing Scotus's claim that there is nothing explanatorily prior from which to deduce contingency, it can be supported by explanations that "emanation," and the like, is internally incoherent. Aquinas proposed to refute Avicenna by showing that his doctrine of the relationship of being and essence in creatures was incoherent. Perhaps there is reasoning elsewhere by Scotus that will do that as well. In any case, such a premise, that some things really are contingent (but that everything could not be), needs some special support in light of its conflict with Avicenna and later with Spinoza.[152]

The final remarks about immortality of the soul illustrate Scotus's originality again and indicate the variety of other topics in natural theology that he treated, including future contingents, divine foreknowledge, the end of the world, and other points not included here.

NOTES

1 That is the order of the main philosophical work, *De primo principio*. That work itself is a compilation, more than half of it word for word, of parts of other things, but from the hand of Duns Scotus. See Wolter 1996, xi. In the other three treatments, *Ordinatio, Reportatio, and Lectura*, all three mainly theological, the order of derivation of divine attributes is from primacy of being to infinity and then to necessity.

2 Wolter 1966, xviii.

3 A recent a priori argument can be found in Plantinga 1974.

4 He accepts "bifurcation": that every well-formed proposition is either true or false, so that, if "not-p" entails a contradiction, then "p" is true. See note 6.

5 *De primo princ.* 3.8.

6 His key reasoning is threatened by a proof that bifurcation does not hold universally, for then, indirect proof is not valid (cf. Dummett 1991). However, his arguments can be reinstated with an additional supposition that the relevant subclass of propositions is bivalent.

7 *De primo princ.* 4.22.

8 *Rep.* 2, d. 1, q. 3, n. 9.

9 "On the First Principle." The standard usage of "principle" in the thirteenth century is "that from which anything proceeds in any way whatever." The First Principle (God) is the explanatory origin of all else by free causation and eminence, and of all being, as such, by its actual infinity. See Wolter 1966, xiii.

10 *In Metaph.* prol., n. 5, trans. Wolter 1993, 2.

11 *Ord.* 1, d. 8, q. 3, trans. Wolter 1993, 3.

12 *De primo princ.* 1.2, trans. Wolter 1966, 2.

13 *De primo princ.* 1.5, trans. Wolter 1966, 2 (italics added).

14 *De primo princ.* 4.2.

15 Gilson seems unduly troubled that the conception of God might have a religious origin (Gilson 1952, 187). The description Scotus uses in his philosophy is framed entirely in terms of metaphysical conceptions: causes and eminence, possibility and necessity. Even his prayer is full of philosophical terminology.

16 We use the phrase "present to the understanding" to convey that a concept is like a lens through which the understanding can think of things; it is an ability of a thinker rather than a label on things. A univocal concept is like a fixed lens; an analogous one is like self-focusing binoculars that adjust to bring the different objects into focus.

17 See Wolter 1966, xv.

18 See the discussion reported in Gilson 1952, 673, and his report of even an Ockhamist interpretation of this work, 674.

19 Gilson 1952, 673, says the *Theoremata* is the "apple of discord" among Scotus interpreters. Much effort was spent on trying to give interpretations concordant with his general doctrines and some were offered that really did consider that he might have changed his mind on his central points (cf. Wolter 1966). Todd Bates, an author here, originated the idea that this work defends Scotus's position on the univocity of being, which is also treated in *Collationes Parisienses*: see Gilson 1952, 674. This work fits with a line of anti-Averroist works from Albertus Magnus, Aquinas, Giles of Rome, and four works by Raymond Lull cited in Copleston 1985, 441, all rejecting key Latin Averroist positions that are anti-Christian. Some of the earlier theorems suggest there may be other objectives as well. That accords with the hostility of his reference to "that accursed Averroës" in *Op. Ox.* 4, d. 43, q. 2, n. 5 (trans. Wolter 1993, 138).

20 Such terms are definitionally interdependent but not mere negations of one another; each has a positive element as does "negative integer" versus "positive integer." Scotus says infinity is a positive mode of being that we, however, comprehend negatively: "nos autem, intelligimus infinitatem negative," from *Doctor subtilis de cognitione Dei*: ms. published in Harris 1927 and cited in Gilson 1952, 192.

21 That accords with the section of *Collationes Parisienses* on whether there is a univocal concept of being. See Gilson 1952, 674, n. 4.

22 Other writers like Aquinas had thought of such series implicitly, having distinguished accidentally ordered causes as well.

23 Wolter 1954, 95.

24 See Alluntis 1965 and Wood 1987.

25 See Brady 1954, 134, commenting on the responses of fourteenth-century commentators: "All recognize the premise of the processus of causes in infinitum is vital to the proof."

26 A coloration was an amendment to another's argument to deflect an obvious objection (Gaunilo's perfect island), but not, by itself, an endorsement. Alluntis thinks Scotus regarded the colorized version as a probable argument (Alluntis 1966, 166). We think he regards it as conclusive for a believer but conjectural for a philosopher.

27 *De primo princ.* 4.22; *Ord.* 1, d. 8, q. 1, nn. 22–25. For him the terms of a proposition (a thought content capable of truth or falsity) present *realities, as conceived,* to judgment; as a result, what is presented in a consistent conception may in fact harbor an inconsistency (cf. Alluntis 1966, 167).

28 It is mistaken to compare formal possibility, which he sometimes calls logical and rational, as if it has anything to do with what is fashionable today. Formal possibility does not guarantee conceptual consistency-for-us (for some people can conceive of the possible (e.g., transubstantiation) as impossible), and we can regard as consistent, as possible (e.g., Descartes's option of human minds without any external world at all, or "uncaused cosmos"), what is really and formally impossible. See other supporting comments in text and notes. So judgments of consistency are not reliable as to formal possibility.

29 Philosophers of religion sometimes adapt the line of reasoning to a new context or try to refine what they take to be "the real strength or force" of what Scotus is doing (cf. Loux 1984; also, Ross 1968). But it is a different matter when one is saying what Scotus said.

30 He does not let "the satanic notation whisper the ontology" (cf. Ross 1989, 271). He acknowledges no domain of "all possible worlds," or of world-relative actuality (as in David Lewis), or "states of affairs."

31 *Ord.* 1, d. 2, q. 1, n. 44.

32 *Ord.* 1, d. 2, q. 1, n. 46.

33 Cf. Brady 1954.

34 *Ord.* 1, d. 2, q. 1.

35 "Formally possible" is superficially like "logically possible" for us in that it is iteratively necessary. But for Scotus it is nonrepugnance to being-as-such, not just a semantic array over domains of propositions (possible worlds). Scotus has no such ontology.

36 Is this a case of concluding to real possibility from consistency-to-us? It would be if Scotus did not, as he does, have particular a posteriori examples to show such a series *can* end; but he does (as we supplied).

But, then, is this cognitively circular, because one would first have to know "there is a first uncaused cause" is formally possible, and that might be what the proof throws into issue? We will see that the answer is no.

37   Cf. "si negatur negatio, ponitur affirmatio": *Ord.* 1, d. 2, q. 1.

38   Cf. Brady 1954.

39   That is why Scotus says, on several occasions, that the cause must lie outside the regress of contingent things.

40   See Loux 1984. Scotus might be thought to make that mistake when he says in *Quodl.* q. 7, n. 72, "[the] totality of effects itself must have a cause which is not part of the whole" (trans. Alluntis and Wolter 1975, 181). But there Scotus is summarizing Aristotle's argument (*Metaph.* 2.2 [994^{a}20]), and though he approves it, it is part of a discussion of divine power, not part of this proof.

41   That is another form of indirect proof he favors: to assume the very thing he thinks is impossible and show that it *still* entails what is false: cf. also the organization of *Theoremata*. He restricts such arguments with impossible suppositions to syntactical and semantic transformations from the "essentials" of the supposition to avoid paradoxes and trivialities (see Calvin Normore, ch. 4 in this volume).

42   If a thing does not exist on account of what it is, there can be no inconsistency in "something causes it." Can it be demonstrated that it is contradictory that there is something that is possible, nonexistent, and uncausable? Yes, because Scotus thinks, as do his contemporaries, that "something comes to be that has no cause" is inconsistent. Presumably an objector would have a clear example of an uncausable event in mind?

43   Remember, the status of a conclusion or reasoning as a posteriori depends on the order of the *knowledge from experience* and not on whether the propositions of the conclusion or the reasoning are contingent or necessary. The mistake that a necessary truth cannot be known a posteriori was only widespread after Kant and till the mid-twentieth century. Now everyone knows two things that Scotus knew: that a necessary truth is implied by everything, that what is true no matter what, is entailed and often can be known from what is true contingently, and also, some necessary truths are known from some things that are contingently false (though that is rarely mentioned).

44   So the first conclusion also follows from the second. He offers a confirming line of thought: "to produce something does not imply any imperfection; it follows that this ability can exist in something without imperfection.... But, if every cause depends on some prior cause, then efficiency is never to be found without imperfection....Therefore, such an efficient power is possible." But that is a conceptual argument

and so clearly subject to his limitations on the 'conceivable-to-us' as to be no more than a confirmation.

45 You cannot have the final mark without the marking pen, the moving pen, the moving hand, the acting person, the free willing, all together. Those are really necessary and essentially ordered. None is formally (absolutely) necessary, yet they are really necessary in the order of nature.

46 Fr. Wolter calls that demonstrating "the source of all possibility" in Wolter 1966, xxi.

47 "secunda conclusio de primo effectivo...est incausabile."

48 Wood 1987, Loux 1984, and others seem to think he does need that. At one point he uses the idea that what begins to be *might* need a cause, but that seems the same as the "nothing comes from nothing" idea.

49 "Aut ergo a se, aut a nihilo, vel ab aliquo alio" and "nullius est causa... illud quod nihil est." *Ord.* 1, d. 2, pars 1, qq. 1–2, n. 43.

50 It *needs to be true* that every contingent being is causable (as a cognitive consequence of the Triple Primacy, and omnipotence, of the First Being), but he does not have to *premise* that as something *already known* in order to establish the existence of the First Being.

51 There is also an implied subargument that "everything that exists is contingent" implies a contradiction because it implies "there might have been nothing at all." Had there been nothing at all, nothing would have been possible. But something exists, and so, necessarily, something is possible. Therefore, there is something that exists necessarily. That seems to be Aquinas's "Third Way" as well.

52 *Ord.* 1, d. 2, qq. 1–2, n. 65.

53 Ibid., n. 68.

54 See Ross 1990.

55 Medieval Aristotelians would have considered an analysis of cause and effect in terms of an antecedent event followed by a later event that succeeded one another according to natural law ("At/then/at, according to law") as laughable. For them causation is production, with substantive power in nature. Contemporary causal theorists – for example, Mackie, Armstrong, and the like would seem as wrong to Scotus as the Arabic occasionalists who denied there are real essences in things. For Scotus, the match burns the hand by *doing* it, not just by a flame's leading a parade of events whose last member is a suppurating wound, where the order of the parade of phenomena is set by "laws of nature" (whose status is unexplained, or treated as a general association of ideas, or as some logical relation of ideas).

56 Brady 1954, 128, quotes Ockham as saying "ratio probans primitatem efficientis est sufficiens et est ratio omnium philosophorum" (*Sent* 1,

d. 2, q. 10), but it is not the "more" evident way of conservation. See also his report of Ockham's commenting that a *probatio*, but not a demonstration, can be offered for divine infinity. Brady also reports that William Rubio (after 1321) says the existence of the First Efficient Being is demonstrable, but in the looser sense, that it is not *so* obvious "quin adversarius posset ipsam evadere aliqualiter cum colore... quia negaret adversaries praedictam assumptum" (Brady 1954, 126).

57 Another function of well-crafted arguments is to alter the cognitive balance of our convictions so that, for example, in light of Scotus's argument and Aquinas's Third Way, a person who thinks things really do exist contingently may become intellectually certain, without serious doubt, that there is a divine being.

58 The reasons he gives in *Ord.* 1, d. 2, qq. 1–2, n. 53, are not the best ones he has, though the first is important: that no matter how many, it must depend on something not in it. That, like the passage from *Quodl.* q. 7, n. 72, cited above, does invite the "fallacy of composition" charge. But it must be remembered that such a fallacy is an informal one and not caused just by attributing to a series what belongs to every member: sometimes, as in this case, that is exactly correct: the modality of the weakest conjunct belongs to the whole conjunction; so does dependence, just as he says. The need for explanation is not eliminated by delaying or extending it, and *ex hypothesi*, there is none; but there is the effect, and thus, a contradiction.

59 Fr. Wolter, at Wolter 1966, xii, summarizes the last step: "whatever is possible is either actual or causable; something possible is not causable; therefore, it is actual."

60 *De primo princ.* 4.22 and *Rep.* 1, d. 35, q. 1, n. 14.

61 Aquinas (*ST* I.2 ff.) uses the same technique to derive the divine attributes, deriving conflicts between denials of the attributes and the lack of act–potency distinction in God.

62 Wolter 1966, 52 (italics added).

63 Ibid.

64 One might wonder at this phrasing. But for something not to exist, it has either to be impossible or preventable. It is not that there has to be a reason for the nonbeing of what does not exist, but that there can be. But there cannot, consistently, be a reason why a First Being does not exist.

65 Ibid.

66 See the argument at *De primo princ.* 4.88–4.90, to "You are one in nature, you are one in number.... you alone are by nature God."

67 *De primo princ.* 4.3, in Wolter 1966, 78–82.

68 God is free of any distinction *in his essence* on the traditional view. But that does not exclude the real distinction, by opposition of relations, among the Persons of the Trinity. Thus, there is real distinction of Persons in God but not any real distinction *in God's essence* among essential divine features; for there is only one such feature, which is inaccessible to us because it is incomprehensible by us. Now Scotus employs that in theology but distinguishes real distinction from "formal distinction *a parte rei.*" That is, he distinguishes "really distinct" as a relation, from "distinct in reality" as a difference and says the divine perfections differ in reality just as the same perfections differ in creatures even when one has both, say, wisdom and goodness.

69 Scotus breaks from Aquinas's view that divine simplicity denies any distinction more than conceptual-for-us among the divine attributes.

70 *Ord.* 1, d. 8, q. 1, n. 6. Scotus has in mind that the individuation principles of material things (haecceities) are completely simple and knowable to God but are not perfect unities of being because they require a nature to contract.

71 Ibid.

72 *Ord.* 1, d. 2, pars 2, qq. 1–4, n. 390: "I understand 'really' in this way, what is in no way through the act of an intellect, such that such an entity would be there even if no intellect were contemplating it."

73 Ibid.

74 Ibid.

75 *ST* I.13.

76 *ST* I.13.

77 *Ord.* 1, d. 8, q. 4, n. 17. We have not derived infinity yet in this presentation, which follows the order of the *De primo principio.* In the *Ordinatio* Scotus follows the order from simplicity, to infinity, to necessity; here the order is from necessity, to simplicity, to infinity.

78 *Rep.* 1, d. 35, q. 1, n. 14.

79 *Rep.* 1, d. 35, q. 1, n. 5.

80 Ibid.

81 Ibid.

82 *Ord.* 1, d. 2, pars. 1, qq. 1–2, n. 106 (trans. Wolter 1993, 61).

83 Ibid.

84 For a reading of Aquinas that makes him in substantial agreement with Scotus on God's knowledge of possibles and of the natures of created things, see Wippel 1984 and 2000.

85 Cf. Aquinas, *De potentia* 3.5 ad 2; and 3.14. See Ross 1990, 176–97. Scotus thinks natures are created *in esse essentiae* along with individuals but also exist eternally in divine knowledge.

86   *In Metaph.* 7, q. 13.

87   It should also be noted that the more common interpretation of Aquinas is the same as what we attribute to Scotus here.

88   Cf. *De potentia* and *ST*.

89   See *De potentia* 1.5 ad 11; and *De veritate* 3.6.

90   *Ord.* 2, d. 3, pars 1, q. 6, trans. Spade 1994, 108. See Timothy B. Noone, ch. 3 in this volume.

91   *Rep.* 1, d. 36, q. 3, n. 20.

92   Ibid. Scotus holds there is direct intuitive knowledge of the existence of perceived singulars.

93   *Ord.* 2, d. 3, pars 1, q. 1, trans. Spade 1994, 64.

94   Scotus uses the same notion in his discussion of freedom and when he speaks of an ordering of "instants of nature" within an instant of time. He also uses it in explaining the order of the created nature to the individual thing: there is a natural priority of instants but no real succession.

95   Ibid. He says we can postulate four "instants" in divine knowing: the first, absolute self-knowledge; the second, say, of 'stone' (a possibility) in 'intelligible being' (*esse intelligibile*) "such that that idea is an intelligible divinely understood, but without any further element"; a third instant in which a merely rational relation of 'being divinely understood' obtains between God and 'stone'; and a fourth in which the rational relation, 'understanding stone' is itself understood. Nothing *happens; this is just what is logically involved.* He is using a metaphor to make clear that there is logical but not entitative complexity to the divine knowing, and no real relation of God to finite possibilities or actualities.

96   *Ord.* 1, d. 45, q. 1, n. 5: "voluntas divina potest in aeternitate sua esse principium volendi quodcumque volibile." Cf. *Lect.* 1, d. 45, q. 1, n. 3.

97   *Quodl.* q. 7, n. 8. The phrase here is used somewhat out of context: Scotus is not circular in his description of omnipotence as power that extends to whatever is possible and not necessary. (See the *Lectura* definition: *Lect.* 1, d. 42, q. un., n. 6.)

98   See the *Lectura* definition of omnipotence: *Lect.* 1, d. 42, q. un., n. 6.

99   *Ord.* 1, d. 43, n. 2.

100   *Rep.* 2, d. 1, q. 3, n. 8.

101   Ibid.

102   *Ord.* 1, d. 43, n. 2.

103   *De primo princ.* 4.71.

104   He says he reserves that for a projected *Treatise on Things Believed: De primo princ.* 4.

105   Ibid.

106 *Lect.* 1, d. 43, q. 1, n. 15.

107 *Ord.* 1, d. 43, q. 1, n. 1174.

108 *Ord.* 2, d. 2, q. 2, n. 5.

109 That position was developed again by Malebranche (ca. 1685) to provide the production missing among physical events in Descartes's account. Hume adopted the same general idea but eliminated God and necessity from the idea of causation, saying causation is a certain kind of regularity instead. And the Humean starting point has dominated since, but with a constant drift toward a priori connections of one sort or another, to explain the regularities in nature.

110 That idea became an essential element of seventeenth-century mechanics, so that Malebranche retreated to occasionalism of his own, and it reappears throughout current philosophy in what is called "At-At causation" (happenings at a place, at a time, successively), so that even force is analyzed through its logical shadows, as points on a curve, without any active natural principle. Cf. Salmon 1977. To the contrary, Avicenna said the nature of a thing is the essence considered as the principle of its operations; see Aquinas, *De ente et essentia.* The absurdity proposed by the Arabic occasionalists is made even more absurd in contemporary philosophy by the simultaneous denial of any divine causation and the claim that all causation is no more than regular succession, usually with some element of logical necessity to ground the regularity, as well, for example, among properties, or propositions – see Mackie, Armstrong, Lewis, and many others. Causation is thus reduced to a semantic relation in parallel with spatiotemporal succession.

111 *Quodl.* q. 7, n. 65, 2nd paragraph.

112 *Ord.* 1, d. 44, q. 1, nn. 5–12. He distinguished the ordained power of God from the absolute power of God that exceeds any created order. The same in *Lect.* 1, d. 44, q. 1, n. 5.

113 *Lect.* 1, d. 39, n. 39. In *Ord.* 1, d. 39, q. 1, n. 1117, he says that the disjunction of 'being' into "necessary/contingent (*possible*)" is *immediate*; there is nothing prior to reply upon.

114 Here he departs as Christian belief requires, but without a crucial argument, from Avicenna, who held, also, that perceived things do not exist on account of what they are but on account of their causes, which, however, are necessitated by the divine being. Other Muslim philosophers held that the secondary causes are only apparently causes because God alone is a real cause of everything immediately (and by emanation). Scotus seems to need an argument as to why the fact that perceived things do not exist on account of what they are entails that they might really not have existed at all, but he insists that he does not.

115   Scotus does not argue that it could not cause by chance, because, like Aristotle, he thinks chance is the intersection of causes "with other ends in view" and thus supposes causation rather than replacing it.

116   That highlights a matter, mentioned in n. 114, about which Avicenna would not yet be satisfied: as to what settles that there really are things that might not have existed at all. It appears that Scotus has not yet eliminated Avicenna's Spinozistic option that everything is one substance and necessary.

117   *Lect.* 1, d. 39, n. 43.

118   Ibid., n. 47.

119   It seems that the logical necessity that there be contingent truth, given that there *is* contingent being, is a sufficient cognitive base for our knowing that a First Causing Being that acts freely by nature, really exists! For if it is possible that there is some contingent truth, then it is necessarily possible. But if nothing comes from nothing, then it is possible that there is a cause of contingent truth; in fact, it is necessarily possible. But that can only be so if some free cause of contingent truth exists no matter what: God. Is that another successful existential argument?

120   Ibid., n. 62.

121   *Lect.* 1, d. 39, n. 53.

122   Ibid., n. 60. Note: Priority of nature is "rational" in these contexts, not causal or entitative.

123   Ibid., n. 49.

124   Ibid. That way of talking, as Aquinas does too, seems awkward. It would be better to say "before" is vantaged in our temporal order and "before the world was" is imaginary, as Aquinas does say. Scotus seems to think that logically (only) there could have been a "before," by a conceptual projection from the actual beginning.

125   Wolter 1993, 59.

126   *Quodl.* q. 16, n. 46.

127   *Coll.* 3.4; *Add.* 2, d. 42, q. 4, n. 11.

128   *Add.* 2, d. 25, q. 1, n. 20.

129   *Ord.* 1, d. 17, pars 1, qq. 1–2, n. 66. Voluntary action is action from and in accord with the will, but it can be determined by desire or other apprehended good. However, *free* action is entirely from the will.

130   *Quodl.* q. 16, n. 35.

131   Ibid., n. 42.

132   *Quodl.* q. 16, nn. 1–50. Also, *Ord.* 1, d. 10, nn. 6–9 and 30–58. *Quodl.* q. 16, n. 44 says "not every necessity destroys freedom."

133   See William E. Mann, ch. 7 in this volume.

134   *Ord.* 1, d. 3, pars 1, qq. 1–2, n. 58 (trans. Wolter 1993, 27). Also, *Quodl.*
      q. 5, n. 10.
135   *Ord.* 1, d. 3, q. 1, trans. Wolter 1993, 75.
136   Ibid., trans. Wolter 1993, 27.
137   *Ord.*, 1, d. 2, q. 1, trans. Wolter 1987, 64–5.
138   Ibid., 65.
139   Ibid., 64.
140   Gilson 1952, 192, is definite that infinity is an intrinsic, positive mode
      of being but conceived "negatively" or "privatively" in contrast to the
      finite things we know.
141   Wolter 1993, 64.
142   Ibid., 68–70.
143   Wolter 1993, 148.
144   Ibid., 150–1.
145   Ibid., 158.
146   Ibid., 163.
147   Ibid. Even though the soul is really distinct from the body, we cannot
      for that reason say the inference to the possibility that the soul may
      pass out of existence is false without begging the question.
148   Ibid., 164.
149   Ibid.
150   Scotus relies upon two iterative modal principles: (1) possibilities and
      necessities are themselves formally necessary; and (2) the weakest
      modal (propositional) operator of any conjunct is the strongest modal
      operator of any conjunction: thus, any conjunction with a contingent
      member is itself contingent (e.g., the regression of causes) and, of course,
      any conjunction with an impossible conjunct is as a whole impossible.
      Those, plus the principle of bifurcation (that every nontensed proposi-
      tion is either true or false) form the structure of his indirect proofs and
      of his arguments from "what entails the false is false."
151   We are not suggesting that such arguments cannot be incorporated into
      a Scotistic framework, say, by deducing a general principle of explica-
      bility from the production of contingent things (cf. Ross 1968). But
      without the root in experience, in the actual production of things, the
      argumentation floats in the dubious realm of speculation based only
      on our conceptions as far as they go: not what Scotus intended at all.
152   It is a matter of wonder that so many technically skilled recent philoso-
      phers are untroubled by stopping at the idea that everything is without
      explanation or is somehow, without further rationale, necessary but
      consider the idea of a Creator somehow irrelevant.

7   Duns Scotus on Natural and Supernatural Knowledge of God

The Earnest Professor begins the lecture by announcing that today we are going to investigate what we can know about God. The Artless Student immediately asks how it is possible that we finite minds can comprehend anything about the infinite. The Professor groans inwardly, resisting the temptation to retort by asking how the finite mind of the Student is so certain that God *is* infinite, given the Student's avowal of doubt about the adequacy of finite minds.

Eager to maintain classroom civility, the Professor might congratulate the Student on fastening on a question discussed at length by John Duns Scotus. It is a sign of the seriousness with which Scotus takes this and related issues that he tackles them immediately in the *Ordinatio* version of his monumental *Commentary on the Sentences of Peter Lombard*. The title of the first question in the Prologue to the First Part is "Whether It Is Necessary for Man in His Present State to Be Supernaturally Inspired with Some Doctrine." The title of the first question of the First Part of the Third Distinction is "Whether God Is Naturally Knowable to the Wayfarer's Intellect."[1] God's existence is not at stake in these questions. Scotus thinks that God's existence can be established as an item of *natural theology*, that part of theological speculation that can be developed by reason alone, independent of any kind of revelation. Scotus takes himself to be in agreement with Aristotle that human sense experience and natural reason are adequate to provide a demonstration of God's existence. Aristotle himself had argued from the existence of changeable, contingent beings capable of initiating change in other changeable, contingent beings to the existence of an immutable, necessary, utterly independent being, an "unmoved mover." Variations on these Aristotelian themes had been played with considerable success a generation before Scotus by Thomas Aquinas.[2] Scotus accepts these arguments, but, because he takes them to depend for their soundness on contingent facts about the created world, he regards them as demonstrating only the relative or conditional necessity of God's existence: God must exist if *this* kind of world is to exist. Perhaps for this reason Scotus favors an argument that purports to establish the absolute necessity of God's existence apart from any contingent facts about the way the world is. Because of this background, I suggest that our two questions should be read in the following spirit: *If*, or *given that*, God exists, what can we know about God, what ought we to know, and how can we know it?

The titles presuppose a distinction between natural knowledge and supernatural knowledge. One of my tasks will be to explicate that distinction. I shall discuss the questions in reverse order, beginning with natural knowledge, then proceeding to supernatural knowledge.

I. NATURAL KNOWLEDGE OF GOD

We may suppose that natural knowledge is knowledge that humans acquire by using their ordinary perceptual and cognitive faculties operating on ordinary physical objects. Scotus seems content to presuppose a generally Aristotelian conception of the scope of natural human intellectual powers, regarding human concept acquisition as based entirely on sense experience. Thus, without some sort of divine supplementation, human reason can only ply its trade with a stock of common, earthly goods. Scotus's notion of natural reason, then, does not go beyond the confines of empiricism, even though Scotus thought that natural reason alone could make more progress in natural theology – by proving the existence of God, for example – than most modern empiricists would accept. If so, it is fair to ask how there could be natural knowledge of God, especially when the natural knowledge is avowed to be knowledge of a supernatural being. The problem is made more acute for Scotus because he does not rely on a powerful tradition, one of whose practitioners was Augustine, that concedes the inadequacy of ordinary knowledge-gathering practices in this area, claiming instead that knowledge of God is innate in the human soul, discoverable by a special meditative technique of inward-turning contemplation.[3] Whatever the merits of this position, Scotus may have thought that it either compromises the claim to naturalness of the knowledge thereby gained or that it is compatible with his own approach. It is easy to interpret Augustine's depiction of the meditative technique as involving divine cooperation in such a way that the meditator will be successful only if God chooses to illuminate the soul in its search.[4] If, on the other hand, the meditative technique does not require divine cooperation, then Scotus can reasonably claim that it is a process not intrinsically at odds with his own naturalistic account. In any event, we will see that Scotus takes himself to be developing conceptual knowledge about God within the confines of ordinary, garden-variety concept-forming procedures.

Although the title of *Ord.* 1, d. 3, pars 1, q. 1 is "Whether God Is Naturally Knowable to the Wayfarer's Intellect," Scotus refines the question, after a series of six preliminary observations, into "Whether the wayfarer's intellect can naturally have some simple concept, in which simple concept God is conceived."[5] The refinement both narrows the search and raises the stakes. First, Scotus makes it clear that what he is after is a *concept*, to be acquired by natural means, which is such that it applies *uniquely* to God. (If it did not apply uniquely to God, then there would be no guarantee that in entertaining the concept, one is thereby conceiving of God.) Second, not just any concept that might (be thought to) apply uniquely to God will do. Scotus explicitly seeks a *simple* concept. What exactly is a simple concept and why is it important to Scotus?

If we hope to find answers, we should look in the preliminary observations. Even though the other five contain important material,[6] it is the first one that is most germane to our question. In the first observation, Scotus dismisses as irrelevant the distinction between knowing God negatively and knowing God affirmatively. There was a view, famously associated with Moses Maimonides, that maintained that the only knowledge we can have about God is negative knowledge. Scotus does not mention Maimonides explicitly.[7] Even so, Maimonides's views provide a foil against which to test Scotus's. According to Maimonides, to say that God is living is to mean that God is not dead; to say that God is eternal is to mean that God is not caused.[8] Maimonides is attracted to this view for a pair of reasons. The first is that any positive attribute is repeatable or shareable: one thing's being good does not preclude many things from being good. The second is that there is no metaphysical composition in God, no distinction between God's essence and existence or God's substance and God's attributes. Kim's goodness is metaphysically separable from Kim, but God's goodness is not metaphysically separable from God. So the metaphysical account of how God is good must differ from the account of how Kim is good. Goodness is a positive attribute of Kim but not of God. For if it were, then by the repeatability criterion for attributes, two or more beings could be good in just the way that God is. Maimonides regards this as a lapse into polytheism. Maimonides's solution is to analyze the claim that God is good into a negation: God is not bad.

Scotus wants to retain that doctrine of God's metaphysical simplicity.[9] I suspect that this desire lies behind his search for a simple concept applicable to God. Scotus is unwilling, however, to accept the negative theology exemplified by Maimonides's approach. He ticks off his objections in rapid order as follows:

1. Negations can only be known through affirmations. Scotus's point seems to be that there can be no simple negative concepts, since every negative concept is logically parasitic on some positive concept. Not-badness, for example, would be at least as dependent on the simpler concept of goodness as not-goodness is; even more so, one can argue, since not-badness would be the negation of badness, which in turn is the negation of goodness. To put the general point in other words, every simple concept must be a positive concept.

2. The only negations we know to apply to God we know solely in virtue of the fact that they deny something of God that would contradict some affirmation we know to be true of God. The sole basis for our knowledge that God is not bad is that it denies "God is bad," which contradicts what we do know about God, namely, that God is good. What stands in need of explanation is how we know this affirmation. An account like Maimonides's has the epistemological dependence precisely backwards.

3. Our greatest love is not directed at negations. When we love God, it is not because God is conceived as not dead or not bad.

4. Negative terms can either be substantival or predicative. 'Not stone', used as a substantive, can be thought to refer to a collection of objects, namely, all those objects that are

not stones. Used predicatively, 'not stone' can indicate that the subject of which it is predicated either is not *a* stone or is not *made of* stone. Think now of some negation applicable to God, such as 'not bad'. Interpreted substantivally, 'not bad' will pick out many things: if Augustine is right, its reference class is everything that exists.[10] Scotus claims that the term extends further than that, even to things that do not exist, for example, a chimera. 'Not bad', then, as a substantive term, does not distinguish God from an avocado or a unicorn. If 'not bad' is interpreted predicatively, then, Scotus claims, the negative attribution must ultimately be grounded in some positive attribute inherent in the subject (in this case, the subject's being good). Once again, the negative cart must be drawn by a positive horse.

Let us take stock. Scotus thinks that no purely negative attribute can adequately convey knowledge of God. That confines his search for an adequate concept to the realm of positive concepts that can be naturally acquired. Maimonides had assumed that any positive *attribute* is repeatable and thus could not represent the essentially unique nature of God. It is a short step from that assumption to the assumption that any positive *concept* of God would also be infected by the repeatability virus. Scotus's strategy is to deny at least one of these repeatability assumptions. There can be a positive concept, naturally acquired, that applies to God and to nothing else. As for the attribute–repeatability assumption, we will see that Scotus's allegiance to the doctrine of God's metaphysical simplicity makes him wary of ascribing any positive attribute to God, except as a *façon de parler*. That same allegiance provides the motivation to find a simple concept. Although there might be complex positive concepts of God, a simple concept will come closer to representing God's own simple nature and will occupy a special epistemological status for Scotus.

The body of Scotus's determination of the question of our natural knowledge of God consists of a series of five theses. The theses are developed in criticism of views attributed to Henry of Ghent. I do not propose to discuss Ghent's views or the accuracy of Scotus's representation of them. Nor shall I give each of the five theses equal treatment. I shall analyze their contents only insofar as they further Scotus's central project.

Here is the first thesis and the justification Scotus offers for it:

Thus I say first that not only can a concept be had naturally in which God is conceived accidentally, as it were, for example, through some attribute, but also that some concept [can be had] in which God is conceived in himself and quidditatively. I prove it thus: in conceiving "wise" a property is conceived, according to him [Henry of Ghent], or a quasi-property, perfecting a nature in second actuality. Thus in understanding "wise" I must understand beforehand some "that which" of which I understand this quasi-property to inhere. And so prior to the concept of each property or quasi-property one must seek the quidditative concept by which it is understood to be attributed. And that other concept will be quidditative of God, because it can be located in nothing else.[11]

To conceive God accidentally is to have a concept of some attribute, for example, wisdom, that applies to creatures and to God. The fact that some creatures are wise is what enables us to acquire the concept of wisdom naturally. In addition to this kind of concept, however, Scotus claims that we can have a quidditative concept of God. Scotus's argument is desperately compressed. I offer the following remarks in hopes of interpreting the passage.

A quidditative concept of a thing represents that thing's quiddity. The quiddity of a thing provides the answer to the question, What (kind of thing) is it? It might be tempting to think that a thing's quiddity is simply the set of properties essential to the thing. But Scotus's notion of a quiddity – and thus of a quidditative concept – runs deeper than that. As a first approximation we may say that the quiddity of a thing explains why the thing's essential properties are essential to it.

To take an example suggested by the passage quoted two paragraphs earlier, compare the proposition "Socrates is wise" with "God is wise." The former proposition records an accidental property of Socrates: it is easy to imagine that Socrates might never have become wise. Although Socrates' wisdom is accidental to Socrates, it is not accidental that Socrates' wisdom depends on his possessing a rational soul. The mere possession of a rational soul, however, is not sufficient to produce wisdom in its possessor. Consider this analogy, adapted from Aristotle's De Anima: "This axe is sharp."[12] Sharpness is an excellence in an axe that perfects its function, to chop. Sharpness must supervene on the right kind of matter – steel will do, congealed chicken fat will not – formed or structured in the right way. (The same steel might have been used to make a golf club.) So although it may be accidental that this axe is sharp, it is not accidental that its sharpness depends on its being made of the right material formed in the right way.

Aristotle said that if an axe had a soul, its soul would be its ability to chop; this would be its "first actuality." The exercise of this ability, the axe's actually chopping, is the axe's "second actuality." Sharpness perfects this second actuality, this activity that is the actualizing of the axe's potential. Like this axe's sharpness, Socrates' wisdom must supervene on "the right stuff," an organic body structured and animated by a rational soul. In the first-actuality sense, a rational soul is a soul that is *capable* of understanding, reasoning, deliberating, and choosing. A soul exercising these capacities is a rational soul in the second-actuality sense. But an exercise of one's understanding can be flawed, one's reasoning can go awry, one's deliberations can be biased, and one's choices can be unduly influenced by emotion. Scotus's view is that the person of wisdom does not exhibit these common human failings in thought or action. Socrates' wisdom perfects the exercise of Socrates' cognitive abilities. But Socrates' having a rational soul does not by itself explain why Socrates is wise. Many fools have rational souls. It is as appropriate to ask how Socrates came to be wise as it is to ask how this axe came to be sharp.

Let us turn now to "God is wise." It cannot be that wisdom is an accidental property of God. It would be misleading, however, to say that wisdom is an essential property of God, inasmuch as that alternative suggests a distinction between a property in God, *being wise*, and God, the bearer of the property. According to the doctrine of God's metaphysical simplicity, a better interpretation of the proposition that God is wise is, not that God *has* wisdom, but that God *is* Wisdom Itself. Scotus never dissents from Ghent's claim that "Whatever is known of God is God."[13] It is the commitment to the doctrine of simplicity that leads Scotus to use the notion of a "quasi-property." The identical surface grammar displayed by "Socrates is wise" and "God is wise" masks an ontological difference between them. What is a property in creatures must be understood as an as-it-were property in the case of God.

Willingness to acquiesce in the judgment that "God is wise" is a necessary truth, even if it is supplemented by the divine simplicity analysis of "God is Wisdom Itself," does not exempt one from facing the question, Why is God wise? For the question need not be interpreted as the fatuous question, How did God become wise? Think of it instead as, What is it about God's nature that entails that God is wise? Scotus's view is that if we consider all the quasi-properties that characterize God – wisdom, power, goodness, and the like – we will discover that they all can be explained by God's quiddity.

Scotus's first thesis does not deliver the quidditative concept it promises. If anything, the first thesis may appear to have made delivery unlikely. For if the way in which Socrates is wise differs so dramatically from the way in which God is wise, what reason have we to think that our concept of wisdom, acquired naturally from our experience of Socrates and other creatures, applies to God? Scotus's second thesis, the determination of which is more than twice as long as the other four theses combined, maintains that we can have not only an analogical concept of God but a univocal concept,[14] that is, a concept that applies to creatures and to God equally, without any shift in meaning. In asserting this possibility, Scotus takes himself to be disagreeing with Ghent; he is certainly disagreeing with Aquinas, who said that "it is impossible to predicate anything of God and creatures univocally."[15] Aquinas offered instead a theory, or some suggestive remarks towards a theory, of analogical predication. I shall not examine any theory of analogical predication here.[16] What I hope to be able to do is provide the motivation behind Aquinas's denial of univocality and the motivation for Scotus's insistence on it.

We have already seen Scotus acknowledging that, unlike Socrates' wisdom, God's wisdom is not an accidental property – in fact, is not a property at all – of God. There are further differences. Socrates' wisdom is the wisdom of an embodied person operating in space and time. God is incorporeal, nonspatial, and nontemporal. Socrates' wisdom includes the operations of reasoning and deliberation, processes that typically take time and begin in ignorance and indecision. God's wisdom is not characterized by these operations. God understands all without need of reasoning and chooses without need of deliberating. Socrates' wisdom is limited; God's wisdom is unlimited. It is easy to sympathize with Aquinas, who, confronted with all these differences, concluded that terms like 'wise', when learned from and applied to persons like Socrates, could not have the same meaning when predicated of God.

Scotus makes two salient critical points in the discussion of his second thesis. Taken together, they clear the way for the second thesis's positive message. The first critical point is that every concept is either univocal or equivocal: there is no third possibility. Either 'wise' has the same meaning when predicated of Socrates and God, or it does not. Call it what you may, analogical predication is still equivocation.[17] Scotus stipulates two tests that a concept must pass if it is to count as univocal.

1. To affirm the concept and to deny it of the same thing must result in contradiction. If it is not contradictory to say "There is a fork in the road but there is no fork in the road," then the concept of a fork is equivocal.
2. The concept must be able to serve as the middle term of a valid syllogism, not allowing one to pass from true premises to a false conclusion. Thus, to coopt a putative example of an analogical concept from Aquinas, in 'This diet is healthy; nothing is healthy unless it is a living organism; therefore, this diet is a living organism', 'healthy' is equivocal in the premises.

The second critical point is that no concept of God naturally acquired can be both simple and equivocal.[18] As the example of forks and health suggest, equivocation feeds on conceptual complexity. Forks in the road and table forks are alike in some important respects but unlike in others. Health is predicated of a diet because of a complex set of causal assumptions about the diet's contribution to physiological well-being. A simple concept, for example, the concept of cerulean blue, provides no conceptual room for equivocation. Thus, if there is a simple concept of God, naturally acquired, it must be univocal between God and natural creatures. One can arrive at the same point by a different route. Suppose, as Scotus never denies, that we can naturally acquire analogical concepts of God. Any such analogical concept will be, by Scotus's lights, equivocal and thus complex. Consider now the conceptual components of any such complex concept. If every component is itself equivocal and does not depend ultimately on some univocal concept, then we have literally no way of telling what the analogical concept is about or even whether it is coherent. For we can understand how equivocation works only when we see how the equivocal term or concept deviates from its

univocal base. Without knowing the patterns that allow for transformations from univocal to equivocal, we would be in the position
of someone who tries to learn a foreign language without knowing
how any term in the language is related to any natural object or to
any term in a language already known. In order to be meaningful,
analogical concepts must be anchored in univocal concepts. Thus,
some component of any analogical concept of God must be univocal.
The combined effect of Scotus's two negative points is that if we are
to have any concept of God, it must either be or contain a concept
univocal between God and naturally known creatures.

But, of course, Scotus has yet to produce a univocal concept of God.
The positive message of the second thesis is contained in its fourth
argument[19] and takes Scotus closer to his goal. Scotus cites with
approval the following paraphrase of a position inspired by Anselm's
Monologion: "Relations excluded, in everything else, whatever is
unqualifiedly better *being this* than *not being this* is to be attributed
to God, just as whatever is not like this is to be denied of him."[20] This
passage alludes to three separate theses. The first is that no relational
property specifies or reveals a thing's essence. In telling you that
Rocky is shorter than, smarter than, and to the left of Bullwinkle, I do
not tell you what Rocky *is*. We will see shortly how Scotus exploits
this thesis.

The second thesis can be more easily expressed if we follow
Scotus in distinguishing a class of perfections called "unqualified
perfections." A perfection – for example, sharpness in an axe – is a
property that aids a thing in performing its functions well. But some
such perfections are limited or qualified. Sharpness can be a perfection only of things made of the right kinds of matter. And sharpness is
not a perfection of every material thing made of sharpness-supporting
material: no one prizes sharpness in a tongue depressor. The ability
to scuttle across the floor quickly is a perfection in cockroaches but
not in dolphins. Yet dolphins possess the same perfection, the ability to avoid predators, that roaches possess. Predator avoidance is a
perfection that is *multiply realizable*, involving legs and carapaces
in some species, fins and sonar in others. For all of that, predator
avoidance carries in its very description an implication of vulnera-
bility. I suggest on Scotus's behalf that an unqualified perfection is
a multiply realizable perfection that has no intrinsic limitation and
does not, in itself, confer an intrinsic limitation on its possessor. We

can now state the second thesis: God possesses all unqualified perfections. The third thesis follows fast on the heels of the second: God possesses nothing that is not an unqualified perfection.

It is important to Scotus that unqualified perfections be multiply realizable. For Scotus puts the following epistemological twist on Anselm's teaching. We have concepts of some of the unqualified perfections because we first find the perfections themselves in creatures. Scotus's examples are wisdom, intellect, and will. Although creatures realize these perfections only to a modest degree, the unqualified perfections, unlike predator avoidance, do not impose any intrinsic limitation on their possessors. We then consider the formal definitions of any unqualified perfection – those characteristics essential to anything's being wise, for example – and ascribe the same perfection to God. In the process, however, we suppose that the perfection is realized maximally in God. (Scotus thinks that this kind of concept manipulation is part of our natural cognitive repertoire. He cites as an example our ability to combine our concepts of goodness, maximality, and act to arrive at the concept of something that is the supremely actualized good.[21]) Throughout this exercise, Scotus insists, we are operating with concepts that are univocal between creatures and God. Multiple realizability underwrites univocality. The fact that predator avoidance can be realized in so many different ways in animals while our concept of predator avoidance remains fixed across species makes it more plausible to believe that wisdom can be realized in vastly different beings – some natural, some supernatural – even though our concept of wisdom is based solely on experience of natural examples.

Anselm's second thesis, supplemented by Scotus's account of concept synthesis, allows us to build up, from a natural base, a concept of God as a being who has all unqualified perfections, each perfection realized to its maximum degree.[22] When we conceive of God in this way, we conceive of God as not merely wise but omniscient, not merely powerful but omnipotent, not merely good but impeccable, and so on. This exercise gives us the most perfect concept we have of God in terms of descriptive content. It does so, however, at a cost. Because the concept is constructed from concepts of indefinitely many unqualified perfections, its very complexity does not match the simplicity of God. We are, Scotus points out, thinking in terms of quasi-attributes attached to a subject. There is an even more perfect, simpler concept we can have of God, a concept less overtly descriptive but more theoretically powerful.[23] It is the concept of God as infinite being. I submit that this is the quidditative concept that Scotus has been seeking. If so, its credentials must be established. The concept must be simple and positive. It must take explanatory precedence over other natural concepts of God. And it must, in a sense to be defined, be more perspicuous than other natural concepts of God.

First, recall that Scotus is in search of a simple, positive concept of God. What reason do we have for thinking that the concept of an infinite being is either simple or positive? One might claim that the concept of infinity is negative, not positive, inasmuch as the word 'infinite' is formed by prefixing the negative particle 'in' to the word 'finite'. Medieval philosophers would hasten to assure us that etymology is a poor guide to the negative–positive distinction, for that distinction is basically metaphysical, not linguistic. To spell out the value presuppositions behind the distinction is a task well beyond the scope of this essay. One analogy may help, however. The etymology of 'incorruptible' is negative, but at least from the time of Augustine forward, incorruptibility was regarded as a positive attribute, while corruptibility was the negative counterpart. In any case, Scotus does not bother to argue that the concept of infinity is a positive concept. We have already seen reason to ascribe to Scotus the thesis that every simple concept must be positive. Scotus should think it sufficient, then, to argue that the concept of infinite being is simple; the concept's being positive would follow as a logical corollary. That is precisely the strategy he adopts. The concept of infinite being

is simpler than the concept of good being, true being, or other similar [concepts], because "infinite" is not a quasi-attribute or property of being, or of that of which it is said. It signifies instead an intrinsic mode of that being, so that when I say "infinite being" I do not have a concept accidentally, as it were, [formed] from a subject and a property, but a concept of a subject in itself with a certain degree of perfection, namely, infinity, just as "intense whiteness" does not signify a concept accidentally, as does "visible whiteness," but rather signifies an intrinsic degree of whiteness in itself.[24]

This much seems clear: visible whiteness is supposed to stand to intense whiteness as good being stands to infinite being. In each pair, the first member is supposed to be metaphysically complex while the second member is not. Scotus tells us that infinity is not a property – not even a quasi-property – of an infinite being, but rather an "intrinsic mode" of that being, just as intensity is supposed to be an intrinsic mode, not a property, of whiteness. Let us see whether Scotus's maneuver is nothing but smoke and mirrors. It seems correct to say that it is one thing for visible whiteness to be visible but another for it to be white. What makes something visible does not thereby make it white, lest all visible things turn out to be white. Scotus wants to say in contrast that it is not one thing for intense whiteness to be white and another thing for it to be intense. Scotus may think that x's intense whiteness is x's *way of being* white, and that a way of being is not a property of x. Inasmuch as 'intense whiteness' seems equivalent to 'whiteness that is intense', and the latter expression suggests a substance bearing an attribute, it might be better, on Scotus's behalf, to think of the concept of *being intensely white*. It is less tempting to think that the concept of being intensely white can be analyzed into a concept of a substance bearing an attribute. If that is so, then a way of being is depicted more adequately by an adverb than an adjective.

Suppose we try to apply this technique to the concept of infinite being. We arrive at the concept of *being (or existing) infinitely*. This concept appears to resist analysis to the same extent to which the concept of *being intensely white* does. But notice that even if the technique purchases some plausibility for Scotus's claim, it does so by converting Scotus's ostensibly substantival phrases, 'intense whiteness' and 'infinite being', into phrases more naturally construed as terms designating some sort of abstract entity, a way of being. The conversion may be harmless enough. The distinction between a concept of a way of being and a concept of something exemplifying that way of being is a subtle one, perhaps discriminable only by philosophers as subtle as the Subtle Doctor.

If the concept of God as infinite being is a quidditative concept, then it must explain why other correct natural concepts of God are correct. Think in particular of the very rich descriptive concept generated by Anselm's second thesis. Scotus can fairly argue that the concept of God as being unlimited in any way explains why each and every element of that descriptive concept is correctly and essentially ascribed to God. God's existing infinitely, for example, explains why

God is omniscient: if some being falls short of omniscience, then, no matter how impressive its other credentials might be, it does not exist infinitely. It is important to note here that the relation between infinite being and omniscient being is asymmetrical. Infinity explains omniscience but not vice versa. It may well be that infinite existence and omniscience are necessarily coextensive, that is, that only an infinite being can be omniscient and only an omniscient being can be infinite. Even so, Scotus is free to maintain that God's omniscience is grounded in God's being infinite, and that it is not the case that God's being infinite is grounded in God's omniscience. We might offer the following observation on his behalf. There are different answers to the questions, What makes God omniscient? and What makes God infinite? God is omniscient, we might say, because omniscience is an entailment of God's infinitude. When we confront the question, What makes God infinite?, we should feel the same sort of one-question-too-many discomfort we feel upon being asked, What makes a triangle have three angles? Explanation must terminate somewhere: Scotus's view is that in the case of natural knowledge of God, explanation stops (and starts) with infinite being.

In virtue of its taking explanatory precedence, a thing's quidditative concept should provide the wherewithal not only for explaining the thing's essential properties but also for showing how other putative quidditative concepts are explanatorily defective. Thus, Scotus entertains the hypothetical case of someone claiming that "highest good" or "highest being" is a quidditative concept of God. These concepts are not untrue of God. It is rather that they are not as perspicuous as the concept of infinite being. Scotus identifies the term 'highest' as the culprit. The term can be understood either comparatively or absolutely. The distinction appears to operate in the following way for Scotus. Taken comparatively, the term 'highest good', for example, is a covertly relational term whose meaning is something like *good that is better than all other existing goods*. It thus does not pass muster by Anselm's first thesis; no relational property can disclose a thing's essence. (Although Scotus does not belabor the point, one problem with 'highest good', construed comparatively, is that in a world composed entirely of swampland and flies, the mantle of highest good would fall either on the species fly or on some individual member of the species.) Understood absolutely, 'highest good' sets a higher standard, something like *good that is better than all other possible goods*. There is no doubt that only God can fill this bill. Even so, Scotus points out, 'highest good' and its confrere 'highest being' do not entail that a being matching those descriptions is *unlimited* in goodness and being, as 'infinite being' does.

The Artless Student's question rightly presupposes a finite human mind whose supply of concepts can only be gleaned from the natural world. The question also presupposes Scotus's thesis that God is an infinite being, although the Earnest Professor might be forgiven for harboring suspicions that the Student had nothing so sophisticated in mind as Scotus's notion of infinite being as a quidditative concept of God. The crux of the Student's question is, How is it possible for a finite mind to take the measure of an infinite being? Of course in one sense it cannot: Scotus concedes that it is impossible for us to have *comprehensive* knowledge of God.[25] Comprehensive knowledge is not necessary, however, in order to know that God is infinite being. One can know that Asia is the largest continent without thereby comprehending all of Asia. Or one can know that there is an infinite number of numbers without comprehending all of them; in fact, if one's mind is finite, no matter how many numbers one comprehends, there will be infinitely many that one does not comprehend. Scotus's diagnosis of the Student's concern, then, is that the Student confuses *knowing that* with *comprehending that*, thinking that the former entails the latter.

II. SUPERNATURAL KNOWLEDGE OF GOD

Scotus believes that natural knowledge of God is not enough – that we humans need to have our natural knowledge of divinity supplemented with supernatural knowledge. In a disarmingly candid paragraph early in the Prologue, Scotus concedes that natural reason is powerless to show (1) that any item of supernatural knowledge can be in the wayfarer, (2) any supernatural knowledge is necessary for the wayfarer's perfection, and (3) that even if there were some supernatural knowledge in the wayfarer, the wayfarer would thereby be aware of its presence. Scotus's tendentious use of the term 'wayfarer', with its connotation that our present earthly existence is but a phase of a much longer journey, shows that he is convinced that humans do have access to some supernatural knowledge. His concession, however, might seem to curtail the enterprise of theology as a rational discipline, especially from the point of view of Aristotle, who for Scotus is the quintessential pagan philosopher. In doing theology, one is confined to the arena of natural reason in sparring with a philosopher like Aristotle, because Aristotelians will not acquiesce in any argument, one of whose premises expresses a supernatural belief. Therefore, Scotus concludes, the arguments made in his *Commentary* in favor of the necessity of supernatural belief are at best "theological persuasions," establishing supernatural beliefs only on the basis of other supernatural beliefs.[26]

In the Prologue, Scotus examines five arguments for the thesis that humans need some knowledge that cannot be obtained by the intellect operating within the confines of its own natural powers. I wish to consider these arguments in turn. Two preliminary remarks are in order.

First, the question set by Scotus in the Prologue, "whether it is necessary for man in his present state to be supernaturally inspired by some special doctrine which the natural light of understanding obviously cannot grasp," raises questions of its own. Doctrine necessary for what? With what kind of necessity? It is instructive to consider the following case imagined by Scotus. Suppose that a person – let us call her Serena – receives no religious training or enlightenment whatsoever and still is able to do right and avoid evil solely by following natural reason. Will Serena be denied salvation? Not by dint of any necessity governing God's actions. To say that God of necessity cannot save Serena would be to deny that God has *absolute power*. Scotus appeals to the notion of God's absolute power here to claim that God can save anyone he chooses to, including a person who, like Serena, lacks faith.[27]

While the hypothetical case illustrates that personal salvation is the goal for which supernatural knowledge is necessary, it might appear at the same time to undermine the necessity for any supernatural knowledge. To see our way clear of this problem, we should distinguish, on Scotus's behalf, between possible constraints on divine actions and on human actions. Because God has absolute power, there are no constraints on what God can do other than those imposed by logical impossibility and logical incompatibility with God's nature. Thus, God cannot make both p and not-p true, nor, if God is essentially omniscient, can God act out of ignorance. If this is so, then God is not constrained to save only those who have supernatural knowledge. In this sense of necessity, Serena does not need supernatural knowledge to enable God to save her.

Now consider our plight from a God's-eye viewpoint. Without supernatural knowledge it is as if we were required to navigate over treacherous terrain without a map, compass, or even a clue that we are embarked. With humans striking out in all directions, there may be an occasional fortunate soul like Serena who chances to make it to the destination. For all of us, the fortunate and the unfortunate, our behavior would be constrained by massive, universal ignorance. The kind of necessity that applies here is *practical necessity*, which is easier to illustrate than to define. If certain kinds of knowledge are practically necessary for successful terrestrial navigation, then certain items of supernatural knowledge are practically necessary for charting the way to our supernatural destination.

Second, Scotus is aware that the expression 'supernatural knowledge' is ambiguous. On the one hand, it can mean any item or body of knowledge that is produced in a knower by supernatural means. In this sense, the content of the knowledge need not itself be supernatural. If an archangel were instantaneously to impart perfect knowledge of linear algebra in me, the knowledge would be supernatural with respect to source but not with respect to content: I might have acquired the knowledge by natural means. On the other hand, 'supernatural knowledge' can mean any item or body of knowledge whose content could never have been discovered by the unaided natural operations of the human intellect and so must have been instilled originally into some human by a supernatural agent.[28] In the remainder of this chapter, I shall understand the notion of supernatural knowledge in this second sense.

Even if God's existence can be demonstrated by natural reason, and so need not be an item of supernatural knowledge, Scotus sees two interrelated problems remaining, problems that require further investigation into the topic of supernatural knowledge. First, is there anything we need to know about God that we cannot know naturally? And second, are our cognitive faculties capable of taking on or assimilating such knowledge if it is necessary? I suggest that the first three of the five arguments examined by Scotus deal with the first question and that the last two address the second.

II.A. The First Argument

The text that contains the first argument is complex, requiring considerable logical reconstruction.[29] But the gist of the argument is simple enough. In order for us to act knowingly, we need to have distinct knowledge about the end for which our actions are undertaken. Our natural faculties cannot give us distinct knowledge about the end. Therefore we need supernatural knowledge about our end.[30]

Setting aside concerns about the validity of this argument, we may still have doubts about the truth – for that matter, the interpretation – of the premises. Consider the first premise. It is easy enough to cite cases in which one knows what one is doing but does not know what end is being served by one's action. Soldiers and even Franciscan friars sometimes follow orders intentionally left unexplained by their superiors. Perhaps Scotus would deny that these cases are really counterexamples to the premise. There are two different directions the denial might take. One might deny that in such cases, the agent is genuinely acting knowingly. Or one might deny that the end envisioned by the agent is identical to the end contemplated by the superiors. If one takes the first approach, one is apt to promote the concept of knowledge, as it occurs in the first premise, to the concept of *comprehension*, insisting that having knowledge about what one is doing is necessary but not sufficient for comprehension of what one is doing. Comprehension requires a clear grasp of the point, purpose, or goal of one's action.

The second approach would emphasize that agents can have relatively local ends for the sake of which they act, and that they cannot act knowingly without their action's being informed by the perception of one or more of those ends. A soldier might not know the overall strategic plan to which his action is subservient. But if his action is performed knowingly, he will be able to cite some goal that he desires – aiding his country, getting promoted, avoiding a court martial – for which his action is a means.

As we have seen, the distinction between knowledge and comprehension that underlies the first approach is an important one, and one with which Scotus is thoroughly familiar.[31] It would be a mistake to confine, on Scotus's behalf, the interpretation of the first premise to comprehension. For Scotus must allow that humans can sometimes have knowledge about an end without having comprehension. Indeed, the cases that are most germane are the ones involving supernatural knowledge, cases in which the agent has true beliefs reliably produced but lacks the clarity and fullness that comprehension requires. It may be that one distinction between knowledge and comprehension is that comprehension entails knowing that one comprehends, whereas knowledge does not entail knowing that one knows. The distinction would help to vindicate Scotus's claim that even if wayfarers have supernatural knowledge, they cannot know that they have it.

The second approach to the first premise yields the claim that acting knowingly entails knowing (and desiring) *some* end or goal that the action is supposed to advance.[32] If that claim seems to be unexceptionable, then so much the better for Scotus. But the more ordinary the first premise seems, the more extraordinary the second premise becomes. While the first premise accommodates all ends known naturally, the second explicitly rules them out, contemplating only ends that cannot be known by our natural faculties. Because there seems to be no natural way to establish it, the second premise is what makes the argument a "theological persuasion." Although Aristotelians are thus entitled to deny the premise, Aristotle's thought influences Scotus's construction of it in two ways. Aristotle had argued that there is one ultimate end for humans, *happiness (eudaimonia)*, to which all other ends sought by humans are subordinate. And Aristotle had argued that happiness consists in rational activity, whose culmination is *contemplation (theoria)* of that which is most noble. The second premise presupposes the first point. It is not just any end that cannot be known naturally. We can have a clear perception of our goals as a student, or teacher, or carpenter. Moreover, we can exercise some voluntary control over the pursuit of these sorts of goals, including rejection of them. But we cannot know our end as a *wayfarer*, a status that we can neither voluntarily adopt nor abandon. Mindful, perhaps, of Paul's pronouncement that now we see through a glass, darkly, but then face to face (1 Cor. 13:12), Scotus transforms happiness, a natural activity that most closely emulates the life of the gods, into *beatitude*, the supernatural state of communion with God enjoyed by the blessed. In similar fashion, contemplation is transformed into the *beatific vision*, the pure, clear, direct perception of the Godhead.

II.B. The Second Argument

Left to our natural devices, we would have no reason to suspect that beatitude is our ultimate end. Once beatitude is proposed, reason is still free to withhold assent. But should one come to believe in the possibility of beatitude, one confronts a practical question: what steps are necessary if one is to attain it? Scotus's second argument addresses this question. To act knowingly for an end requires not only knowing the end itself, but also how one should dispose oneself to attain it, and what steps are necessary and sufficient for its attainment. In the case of beatitude, none of these items can be known naturally, for the same basic reason. Whether one achieves beatitude is entirely dependent upon God's free acceptance. Nothing we can do will induce beatitude from God as a matter of natural necessity; hence, no actions we can perform are either causally necessary or sufficient.[33]

Scotus does not elaborate on it, but we can interpret the second argument as delivering two messages. They can be described by invoking the distinction between *algorithms* and *heuristics*. The first message is negative: we possess no algorithm, no precisely defined procedure, the careful following of which will produce salvation.[34] To believe that we have some procedure that is causally sufficient is to lapse into magic. To believe that some procedure is causally necessary is to ignore the case of Serena. But if we extract only this negative message from the second argument, we are left with a devastating result. Having been informed about beatitude, we would be stranded without any rational guidance about reaching it. The second message is intended to resolve this quandary. We can think of Scripture as containing divinely revealed heuristics, precepts and rules intended to guide human conduct. The Decalogue and the Sermon on the Mount provide examples. The virtues of heuristics are that they are easily comprehended by beings with adequate but finite cognitive resources and that they apply noncontroversially to a large number of cases. But the richness of experience makes it hard for fallible humans to see how they apply in many other cases: Torah begets Talmud.

II.C. The Third Argument

Aristotle would accede to the assumption that forms the basis of the third argument, namely, that there are "separated substances" or immaterial, wholly spiritual agents. Aristotle would have cited the intelligences that move the heavenly bodies. As we will see momentarily, Scotus has other beings in mind. Scotus argues that we cannot have natural knowledge of the *propria* of separated substances, where a *proprium* is, roughly, an attribute unique to a kind of entity.[35] Because the separated substances are not empirical entities, we are not in a position to give a scientific, explanatory account of their *propria* in the way, for example, in which we can give an explanation of what is distinctive about the digestion of cows from an examination of bovine anatomy. But neither can we infer the *propria* of the separated substances from their effects, as a physicist might infer the properties of a subatomic particle.[36] In elaborating on this point, Scotus descends from the philosophical stratosphere in which the argument has proceeded so far to provide some examples. Creatures are the effects of God, the primary immaterial substance itself, but no examination of them would give us reason to believe that God is triune or that the whole of creation is the result of a contingent, freely chosen act. Scotus believes that there are other separated substances. Various Aristotelian teachings, such as the doctrine of the eternity of the world and the assimilation of necessity to omnitemporality, would lead one to think that the other separated substances must be everlasting and necessary beings. But it is an item of revelation that they too were created and are contingent. Similarly, one might expect that because the angels see God more clearly than humans do, all angels would be incapable of sin and acquire beatitude of their own nature. Once again, revelation says otherwise.

To sum up the first three arguments: without supernatural aid we can know that omniscient, omnipotent God exists but not that God is triune and the contingently acting creator of all else that exists. Nor would we know that there is an end offered to us along with a set of heuristic prescriptions about how we might obtain that end.

Scotus segregates the last two arguments from the first three by characterizing the first three as "more probable" (*probabilior*) than the last two.[37] The standard way to understand "more probable" is as "more likely to be true." In the present context, however, it is possible that Scotus intends a narrower, more technical sense of "more probable." In the Aristotelian theory of demonstration with which Scotus is familiar, "more probable" could mean "more directly demonstrable." Suppose, for example, that a theorem establishing the sum of the interior angles of a hexagon makes use of a previously proved theorem about the sum of the interior angles of a triangle. Then the triangle theorem is "more probable" than the hexagon theorem, even though both theorems are necessarily true, because the hexagon theorem depends on the triangle theorem but not vice versa. Indeed, when Scotus criticizes the two arguments, the criticism includes (but in the case of the fifth argument, is not limited to) pointing out how many and what other revealed propositions the two arguments presuppose.[38]

The two arguments shift their focus from what we *need* to know to whether we *can* know.

II.D. The Fourth Argument

Whatever is ordained but not disposed to an end must be gradually disposed to it. Humans are ordained but not disposed to a supernatural end. Therefore, humans must be gradually disposed to it, for which imperfect supernatural knowledge is supposed to be necessary.[39]

II.E. The Fifth Argument

Any agent using an instrument in acting cannot use the instrument to do something that exceeds the nature of the instrument. The soul uses the light of the intellect to understand things naturally. This instrument is limited to acquiring knowledge through the senses. Therefore, the soul cannot have knowledge other than through the senses.[40]

As Scotus points out, the fifth argument shoots itself in the foot. If wayfarers need to have knowledge that cannot be acquired by the senses and yet are not equipped to receive such knowledge, then not even omnipotent God can impart the knowledge to them *as long as they remain wayfarers*.[41] God may be able to make a silk purse out of a sow's ear if all that is required is that the same atoms that once composed the ear now constitute the purse. But God cannot teach an igneous rock to play chess without conferring capacities on it that turns it into something that is no longer simply an igneous rock. Scotus's point is that we need supernatural knowledge in our present status as wayfarers. In the ordinary course of events – barring cases like Serena's – that knowledge is essential if we are to transcend this status. The fifth argument, however, would deny us the appropriate intellectual provisions.

Scotus has no similar criticism of the fourth argument. I wish to conclude by suggesting that it may contain an important insight. The argument can be interpreted simply as pointing out the problem of cognitive overload. Remember Plato's description of the denizen of the cave who is forced to leave it. Upon first emerging into the world of real objects illuminated by the sun, the cavedweller would be unable to stand the brightness: it would take time for vision to acclimate itself to its new surroundings and to begin to perceive those surroundings correctly.[42] The fourth argument can be seen as making an analogous point about the brilliance of the beatific vision: beatitude must be preceded by intellectual tempering to make the soul fit to absorb and comprehend it.

I do not wish to quarrel with the claim made by this interpretation so much as I wish to supplement it with another consideration. Scotus must surely think that the will needs tempering at least as much as the intellect. One way in which Christian beatitude is distinguished from Aristotelian *eudaimonia* is that beatitude has an essential component of *love* for the agent who is the object of the beatific vision. There are good reasons for maintaining that this love, if it is to be genuine, can neither be coerced nor have personal gain as its principal motivation.[43] If that is so, then there is a further point to God's *gradually* dispensing *imperfect* knowledge to humans. The razzle-dazzle of a full-blown theophany might compromise either the voluntariness or the motivational purity of the love.

After some reflection it may occur to the Artless Student to query the Earnest Professor about some of the hefty philosophical assumptions playing a significant role in the construction of Scotus's views. The doctrine of God's simplicity, the distinction between positive and negative attributes, and the thesis that some perfections are unqualified may seem to cry out for justification. At that point, the Student will no longer be artless. Philosophy will have settled in.[44]

NOTES

1   Translations are mine. The first question of the Prologue has been trans-
    lated by Allan Wolter in Wolter 1951. Wolter has also translated portions
    of *Ord.* 1, pars 3, d. 1, q. 1, in Wolter 1987.
2   See Aquinas's *SCG* I.13 and 15, and *ST* I.2.3.
3   See Menn 1998.
4   One might so interpret Augustine's *De libero arbitrio* II and *De magistro*
    11 ff.
5   *Ord.* 1, pars 3, d. 1, q. 1, n. 19.
6   *Ord.* 1, pars 3, d. 1, q. 1, nn. 10–15.
7   Maimonides is on Scotus's mind in the related discussion of the unique-
    ness of God; cf. *Ord.* 1, d. 2, q. 3.
8   See *The Guide of the Perplexed*, I, 58.
9   For explication and defense of this doctrine, see Mann 1982 and Stump
    and Kretzmann 1985.
10 See Mann 2001.
11 *Ord.* 1, pars 3, d. 1, q. 1, n. 25.
12 See Aristotle, *De an.* 2.1 ($412^{b}12$–$413^{a}3$).
13 *Ord.* 1, pars 3, d. 1, q. 1, n. 20.
14 *Ord.* 1, pars 3, d. 1, q. 1, n. 26.
15 See *ST* I.13.5.
16 For a definitive modern discussion, see Ross 1961.
17 *Ord.* 1, pars 3, d. 1, q. 1, n. 26.
18 I am relying principally on n. 35. This paragraph is very complex, even
    by Scotistic standards. I shall not present all its argumentation. I hope I
    am presenting *some* of it.
19 *Ord.* 1, pars 3, d. 1, q. 1, nn. 38–40.
20 See *Monologion* 15. For an insightfully alternative version of Anselm's
    passage, see Thomas Williams's translation in Williams 1995a, 28.
21 *Ord.* 1, pars 3, d. 1, q. 1, n. 61.
22 *Ord.* 1, pars 3, d. 1, q. 1, n. 58.
23 The crucial passage is n. 58. Wolter's translation is misleading here,
    confusing Scotus's identification of the most perfect *descriptive* concept
    with the most perfect concept *tout court*. Thus, when Scotus says that
    the concept of God as infinite being is *perfectior* than the Anselmian
    descriptive concept, Wolter feels compelled to translate *perfectior* as
    "less perfect"!
24 *Ord.* 1, pars 3, d. 1, q. 1, n. 58.
25 *Ord.* 1, pars 3, d. 1, q. 1, n. 65.
26 *Ord.* prol., pars 1, q. un., n. 12.
27 *Ord.* prol., pars 1, q. un., nn. 54–55.

28 *Ord.* prol., pars 1, q. un., nn. 57–65. It is a fine question whether supernatural knowledge in this second sense, once acquired, can be transferred to other knowers by natural means.

29 I have analyzed this argument in Mann 1992.

30 *Ord.* prol., pars 1, q. un., nn. 13–16.

31 In deference to Scotus I have described the distinction as one between *scire* and *comprehendere* rather than *intelligere*. *Intelligere* for Scotus need involve nothing more than linguistic competence without epistemically grounded propositional assent. See Mann 1992, Section IV, for further discussion.

32 "Supposed to advance" flutters between "is known to advance" and "is believed to advance." For my immediate purposes it is not important that we pin down this issue.

33 *Ord.* prol., pars 1, q. un., nn. 17–18.

34 The message claims that we *possess* no algorithm, not that there *is* no algorithm. But even if there are such algorithms, they may be beyond our cognitive powers to store and retrieve. I can write an algorithm the following of which will ensure that you never lose at ticktacktoe. No one (yet!) can write a similar algorithm for chess, and if one were to be written, it would surely exceed the capacity of any individual's memory.

35 But only roughly. See Mann 1987 for refinements.

36 *Ord.* prol., pars 1, q. un., nn. 40–1.

37 *Ord.* prol., pars 1, q. un., nn. 53–4.

38 But not entirely. As we will see, Scotus pins an absurdity on the fifth argument.

39 *Ord.* prol., pars 1, q. un., n. 49.

40 *Ord.* prol., pars 1, q. un., n. 51.

41 *Ord.* prol., pars 1, q. un., n. 52.

42 Plato, *Republic* 514a–517a.

43 See Mann 1993 and 1998.

44 This essay incorporates, in modified form, Mann 1999. Research on this essay was supported by a University of Vermont Summer Research Grant, hereby gratefully acknowledged.

8   Philosophy of Mind

As many commentators have noticed, medieval views on the relation of mind and body occupy a strange territory somewhere between substance dualism, on the one hand, and some form of materialism, on the other.[1] On the one hand, the medievals were convinced that the soul is an immaterial agent, causally responsible for our intellectual activities – causally responsible independently of the body – on the other hand, they were all convinced that body and soul are united in such a way as to form one (composite) substance. While there was widespread agreement about the correct understanding of the first of these two claims – that the soul is an individual immaterial object – there was considerable disagreement about the correct understanding of the second. The consensus was that the soul is in some sense an (Aristotelian) form of the body. But there was no corresponding consensus about what it is to be a form.[2]

I. THE IMMATERIALITY OF THE SOUL

Scotus's account of the immateriality of the soul springs from a discussion of the immateriality of human cognition and will. The argument from cognition focuses on an argument proposed by Aquinas in defence of the immateriality of the soul. According to Aquinas, we can infer the immateriality of the soul from the immateriality of mental acts. For example, Aquinas argues that the universality of the concepts known by the intellect is sufficient to allow us to infer that the intellect must be immaterial:

The intellective soul knows a thing in its nature, absolutely [i.e., as universal]. . . . If the soul were composed of matter and form, forms of things

263

would be received in it as individuals. . . . So the intellective soul, and every substance that can know forms absolutely, lacks composition of form and matter.[3]

Scotus is happy to accept both of these immateriality claims. But he is ambiguous about the argument itself. As he spots, the argument relies on an equivocation in the senses of 'immaterial'. Scotus distinguishes three ways in which a mental act could be thought to be immaterial. First, an act can be said to be immaterial if it is not exercised through a bodily organ.[4] Secondly, an act can be said to be immaterial if it is not an accident of an extended substance – a substance, in other words, that includes matter as a part.[5] The third way in which an act can be said to be immaterial is if the act's content is abstract:

Immateriality can be understood in a third sense, namely with reference to the object, inasmuch as this knowledge considers the object under immaterial aspects, as for instance, abstracting from the "here and now" and such like, which are said to be material conditions.[6]

An analysis of Scotus's views here is made harder by the fact that he offers two separate and rather different assessments of the Thomist argument. In the *Ordinatio*, Scotus is happy to accept a version of Aquinas's argument (though I shall argue that he should not be); in the later *Quodlibet*, Scotus is more reluctant to accept the argument. I shall look at the two versions in turn, beginning with the later account, and then going back to assess the earlier one.

In the *Quodlibet*, Scotus claims that Aquinas's argument from the immateriality of mental acts to the immateriality of the soul is acceptable provided we understand the immateriality of mental acts to mean that such an act is not an accident of a substance that includes matter.[7] Understanding 'immaterial' in this sense, Scotus accepts as factually true both the premise and the conclusion, and he accepts the validity of the inference. The problem he sees is that, to infer the nonbodily nature of the intellect from the abstract nature of mental content, we would have to be able to show that abstract mental content could only be possessed by a nonbodily substance – and in this late text Scotus claims not to know any such argument.[8]

This represents an unequivocal rejection of Aquinas's argument.[9] In the slightly earlier account in the *Ordinatio*, Scotus offers an argument in favour of the immateriality of the soul. The argument attempts to find a way to bridge the gap between abstract mental content and nonbodiliness – that is, between the third and second senses of 'immaterial'. The argument, however, does not seem to fare any better than Aquinas's:

1. A human being possesses knowledge with abstract content (assumption).
2. No sense knowledge has abstract content (assumption).
3. A human being possesses knowledge that is not sense knowledge (from 1 and 2).
4. Necessarily, knowledge that is not sense knowledge is not extended (assumption).
5. Every nonextended property is possessed by something nonextended (assumption).
6. Necessarily, something possessing knowledge that is not sense knowledge is nonextended (from 4 and 5).
7. A human being includes something nonextended (from 3 and 6).[10]

I will consider the claim made in 7 later, since how we understand 7 will depend on how we understand the relation of a human being to his or her soul – a topic that I will look at in Section III.[11] For now I want to focus on other parts of the argument. In fact, several steps of the argument might demand comment. For example, 2 might require some justifying. But Scotus offers an argument for 2 that, supposing Scotus's moderate realism, seems to me to be acceptable. Scotus lists eight sorts of abstract mental contents and proceeds to show that none of these can be sense knowledge. The eight objects are (i) the actual universal, (ii) being and quality as such, (iii) relations, (iv) distinctions between the sensible and nonsensible, (v) logical intentions (universal, genus, species, judgment), (vi) our act of knowledge, (vii) first principles, (viii) our deductions.[12] Here is how Scotus shows that (i) the actual universal and (v) logical intentions cannot be sense knowledge:

The senses can only be moved to perceive what is included in a sensible object as such. But conceptual relations are not included in any existing thing as such, whereas the senses do have to do with existing things as existing. The same argument can be applied to the actual universal, for it is absurd that the actual universal should exist as such.[13]

The idea here is that the senses cannot be the subject of a mental act with abstract content. This seems fair enough: the abstract objects Scotus lists simply are not the right sort of things to be sensed.

The difficulty I would like to focus on here lies elsewhere in the argument – specifically with 4, the assumption that knowledge that is not sense knowledge cannot be extended. Scotus puts it as follows:

[The subject of our cognitive acts] cannot be something extended, whether it be a part of the organism or the whole composite, for then this operation would be extended and lack the prescribed characteristics [of an intellectual operation].[14]

Scotus here seems to be happy to accept an argument from the abstract content of an act to its being nonextended – that is to say, from sense-three immateriality to sense-two immateriality. This is just the mistake Scotus will later – in the *Quodlibet* – accuse Aquinas of making. And it is curious to find Scotus here equivocating on the senses of 'immaterial', since part of the thrust of the argument in the *Ordinatio* is that a clear distinction should be made between these various senses. Scotus elsewhere proves that the act is nonorganic.[15] But, as he himself is aware, nonorganic and nonextended are not logically equivalent. Indeed, Scotus sees in this very text that an argument is needed to get from a claim about the nonorganic nature of an act with abstract content to the claim that it is nonextended:

If we could prove this knowledge [viz. a mental act with abstract content] to be immaterial in the second sense, and not merely in the first, our proposed conclusion would follow all the more.[16]

And in the *Quodlibet*, Scotus notes that there are clear cases of extended nonorganic things. He cites the form of fire – this fire, not fire as such – and of course any homogeneous substance will be an example of the sort of thing Scotus has in mind.[17] As far as I can see, Scotus offers no attempt to justify the inference to the nonextended nature of our intellectual mental acts.

Scotus does, however, have an unequivocally successful argument in favour of the immateriality of the soul:

Man is master of his acts to such an extent that it is within his power to determine himself at will to this or to its opposite.... And this is something known by natural reason and not merely by faith. Such a lack of determination, however, cannot exist in any organic or extended appetite, because every organic or material appetite is determined to a certain class of suitable objects so that what is apprehended cannot be unsuitable nor can the appetite fail to seek it. The will, therefore, by which we can will in such an indeterminate way, is not the appetite of a material form, and in consequence it belongs to something which excels every such form.[18]

The idea is that all material objects function deterministically such that genuine nonrandom indeterminism can only be explained by the presence of an immaterial – nonbodily – agent. Given that, as Scotus claims here, human beings have contracausal freedom, there must be at least a component of a human being that is utterly nonbodily.

How does Scotus justify the two controversial claims in this argument – namely, that human beings have contracausal freewill and that all material objects function deterministically? Scotus offers two arguments in favour of contracausal freewill. First, we know introspectively that, when we do action a, we have the power to do not-a or to refrain from acting altogether.[19] Secondly, if the will were not free, it would automatically tend to happiness. And, since the will exercises some control over the intellect, the will's failing to be free would result in the will's constraining the intellect to consider happiness all the time. But we know that this is not the case. So the will must be free.[20]

In favour of the deterministic functioning of material objects is a central Aristotelian insight about natural teleology. All material substances have unavoidable natural inclinations towards their self-fulfillment.[21] We might be a bit unhappy about the argument here; but I do not suppose that this premiss itself would hold many substantive difficulties for us.

II. THE POWERS OF THE SOUL

Given that the soul is an immaterial agent, the Schoolmen debated at some length the correct analysis we should give of the relation of the soul to its powers. After all, the argument in favour of the immateriality of the soul relies on the claim that the soul has powers – specifically, cognitive and appetitive powers – in virtue of which it can bring about immaterial effects.[22] The question, as we shall see, turns out to have some interesting metaphysical consequences, at least in Scotus's account, since Scotus seems to believe that the relation he describes is simply a particular instance of a general relation between substances and certain of their properties. Equally, the account can be generalized to cover all substances and all of their essential causal powers. For example, sense powers will have this sort of relation to the organs and bodies that possess them.

As the Schoolmen discuss the question, there appear to be two quite distinct issues at stake – issues that the Schoolmen did not always keep separate. The first is the question of the relation between the essence of the soul and its powers: whether a definition of the concept of a human soul would include causal powers as such. The second, assuming a negative answer to the first, is the question of the relation between the (individual) soul and its (individual) causal powers. Generally, the Schoolmen would deny that the definition of the concept of a human soul would include causal powers as such. The powers of the soul are *propria* – necessary properties of the soul that are not part of its essence.[23] But they drew very different conclusions from this in relation to the second question.[24]

Scotus's main targets are the theories of Aquinas and Henry of Ghent. According to Aquinas, the essence of the soul – the definition of the concept 'soul' – cannot include causal powers as such. Since the essence of the soul does not include the soul's powers as such, Aquinas argues that the individual soul must be distinct from its individual powers in some way. According to Aquinas, a soul's powers are "received into" the soul in the same sort of way as accidents are "received into" a substance: the powers of the soul actualize some passive potency or capacity in the soul.[25] This does not mean, however, that the soul's powers are in any sense contingent features of the soul. Rather, the soul's powers are necessary features of it – features it cannot be without. Indeed, the soul's powers are explained by its essence – its having the essence it has is sufficient for its possessing the powers it possesses.[26]

Aquinas's basic reason for holding that the essence of the soul cannot include powers as such is that the essence of the soul is to be the form of the human body.[27] Scotus likewise argues that the powers of the soul are *propria* of the soul. He argues that the soul as such is in some sense logically prior to its possession of causal powers.[28] But he insists that this does not entail a real distinction between the individual soul and its individual powers. *Propria* are inseparable properties, and real distinction requires real separability.[29] Scotus uses this insight to argue that Aquinas's view of the powers of the soul entails – absurdly – that the powers themselves are causal agents. Arguing against Aquinas's view, Scotus worries that, if the soul is really distinct from its powers, then the soul "operates and acts by the mediation of some accident really distinct from it,"[30] and that it would follow that "some form lower than the soul could be the immediate principle of acting."[31] On the face of it, this scarcely does justice to Aquinas's claims about the status of causal powers. Aquinas would doubtless want to deny that causal powers are in any sense *numerically* distinct from their substances, and he would doubtless want to deny too that there is any sense in which the accidents of a substance can be said to be causes of the actions brought about through them.[32]

Given a rejection of Aquinas's claim that the powers of the soul are inherent accidents, both Henry and Scotus propose alternative accounts of how the powers of the soul are related to the soul. Henry argues that the powers of the soul are just the soul's being related in various ways to various sorts of possible action: "The powers add to the essence only a relation to specifically different acts."[33] These relations are not in any sense things over and above the soul, and Henry denies that they inhere in the soul.[34]

Scotus's main argument against Henry's theory is metaphysical. Henry's theory entails that an agent is an aggregate of essence + relation. But no agent is an aggregate. Agents are numerically one.[35] Scotus argues instead that the soul and its powers are one substance, such that the powers of the soul "are not really distinct in themselves or from the essence."[36] Scotus argues that the soul and its powers are formally distinct – that is to say, the definition of the essence of the soul does not include the soul's powers as such, even though the soul's powers are not really distinct from its essence.[37] It is in this sense that, according to Scotus, we should understand the claim that the powers of the soul are *propria* of the soul. Scotus goes into some detail explaining the sort of relation that we should posit between the soul and its powers. He speaks – following a rather odd exegesis of a passage from pseudo-Dionysius[38] – of the powers of the soul being "unitively contained" within the soul itself. He gives two examples of this sort of relationship: a determinate unitively contains all its determinables, and an object unitively contains all of its proper passions.[39] It is the second case that is relevant here. Scotus gives two examples: God and his attributes, and being and its convertible

properties (one, good, and true). When discussing the relation between God and his attributes, Scotus shows in some detail how a substance is related to its necessary but nonessential (nondefining) attributes. And the discussion shows just in what way Scotus's account
of the powers of the soul will turn out to be different from Aquinas's.

According to Scotus, following a claim in John of Damascus, the
divine attributes are "circumstances" of the divine essence: they are
not identical with the divine essence in every way since they admit
of definitions that are different from any possible definition of the
divine essence.[40] An objector claims that this entails that the divine
attributes inhere in the divine essence – a claim that would be inconsistent with the pure actuality of the divine essence, since inherent forms always actualize some passive potency in their subjects.[41]
Scotus replies by distinguishing three aspects of a form's relation to
its subject: (i) a form 'informs' its subject, (ii) a form is a part of a composite whole, and (iii) a form F-ness is a truthmaker: it is in virtue
of a form – F-ness – that something is F. The first two of these features of a form's relation to its subject entail imperfections – passive
potency and composition, respectively. But the third is a perfection,
and there is no objection to the divine attributes' exhibiting this feature in relation to the divine essence.[42] Neither should we think of
truth making as entailing the informing of a subject. 'Animate' is a
truthmaker for a human being without its being the case that the
human soul informs the human being (though it does, of course, in
some sense inform the body – of which more in Section III).[43]

Presumably Scotus wants to make the same claim about the powers of the soul – and indeed about *propria* in general. The powers
of the soul are those things in virtue of which the soul can perform
certain sorts of activity, without this entailing that the powers of
the soul inhere in the soul. And this marks a – perhaps *the* – crucial
difference between Scotus's account and Aquinas's. It is worth keeping in mind that Scotus's account precludes any sort of composition
between the soul and its powers: the soul and its powers are, as such,
no more complex than God and his attributes. Insofar as Scotus is
right in supposing Henry's rival account to entail that the soul and
its powers are some sort of aggregate of substance and relation, the
sort of soul that Scotus envisages is simpler than that envisaged by
Henry. (I doubt that Scotus is right in his reading of Henry here, since
Henry explicitly thinks of relations as modes.)[44]

Scotus – like Aquinas – would probably want to think of the powers of the soul as *particulars* – in this case, necessarily dependent particulars. I believe that Scotus's standard account of the formally distinct features of a thing entails that those features are (at least in normal cases) particulars. Scotus is explicit that accidents are particulars.[45] And when discussing the ways in which unitively contained attributes are and are not like accidents, Scotus clearly seems to suppose – though he does not say this explicitly – that there is no distinction between accidents and unitively contained attributes to be drawn in terms of the particularity or universality of these attributes. He certainly does not criticize Aquinas's position by arguing that Aquinas has wrongly hypostatized the soul's powers. So I would suggest that, just as accidents are individualized particulars for Scotus, so too are the powers of the soul.[46] (The difference between accidents and unitively contained attributes lies rather in the inseparability of such attributes from their subjects.)

III. THE SOUL'S RELATION TO THE BODY

The medievals, following Aristotle, analyse substances into two components: matter and form. Like Aristotle, they believe that an analysis of this sort is necessary to explain change. When one substance changes – through some process – into another, something remains constant over the change. This "something" is *matter*. But this matter is arranged in different ways – perhaps very different ways – before and after any change. This arrangement of matter is known as form, or more properly substantial form (though, as we shall see, not all forms are just ways in which matter is arranged). Form is supposed to explain why a given substance is the sort of thing it is.[47] The medievals – again following Aristotle – label the forms of living things 'souls'. Thus, the form of Felix the cat could be called Felix's 'soul', for example. A soul is the sort of form in virtue of which a substance is alive.

This account of the soul as both Aristotelian form and subsistent agent is open to an objection. On the face of it, form is something abstract and universal: an arrangement of matter. But an individual subsistent is not something abstract or universal: it is a particular, as individual as a material body. In the Middle Ages, the claim that form is just something abstract was generally rejected, though traces of it

can be found in Richard of Middleton.[48] Scotus rejects this view by
focusing on the *explanatory* role form is supposed to play. Substantial
form is supposed to explain the fact that a substance belongs to a
natural kind. And, as Scotus sees it, it can only do this if it is an
individual.[49]

None of this means that an individual form does not have a universal or common constituent. Scotus believes that substantial form as
such is common – really shared by different substantial forms of the
same kind. He argues that an individual substantial form includes
both a common (form-)nature and an individuating haecceity.[50]

On the account I have just been sketching, a human being is a
composite of matter and soul. Aquinas accepts this sort of account
straightforwardly. As Aquinas spotted, one of its advantages is that
it can offer a clear account of the unity of a human person.[51] Despite
its obvious appeal, most thinkers of the late-thirteenth and early-
fourteenth centuries believed that this straightforward account of
matter–form composition accorded ill with the requirements both of
theological orthodoxy and of empirical experience. Both theological
and philosophical objections turn on the same worry: that Aquinas
cannot give an account of the identity of a body through death. According to Aquinas, a corpse is in no sense identical with the living
body it succeeds. The identity of a body requires the identity of its
form. But, as we have seen, death is explained by matter's losing one
sort of substantial form and its gaining another. So a living body and
a corpse are wholly distinct.[52]

There are obvious difficulties with this theory of Aquinas's. The-
ologically, it means that Christ's dead body is numerically distinct
from his living body – a claim that was condemned by Robert
Kilwardby, Archbishop of Canterbury, in 1277.[53] Philosophically, we
might well want to claim that bodies – though not the substances
of which they are parts – retain their identity through death. In order to allow for these various theological and philosophical insights,
Scotus – following a standard line adopted by the majority of later
thirteenth-century thinkers – holds that we need to posit (at least)
two substantial forms in any animate composite: a *bodily form*, explaining the identity of the body and its basic bodily structure, and
an *animating soul*, explaining the fact that the body is alive.[54]

Scotus's arguments for this position all focus on the apparent persistence of a body through death. The bodily form and the animating

soul must be distinct, since the body (including the bodily form) persists through death, whereas (by definition) the animating soul does not.[55] The argument relies on the presupposition that the same body does indeed remain – a presupposition that Aquinas would want to question. After all, while a living body and a dead one have very similar structural properties, right down to the molecular level, they behave in very different ways: and this might make us want to claim that they are numerically distinct from each other. So a second argument attempts to show that we have good reason for supposing that the body remains. Various sorts of cause of death (stabbing or drowning, to use Scotus's examples) always produce bodies of the same kind. But agents as different as water and a knife do not on the face of it look to be the sorts of thing that could produce the same sort of effect. So we can only explain the presence of a corpse after the proposed forms of killing by appealing to the persistence of some other form – namely the bodily form.[56] The water, and the knife, do not actually produce anything at all. Aquinas, I think, would have simply to claim that, under the right circumstances, knives and ponds can indeed produce specifically the same effects (where "the right circumstances" might include a consideration of the nature of the form of the living being prior to its death).

This sort of view, according to which there is a *plurality of forms* in an animate composite, makes it harder to give an account of the unity of a composite. In fact, we might find it hard to see what sense can be made of calling the animating soul a 'form' at all, given the basic claim that the forms of material objects ought to have some role in the structuring of a body. Scotus is well aware of both of these two difficulties and spends some time trying to work out a philosophical solution to them – though it must be admitted that his solution to the second is ultimately aporetic.

As we saw above, Aquinas believes that a pluralist position cannot give an account of the unity of an animate composite. Scotus's initial response to Aquinas is to deny any straightforward identification of *simplicity* and *unity*: "I agree that one thing has one existence, but I deny that one existence requires just one [substantial] form."[57] Clearly, Scotus needs to be able to show how even quite complex objects can still satisfy requirements for substantial unity. His basic strategy is to argue that two or more objects – say body and soul, or matter and bodily form – unite to form a substance (rather than, say,

an aggregate) if the whole formed from them has some properties
that could not be had by the parts alone. Scotus supposes that the
parts of a substance simply are not the right sorts of things to be
subjects of the properties of the whole substance.[58]

This account is strongly antireductionistic: a substance is more
than just the sum of its parts. The account does not explain what it
is about substantial forms that allows them to be parts of unities of
this type. Scotus, as a good Aristotelian, talks of a form's actualizing
some passive potency in its subject.[59] As Scotus understands this,
it means that a form begins to inhere in a preexistent object (be it
matter or body), such that the union of the two (the form and the
preexistent object) forms a third thing really distinct from them.[60]
Clearly, the set of potency–actuality relations in a composite that
includes many substantial forms will be of some complexity. (It is
this complexity that Aquinas would regard as inconsistent with any
talk of substantial unity.[61]) The union of bodily form and matter
results in the existence of a body, such that the bodily form actualizes
the matter's potency to be the subject of the bodily form. The union
of this body with the intellective soul results in a whole living human
being. The intellective soul actualizes the potency of the body to be
the subject of the intellective soul. But these actualization relations
are transitive, such that the soul's actualization of the body's potency
entails the soul's actualizing a potency in matter too. To this extent,
then, the soul is a bodily form.[62]

Given that the presence of properties that could not be had by
any of the parts is sufficient for the substantial unity of a composite
object, Scotus has a sufficient response to any theory that the soul
and body are irreducibly two substances if he can show that a human
being has some properties that could not be had by either body or
soul alone. Scotus believes that there are some such properties –
specifically, our vegetative and sensitive powers:

The natural operations which consist in acting and suffering – e.g., sensory
operations – ... can be received only in something composed of an organ
(perfectly mixed) and the soul (insofar as it has perfective potency). Neither
of these is present [in the case of the assumption of a dead body by an angel].[63]

The proximate recipient of any sensitive operation, however, is composed
of matter and form, as is clear from the opening passages of De sensu et
sensato.[64]

The idea is that an inanimate organ – the eye of a corpse, for example – cannot function; it cannot sense things. Of course, if it were transplanted into the body of a living person, it could; but this only bears out Scotus's point that the functioning of the eye depends on the eye itself being a composite of bodily part and soul.

If Scotus is to be able to show that this animating soul is identical with the intellective soul discussed in Section I, he will need to be able to show that these vegetative and sensory functions somehow require the presence of a specifically intellective soul. He will need, in other words, to show that the intellective soul is numerically identical with the animating and sensory forms alluded to in the preceding two passages. Scotus clearly believes that the intellective soul is identical with the animating and sensory forms: "The sensory and vegetative souls are the same soul as the intellective in man."[65] But Scotus never provides an argument to show this identity. To this extent, his account is aporetic. In fact, Scotus's failure to provide an argument is extremely puzzling. Many of his Franciscan predecessors wanted to distinguish vegetative, sensory, and intellective souls in human beings. And these people will have much more difficulty showing how we might plausibly talk of the intellective soul as some kind of (Aristotelian) form at all, rather than as – say – the Platonic mover of a living body. Perhaps Scotus could appeal to some of the empirical facts about death: namely, that all animate functions cease at once. (But I do not know what he could say about people who exist in a persistent vegetative state.)[66]

Nevertheless, it is clear that Scotus's general strategy allows him to provide some principled and coherent way of claiming that the intellective soul – as described by him – is really a *form*. When discussing – in a passage just quoted – the possibility of an angel's assuming a dead body, Scotus notes that such a body would be "imperfectly mixed": it would not be a properly structured (human) body at all. Calling the soul a form here is a way of stressing that it allows the composite to function in certain ways: not that the soul is the *cause* of this functioning, but that it structures the whole in such a way that the whole – body and soul – can together function in certain ways. But there cannot be a difference merely in function – or at any rate, there cannot be one that is spelled out merely in terms of *form*. So Scotus ought to be committed to the view that the soul must itself have a role in structuring the organism: it must be responsible for tweaking the structure of the body such that the body thus structured will function in certain ways. If Scotus does not think this, then it will be difficult to see how his understanding of form can be distinguished from a straightforward Platonic mover.[67]

As Aquinas presents his position, one of its advantages is that it allows an explanation of the causal links between soul and body:

The soul moves the body . . . by its motive power, the action of which presupposes a body already made actual by the soul, so that thus the soul according to its motive power is the moving part, and the animated body the moved part.[68]

On Scotus's account of the union of soul and body, the soul is that in virtue of which the body is alive, such that the soul in some sense contributes to the structure of the body and is responsible as formal cause for the various microstructures that distinguish a living body from a dead one. To this extent, Scotus's theory could explain the causal interaction of body and soul just as effectively as Aquinas's. Scotus does not, however, appeal to this explanatory capacity of his account, since he does not seem to believe that there is a causal difficulty in the interactions of soul and body. Thus, he is happy merely to stipulate that the soul can move the body ("There is a power in the soul for moving the body organically, by means of other organic parts"),[69] and he is equally happy to make the same stipulation for an angel united to an inanimate human body. Since an angel united to an inanimate human body will have plenty of surface similarities to a Platonic sort of soul, a mere mover of its body, I take it that Scotus would have been unimpressed by modern causal worries about substance dualism.

IV. A DISEMBODIED SOUL

According to Scotus the soul is both an immaterial agent and a substantial form of a human being. These two features of the soul pull in rather different directions. We would certainly expect an immaterial agent to be able to exist apart from any body; we would certainly not expect the substantial form of a human being to be able to exist apart from a human body, since human beings are necessarily bodily. Aquinas presents an argument to try to show that the immateriality of the soul is sufficient for its incorruptibility and thus for its natural survival of the body's demise:

It is clear that that which belongs to something in itself is inseparable from it. Existence however belongs in itself to form which is act. Whence matter acquires existence in act in virtue of its acquiring form; and corruption happens to it in virtue of form's being separated from it. It is however impossible that form is separated from itself. Whence it is impossible that a subsistent form ceases to be.[70]

The soul is form; corruption requires the separability of form and matter. So the soul cannot be corrupted. Scotus is unconvinced:

Not all destruction is the result of separating one thing from another. Take the being of an angel, and let it be assumed as some do that its existence is distinct from its essence. Such a being is not separable from itself and nevertheless it can be destroyed if its existence is succeeded by the opposite of existence.[71]

This seems spot on (though Scotus does not need the counter-factual assumption that essence and existence are distinct). One way in which a soul could be destroyed would be if it loses one of its essential properties. For example, if being a form that is in some sense the form of a body is essential to the soul, we would expect the soul to perish when its body perishes. And this gives us good reason for wanting to deny that the loss of form is necessary for destruction. A subsistent form – one that cannot "lose its form" – would perish if one of the conditions necessary for its existence ceased to obtain.[72] Of course, this does not mean that the intellect, in Scotus's account, cannot survive the death of the body; just that there are no proofs that it will do.[73]

Sometimes, however, Scotus approaches the topic from the other side. Rather than focus on the soul's role as form, he focuses instead on its immaterial function. In the *Quodlibet*, he accepts the following argument:

What can function without matter can exist without matter. Therefore that nature whose proper function is understanding can exist without matter.[74]

Curiously, Scotus rejects exactly this argument in the *Ordinatio* on the grounds that the soul is necessarily "a principle which has an operation proper to the composite as a whole" – namely, sensation. Nothing disembodied can be such a principle.[75] This rejection seems to show too much, since it makes the survival of the soul after the death of the body impossible, and Scotus certainly believes that the soul (factually) survives the death of its body. In the *Quodlibet*, however, Scotus appears to accept the inference. This does not mean that he becomes more optimistic about proving the soul's survival, since, as I tried to show in Section I, Scotus in the *Quodlibet* is less optimistic about the possibility of showing that the soul's operations are immaterial in the relevant sense.[76]

According to Aquinas, a disembodied soul has no natural way of gaining new knowledge, since it has no senses, and thus no access to the material world. Scotus disagrees. Physically extended sense data are the immediate objects of the intellect. And these sense data are representations (presumably, natural likenesses) of physical objects. So physical objects can present themselves directly to the disembodied intellect just as well as they can be iconically represented, by sense data, to the embodied intellect.[77] A disembodied soul, then, can gain – without any divine intervention – all the sorts of intellectual knowledge that an embodied one can.

NOTES

1 See most notably Stump 1995, though her detailed analysis is in part vitiated by some serious misinterpretations of Aquinas. See also Pasnau 1997a, 109–11, for a summary of some of the literature on Aristotle and for a brief discussion of some conflicting medieval views on the soul's role as form.

2 Some of these issues are discussed by Adams 1992; Bonansea 1983, 19–36; Bridges 1965; Bettoni 1961, ch. 3; Gilson 1952, ch. 7; and Cross 1999, ch. 6.

3 *ST* I.75.5, summarized by Scotus at *Quodl.* q. 9, n. 7. For a discussion of this difficulty in Aquinas, with exhaustive textual evidence, see Pasnau 1998.

4 *Quodl.* q. 9, n. 9; see also *Ord.* 4, d. 43, q. 2, n. 9. We should not understand this immateriality claim to entail no more than lack of *dependence* on something material, as suggested in the recent interpretation in Priest 1998, 370–1. For Scotus, an organic act should be understood to be the act of an organ – to be in some sense an *accident* of the organ: see *Ord.* 4, d. 13, q. 1, n. 10; *In De an.* q. 6, n. 3. And as Scotus understands it, being an accident requires more than dependence: it requires inherence

too. And Scotus is aware that the sort of dependence involved in being an accident should be distinguished from causal dependence: see *Ord.* 3, d. 1 q. 1, n. 3 for both of these points.

5   *Ord.* 4, d. 43, q. 2, n. 9. This passage makes it clear that lack of extension is the crucial feature of the immaterial in this second sense. The parallel passage in the *Quodlibet* suggests that lack of matter is the crucial feature (*Quodl.* q. 9, n. 11). The two claims are not in fact quite equivalent, since elsewhere Scotus suggests that there is at least a conceptual distinction between extension and materiality. On this, see Cross 1998, 151–2.

6   *Ord.* 4, d. 43, q. 2, n. 9; see *Quodl.* q. 9, n. 11.

7   *Quodl.* q. 9, n. 12.

8   *Quodl.* q. 9, n. 11.

9   For similar modern criticisms of Aquinas's argument, see Novak 1987 and Pasnau 1998.

10 Steps (1) to (3) come from *Ord.* 4, d. 43, q. 2, n. 9; steps (4) to (7) from *Ord.* 4, d. 43, q. 2, n. 12. Scotus also suggests a further argument to show (3): see *Ord.* 4, d. 43, q. 2, n. 7. The argument relies on the claim that the comparison of different sorts of sense data is an intellectual (and thus immaterial) function and not a matter for the (internal) common sense, a claim that is denied at *In De an.* q. 9, n. 3, and q. 10, n. 3; *In Metaph.* 1, q. 3, n. 9; 9, q. 5, nn. 28–9. For the materiality of the common sense, see *In De an.* q. 9, n. 4. On the five external senses, see *In De an.* q. 6.

11 See below, n. 66.

12 *Ord.* 4, d. 43, q. 2, n. 10.

13 *Ord.* 4, d. 43, q. 2, n. 11.

14 *Ord.* 4, d. 43, q. 2, n. 12.

15 Scotus argues that the claim that all sense knowledge is organic "is proved from the fact that every organ is determined to a certain kind of sensible" (*Ord.* 4, d. 43, q. 2, n. 7). Scotus is mistaken about this. The claim to be proved is that all sense knowledge is organic; the proof amounts to no more than an assertion of the (logically independent) claim that all organic knowledge is sense knowledge.

16 *Ord.* 4, d. 43, q. 2, n. 9.

17 For the form of fire, see *Quodl.* q. 9, n. 10; on homogeneous substances, see Cross 1998, chs. 7 and 8.

18 *Ord.* 4, d. 43, q. 2, n. 26. Of course, this is an argument in favour of the will's being immaterial; it is an argument for the soul's immateriality only if we can show that will (appetite) is a property of the soul, and likewise an argument for the intellect's immateriality only if we can show

that both will and intellect are properties of the soul. Scotus certainly assumes that intellect and will are properties of the soul, as I discuss in Section II. But he does not offer an argument to show that this is so.

19 *Lect.* 1, d. 39, qq. 1–5, nn. 40, 54; also *In Metaph.* 9, q. 15, n. 30.

20 *Ord.* 4, d. 49, qq. 9–10, n. 5.

21 *Ord.* 4, d. 49, qq. 9–10, nn. 2–3; *Ord.* 2, d. 6, q. 2, n. 8. I discuss all of this in more detail in Cross 1999, 84–9.

22 The relevant powers are intellect and will: see *Ord.* 2, d. 1, q. 6, n. 316; *Ord.* 2, d. 16, q. un., nn. 15–16, 18. See also Aquinas, *ST* I.77.1, esp. ad 5. Scotus sees the intellect as containing various sub-powers. In addition to the agent intellect, responsible for abstracting intelligible species from phantasms (see *Ord.* 1, d. 3, pars 3, q. 1, nn. 359–60), Scotus accepts Augustine's analysis of intellect into memory and intelligence, the first of which is responsible for storing species and forming concepts, and the second of which is responsible for the act of understanding: see *Ord.* 1, d. 2, pars 2, qq. 1–4, nn. 221 and 291; *Ord.* 1, d. 3, pars 3, q. 4; *Ord.* 1, d. 27, qq. 1–3, n. 46. Scotus puzzles about how to fit memory and intelligence into the Aristotelian categories of agent and possible intellects. He is convinced, following Aristotle's belief that the intellect can be made all things (Aristotle, *De anima* 3.5 [430^{a}14–15]), that the intelligence (the Augustinian faculty that actually understands) is part of the possible intellect. He believes too that the aspect of memory that is responsible for storing intelligible species is part of the possible intellect. But he is unsure whether the aspect of the memory that is responsible for concept formation should be classified as agent intellect or as possible intellect: for the whole discussion, see *Quodl.* 15, a. 3, nn. 13–20. (Scotus even suggests in passing that the agent intellect, if deemed to be responsible for concept formation, could be simply a part of the memory [*Quodl.* 15, a. 3, n. 20], but since he nowhere suggests that the memory is responsible for abstracting species, I doubt that this is anything other than a slip: agent intellect is either partly included in memory, or not included at all.) The reader is left with the decided impression that, with the exception of the abstractive agent intellect, Scotus regards Augustine's analysis as far more useful than Aristotle's – presumably because Scotus's real interest lies in the process of concept formation, and Augustine's analysis is itself aimed, to a greater extent than Aristotle's, at proving an account of this process. For a discussion of the powers of the soul in Duns Scotus, Aquinas, and Henry of Ghent, see A. Broadie 1995, 28–9; see also Grajewski 1944, ch. 8.

23 We would want to talk about essential properties that are not part of its kind–nature. But the difference is merely terminological.

24 We should keep in mind that the thinkers I examine here did not always have a clear grasp of this distinction and often (as we shall see) slip between the two senses quite easily. I will not always be very systematic about this, sometimes following their usage without comment, and sometimes – when necessary to avoid equivocation – trying to get clear about the relevant sense.

25 *ST* I.77.1 ad 6.

26 *ST* I.77.1 ad 5.

27 *ST* I.76.1 ad 4.

28 *Ord.* 2, d. 16, q. un., n. 18; n. 12.

29 See *Quodl.* q. 3, n. 15, for the sufficiency of inseparability for real identity (and therefore the necessity of separability for real distinction).

30 *Ord.* 2, d. 16, q. un., n. 15.

31 *Ord.* 2, d. 16, q. un., n. 16.

32 For the first point, see for example *ST* IaIIae.55.4 ad 1; *ST* IaIIae.110.2 ad 3. On the second point, Aquinas claims that only actual things (by which he means to exclude accidents) actually do things: see *ST* I.75.2 in corp. On the other hand Aquinas is happy to make a distinction between properties that inhere in the essence of the soul and properties that inhere in the powers (and *not* in the essence): see *ST* IaIIae.110.4 c; whereas Scotus argues that talk of something inhering in the powers is just a way of talking about certain sorts of properties' inhering in the essence: an inherence relation that they have specifically in virtue of their inherence in the powers: see, for example, *Ord.* 3, d. 2, q. 1, n. 14.

33 Henry, *Quodl.* 3, q. 14 (1:66ʳS; see also 1:68ᵛZ, 1:69ʳZ).

34 Henry, *Quodl.* 3, q. 14 (1:71ʳF).

35 *Ord.* 2, d. 16, q. un., n. 13. See also *In Metaph.* 9, q. 5, nn. 12–15.

36 *Ord.* 2, d. 16, q. un., n. 15.

37 *Ord.* 2, d. 16, q. un., n. 17; see also *In Metaph.* 9, q. 5, nn. 12–14.

38 See *De Div. Nom.* 5 (Pseudo-Dionysius 1857, 820D).

39 *Ord.* 2, d. 16, q. un., n. 17. For other discussions of unitive containment, even more tantalizingly brief, see *Ord.* 4, d. 46, q. 3, n. 4; *Rep.* 2, d. 1, q. 6, n. 14; *In Metaph.* 4, q. 2, nn. 143, 159–60.

40 *Ord.* 1, d. 8, q. 4, n. 198, with reference to *De Fide Orth.* 1, c. 4 (John of Damascus 1864, 799C); c. 4 (John of Damascus 1955, 21); I examine the distinction between the divine essence and attributes in more detail in Cross 1999, 43–4. Scotus identifies the divine essence as such with the Trinity: see Cross 1999, 7, and the texts cited there.

41 *Ord.* 1, d. 8, q. 4, n. 210.

42 *Ord.* 1, d. 8, q. 4, n. 213; see also the text cited at n. 4 above.

43 *Ord.* 1, d. 8, q. 4, n. 214.

44 On this, see Henninger 1989, ch. 3.

45 On this, see Cross 1998, 95–100.

46 For a different interpretation, see A. Broadie 1995, 28.

47 For Scotus's account of matter and form, see Cross 1998, chs. 2 and 3.

48 See Cross 1998, 35–7.

49 See Cross 1998, 37–8 for a discussion and assessment of this claim.

50 For the claim that substantial form, matter, and composite substance all require explanations of their individuation, see *Ord.* 2, d. 3, pars 1, q. 4, n. 187.

51 *ST* I.76.3.

52 Aquinas, *Quodl.* 3, q. 2, a. 2.

53 Compare proposition 13 "in naturalibus" condemned by Kilwardby at Oxford in 1277, printed in Denifle and Chatelain 1889–1897, 1:559.

54 Scotus believes it "probable" that each bodily organ has its own substantial form too. I discuss this in detail in Cross 1998, 68–70. I discuss Scotus's general theory of the plurality of forms, along with his arguments against the opposing positions held by Aquinas and Henry of Ghent, in Cross 1998, 47–68.

55 *Ord.* 4, d. 11, q. 3, n. 54.

56 *Ord.* 4, d. 11, q. 3, n. 38. There are some textual difficulties with this passage, which I discuss in Cross 1998, 57, n. 27.

57 *Ord.* 4, d. 11, q. 3, n. 46.

58 *Ord.* 3, d. 2, q. 2, n. 7. I discuss this theory in Scotus in great detail in Cross 1995 and Cross 1998, ch. 5.

59 See, for example, Aristotle, *Metaph.* 7.6 (1045^{b}17–21); Scotus, *Lect.* 2, d. 12, q. un., n. 37.

60 *Lect.* 2, d. 12, q. un., n. 50; see also the texts cited in Cross 1998, 91, n. 44.

61 Henry of Ghent uses the complexity of these relations as a way of arguing against the plurality view: see Cross 1998, 49–55. Essentially, Scotus argues that the basic subject for all of these forms is matter: see Cross 1998, 67–8.

62 For the whole discussion, see Cross 1998, 67–70. This analysis makes Scotus immune to the condemnation of Olivi's position at the Council of Vienne in 1312. According to the condemned position, "the substance of the rational or intellective soul is not of itself and essentially the form of the human body": Tanner 1990, 1:361. See the discussion in Pasnau 1997a, 110–11, though note that Pasnau incorrectly refers to the (nonexistent) Council of *Vienna*.

63 *Ord.* 2, d. 8, q. un., n. 4.

64 *Quodl.* q. 9, n. 11, referring to Aristotle, *De Sensu* 1 (436^{a}11–12, 436^{b}1–10); see also *Ord.* 4, d. 44, q. 2, n. 6.

65   *Ord.* 4, d. 44, q. 1, n. 4.

66   In fact, there is an objection to an identification of the vegetative, sensory, and intellective souls that Scotus does not deal with. As we have seen, the intellective soul is unextended. Technically, it exists whole in the whole body, and whole in each part of the body (see, e.g., *Ord.* 1, d. 2, pars 2, qq. 1–4, n. 386). But other substantial forms – for example, the vegetative soul in plants or the bodily form – are physically extended (see *Lect.* 1, d. 17, pars 2, q. 4, n. 228). (Equally, Scotus's arguments outlined in Section I rely on the presupposition that the bodily form is extended; otherwise, there would be no reason why this form could not be the subject of intellectual cognition.) But nothing can be both extended and nonextended. So it is hard to see how the intellective soul could be identical with the vegetative soul. Since, for reasons I am about to outline, identifying these souls has some philosophically highly desirable results, it is a shame that Scotus did not consider the whole issue in more depth.

67   Scotus cannot appeal to the transitivity of the actualization relations that exist between soul, bodily form, and matter, since this transitivity is precisely what requires explaining.

68   Aquinas, *ST* I.76.4 ad 2.

69   *Ord.* 4, d. 49, q. 14, n. 4.

70   Aquinas, *ST* I.75.6 c.

71   *Ord.* 4, d. 43, q. 2, n. 17.

72   I argue this at length in Cross 1997b.

73   For Scotus's belief in the factual postmortem survival of the soul, see *Ord.* 4, d. 43, q. 2, n. 28.

74   *Quodl.* q. 9, n. 12; see *Ord.* 4, d. 43, q. 2, n. 13, citing Aristotle, *De an.* 2.2 (413^{b}29–31).

75   *Ord.* 4, d. 43, q. 2, n. 17. Note that the relevant senses here are not the five exterior senses but the interior senses.

76   Adams sees the *Quodlibet* account as moving "closer to that of Aquinas" (Adams 1992, 14). In this account, Scotus is unequivocal that the soul by its nature does not depend on matter (*Quodl.* q. 9, n. 4). But in holding that the soul is unextended, the *Ordinatio* account appears to make just this claim too. Scotus is, in the later account, less optimistic about being able to *show* the truth of the claim. Nevertheless, the argument from functional immateriality to existential independence is a concession towards Aquinas – though not one for which Scotus offers any justification. Perhaps we could see the modalities in the *Quodlibet* passage as in some sense nomological, not metaphysical, in which case the sense would be that, if the soul can survive the demise of its body, then, since the soul has immaterial functions, its survival is natural, not requiring a

miracle. (Contrast disembodied fire-form, the existence of which would certainly require special divine intervention. For the possibility of such disembodied form, see Cross 1998, 38–40.) Nevertheless, Scotus always insists that the soul has a natural inclination for union with the body: see *In Metaph.* 4, q. 2 n. 26; *Ord.* 3, d. 1, q. 1, n. 8; *Quodl.* q. 9, n. 4.

77   *Ord.* 4, d. 45, q. 2, n. 8. Note of course that this sort of direct presence does not issue in any sort of *sensation*: see *Ord.* 4, d. 49, q. 2, n. 6.

9 Cognition

The traditional philosophical category of epistemology serves medieval philosophy poorly. The medievals were concerned with most of what now falls within the theory of knowledge, but they never thought of knowledge as the sort of integrated topic around which one might construct a philosophical theory.[1] Much the same might be said about philosophy today. In place of knowledge, philosophers now focus their energies on cognition; in place of the theory of knowledge, we now have cognitive theory. This way of dividing up the philosophical terrain turns out to be well suited to the study of medieval philosophy. The medievals, rather than focusing on how knowledge differs from mere true belief, focus on how we manage to form true beliefs: How does the process work? To answer this question is to develop a theory of cognition.

As in most matters, John Duns Scotus does not distinguish himself in cognitive theory by adopting a radically new perspective. Scotus accepts the general cognitive framework set out by his most distinguished recent predecessors, Thomas Aquinas and Henry of Ghent; where he disagrees, he does so in ways that reinforce the broader contours of the theory.[2] Scotus is interesting, then, not because he offers any startlingly new ideas about cognition, but because he gives a careful and penetrating analysis of the field as it stood at the end of the thirteenth century. In many ways, he sees the issues in more depth than had anyone before him.

I. THE COGNITIVE FRAMEWORK

Medieval cognitive theory takes its primary inspiration from Aristotle, with significant modification and supplementation from

Augustine and Avicenna. The history of thirteenth-century cognitive theory largely consists in progressively more sophisticated efforts at combining these various influences into a systematic and harmonious account of how animals (including, especially, human beings) process information about the world around them. By the end of the thirteenth century, there was substantial consensus among the Scholastics about the proper way of understanding the basic components of our cognitive systems. Scotus endorses the consensus view in most of its basic details.

First, and most basically, Scotus endorses a distinction between the sensory and the intellective components of cognition. The sensory powers consist of the usual five external senses and the internal senses of the brain: common sense, phantasia, imagination, the estimative power, and memory.[3] As we will see, Scotus rejects one standard way of drawing the distinction between sense and intellect: he denies that material individuals are the object of the senses exclusively, and he denies that universal essences are the exclusive object of the intellect (see Section IV). Still, Scotus does accept another standard basis for the sensory–intellectual distinction: he agrees that the sensory powers have physical organs whereas the intellect is immaterial.[4] This leads to the further conclusion that the senses, owing to their materiality, cannot act directly on the intellect, owing to its immateriality.[5]

Among animals, only human beings have an intellect. Like most of his contemporaries, Scotus accepts the familiar Aristotelian distinction between the intellect's receptive component (the possible intellect) and its active component (the agent intellect). Again like most of his contemporaries, Scotus takes both the agent and possible intellect to be enduring powers within the human mind. He rejects readings of Aristotle on which the possible intellect exists only when it is actually thinking,[6] or on which the agent intellect is not a part of the human mind.[7] Scotus is reluctant, however, to describe these as two separate powers within the mind: he postulates a formal rather than a real distinction between the possible and agent intellects.[8] But the ontological status of the distinction has little bearing on Scotus's theory of cognition: even a merely conceptual distinction would require a difference in function. The function of the agent intellect, in Averroës's words, is "to transfer from order to order," to make the transition from sensory images to universal concepts.[9] The function of the possible intellect is to receive and then to store this information; human thought occurs in virtue of these intelligible forms (or *intelligible species*) being actualized in the possible intellect.[10]

In this life, the intellect derives its information from the senses (see Section V). But even before the intellect begins to classify and conceptualize the sensory data, the senses themselves process that information in various complex ways. The simplest form of sensation, sensation *per se*, occurs when one of the five external senses apprehends the sensible quality that is its proper object: when sight sees color, for instance, or hearing hears sounds. Speaking more broadly, one sees darkness, or sees a human being. This is sensation *per accidens*.[11] When the internal senses of the brain store and reimagine this information (in the internal sense of *phantasia*), they generate *phantasms*.[12] These phantasms, abstracted by the agent intellect, are in this life the intellect's sole source of information:

A real concept is caused naturally in the intellect of a wayfarer only by the things that are naturally capable of moving our intellect. These are (a) the phantasm (or the object depicted in phantasms) and (b) the agent intellect.[13]

With this, Scotus endorses Aristotle's well-known remark that "the soul never thinks without a phantasm."[14] Scotus takes this remark one step further. It was Avicenna's view that the intellect, once given its initial data, can operate entirely on its own, free from any sensory influence.[15] Scotus rejects this, holding instead that the intellect must continually turn back toward phantasms. Following Thomas Aquinas,[16] but explaining the idea rather more clearly, Scotus maintains that the senses and intellect work in tandem:

The intellect understands nothing except by turning toward phantasms: not that this turn (*conversio*) belongs to intellect alone, [looking] over phantasms; rather it belongs to the soul as a whole, so that the intellect understands nothing except while *phantasia* forms phantasms (*phantasiatur*).[17]

Our conceptual thoughts are guided by our sensory images, not just as a starting point but as a constant touchstone and inspiration.

II. MENTAL REPRESENTATION

In the long, unrelentingly difficult thirteenth question of his *Quodlibeta*, Scotus asks whether the act of knowledge is absolute or relative. This is to ask whether having knowledge consists in some sort of relation to another object, or whether it consists in an absolute, nonrelational quality of the mind. Scotus's answer is that all cognition, sensory and intellectual, involves both of these components.[18] There must be a relation, first, because it is essential to all cognition that there be some object toward which the action tends. Contrary to the more familiar Aristotelian suggestion that cognition consists in a certain kind of reception of form, Scotus defines cognition in terms of an intentional relationship to other things:

A cognitive power must not only receive the species of its object, but also tend through its act toward the object. This second is more essential to the power, because the first is required on account of the power's imperfection. And the object is the object less because it impresses a species and more because the power tends toward it.[19]

Here to tend (tendere) has all of the contemporary implications of intentionality. To tend toward another is to represent another, to be about another – not in the way that a word or a picture represents something else, but in the distinctive (and highly mysterious) way in which thoughts and perceptions are about things. Words and pictures do not themselves tend toward what they represent; they do so only through the mind of an interpreter. Thoughts and perceptions need no interpreter, for they are the interpretation; they themselves tend toward other things. In this sense, they have intentionality.

So cognition essentially involves a relation to an object. But that is not to say that a cognitive act just is a relation. The act itself is an absolute entity, existing wholly within the cognitive power. We do not usually conceive of cognition in this way because "an operation is generally understood in respect of its tending toward an object."[20] But the foundation of this intentional relationship is a nonrelational quality existing within the cognitive agent. It is this absolute quality that should be the locus of any attempt to give a meaningful explanation of intentionality. How do thoughts and perceptions tend toward things? The answer Scotus gives is in basic respects the same one that philosophers had been giving throughout the thirteenth century: he appeals to sensible and intelligible species that inform our cognitive powers and thereby cause acts of cognition tending toward the objects that the species are a likeness of.[21] The difficulties with this sort of theory were by this time well known;[22] Scotus offers what is in many respects the most sophisticated medieval attempt to defend the theory.

One of the most common complaints about the species theory was its apparent superfluousness. Scotus considers the objection:

The presence of the object is the cause of the presence of the species, and not vice versa. For it is not because the species is in the eye that white is present, but vice versa. Therefore the first representation of the object is not through the species, and therefore it is superfluous to posit the species for the sake of the object's presence.[23]

Some sort of image may be necessary in cases where the object has disappeared. But as regards the initial apprehension ("first representation") of the object, there is no need for species. The object itself is there, exercising its own causal influence on the cognitive process.

Scotus does not make the most obvious reply: he does not insist that the object is not immediately present, and that the species is needed as an intermediary, a likeness standing in for the thing itself. Critics of the species theory often assumed that such a causal role was the *raison d'être* of species.[24] But this is not Scotus's view. He gladly allows that the external object is present – that it has *real presence* – and that it is the efficient cause of the cognitive act. Still, Scotus insists that this is not enough to account for cognition. Another kind of presence is needed, the presence of the object-as-cognized:

This doesn't require the real presence of the object in itself, but it requires something in which the object is displayed (*relucet*). . . . The species is of such a nature that the cognizible-object is present in it not effectively or really, but by way of being displayed.[25]

Of course the object in itself can be present and can make an impression on our cognitive faculties. But that does not explain cognition: that sort of relationship obtains throughout the natural world, between the sun and a rock, or waves and a beach. To account for the special sort of relationship at work in cognition, Scotus appeals to a further kind of presence, which he describes as the object's presence *sub ratione cognoscibilis seu repraesentati*.[26] It is this sort of presence, here said to be brought about through species, that is required for the intentional relationships found in all cognition.

The need for this special kind of presence is more clear in cases in which the object of thought is not itself present. Even here, thought has a kind of relationship to an object: one must be thinking about something. But since the object has no *real* presence, and so exerts no causal influence, the relationship is entirely conceptual. "A relation can have no truer being than does the term to which it relates";[27] since the object's existence is merely conceptual, so too is the relationship. In such cases, the basis for the conceptual relationship must be entirely within the cognitive power. Scotus again appeals to the presence of the object-as-cognized: when we manage to think about objects, those objects have what Scotus calls *esse cognitum* within intellect.[28]

This appeal to a special sort of existence, to the presence of the object-as-cognized, is mysterious on its face and perhaps ultimately obscure. But there is something to be said for Scotus's approach. When we perceive or think about objects in the world, we are not perceiving or thinking about likenesses or representations of those things. Our object is rather the things themselves: our perceptions and thoughts tend outward; our intentional relationship is with the world, not with our inner mental states. At the same time, the cognitive act is grounded in what we have seen Scotus describe as an absolute (nonrelational) quality within the mind. It is this quality that somehow explains the intentional relationship – but how? We want to avoid the conclusion that "each intellection will be its own absolute action, a form stopping with itself, having no outside terminus."[29] And it seems plainly inadequate to appeal to mere likenesses, as if we grasp the things in themselves in virtue of having access to pictures of them. This sort of move is inadequate, not so much because it sets off well-known skeptical alarms,[30] but simply because it fails to do justice to the phenomenon. We perceive and think about objects in the world; the content of our thoughts is the world itself, not pictures of the world. Scotus's appeal to the presence of the object-as-cognized is obscure, but it has the virtue of making manifest what any satisfactory account of cognition must explain, and what to this day no account of cognition has explained.

III. IS COGNITION ACTIVE OR PASSIVE (OR BOTH)?

It was axiomatic, for most medieval philosophers, that cognition consists in being acted on in a certain way. This was how Aristotle had described both sensation and intellection,[31] and throughout the Middle Ages few would disagree. But there was considerable disagreement regarding how exactly to characterize the passive character of cognition. When Scotus comes to consider the causal role played by intellect in cognition, he begins with a detailed discussion of six views being defended at the time. At one extreme, Godfrey of Fontaines argued for the complete passivity of both the senses and intellect. Scotus is not exaggerating when he writes that, on Godfrey's view, "nothing in the intellective part (including both agent and possible intellect) will have in any way an active character... with respect to any intellection or with respect to the object of intellection."[32] For Godfrey, the phantasm is what causes cognition, and the possible intellect merely receives that impression.[33] At the opposite extreme lies Peter John Olivi, who simply rejects Aristotle's authority with regard to the passivity of cognition. Olivi mockingly describes Aristotle as "the god of this era," and says that his views in this area are based upon "no adequate argument, indeed virtually no argument at all."[34] Scotus fairly characterizes Olivi as "attributing all activity in intellection to the soul itself"; the same goes for sensation.[35]

In the face of such wildly contrasting views, Scotus takes a characteristically moderate stance, and he takes characteristic delight in working out the intricate metaphysical details. Olivi's position is untenable because it leaves no coherent causal role for external objects and so forces him to postulate some novel fifth kind of cause.[36] Moreover, once external objects fall out of the picture, there is no way of explaining why the intellect is not always capable of thinking whatever it likes.[37] Further, there would be no way to account for how the act of cognition takes on the likeness of its object.[38] Godfrey's view fares no better. First, "it utterly degrades the nature of the soul."[39] Moreover, it would leave us unable to think whenever we wanted to[40] and would leave no room for intellectual reasoning and deduction.[41] Further, it leaves no way of accounting for cognitive error because acts of cognition will necessarily conform with the phantasms (and if the phantasms are themselves in error, there is no way to account for how we may or may not come to grasp as much).[42]

Scotus proposes a compromise account of intellectual cognition, according to which the soul and the object (by way of an intelligible species) must cooperate in producing the act. There are various ways in which two causes cooperate in producing one effect:[43]

A. Cooperating equally *(two people pulling a boat)*
B. Essentially ordered

    1. The higher cause acts on the lower
        1a. The higher cause gives the lower the power or form by which it acts *(God and creatures; sun and man in procreation)*
        1b. The higher cause simply puts the lower in motion *(hand and stick, hitting a ball)*
    2. The higher cause does not act on the lower but has a greater causal power than does the lower *(man and woman in procreation)*

In type (A) cases, the causes are of the same kind and order. Either might produce the effect on its own, if its present causal power were simply increased.[44] In type (B) cases, there is no such symmetry. The lower cause in these cases is essentially dependent on the higher cause, either as its cause (1a, 1b) or merely as its essential complement (2). Intellect and object (or species) cooperate in this last way:

They are causes essentially ordered, in the last way, so that one is unconditionally more perfect than the other, and yet each is complete in its own causality, not dependent on the other.[45]

In standard cases (ignoring, for instance, the beatific vision), the intellect is the more perfect cause, and it uses the intelligible species as its instrument.[46]

In type (B) cases, two causes do the job better than could one cause alone.[47] What then does the intelligible species contribute? In what sense is it an instrument? A species is a form, not an object that can be wielded like a stick. Scotus answers this question by drawing an analogy to the way the hand might use the *sharpness* of a knife. Changing the scenario, he imagines this sharpness transferred to the hand itself, in which case the hand would use its sharp edge in much the way that the mind uses an intelligible species. The hand would be the principal cause, in virtue of its moving power, and its sharpness would be a secondary cause. It is in precisely this sense that the intellect and intelligible species jointly produce an act of cognition.[48]

Scotus goes on to make a startling suggestion. Just as it makes perfect sense, in the initial scenario, to think of the hand using the sharpness of the knife, so we can (at least in principle) conceive of intelligible species being somehow connected to the intellect without actually informing it.

If a species could exist (*inexsistens*) for intellect without inhering as a form, and if that manner of existing were or could be sufficiently connected to intellect, then these two partial causes (intellect and species), connected to one another, could have the same operation that they can have now when the species informs the intellect.[49]

This is to say that in principle there is no causal objection to the idea that the content of our thoughts might be determined by features outside the mind. Scotus concedes that it is not clear how a species, as an accidental form, could be connected to the intellect without actually informing it. But Scotus is after another conclusion: his view is that the intellect can (in special cases) operate without being essentially ordered to *any* intelligible species. He believes that an intelligible object might be immediately present to the intellect, without species, and might produce an act of cognition without informing the intellect.[50] In this way, the intellect could have an immediate vision of external objects. The term Scotus coined for this sort of vision is *intuitive cognition* (see Section V).

IV. THE OBJECT OF INTELLECT

What is the function of the senses? What is the function of the intellect? The first question is relatively easy to answer: each of the five external senses functions so as to convey a certain sort of information about the external world. In the Aristotelian tradition, the senses are individuated by the fact that each has its own object(s): sight has color, hearing sound, and so forth. Scotus offers a variation of this strategy, proposing to individuate the senses in terms of the different way that each sense is equipped to receive information from without.[51]

What about the intellect? Aquinas had proposed that the intellect's proper object is the quiddity of material substances. The function of intellect, in other words, is to grasp the essences of objects in the material world.[52] Understandably, this met with opposition from other Christian theologians, who questioned whether such a view could be squared with the doctrine of the beatific vision. How could the intellect's proper function be tied to life on earth, when human happiness is directed entirely toward the next life, toward intellectual union with God? In light of these concerns, among others, Henry of Ghent identified God as the proper object of intellect.[53]

Scotus finds neither view satisfactory, and so he proposes a characteristically subtle middle ground. The proper object of intellect – that is, the object that is primary in virtue of being most suited to intellect (*primum obiectum adaequatum*)[54] – is being (*ens*) taken in its most general sense. In this sense, Scotus argues that being is common to everything that the intellect could potentially conceive. It is common to God and God's attributes, to the essences of created substances, and to all the accidental features of created substances.[55] (Here Scotus must make his controversial claim that the concept of being is univocal between God and creatures.[56]) What unifies the intellect's diverse operations is its grasp of being in all of its various manifestations. Just as sight has color as its object, so the intellect has being, and it is capable of grasping all being in just the way that the eye is capable of grasping all colors.[57]

Ghent's view fails, most basically, because God is not the most common feature of everything intelligible. All things have their being from God, but still we grasp objects in virtue of their own created being:

God contains virtually within himself all things that are intelligible *per se*. But he is not for this reason the adequate object of our intellect, because other beings move our intellect through their own power.[58]

Aquinas's view fares no better. First, it takes too limited a perspective. Even if the essences of material objects were the proper object of intellect in this life, that would not account for the capacities of the blessed in heaven, or even the capacities of separated souls. "The first object assigned to a power is what is adequate to the power *given the nature of the power*, not what is adequate to the power *in a particular state*."[59] To say that in the next life the human intellect will be given a new object and a new function is in effect to claim that the intellect will be made into a different power.[60] So if the intellect has a capacity in the next life, it must have it in this life as well. Moreover, even if in this life the intellect must *begin* with ideas drawn from the material world, still it can develop those ideas in such a way as to transcend the sensible and achieve a real (albeit indirect) understanding of God's nature.[61] Therefore the intellect's proper object is not the quiddities of material objects but instead all being, including God and the angels.

Scotus believes that there is nothing intelligible to any intellect that is unintelligible to us. (Even God's essence is intelligible, albeit never completely, to the blessed in heaven.) Whatever any mind can know, our minds can know.[62] But of course this holds only in principle. In this life there are many things that we have no knowledge of, and many things that we cannot possibly grasp directly (above all, God's essence). As things stand, the intellect's powers are limited to the world around us, in just the way that Aquinas's account describes. This suggests an objection: if Scotus is right that the intellect's proper object is being in general, then why does the intellect not have access, even in this life, to all forms of being? Scotus handles this objection by distinguishing between the intellect's natural power, which extends to all being, and its presently limited power:

Our intellect understands in its present state only things whose species are displayed in the phantasm. This is so either because of the punishment of original sin, or because of a natural correspondence in operation between the soul's powers, in virtue of which we see that a higher power operates on the same thing that a lower power operates on (assuming that each is operating perfectly).[63]

As far as this life is concerned, the intellect must work through the senses. For now, its proper object is the material world. This seems to be a considerable concession to Aquinas and other advocates of the traditional Aristotelian model. At this point, Scotus's claims about being as the proper object of intellect appear to be highly theoretical, with no direct application to our lives at present.

But the concession is not nearly as considerable as it seems. As we will see in the next section, Scotus is at least tempted to postulate a form of intellectual cognition – intuitive cognition – that grasps objects directly, bypassing phantasms. Moreover, quite apart from intuitive cognition, Scotus rejects a key Aristotelian principle: that the intellect concerns the universal, the senses the singular. Scotus holds that although the senses are limited to grasping the singular, the intellect is capable of grasping both the singular and the universal.[64] Since "intelligibility follows being," and since singular entities have being above all else, the singular must at least in principle be intelligible.[65] Moreover, Scotus argues that we in fact do grasp the singular through intellect. Otherwise there would be no explanation for some of our most basic mental capacities: How could we draw inductive conclusions on the basis of particulars? How could we love individuals?[66] So even if the intellect is for now limited to cognition through phantasms, Scotus still denies that the intellect's only proper object is quiddities or universals.

If there is anything to the idea that the intellect is incapable of grasping the singular, it is that the intellect cannot grasp the singular *as singular*. But this is something that the senses are likewise incapable of. Scotus argues as follows:

Suppose that two white things are put in front of sight, or two singulars of any sort in front of intellect. Let them be in reality essentially distinct, but with exactly similar accidents, including place (two bodies in the same place, or two rays in the same medium), and with exactly the similar shape, size, color, and so on for any other conditions that might be listed. Neither intellect nor sense would distinguish between them; instead, they would judge them to be one. Therefore, neither one cognizes any such singulars in terms of its proper aspect of singularity.[67]

It is a tenet of Scotus's metaphysics that two individuals might be exactly similar in all their accidental features and yet be individuated by some further element, their haecceity. Yet it is a tenet of his cognitive theory that we cannot know this haecceity (at least in this life), even though we can know singulars.

V. INTUITIVE COGNITION

Scotus's famed distinction between intuitive and abstractive cognition makes its first explicit appearance in Book 2, Distinction 3 of his *Lectura*:

We should know that there can be two kinds of cognition and intellection in the intellect: one intellection can be in the intellect inasmuch as it *abstracts* from all existence; the other intellection can be of a thing insofar as it is present in its existence.[68]

This would prove to be, by far, Scotus's most influential contribution to the theory of cognition. As Katherine Tachau has shown in detail, "the history of medieval theories of knowledge from ca. 1310 can be traced as a development of this dichotomy."[69]

It is surprising that this is so. Although Scotus was the first to use this terminology to make this distinction, the distinction itself had been made by earlier Scholastics.[70] Moreover, Scotus himself devotes relatively little space to the topic; when he does take up the distinction, he generally employs it in quite modest ways, in contexts peripheral to the subjects of knowledge and cognition. Moreover, the distinction itself is a rather pedestrian one. When Scotus describes intuitive cognition as being "of a thing insofar as it is present in its existence" (as in the preceding excerpt from his *Lectura*), he is simply describing the mode of cognition that we associate with perception: cognition that yields information about how things are right now.[71] In fact, Scotus explicitly counts sensation as a form of intuitive cognition, and he describes imagination as a kind of abstractive cognition.[72] Although Scotus's followers like to say that intuitive cognition was a "revolutionary" development in medieval philosophy,[73] it is hard to acquire that impression simply by studying Scotus's texts.

What makes intuitive cognition so interesting? First, and most obviously, there is Scotus's claim that the human intellect can in principle have intuitive cognition: that our intellects are capable of a kind of intellectual *vision*. (Of course it would not truly be visual, no more than it would be, say, auditory. But the analogy to sight is irresistible.) Our ordinary mode of intellectual operation is abstractive. We grasp the nature of triangles and dogs via phantasms, and this mode of cognition leaves us incapable of determining whether any such things actually exist right now. I can think about dogs in general, or even about one dog in particular. But to know whether a particular dog (or even any dogs) exist right now, I need the senses. Scotus's surprising claim is that in principle the intellect could have such information without the senses. In effect, Scotus is arguing for the theoretical possibility of some form of extrasensory perception.[74]

There are two main arguments for this claim. First, Scotus argues that the intellect, as a higher cognitive power, should be able to do whatever our lower cognitive powers, the senses, can do.[75] Second, he appeals to a point generally accepted by his contemporaries: that the blessed in heaven *will* have an intellectual, intuitive cognition of the divine essence.[76] These arguments are weak, but they are perhaps strong enough to reach Scotus's modest conclusion. This modest conclusion requires establishing only that it is *conceivable* for our intellects to have some kind of direct, perceptual acquaintance with reality. If God can make it happen, then it is at least conceivable. And if the senses can have this kind of cognition, then surely it must be possible, at least in principle, for the intellect to do so as well. All that would be required, presumably, is the right sort of causal influence from object to intellect (see the end of Section III).

Taken only this far, the argument for intuitive cognition is intriguing in an abstract, theoretical way. But the doctrine never would have received such attention if there were nothing more to it. What captured the imagination of later Scholastics was Scotus's suggestion, in some of his latest writings, that intuitive cognition is not just a theoretical possibility but an essential and utterly ordinary aspect of our everyday cognitive lives. He seems to claim, for example, that self-knowledge is a kind of intuitive intellectual cognition:

If we were not to have intuitive cognition of anything, we would not know whether our own acts were present to us, or at least would not know about those acts with any certainty. But this is false, therefore etc.[77]

In an even more striking passage, Scotus seems to contend that the human intellect, in this life, has intuitive cognition not just of its inner states ("sensations") but of the ordinary material objects perceived through the senses: "the intellect not only cognizes universals, which is of course true for abstractive intellection..., but it also intuitively cognizes what the senses cognize." As evidence for this claim, Scotus appeals to the intellect's need to reason about particular objects with the knowledge of whether or not they exist.[78] This last passage would exert a tremendous influence on later medieval philosophy. William Ockham quotes it at length, twice, to ensure that his own views about intuitive intellectual cognition "would not be condemned as new."[79]

Scotus's bold claims for intuitive cognition do in some ways look revolutionary. He repeatedly stresses that intuitive cognition differs from abstractive cognition insofar as the former occurs without an intervening species:

An abstractive and an intuitive act differ in kind, because there is a different thing producing the movement in each case. In the first, a species that is similar to the object produces the movement; in the second, the object present in its own right produces the movement.[80]

Intuitive intellectual cognition appears to bypass phantasms and intelligible species, reaching out directly to the things themselves. Such ideas led later Scholastics to become increasingly suspicious of sensible and intelligible species and to give sustained attention to the epistemological problems surrounding the standard Aristotelian account.

Yet these bold passages, as I'll call them, are hard to reconcile with the rest of Scotus's work. In some places, Scotus explicitly denies that intuitive intellectual cognition is possible in this life.[81] Elsewhere, he implicitly makes this denial by insisting that for now our intellects cognize only via phantasms:

In this life, our intellect cognizes nothing except for what a phantasm can produce, because it is acted on immediately only by a phantasm or by what can be captured by a phantasm (vel a phantasiabili).[82]

He even makes this point specifically with regard to self-knowledge:

The intellect cannot immediately understand itself, without understanding anything else, because it cannot immediately be moved by itself, given its necessary relationship in this life to what is imaginable.[83]

Sebastian Day has attempted to show that the bold passages are consistent with the rest of Scotus's writings.[84] More recently, and more persuasively, Allan Wolter has argued for a gradual evolution in Scotus's thought.[85] But even this much is doubtful. In his *Quodlibeta*, which date from the last two years of his life, Scotus consistently limits himself to arguing for the mere possibility of intuitive intellectual cognition. In contrast to abstractive cognition, the existence of which "we frequently experience within ourselves," the reality of intuitive cognition is far less clear: "Even though we do not experience it within ourselves with as much certainty, such [cognition] is possible."[86] This seems to be in conflict with the bold claims quoted earlier. For example, if intuitive cognition accounts for self-knowledge, then each of our frequent experiences of abstractive cognition would itself be an instance of an intuitive cognition and ought to be every bit as evident as abstractive cognition. Even if his bolder remarks were written after the *Quodlibeta*, it is hard to believe that Scotus could have changed his mind so dramatically in such a short time.

Moreover, even if Scotus did change his mind, his claims about intuitive cognition are fraught with difficulties. First, despite his claim that intuitive cognition is direct and unmediated by species, he shows no signs of eliminating sensible species from intuitive sensory cognition. (Does he perhaps think that only certain kinds of species are problematic?)[87] Second, his bold claims for intuitive intellectual cognition provide no indication of how the intellect could possibly function without going through the senses. In the case of self-knowledge, the problem is perhaps less acute. But it is not at all clear how Scotus can account for intuitive intellectual cognition of the material world. Obviously, some sort of causal connection must be in place.[88] Yet he explicitly holds that intuitive intellectual cognition is immediate and that it does not work through species (see Note 80). If Scotus is in fact committed to his bold view, then the only position that seems at all reasonable is to allow that, in this life, intuitive intellectual cognition comes via the senses. This is how Ockham, for instance, would later account for intuitive intellectual cognition.[89] But this solution would require Scotus to revise some of his claims about intuitive cognition: he would have to concede that it does take place through species (or he would have to abandon species entirely), and he would have to give up the claims of immediacy that he makes for intuitive cognition.[90] So understood, intuitive intellectual cognition becomes at once more plausible and less interesting.

VI. DIVINE ILLUMINATION

Although later Scholastics would increasingly turn to intuitive cognition in their analyses of knowledge and certainty, Scotus makes no such appeal. His most detailed and interesting discussion of these topics comes in reply to Henry of Ghent. Ghent had argued that human beings cannot attain "certain and pure truth" without a special divine illumination. (By a "special" illumination he means something over and above the natural light with which human beings have been endowed. Fire, for example, needs no special illumination in order to burn.[91]) This would turn out to be the last hour of daylight for divine illumination. And it was Scotus who was responsible for quenching the theory, once and for all.

Scotus's argument consists partly in a refutation of skepticism and partly in a refutation of Ghent's case for a special divine illumination.

In doing the latter, Scotus works his way through Ghent's own arguments for the fallibility of unaided human cognition (arguments based on the constant changeability of the human mind and its objects).[92] Scotus also makes a more general claim: if human cognition were fallible in the way Ghent argues, then outside illumination could not, even in principle, ensure "certain and pure knowledge." On Ghent's account, the human mind cooperates with the divine light in achieving such knowledge. Scotus replies:

When one of what comes together is incompatible with certainty, then certainty cannot be achieved. For just as from one premise that is necessary and one that is contingent nothing follows but a contingent conclusion, so from something certain and something uncertain, coming together in some cognition, no cognition that is certain follows.[93]

If one part of a system is fallible, then that fallibility infects the process as a whole. Scotus's bold – but reasonable – claim is that if the human mind were intrinsically incapable of achieving certain knowledge, then not even divine illumination could save it.

Scotus's own view is that the human mind is capable of such knowledge on its own. If by "certain and pure truth" Ghent means "infallible truth, without doubt and deception," then Scotus thinks he has established that human beings "can achieve this, by purely natural means."[94] How *can* such a thing be established? How can the skeptic be refuted without appealing to divine illumination? Scotus distinguishes four kinds of knowledge:

- a priori (*principia per se nota*)
- inductive (*cognita per experientiam*)
- introspective (*cognoscibilia de actibus nostris*)
- sensory (*ea quae subsunt actibus sensus*)

The general strategy is to show that sensory knowledge rests on inductive knowledge, that inductive knowledge rests on a priori knowledge, and that introspective knowledge can be defended as analogous to a priori knowledge.[95] Scotus's implicit aim is to shift as much weight as possible onto the broad shoulders of a priori knowledge.

This entire discussion – by far the most sophisticated of its kind in the Middle Ages – merits more careful study than it has yet received. Here I want to focus on how Scotus makes the case for "infallible truth" with respect to a priori claims. Notice, initially, that 'a priori' is not Scotus's own phrase: he speaks of "principles known (*nota*) *per se.*" One might initially think that such principles should be described as analytic truths. But that will not do. To say that these principles are "known *per se*" or "self-evident" is to give them a certain *epistemic* status, to make a point about how they are known. Take, for instance, the a priori principle that inductive knowledge rests on, that *whatever is the usual result of a nonfree cause is the natural effect of that cause.*[96] Perhaps this can be construed as analytic, on some notions of analyticity. But Scotus is committed to something else: that this is a principle that "has evident truth" in virtue solely of its terms.[97] This is a point not about what makes the sentence true, but about how we grasp its truth. Scotus is saying that anyone who understands the terms will immediately see that the sentence is true.

For Scotus, the a priori is the bedrock on which other sorts of knowledge rest, and so he does not attempt to locate some further set of even more basic truths. Instead, he argues that our a priori knowledge is foolproof because of certain psychological facts. When one considers a proposition like *Every whole is greater than its part*, one immediately grasps that the terms are related in such a way that the proposition must be true:

There can be in the intellect no apprehension of the terms or composition of those terms without the conformity of that composition to the terms emerging (*quin stet conformitas*), just as two white things cannot arise without their likeness emerging.[98]

The relationship between terms in an a priori proposition is like the resemblance between two white objects. As soon as we grasp an a priori truth, we immediately grasp its truth: we simply see that the proposition must be true, "without doubt and deception." Of course, we will not grasp its truth if we do not understand the meaning of its terms, but in that case we will not have truly formed the proposition in our mind. And in contrast to the analogous case of recognizing similarity, there is no room for sensory error here. The senses help us acquire certain concepts, but once we have those concepts, the senses drop out of the picture: sensory reliability becomes irrelevant. Scotus offers the example of a blind man miraculously shown in his dreams an image of black and white. Once he acquires these concepts, he can recognize as truly and infallibly as anyone – his blindness notwithstanding – that white is not black.[99]

It was conceptual truths of this sort that led Augustine to his famous question:

If we both see that what you say is true and what I say is true, then where do we see it? Not I in you, nor you in me, but both in that unchangeable truth that is above our minds.[100]

Unwilling to discard such a prominent Augustinian theme, Scotus articulates four senses in which the human intellect sees infallible truths in the divine light. In each sense, the divine light acts not on us but on the objects of our understanding. By giving objects their intelligibility (*esse intelligibile*), the divine intellect "is that in virtue of which secondarily the objects produced move the intellect in actuality."[101] When the human mind grasps an a priori truth, it does so immediately and infallibly not because the mind has received any special illumination, but because the terms of the proposition are themselves intelligible: our grasp of a proposition "seems to follow necessarily from the character of the terms, which character they derive from the divine intellect's causing those terms to have intelligible being naturally."[102] It is not that we are illuminated by the divine light, but that the truth we grasp is illuminated.

This marks a turning point in the history of philosophy, the first great victory for naturalism as a research strategy in the philosophy of mind. From the beginning, philosophers had appealed to the supernatural in their accounts of cognition. Socrates had his "divine sign,"[103] Plato had recollection, Aristotle the agent intellect. It was a step toward naturalism when Aquinas located the agent intellect within the human soul and refused to postulate any special divine illumination. But Aquinas simply repositioned this illumination, making it innate rather than occasional. For Aquinas it was still a fundamentally miraculous fact that our intellect manages to grasp unchanging truths.[104] Scotus is the first major philosopher to attempt a naturalistic account of the human cognitive system. When we grasp some conceptual truth, nothing miraculous or divine happens within us: "the terms, once apprehended and put together, are naturally suited (*sunt nati naturaliter*) to cause an awareness of the composition's conformity with its terms."[105] Scotus says that the intellect's operation is, if anything, more natural, less in need of some special intervention, than are other natural actions, such as fire's producing heat.[106] It is of course God who gives the world its intelligibility, just as it is God who creates our cognitive powers. But what is new in Scotus is the idea that the mind is not a special case. From this point forward, divine illumination would cease to be a serious philosophical possibility.

NOTES

1   It is a credit to the ingenuity of Scott MacDonald that he was able to construct for Thomas Aquinas such a coherent theory of knowledge in his chapter by that name in Kretzmann and Stump 1993. But it is a sign of how far these issues are from Aquinas's main concerns that MacDonald has to draw almost exclusively on an obscure source, Aquinas's commentary on the *Posterior Analytics*.

2   Cf. Wolter 1990b, 104: "Like most of his contemporaries, Scotus held a basically Aristotelian theory of knowledge, which he modified only slightly in the interests of an earlier Franciscan–Augustinian tradition."

3   On the external senses, see *In De an.* q. 6. On the common sense, see *In De an.* qq. 9–10. Scotus mentions other internal senses in scattered passages, but he never develops a view of his own. See Steneck 1970, 127–37.

4   See, for example, *Ord.* 1, d. 3, pars 3, q. 4, n. 594; *Ord.* 2, d. 3, pars 2, q. 1, n. 296; *In De an.* q. 5, nn. 3–4; *Quodl.* q. 13, n. 62.

5   See, for example, *In De an.* q. 11, n. 4.

6   See *Ord.* 2, d. 3, pars 2, q. 1, n. 297 and *Ord.* 1, d. 3, pars 3, q. 2, nn. 541–42 commenting on *De anima* 3.4 (429^{a}24): "[the intellect] is not actually, before it thinks, any of the things there are."

7   See, for example, *In De an.* q. 13, nn. 1–2.

8   See, for example, *Rep.* 2, d. 16; *Quodl.* q. 15, nn. 60–63.

9   See, for example, *Ord.* 1, d. 3, pars 3, q. 1, nn. 359–63; *Lect.* 1, d. 3, pars 3, q. 1, n. 275; *Quodl.* q. 15, nn. 46–47, 51; *In De an.* q. 11, nn. 4–5; *In Metaph.* 1, q. 4, n. 14; 8, q. 18, nn. 48–57. Cf. Averroës, *De an.* III comm. 18 (439).

10 See, for example, *Ord.* 1, d. 3, pars 3, q. 1, nn. 363, 370, 388, *textus interpolatus* at n. 378 (Vatican 3: 364–66); *Quodl.* q. 15, n. 52; *In Metaph.* 7, q. 18, n. 51; *In De an.* q. 14 and q. 17; *In Periherm.* I, 1, q. 2; *In Periherm.* II, q. 1; Perler 1996.

11 See, for example, *In Metaph.* 2, qq. 2–3, n. 80. At *In Metaph.* 7, q. 15, n. 20, Scotus proposes a test for cognition *per se*: "for a power cognizing *per se* some object under some account, it will cognize that *per se* which remains when everything else is stripped away." In the case of vision, then, its *per se* object(s) would be the bedrock feature(s) that cannot be

removed from the perception, such as color, shape, size, motion. Take away any one of these, and vision is no longer possible.

For further discussion of sensation *per se* and *per accidens*, see *In De an.* q. 6, n. 6, where Scotus offers a different test: something is sensible *per se* if it makes a difference to the impression received by the sense. (The forthcoming edition of *In De an.* shows that the text here should read "*quia sensibilia communia immutant per se sensus proprios*," omitting *non* from that phrase.)

12 See, for example, *Ord.* 1, d. 3, pars 3, q. 1, nn. 352, 357, 365; *In Metaph.* 1, q. 4, n. 14.

13 *Ord.* 1, d. 3, pars 1, qq. 1–2, n. 35. Cf. *Ord.* 1, d. 3, pars 1, q. 3, n. 187; 1, d. 3, pars 3, q. 1, nn. 366, 392; *In De an.* q. 11, nn. 4–5.

14 *De anima* 3.7 (431^{a}16–17). Cf. 431^{b}2, 432^{a}8–9, ^{a}13–14; *De memoria* 450^{a}1.

15 *Liber de anima* V.3 (105).

16 *ST* I.84.7.

17 *Lect.* 2, d. 3, pars 2, q. 1, n. 255; cf. *Lect.* 1, d. 3, pars 3, q. 1, n. 300; *Ord.* 1, d. 3, pars 3, q. 1, n. 392; *Ord.* 1, d. 3, pars 1, q. 3, n. 187; *In De an.* q. 17, n. 13; q. 18; *Op. Ox.* 4, d. 45, q. 1. For further discussion see R. Dumont 1965, 620–4; Honnefelder 1979, 178–81.

18 *Quodl.* q. 13, n. 69.

19 *In Metaph.* 7, q. 14, n. 29. For further discussion of the role of intentions in cognition, see *Ord.* 2, q. 13 (McCarthy 1976, 26).

20 *Quodl.* q. 13, n. 96.

21 For intelligible species see, for example, *Quodl.* q. 13, n. 97; *In Periherm.* II, q. 1; *Ord.* 1, d. 3, pars 3, q. 1 passim; *Ord.* 1, d. 3, pars 3, q. 2, nn. 487, 541; *Lect.* 1, d. 3. pars 1, q. 3, n. 185; *Lect.* 1, d. 3, pars 3, q. 1 passim; *Lect.* 2, d. 3, pars 2, q. 3, n. 345. For sensible species see, for example, *In De an.* q. 5; *Lect.* 1, d. 3, pars 3, q. 1, nn. 283–4; *Lect.* 2, d. 3, p. 2, q. 1, n. 261; *Ord.* 1, d. 3, p. 1, q. 4, n. 239; *Ord.* 1, d. 3, pars 3, q. 2, nn. 471–3, 504–5. In this last passage, Scotus holds that 'species' can refer either to the act itself of cognition, or (more customarily) to the prior likeness in virtue of which the act occurs.

22 See Pasnau 1997b, part two.

23 *Ord.* 1, d. 3, pars 3, q. 1, n. 334. The argument is drawn from Henry of Ghent, *Quodlibet* V.14 (f.174^{v}Z). Ghent's concern is with rejecting one particular aspect of the standard species theory, the role given to intelligible species (see Pasnau 1997b, Appendix B). Scotus repeatedly defends the standard theory against Ghent's attacks: see *Ord./Lect.* 1, d. 3, pars 3, q. 1; *In De an.* q. 17.

24 See Peter John Olivi, *II Sent.* q. 73 (3: 55); William Ockham, *Rep.* II.12–13 (5: 274), *Rep.* III.2 (6: 59).

25 *Ord.* 1, d. 3, pars 3, q. 1, *textus interpolatus* at n. 382 (Vatican 3:366–67). Cf. *Ord.* 1, d. 3, pars 3, q. 1, n. 386; 1, d. 36, n. 28; *Lect.* 1, d. 3, pars 3, q. 2, n. 392; and Perler 1994.

26 *Ord.* 1, d. 3, pars 3, q. 1, n. 382. Cf. *Ord.* 1, d. 3, pars 1, q. 4, n. 260; *In De an.* q. 17, n. 6.

27 *Quodl.* q. 13, n. 43.

28 *In Metaph.* 7, q. 18, n. 51; *Quodl.* q. 13, n. 33, nn. 41–7 and 60–1; *Ord.* 1, d. 3, pars 3, q. 1, nn. 386–7, *textus interpolatus* at n. 359 (Vatican 3: 363). Sometimes, Scotus speaks of the object as having diminished existence (*esse deminutum*): see, for example, *Ord.* 1, d. 36, n. 34; *Ord.* 2, d. 3, pars 2, q. 1, n. 271; *Lect.* 2, d. 3, pars 2, q. 1, n. 246.

29 *Ord.* 1, d. 3, pars 3, q. 1, n. 336.

30 Scotus considers this issue at *Lect.* 1, d. 3, pars 3, q. 2, nn. 390–3. See also *Quodl.* q. 14, a. 3; *In Periherm.* II, q. 1; *Lect.* 2, d. 3, pars 2, q. 2, n. 283.

31 See *De an.* 2.11 (423^{b}32); 3.4 (429^{a}15).

32 *Ord.* 1, d. 3, pars 3, q. 2, n. 428; cf. *Lect.* n. 326. Godfrey's views are presented throughout his *Quodlibeta* – see, for example, 8.2, 9.19, 10.12, 13.3.

33 Like Henry of Ghent (see note 23), Godfrey contends that the phantasm itself can act on the possible intellect, and that intelligible species are superfluous. The agent intellect does play an active role in preparing the phantasm, but merely insofar as it separates the phantasm's intelligible content from the sensible accidents. See *Ord.* 1, d. 3, pars 3, q. 2, n. 427, and Wippel 1981, 194–200, especially note 78.

34 *II Sent.* Q58 ad 14.3 (2: 482).

35 *Ord.* 1, d. 3, pars 3, q. 2, n. 407; cf. *Lect.* n. 313 and Pasnau 1997b, 130–34, 168–81.

36 *Ord.* 1, d. 3, pars 3, q. 2, n. 415; cf. *Lect.* n. 324 . Olivi himself says that on his view "the soul's apprehensive powers are the complete efficient cause of their actions: objects cooperate with them not in the manner of an efficient cause but in the manner of an object" (Olivi 1998, 55).

37 *Ord.* 1, d. 3, pars 3, q. 2, n. 414.

38 *Ord.* 1, d. 3, pars 3, q. 2, n. 490; cf. *Lect.* n. 360; *Quodl.* q. 15, n. 30.

39 *Ord.* 1, d. 3, pars 3, q. 2, n. 429; cf. *Lect.* nn. 336, 403; *Quodl.* q. 15, n. 27; *In De an.* q. 12, n. 7.

40 *Ord.* 1, d. 3, pars 3, q. 2, n. 486; cf. *Ord.* 1, d. 3, pars 3, q. 4, n. 578.

41 *Ord.* 1, d. 3, pars 3, q. 2, n. 440; cf. *Lect.* n. 333.

42 *Ord.* 1, d. 3, pars 3, q. 2, n. 435; cf. *Lect.* n. 332. One fascinating aspect of Scotus's work is that he frequently adds later remarks undermining his earlier arguments. In this case, he remarks retrospectively that the argument "is not compelling against them [Godfrey], because it raises

a difficulty common to every view" (n. 444). Regardless of whether one posits phantasms, intelligible species, or the intellect as the active cause, the process will be an entirely natural one, not a free one. Therefore, it should determinately produce the same result, time after time. Therefore, there will always be a puzzle about how thought sometimes goes right, sometimes goes wrong. Yet, as is often the case with Scotus's "extra" remarks, this is surely not intended to be conclusive. For whereas Godfrey's view leaves little room to explain the variable, unpredictable nature of our thoughts, a less passive account, like Scotus's, could appeal to the will's influence on the intellect. For a move in this direction, see *Quodl.* q. 15, n. 28.

43 *Ord.* 1, d. 3, pars 3, q. 2, n. 496; cf. *Lect.* nn. 366–7.

44 *Lect.* 1, d. 3, pars 3, q. 2, n. 366: "if the entire power that is in all were in one, that one would pull the boat." Cf. *Ord.* 1, d. 3, pars 3, q. 2, n. 497.

45 *Ord.* 1, d. 3, pars 3, q. 2, n. 498. See also *Ord.* 2, d. 3, pars 2, q. 1, nn. 270, 278–85. Scotus presumably has in mind the object (or species) and the possible intellect. The agent intellect, in contrast, is responsible for producing intelligible species (see *Quodl.* q. 15, n. 51), and so this pairing would apparently fall into class B1a.

46 *Ord.* 1, d. 3, pars 3, q. 3, nn. 559–62; *Lect.* nn. 379–81.

47 *Lect.* 1, d. 3, pars 3, q. 2, n. 367.

48 *Ord.* 1, d. 3, pars 3, q. 2, n. 500; cf. *Lect.* n. 372.

49 *Ord.* 1, d. 3, pars 3, q. 2, n. 500; cf. *Lect.* n. 370.

50 *Ord.* 1, d. 3, pars 3, q. 2, nn. 500–1; *Lect.* n. 370; *Lect.* 1, d. 3, pars 3, q. 1, n. 305.

51 See *In De an.* q. 6, n. 3: "The adequacy of the [five] senses is in this way drawn from the variety of impressions on the organ from the object, and from the variety of ways the two conform."

52 See, for example, *ST* I.84.7, 88.3, and Scotus's discussion at *Ord.* 1, d. 3, pars 1, q. 3, nn. 110–24; *In Metaph.* 2, q. 3, nn. 22–75; *In De an.* q. 19, nn. 2–4; *Quodl.* q. 14, n. 40. The bulk of *Ord.* 1, d. 3, pars 1, q. 3 is translated in Hyman and Walsh 1973, 614–22.

53 *Summa quaestionum ordinariarum* 24.8–9. See Scotus's discussion in *Ord.* 1, d. 3, pars 1, q. 3, nn. 125–127; *Lect.* nn. 88–91.

54 *Ord.* 1, d. 3, pars 1, q. 2, nn. 69–70; *Ord.* 1, d. 3, pars 1, q. 3, n. 108. For an account of what is meant by *primum obiectum adaequatum*, see *In De an.* q. 21, n. 2; *Lect.* 1, d. 3, pars 1, qq. 1–2, n. 90. See also Honnefelder 1979, 55–98.

55 *Ord.* 1, d. 3, pars 1, q. 3, n. 137; *In De an.* q. 21, nn. 4–8.

56 *Ord.* 1, d. 3, pars 1, q. 1, nn. 26–55; *Ord.* 1, d. 3, pars 1, q. 2, nn. 129, 152–66.

57 *Ord.* 1, d. 3, pars 1, q. 3, nn. 117, 151, 186.
58 *Ord.* 1, d. 3, pars 1, q. 3, n. 127; cf. nn. 128, 190, 195; *Lect.* 1, d. 3, pars 1, q. 2, n. 91; *In De an.* q. 21, n. 3.
59 *Ord.* 1, d. 3, pars 1, q. 3, n. 186. Cf. *In De an.* q. 19, n. 2.
60 *Ord.* 1, d. 3, pars 1, q. 3, n. 114; *Lect.* 1, d. 3, pars 1, q. 1, nn. 40, 92; *Quodl.* q. 14, nn. 41–2.
61 *In De an.* q. 19, nn. 5–8.
62 *Quodl.* q. 14, n. 6 and n. 43; *Ord.* prol., pars 1, n. 7.
63 *Ord.* 1, d. 3, pars 1, q. 3, n. 187. Cf. *Quodl.* q. 14, n. 44; *In De an.* q. 18, n. 4.
64 See, for example, *Quodl.* q. 13, n. 32, and *Op. Ox.* 3, d. 14, q. 3: "there are two kinds of cognition, abstractive and intuitive,... and each can cognize both the nature, as it precedes singularity, and the singular, as a this." For Aristotle, see *Phys.* 1.5 (189^a6–8); *De an.* 2.5 (417^b19–29). For the medieval history of this question, with particular attention to Scotus's position, see Bérubé 1964.
65 *In De an.* q. 22, n. 4; *In Metaph.* 7, q. 15, n. 14.
66 *In De an.* q. 22, nn. 4–5.
67 *In De an.* q. 22, n. 6; cf. *In Metaph.* 7, q. 13, n. 158; q. 15, n. 20.
68 *Lect.* 2, d. 3, pars 2, q. 2, n. 285. Cf. *Ord.* 1, d. 1, pars 1, q. 2, nn. 34–6; *Ord.* 2, d. 3, pars 2, q. 2, n. 321(translated in Hyman and Walsh 1973, 631–2); *Quodl.* q. 6, nn. 18–19; *In Metaph.* 7, q. 15, n. 18; *Collatio* 36, n. 11.
69 Tachau 1988, 81.
70 In particular, in Henry of Ghent. See S. Dumont 1989, 592–3. The terms *intuitiva* and *intuitio* were likewise common: see Tachau 1988, 70, n. 58. Lynch 1972 argues for the importance of Vital du Four's theory of intuitive cognition.
71 Often, especially in his earliest works, Scotus uses the term 'vision' to refer to intuitive cognition (see S. Dumont 1989, 581). I am focusing here solely on what Scotus calls perfect intuitive cognition, ignoring what he calls imperfect intuitive cognition, which gives us information about the existence of things in the past or future. For a discussion of the latter, see Wolter 1990b, 115–17.
72 *Ord.* 2, d. 3, pars 2, q. 2, n. 323; cf. *Lect.* n. 290; *Quodl.* q. 13, n. 27; *In Metaph.* 2, q. 3, nn. 80, 109.
73 See, for example, Day 1947, 139.
74 Even this is not original with Scotus. Olivi, for example, devotes a short quodlibetal question to considering "whether our intellect can immediately see external sense objects without any sensory act" (*Quodlibet* I.5 [Venice, 1509], f.3^r). He concludes that the answer is no, in our present state, but he leaves open the question of whether it might be within the intellect's absolute power.

75 *Quodl.* q. 6, nn. 18–19; q. 13, n. 29; *Ord.* 2, d. 3, pars 2, q. 2, n. 320; *Lect.* n. 287; *In Metaph.* 2, q. 3, n. 112; *Ord.* 4, d. 45, q. 3 (Wolter and Adams 1993, 205); *Op. Ox.* 4, d. 49, q. 8; 4, d. 49, q. 12.

76 See *Quodl.* q. 6, n. 20; q. 13, n. 28; *Ord.* 2, d. 3, pars 2, q. 2, n. 322; *Lect.* n. 289. On the claim's general acceptability, see S. Dumont 1989, 583.

77 *Op. Ox.* 4, d. 49, q. 8. Cf. *Op. Ox.* 4, d. 43, q. 2, where Scotus makes it clear that such self-knowledge is intellectual (although there he does not explicitly speak of intuitive cognition).

78 *Ord.* 4, d. 45, q. 3 (Wolter and Adams 1993, 205): "Supposito enim quod intellectus non tantum cognoscat universalia (quod quidem est verum de intellectione abstractiva, de qua loquitur Philosophus, quia sola illa est scientifica), sed etiam intuitive cognoscat illa quae sensus cognoscit (quia perfectior et superior cognoscitiva in eodem cognoscit illud quod inferior), et etiam quod cognoscat sensationes (et utrumque probatur per hoc quod cognoscit propositiones contingenter veras, et ex eis syllogizat; formare autem propositiones et syllogizare proprium est intellectui; illarum autem veritas est de objectis ut intuitive cognitis, sub ratione scilicet existentiae, sub qua cognoscuntur a sensu). . . . "

This passage is embedded within a larger argument for the presence of memory within intellect: Scotus contends that there could be no intellectual memory if the intellect had only abstractive cognition (205–6). See also *Op. Ox.* 3, d. 14, q. 3, where much the same argument is made in the context of Christ's intellect. (For the *Ordinatio* text of 3, d. 14, q. 3, see Wolter 1990b, 101–2, 116–17.) Another intriguing text is an addition to *In Metaph.* 7, q. 15, where Scotus first denies the possibility of intuitive intellectual cognition in this life (n. 26), then seems to embrace it (nn. 27–8), and then adds further remarks (nn. 28–9) that muddy the waters to such a degree that I cannot see where he ultimately stands.

79 *Ord.* prol., pars 1, q. un. Cf. *Rep.* 4, q. 14.

80 *Op. Ox.* 4, d. 49, q. 12, n. 6. Cf. *Quodl.* q. 13, n. 33; q. 14, n. 36; *Op. Ox.* 4, d. 45, q. 2, n. 12; *Ord.* 2, d. 9, qq. 1–2, nn. 65, 98; *De primo princ.* 4.89 (Wolter 1966, 149).

81 *In Metaph.* 2, q. 3, n. 81: "within intellect, no visual or intuitive apprehension – a first cognition – is possible in this life." But then a few pages later (n. 111), Scotus remarks that the issue "is in doubt," and he gives arguments for each side. (Both of these passages are later additions.) See also *Lect.* 2, d. 3, pars 2, q. 1, n. 250: "but now, since we understand nothing except through abstraction. . . . " But this claim does not appear in the *Ordinatio* (cf. n. 277).

82 *Op. Ox.* 3, d. 14, q. 3, n. 9. Cf. *Lect.* 2, d. 3, pars 2, q. 1, nn. 253–5; *Ord.* 1, d. 3, pars 1, qq. 1–2, n. 35 (as quoted in Section I); *Ord.* 1, d. 3, pars 1,

q. 3, n. 187 (as quoted in Section IV); *Ord.* 1, d. 3, pars 3, q. 1, n. 392; *Ord.* 1, d. 3, pars 3, q. 2, n. 487; *In Metaph.* 1, q. 4, n. 14; *In De an.* q. 11, nn. 4–5; q. 19, n. 5.

83 *Ord.* 2, d. 3, pars 2, q. 1, n. 293. Cf. nn. 289–92; *Lect.* 2, d. 3, pars 2, q. 1, n. 256, *In De an.* q. 19, n. 6.

84 Day 1947. He presents it as Scotus's consistent position that intuitive intellectual cognition "is a fact of everyday experience" (86). Although Day's book remains the most useful single source for information on Scotus's theory in virtue of its thorough collection and analysis of texts, his conclusions should be treated with great suspicion. For a more balanced treatment, see Bérubé 1964, ch. 7.

85 Wolter 1990b.

86 *Quodl.* q. 6, nn. 18–19.

87 On sensible species, see note 21. On intuitive cognition without species, Day 1947 remarks, "this is a problem that has exercised the ingenuity of Scotistic commentators for centuries" (105). Some contend that intuitive intellectual cognition must involve at least intelligible species (Gilson 1952, 542, 549–50, 553n; Langston 1993), but see Honnefelder 1979, 244–52.

88 See *Quodl.* q. 14, n. 36, and *In Metaph.* 7, q. 15, n. 22: "No cognitive power within us cognizes a thing in virtue of its absolute cognizability – that is, inasmuch as it is apparent in its own right. We cognize it only inasmuch as it is capable of moving our cognitive power."

89 See the discussion in Adams 1987, 506–9. Ockham explicitly raises the worry that Scotus "elsewhere claims the opposite." Then he dismisses the worry, explaining that he is relying on Scotus not as an authority but merely as a precedent for his own views: "if elsewhere he said the opposite, I do not care; here he nevertheless held this view" (*Ordinatio* 1, pro., q. 1 [1: 47]).

90 John Marenbon reaches a similar conclusion. His interesting suggestion is that, for Scotus, intellectual intuition of material particulars occurs in virtue of the intellect's directly and intuitively apprehending occurrent acts of sensation: this "may seem to be indirect; but how could it be conceived more directly?" (Marenbon 1987, 168–9). Bérubé likewise holds that in this life the intellect acquires its information through the senses, even in cases of intuitive cognition. But he takes issue with an interpretation like Marenbon's and insists that the intellect still manages a direct grasp of particulars (Bérubé 1964, 201). Wolter perhaps has in mind a similar balancing act when he denies that "Scotus believed our intellect was ever in direct causal, as opposed to intentional, 'contact' with the extramental object in the physical world" (Wolter 1990b, 122).

91 *Lect.* 1, d. 3, pars 1, q. 3, n. 144. Ghent's own discussion comes in the first article of his *Summa quaestionum ordinariarum*. See Pasnau 1995.

92 *Ord.* 1, d. 3, pars 1, q. 4, nn. 246–57; *Lect.* 1, d. 3, pars 1, q. 3, nn. 157–9. For a detailed discussion of divine illumination, see Marrone 2001. Wolter translates *Ord.* 1, d. 3, pars 1, q. 4 in Wolter 1987, 97–131.

93 *Ord.* 1, d. 3, pars 1, q. 4, n. 221. Cf. *Lect.* 1, d. 3, pars 1, q. 3, nn. 168–70.

94 *Ord.* 1, d. 3, pars 1, q. 4, n. 258.

95 *Ord.* 1, d. 3, pars 1, q. 4, nn. 229–45; cf. *Lect.* 1, d. 3, pars 1, q. 3, nn. 172–81, translated in Frank and Wolter 1995. For another fascinating treatment of these same issues, see *In Metaph.* 1, q. 4. See also Effler 1968 and Vier 1951, 153–65 (sensory knowledge), 136–52 (induction), 125–30 (introspection).

96 "Quidquid evenit ut in pluribus ab aliqua causa non libera est effectus naturalis illius causae" (*Ord.* 1, d. 3, pars 1, q. 4, n. 235).

97 *Ord.* 1, d. 2, pars 1, qq. 1–2, nn. 15, 21. For discussion of *per se nota* in Scotus, see Vier 1951, 66–91, and Van Hook 1962, neither of whom raises the issue I address here.

98 *Ord.* 1, d. 3, pars 1, q. 4, n. 230. *Lect.* 1, d. 3, pars 1, q. 3, n. 174 presents much the same account, but without the compelling analogy of "two white things." See also *In Metaph.* 1, q. 4; 6, q. 3, nn. 50–60.

99 *Ord.* 1, d. 3, pars 1, q. 4, n. 234; *Lect.* 1, d. 3, pars 1, q. 3, nn. 175–6 says much the same, but without the clever case of the blind man. See also *In Metaph.* 1, q. 4, nn. 43–6, where the blind man makes another appearance.

100 *Confessions* XII.25.35, partially quoted at *Ord.* 1, d. 3, pars 1, q. 4, n. 206.

101 *Ord.* 1, d. 3, pars 1, q. 4, n. 267.

102 *Ord.* 1, d. 3, pars 1, q. 4, n. 268; cf. *Lect.* 1, d. 3, pars 1, q. 3, nn. 191–2.

103 *Apology* 31d.

104 See, for example, *De veritate* 10.6 and 11.1. I argue for this interpretation in Pasnau 2002, ch. 10, sec. 2.

105 *Ord.* 1, d. 3, pars 1, q. 4, n. 269.

106 *Lect.* 1, d. 3, pars 1, q. 3, n. 201. The point is that fire is only contingently hot, whereas the mind cannot help but see certain truths. Scotus drops this line in the *Ordinatio*, perhaps thinking that it pushes matters too far, but he continues to stress that the intellect exhibits "maxima naturalitas" (*Ord.* 1, d. 3, pars 1, q. 4, n. 269; cf. n. 272).

10 Scotus's Theory of Natural Law

The theory of natural law is the heart of the ethics of John Duns Scotus. Unlike other approaches in medieval ethics, Scotus's framework is not that of an ethics of virtue. One reason for this is Scotus's innovative concept of will, which diverges significantly from its classical and medieval predecessors. This new conception of will, and the assumptions for action theory that arise from it, require a different systematic role for the concept of virtue, one that accords greater weight to the judgment of reason than to the natural goal-directedness of purposive action. What takes center stage in Scotus's ethics is the obligation on the part of reason to what is apprehended in the natural law as a practical truth, rather than what befits the agent's end-directed nature as it is manifested in the virtues.

A second theme that determines the fundamental orientation of Scotus's practical philosophy arises from the twofold task that confronted Scotus as a theologian. On the one hand, because of the influence of the Aristotelian conception of science, he had to show that the claim of theology to be a science could be made good. On the other hand, because he belonged to the Franciscan tradition, he also had to emphasize the practical character of theology. As a result, Scotus was faced with the task of developing an understanding of practical science that would show how both demands could be consistently met.[1] As I show in detail in this chapter, Scotus's theory of natural law is precisely a response to this higher standard for rational acceptability.

The 'nature' appealed to by classical and medieval theories of natural law – however it might have been conceived by any particular thinker – was invariably associated with two criteria: it represented an authoritative standard, with determinate content, that was understood as both universal (that is, not prescriptive for just one individual) and accessible to human beings through their natural powers. Because natural law rests on a nature that cannot be changed by human action, it has universal validity. Because human beings themselves belong to that nature, they are in principle capable of knowing the corresponding law.

In the Christian context the content of nature is determined by God's initial plan of creation. According to this understanding, God's creative act, which is anchored in an eternal law, provides the only link for the validity of a universal natural law. This conception is given concise expression in Thomas Aquinas's claim that the natural law should be understood as a participation in the eternal law. Although the fundamental natural structure of human beings is mirrored in their natural inclinations, the natural law is constituted in them only through reason; for it is only as rational beings that they participate in the eternal law.[2]

This linking of natural law to eternal law does not merely place the natural law beyond the power of human beings to change. It also raises most pointedly the question of whether, and in what way, the natural law can be changed by *divine* action. For this reason the biblical "scandals," which offer apparent exceptions to the commandments of the Decalogue, became for the Christian authors of the Middle Ages the touchstone for the immutability of the natural law. The divinely commanded cases of Hosea's unchastity, the plundering of the Egyptians, and above all the sacrifice of Isaac, had to be incorporated into the understanding of the natural law if every commandment of the Decalogue was to be reckoned as belonging to that law – as most authors, and especially Thomas Aquinas, insisted. The apparent exceptions that God made in what is prescribed by natural law also presented a special problem for another reason: such an act of divine will seems to preclude human knowledge of what grounds the Commandments, unless we have some sort of insight into God's activity.

Scotus follows the main thread of this way of posing the problem when he devotes *Ordinatio* 3, d. 37, the central text in which he develops his conception of natural law, to the question of whether all the commandments of the Decalogue belong to the natural law.[3] In opposition to the view that assigned the Ten Commandments in their entirety to the natural law arising out of God's unalterable plan for creation, Scotus's conception represents in many ways a clear break and a new beginning. In recent years there has been widespread controversy in the secondary literature about how to assess Scotus's view against the background of the connection between God's act of will and the ability of human beings to know the natural law through reason.[4] Scotus's push to "denaturalize" not only natural law theory[5] but indeed his whole ethical system seems to open up three possibilties for interpretation, all of which are more or less clearly put forward in the secondary literature: either (1) the rational accessibility of ethics is subantially reduced, or (2) in the extreme version, moral knowledge is held to be attainable only through divine revelation, or finally (3) one attempts to hold fast to some residual naturalism in Scotus's thought, which is then contrasted with a radical voluntarism. This chapter undertakes to show the consistency of the voluntaristic elements in Scotus's teaching – elements that must not be ignored, that indeed need to be elucidated in detail – with the demands of a rational ethics that is intended to be philosophical and not theological. Scotus's doctrine of natural law is the cornerstone of this undertaking. In my first section I lay out that doctrine, and in the second I show how it is integrated into Scotus's ethics as a whole.

I. THE DOCTRINE OF NATURAL LAW

The question that arises in connection with the biblical problem cases discussed in *Ordinatio* 3, d. 37, is, at its core, about the possibility of a divine dispensation from the Ten Commandments.[6] The position that Scotus chooses as a foil is substantially that of Thomas Aquinas, who held that all the commandments of the Decalogue belong to the natural law. According to this view, the apparent exceptions are not dispensations in a strict sense; instead, they can be explained by reference to the real intention behind the commandment in question. To safeguard this original intention there can be dispensations in a broader sense, namely, insofar as permission is given to perform acts that, considered generally and without reference to their specifying circumstances, had originally been forbidden.[7]

Scotus's original formulation of the question (including the contrary position) concerns the scope of the commandments that belong to the natural law; he asks whether this or that commandment belongs to the natural law, not what the natural law as such amounts to. It is Scotus himself who transforms this original question about the scope of the natural law into a question about the essence of the natural law. He does so by making the possibility of dispensation a basis for defining natural law itself. This happens in two steps. First Scotus lays out the way in which he understands the concept of dispensation (*dispensatio*). Dispensation can be understood in either of two ways: as an additional elaboration of some commandment (*declaratio*) or as the abrogation of an existing commandment (*revocatio*). He thereby excludes the interpretation according to which a dispensation involves allowing an exception in the observance of an existing commandment.[8] In the second step Scotus limits natural law in the strict sense to those commandments that either are *per se notum ex terminis* – that is, can be seen to be true simply in virtue of the concepts used in formulating them – or follow necessarily from such self-evident practical principles. If one understands 'dispensation' in the way discussed here, it is obvious that there can be no dispensation from such commandments.[9] For that which can be seen as self-evident needs no elaboration and cannot be thought to be invalid.

Thus, Scotus first offers a purely formal criterion for belonging to natural law: a commandment belongs to natural law in the strict sense if, simply on the basis of the content expressed in the commandment, it is conceptually necessary that the commandment be valid. Nowhere in his work does Scotus trace the content of the natural law back to the eternal law; in fact, the doctrine of eternal law has no importance in his system. Neither the context in which a commandment is operative, nor the intention with which it is laid down, is relevant to its validity, if it is to count as belonging to the natural law in the strict sense. Scotus then makes clear what he means by this conceptual necessity when he goes on to discuss whether following the commandments is necessary for attaining the ultimate end. Only for these self-evident principles, he concludes, is it the case that what they prescribe is unqualifiedly necessary in order to attain the ultimate end. "Unqualifiedly necessary," as the context makes clear, means that it is inconceivable that one could repudiate the goodness prescribed in these commandments without thereby also repudiating the goodness of the ultimate end itself.[10]

Since the ultimate end of all action is the attainment of the highest good, and the highest good is identical with God, the only commandments that can belong to natural law in the strict sense are those that have God himself as their object. As far as the Decalogue is concerned, the result of Scotus's reflections is that only the commandments of the first table belong to natural law in the strict sense. The commandments of the second table can be counted as belonging to the natural law only in a looser sense. So only the first two commandments – Scotus is uncertain about the third – belong to the natural law in the strict sense, since only "these regard God immediately as object."[11] The content of the natural law in the strict sense can be summarized in the formulation that "God is to be loved"[12] – or rather, in the more precise negative formulation, that "God is not to be hated."[13] This commandment meets the formal criterion of self-evidence because in essence (as Scotus emphasizes in Ord. 3, d. 27) it simply states that "what is best must be loved most." On this interpretation it becomes obvious that the commandment to love God is a self-evident practical principle and therefore meets the formal criterion for belonging to the natural law.[14]

All the other commandments belong to the natural law in a wider sense. The criterion in virtue of which they belong is not their conceptual necessity but their broad agreement (consonantia) with natural law in the strict sense.[15] Scotus understands all the commandments, both those that belong to natural law in the strict sense and those that belong to it only in the wider sense, as practical truths (vera practica): the former because they are self-evident, the latter because of their accordance or agreement (consonantia) with the former.[16] Scotus's concept of agreement is defined negatively insofar as it implies that there is no strict deductive connection that would permit a necessary inference from overarching self-evident principles. More positively, these commandments can be understood as elaborations (declaratio) or explanations (explicatio) of some overarching general commandment – as Scotus makes clear in an example.[17] Commandments with this sort of consonantia extend general commandments by making them applicable to specific cases.

To elucidate this procedure, Scotus employs a comparison from the realm of positive law.[18] Assuming the validity of a general prescription that human beings ought to live peacefully in community, one can extend this rule through a more specific command that everyone is to enjoy control over his or her personal property. The introduction of such a command depends upon a prior judgment:

whether one regards the members of the community as weak in such a way that they care more for their own possessions than for what belongs to the community. The more specific injunction concerning private property is not deduced from the general commandment about living together peacefully; rather, it requires an additional assumption – that the citizens are weak – which represents a substantive addition to a situation that was conceived at the outset only quite generally.

As Scotus makes clear in another context, this conception of *consonantia* allows for two interpretations.[19] On the one hand, there are commandments that accord with general commandments but whose opposites would also be compatible with those same general commandments; on the other hand, there are those whose opposites are not compatible with the overarching general principles. Only the latter belong to the natural law in the wider sense; the former belong only to positive law. On this understanding, a commandment prescribing certain ceremonies or customs belongs to positive law, since a comparable commandment prescribing other ceremonies – and perhaps even forbidding the practice of ceremonies of the first sort – can also be conceived as being in accordance with natural law in the strict sense.

A more fundamental understanding of this interpretation of the natural law appears when one considers the background of Scotus's doctrine of natural law in *Ord.* 1, d. 44, on which his doctrine rests. Existing commandments can be obeyed, transgressed, or replaced by others. One commandment is replaced by another when another commandment is established by an act of the one who has the authority to issue commandments. When, for example, God commands Abraham to kill his son Isaac, the original prohibition of murder is set aside and replaced by another commandment corresponding to the divine act.[20] Now if an agent does not have the power to issue commandments, he or she can only either obey or "inordinately" transgress existing commandments. If someone acts within the bounds of the order established by existing law, that person acts by "ordinate power" (*potentia ordinata*); if someone either transgresses the existing order or replaces the commandments that constitute that order, that person acts by "absolute power" (*potentia absoluta*). All agents endowed with the powers of intellect and will have at their disposal the ability either to act within the bounds of an existing order or to transgress that order, whether ordinately or inordinately.

When this *locus classicus* for the distinction between ordinate and absolute power is applied to the discussion of the natural law, the following connections become evident. The entire realm is in principle subject to change; it is open to an act of God's absolute power. Divine omnipotence can dispense from every commandment that in part constitutes a given order. The only limit is the limit of God's absolute power itself; there can be no dispensation from commandments whose validity is outside the domain of God's absolute power. And the only constraint on God's absolute power is the requirement of freedom from contradiction. In virtue of his infinite power, God can replace any created order with another, provided only that there is nothing self-contradictory about his action. Everything that contains such a contradiction falls outside the scope of God's infinite power. Applied to the doctrine of natural law, this means that the natural law in the strict sense comprises all commandments that are such that any dispensation from them would involve a contradiction. Such is the case for the commandment prescribing love of God, since it requires that the greatest good be loved in the highest degree. The contradictory character of any possible dispensation follows self-evidently from the content of the concepts "greatest good" and "love in the highest degree."

Whatever does not involve a contradiction is in principle subject to God's omnipotence. And yet even this domain is not simply arbitrary. God can, to be sure, replace existing orders with others; but then it is in every case an *order* that is being replaced.[21] The notion of *potentia ordinata* does not refer to a law governing a single case but rather to some general ordering.[22] On Scotus's reading, the dispensation involved in the sacrifice of Isaac comes about when God, by his absolute power, sets aside his original ordering, which contains a general prohibition of murder, and replaces it with an ordering in which that prohibition is no longer in force. The command to kill Isaac and the general prohibition of murder cannot coexist in a single ordering. That what is changed is in every case an ordering – that is, a general law – therefore rests upon the fact that there are criteria of coherence that govern the compatibility of the more specific precepts. That is the significance of Scotus's conception of dispensation, which excludes the possibility that a dispensation would permit an exception to an existing law without setting aside that law altogether and replacing it with another.

This requirement of coherence can also, in a certain way, be understood as an interpretation of the *consonantia* that characterizes precepts that belong to natural law in the broader sense. If these commandments are in accordance with – but not deducible from – the overarching commandments of the natural law in the strict sense, they must also be compatible with each other. This requirement is a consequence of the noncontradictory character of divine action: if God were to create an ordering that contained precepts that could not be reconciled with one another, a contradiction would thereby exist. Within a single ordering, not only must direct contradiction be excluded, but the various commandments and the goods that they enshrine must also be brought into a coherent hierarchy. In accordance with this coherence criterion there is room for a weighing of goods, which – by contrast with the commandments of natural law in the strict sense – allows for the possibility of dispensation in order to avoid a greater evil. So, for example, there is the possibility of dispensation from the indissolubility of marriage if otherwise there is the danger that the displeasure of the spouses might end in murder.[23] As this example makes clear, the individual commandments are subject to a reciprocal weighing that is the prerequisite for a noncontradictory and meaningful ordering of the whole. Insofar as a comparative weighting of various goods proceeds by discursive argument, we are here dealing with a rational procedure that is brought to bear on the commandments of the natural law in the wider sense.

So although these commandments cannot be deduced from the overarching commandments, this does not mean that there are no rationally ascertainable reasons why certain commandments should be in force, or – above all – why only certain commandments should coexist in one coherent system. It is true, to be sure, that the validity of the commandments belonging to natural law in the wider sense cannot be explained by appeal to any facts having to do with human nature – as created, human nature is contingent; but on the other hand, it is also true that knowledge about the interplay between the presupposed facts and the valid commandments can be gained discursively. This knowledge is neither purely intuitive nor deductive.[24] Scotus's discussion of property rights makes this clear.[25] The right to private property cannot in any way be derived from some rational ordering that precedes the divine action. God's action is irreducibly free, and so creation is radically contingent; consequently, any commandment that does not have God himself as its object has force only in virtue of an act of divine will. How, then, can such commandments be regarded as rationally knowable without introducing determination into the divine will?

Even though we cannot answer the question why the creation is the way it is, we can nevertheless to a certain extent know the way it is. Thus, we have a certain acquaintance with what we as human beings are.[26] From the premise that human beings are more concerned about their own possessions than about those of the community, one can build an argument for the validity of a law establishing private property. If one takes as a premise some other picture of human beings, one can develop possible arguments against such a law. In either case, however, the arguments one offers will not have a strictly deductive character but will nonetheless be rational. These arguments do not make reference to the divine plan for creation, that is, to an eternal law, but rather to our limited knowledge of reality. This argumentative structure thus gives Scotus complete freedom to show the legitimacy of a plurality of orderings, but each of these must be shown to be rational in its own right.[27]

General laws can to a certain extent be reconstructed by noting how particular cases are governed. Thus, Judas, who was a sinner to the end (finaliter peccator), can in principle be saved – but not in an ordering that contains a law prescribing that every unrepentant sinner be damned. Once the particular judgment that Judas is such a sinner has been made, his salvation can take place only in an ordering that does not contain the general law prescribing that every unrepentant sinner be damned.[28] Similarly, a king's particular judgment that this specific murderer is to be put to death is in keeping with a general law (iudicium secundum legem). The individual judgment makes reference to a law that in turn must make reference to that judgment if the law is to be applicable to a specific case.[29]

This interplay of both vertical and horizontal consonantia between different levels of law allows an interpretation of Scotus's ethics that eliminates the apparent one-sidedness and lack of content in what appears at first glance to be the purely formal formulation of Scotus's natural law theory.[30] On this interpretation, the strongly formal deduction of concrete laws from self-evident general principles derives entirely from the reason why those particular laws are in force: they are in force only insofar as they can be traced back to the highest practical principles. They can be discovered (that is, rationally reconstructed) in a more broadly interpreted framework. The *consonantia* that Scotus invokes in characterizing them allows one to ascend from concrete reality to the principles that must be presupposed in any interpretation of that reality if the minimal requirement of internal coherence is to be met. Through this ascent one arrives at obligations with a determinate content.

Once we realize that on this theory of natural law rational discourse is by no means precluded, the debate over whether to treat the dependence of the second table on the divine will as a voluntaristic element in Scotus's ethics loses a good deal of its explosiveness. Similarly, rationality is not limited to the purely formal formulations of the law, with their largely indeterminate content. Scotus's theory of natural law offers a multilevel argumentative structure: alongside the supreme principles, which are grasped by formal deduction, he recognizes other basic principles. These are recognized both by their meaningful elaboration of the most general principles and by their mutual balancing and coherence; and in addition to this, they can serve as justifications for the everyday moral intuitions that are manifested in our particular moral judgments.

The issue of monogamy, which Scotus discusses in *Ord.* 4, d. 33, can serve as an example of the way in which overarching principles work in conjunction with the particular judgments that describe contingent reality.[31] Two aspects of the question of monogamy, and its abolition in favor of polygamy, require investigation: the reciprocal justice of the partners who are bound together in the marriage contract,[32] and the requirements for dispensation from the law enjoining monogamy.[33] In both investigations Scotus proceeds by assuming a general practical principle whose validity does not depend on its application to any specific case. These principles do not of themselves provide any information about whether monogamy or polygamy can be legitimate in a particular case. Nevertheless, these basic principles serve as rational procedural rules that make possible a decision about the individual case by reference to the demands of a given situation.

For the first part of the question the underlying principle is that in every exchange (Scotus discusses the marriage contract under the heading of commutative justice[34]) there should be the greatest possible equality in what is exchanged by those making the exchange, as judged in light of the purpose of the exhange.[35] Whether monogamy or polygamy is licit depends on what one takes the goal of the exchange to be: the procreation of the greatest possible number of offspring, or the restraint of unchastity. If the first, polygamy is licit; if the second, monogamy is required. Either way, whichever purpose is regarded as definitive, there are rationally identifiable grounds for or against a commandment, or, in other words, the observance of strict justice.[36]

As for the second aspect of the question, the possibility of dispensation from the commandment enjoining monogamy, Scotus again proceeds on the basis of an overarching principle. This general and largely formal principle states that if something is ordered to two ends, one of which is more fundamental than the other, it should be used in such a way as to contribute more to the more fundamental end, even if that comes at the expense of the subordinate end.[37] To act on this rule is in accordance with right reason; it also depends on a paradigmatically rational judgment. If one applies this principle for the weighing of goods to the case at hand, whether monogamy or polygamy is preferable will depend on the actual evaluation of the ends of marriage. If the situation is such that the primary goal must be the procreation of the greatest possible number of offspring, polygamy is the preferable solution; if that is not the case, monogamy is the more suitable way of realizing the other end of marriage, the avoidance of unchastity.[38]

So Scotus does not answer the original question about the possibility of dispensation simply by referring to the unknowable decision of the divine will. Instead, he has recourse to the reasons that can be offered for or against supposing that a corresponding command is in force. It is these reasons that enable one to reconstruct the rational structure of the corresponding ordering of laws.

As the discussion in *Ord.* 4, d. 33, makes clear, the principles that underlie such argumentation do not make reference to any presupposed natural human teleology. Rather, we are dealing here with principles of argumentation that can be understood as principles of consistency for any given ordering. The validity of the principles of commutative justice and the weighing of goods that Scotus brings forward in this connection are not themselves called into question in his discussion of the possibility of dispensation. Instead, those principles are used in order to make clear the coherent stucture of a whole ordering that is subject to dispensation. For this reason comparable principles can be retained for rational argumentation without calling into question Scotus's distinctive emphasis on divine freedom. As the argumentative structure of Scotus's ethics makes clear, these very same principles both underlie the rationality of divine action and guarantee that human beings can know the moral law through reason.

II. THE RELATION OF NATURAL LAW THEORY TO OTHER ASPECTS OF SCOTUS'S ETHICS

As this sketch of the theory of natural law makes clear, the concept of nature that Scotus sets forth differs in significant ways from the Aristotelian–Thomistic understanding. Scotus makes no reference at all to the agent's nature interpreted teleologically.[39] This aspect of Scotus's view is closely connected with his distinctive conception of action and willing, with a revised view of moral goodness, and with specific epistemological presuppositions about ethics as a whole.[40]

Scotus understands voluntary actions as "praxeis" in a specific sense that – as Scotus explicitly states – differs fundamentally from the Aristotelian understanding of action. Whereas Aristotle understands actions as simple, natural movements (motio simplex naturalis), Scotus understands them as acts of will that are by nature apt to be determined in their morally relevant features by an act of intellectual understanding.[41] The decisive difference between the two views is that Scotus locates the origin of actions in a freely acting power of will, whereas the Aristotelian view traces actions to the cooperative activity of the intellect with a naturally functioning appetitive power. For Scotus, actions are not the productions of a teleologically constituted natural appetite determined by its inherent end, but rather acts of a free power that does not aim at natural ends but at objects of action presented to it by the intellect. These objects do not act as final causes on the will, since only the will itself, understood as efficient cause, is responsible for an action. The intellect comes into play as a partial cause that motivates, but does not in the end determine, the will to determinate actions. Thus, the will is the cause of action in a more fundamental sense (*causa principalior*).[42]

Because this often misunderstood account of the cooperative activity of will and intellect does not ignore the characteristic modes of action of intellect and will, but instead limits them to their respective domains, it entails neither intellectual determinism nor a voluntarism that destroys the rationality of action. The intellect acts naturally: that is, it necessarily cognizes those objects to which its attention is directed, and this necessity applies both to the exercise of its act and to the content of its cognition. The will, by contrast, acts contingently, so that it is free with respect to both the exercise of its act and the object of its willing.[43] The intellect cognizes a possible object of action that need not stand in any particular relation to the appetite of the agent. The intellect cognizes objects, not ends, since an object of action (*obiectum*) is not of itself an end for action (*finis*). An object becomes an end only when it is sought after by the will. What an object is – what its quidditative character and distinctive qualities are – is a necessary feature of the way in which it is constituted. Its status as an end comes only from an act of will and is therefore contingent.[44]

Two main consequences follow from this account. First, the objective character of what is cognized by the intellect allows Scotus to retain his demand for truth in practical knowledge. Behind Scotus's provocative thesis that there are necessary truths even about contingent matters, such as acts of will,[45] is this assumption that what is cognized is independent of any prior relation to the will. A second consequence of, or perhaps a corollary to, this understanding of the object of voluntary action is that the will is to be understood as the efficient cause of free actions. The distinctive character of freedom is seen in the fact that the will is not aimed at naturally impressed ends that are themselves to be understood as final causes, as Aristotelian–Thomistic naturalism would have it; instead, the will can determine itself to action in complete independence from any final cause as coprinciple. This last point implies a thoroughgoing break with a foundational principle of Aristotelian physics and metaphysics that had also been taken as binding by medieval thinkers.[46] Scotus's interpretation of the will as a power that can move itself from potentiality to actuality without any prior cause directly contradicts the Aristotelian axiom that whatever is moved is moved by another (*omne quod movetur ab alio movetur*).[47] It is his break with this fundamental principle and the teleological interpretation of voluntary action implied by it that permits Scotus to conceive the will as a power for free self-determination.

This Scotist doctrine goes hand in hand with a thoroughgoing critique of the concept of final causality, which is so important in Aristotelian–Thomistic ethics. Unlike his medieval predecessors and contemporaries, Scotus considers the idea of a cause that exercises its causality as an end to be purely metaphorical, corresponding to no actual reality. With reference precisely to the Aristotelian conception of rational appetite, Scotus criticizes the notion that such an appetite acts in virtue of its relation to a final cause. The end at which an appetite aims can be considered a motive cause only in a metaphorical sense. In reality, one can say only of a power considered as efficient cause that it moves itself.[48] In an uncharacteristically harsh tone Scotus criticizes the appeal to final causes as a flight into fantasy (*fugiendo finguntur viae mirabiles*).[49] Against the backdrop of this altered understanding of what sorts of cause can legitimately come up for discussion, Scotus develops an interpretation of the will that conceives it in sharp distinction to the Aristotelian–Thomistic conception of a rational appetite. Here lies the root of Scotus's denaturalized conception of the will.

This difference from the doctrine of Thomas Aquinas in particular becomes especially clear when one examines the consequences it entails for Scotus's teaching about happiness. According to the Thomist view, the will must necessarily aim at happiness as the epitome of all goods, since an aversion of the will is conceivable only when the object presented to it by the intellect is in some respect lacking in goodness, which by definition cannot be the case for perfect happiness.[50] On Aquinas's view, the activity of a rational appetite with respect to its complete end or perfect fulfillment is necessarily determined. It has room for freedom because of the deficiency of the particular good that is only imperfectly conceived by the finite intellect. The appetite is necessarily determined to action by the natural tendency that is innate in it and fixed by its end. In this way a natural disposition underlies both the content and the exercise of volition.

Scotus understands the will's relation to its object fundamentally differently. By contrast with the intellectual power, which is necessitated to an act of assent by the evidentness of its objects, there is no object that determines the will to act. Its assent is given freely, no matter what degree of goodness a given object possesses.[51] Aquinas understands the relationship of a rational appetite to its end as determining the will by a natural necessity (*necessitas naturalis*), so that the will necessarily cleaves to its ultimate end, happiness, as well as to any goods that are necessarily connected with happiness.[52] Scotus breaks this unmediated connection between an end cognized as good and the corresponding act of will by introducing an element of reflexivity that is unique to the will as distinct from mere appetite. The will that wills an object also always wills its willing of that object (*vult se velle illud*). But since the will always acts freely, it can also refrain from willing (*non velle*) the willing of any given object; in other words, it always has the power to abandon or suspend its own willing. For this reason, the will does not necessarily will even the epitome of good, happiness – and this lack of necessity does not depend on someone's having a merely partial understanding of happiness.[53] On Scotus's view the will has a reflexive act (*actus reflexus*), as Scotus calls it, bearing on its own willing. The first-order willing that is directed at a particular object becomes, at the second-order level, itself an object of the will, which can determine itself either to will or to refrain from willing this object.[54] This two-tiered character and reflexivity are what make the will, as Scotus understands it, a free, self-determining power.

How can this theory of the will's free self-determination be conjoined with the formulation of a rational ethics? Scotus's view certainly severs the natural connection between the end of action, cognition, and appetite; but it by no means abandons the claim to provide a rational theory of action, as opposed to a voluntaristic theory that undermines moral requirements. Scotus's account of the will does not proceed from the assumption that the will can reject (*nolle*, will against) an object that is cognized as good. If that were the case, one could hardly speak of an action that is to be controlled by reason. No matter how well reason might come to understand the good, the will could elicit its acts in opposition to such understanding, so that every basis for ethics as a rational standard guiding conduct would be undermined. The success of Scotus's natural law theory in safeguarding our ability to come to know particular commandments through discursive reason would be meaningless, since the possibility that what is cognized as good would have its proper influence on our conduct would be nullified.

This model of the mediated, reflexive determination of the will in no way entails that the will can explicitly refuse an object that is cognized as good, that is, that it can have an act of *nolle* with respect to that object. Rather, Scotus's position admits only that the will, because of this reflexivity, can refrain from a positive act of willing the object. By thus refraining from an act of assent, it can direct the intellect to other objects, as *Add.* 2, d. 42, q. 4 makes clear. The content of the intellect's cognition is not thereby turned into its opposite; that is, the cognized good is not turned into an evil by fiat of the will. The objective value of the cognized object remains intact, even though it is in the will's power to direct the intellect to considering some other object instead.[55] The denaturalizing of the concept of object – that is, the detaching of the intellectually cognized good from any necessary exercise of the act of will – allows Scotus to posit the free self-determination of the will without having to give up on the objectivity of practical cognition.

This view has wide-ranging consequences for the concept of moral goodness. Whereas in the Aristotelian–Thomistic tradition moral goodness involves the fulfillment of an appetite that is aimed at its own perfection, Scotus's concept of will does not permit any sort of appeal to fulfillment understood in terms of a nature. In Aquinas's system moral goodness is understood ontologically, as being that contributes to perfection and is operative as final cause: as *ens perfectivum per modum finis*.[56] Scotus, by contrast, understands moral goodness as a relational concept. The morally good is constituted by a *convenientia* that is to be ascertained in a judgment. This *convenientia* is the integral possession of those features that ought to hold true according to the right reason of the agent.[57] Moral goodness is not something in its own right, *aliquid absolutum*, but a relation that holds between an act and the feaures that it ought to have.[58] This relation of *convenientia* or *conformitas* (Scotus uses both expressions) is not by itself sufficient for moral goodness. It is also necessary that the agent's reason correctly judge that this *convenientia* is present.[59]

By making the judgment of right reason (*dictamen rectae rationis*) the fundamental determinant of moral goodness, Scotus gives the concept of virtue a different role in his ethical theory from that which it had in the Aristotelian–Thomistic system. Moral goodness does not arise from the correspondence of right appetite and right reason, as is the case in Aristotle; nor is the role of reason confined to the choice of means, while the ends of moral action are given by the natural inclinations, as Aquinas holds.[60] For Scotus, prudence as an intellectual habit is given unequivocal priority, and thus the goodness of an action comes not from its relation to virtue but solely from its agreement with the judgment of reason.[61] If one examines these implications of Scotus's theory of will – which does not merely emphasize a different account of how the will operates but gives a new account of the role of reason in originating moral action – one sees that the possibility of a rational ethics is by no means called into question. It is precisely because Scotus excludes all natural determination from the will that reason becomes all the more significant. This is true, first of all, in his theory of action insofar as reason can no longer be merely a sine qua non cause of volition; instead, reason is a partial cause that for Scotus safeguards the teleological orientation of the will, which can no longer be accounted for in merely natural terms.[62] This is also true for his understanding of the natural law and the conceptions of law that make reference to it (lex positiva). Once again, the faculty of intellect, understood as the capacity to draw conclusions or as reason working discursively, compensates for the absence of a natural point of reference from which the precepts of the natural law could be reconstructed. In this account reason appears as a natural power of human beings that can exercise its activity without having to rely exclusively on divine revelation. Scotus's theory of will therefore leads neither to the abandonment of rational ethics nor to the destruction of its philosophical character.

NOTES

1 Cf. *Ord.* prol., pars 5, nn. 217–366; cf. Möhle 1995, 13–157.
2 *ST* IaIIae.91.2.
3 See *Ord.* 3, d. 37, in Wolter 1986, 268–7. Wolter offers a revision of the Wadding edition based on the Assisi Codex and a manuscript from Rome (cod. vat. lat. 883). Mercken 1998 has commented critically on Wolter's text.
4 Cf. Honnefelder 1996 and more recently Williams 1998a.
5 This tendency in Scotus's thought is encapsulated in the title chosen by John Boler for his much-discussed contribution, "Transcending the

Natural: Duns Scotus on the Two Affections of the Will" (Boler 1993).
Cf. Williams 1995b and Lee 1998.

6 For Scotus's doctrine of natural law, see Boulnois 1999, esp. 62–72;
   Wolter 1986, 57–75; Möhle 1995, 338–89; Shannon 1995, 56–68; and
   Prentice 1967.

7 *Ord.* 3, d. 37, n. 2.

8 *Ord.* 3, d. 37, n. 3.

9 *Ord.* 3, d. 37, n. 5.

10 *Ord.* 3, d. 37, n. 5.

11 *Ord.* 3, d. 37, n. 6; trans. Wolter 1986, 277.

12 *Ord.* 3, d. 37, n. 6.

13 *Ord.* 3, d. 37, n. 7.

14 *Ord.* 3, d. 27, n. 2.

15 *Ord.* 3, d. 37, n. 8.

16 *Ord.* 4, d. 17, n. 3.

17 *Ord.* 3, d. 37, n. 8.

18 Ibid.

19 *Rep.* 4, d. 17, n. 4.

20 *Ord.* 1, d. 44, n. 8.

21 Hence, I say that many other things can be done orderly; and many
    things that do not include a contradiction other than those that
    conform to present law can occur in an ordained way when the
    rectitude of such law – according to which one acts rightly and
    orderly – lies in the power of the agent himself. And therefore such
    an agent can act otherwise, so that he establishes another upright
    law, which, if it were set up by God, would be right, because no law
    is right except insofar as the divine will accepts it as established.
    And in such a case the absolute power of the agent in regard to
    something would not extend to anything other than what might
    happen ordinately if it occurred, not indeed ordainedly with respect
    to this present order, but ordinately with reference to some other
    order that the divine will could set up if it were able to act in such
    a way. *Ord.* 1, d. 44, n. 8; trans. Wolter 1986, 257.

22 *Ord.* 1, d. 44, n. 11.

23 *Ord.* 4, d. 33, q. 3, n. 9.

24 On this understanding the dispute between Allan B. Wolter and Thomas
    Williams over the ontological and epistemological status of the natural
    law can be resolved by appeal to a more precise characterization of the
    issues. Cf. Williams 1997, especially 84–93.

25 Cf. *Ord.* 3, d. 37, n. 8. Scotus frequently explains the connection among
    commandments of the natural law by reference to structurally similar
    cases in positive law.

26 We possess such knowledge either naturally or by way of revelation.

27 Cf. Kluxen 1998, especially 108–9.

28 *Ord.* 1, d. 44, n. 11.

29   *Ord.* 1, d. 44, n. 9.
30   Cf. Möhle 1999, 47–61.
31   *Rep.* 4, d. 33, considers the issue in greater detail.
32   *Ord.* 4, d. 33, q. 1, n. 2.
33   *Ord.* 4, d. 33, q. 1, nn. 4–6.
34   *Ord.* 4, d. 33, q. 1, n. 2.
35   Ibid.
36   For the completion of justice – so says an *additio* to the text – the law-
     giver's intention with respect to the exchange must be carried out. That
     the purpose can derive from a superior lawgiver (e.g., God) and not only
     from the participants in the exchange does not in principle undermine
     rationality, for this sort of intervention in the fundamental requirements
     is implied by the marriage contract's dependence on the agreement of
     the superior master (*dominus superior*).
37   *Ord.* 4, d. 33, q. 1, n. 5.
38   Ibid.
39   Cf. Boler 1993.
40   For Scotus's ethics as a whole, see Möhle 1995, Shannon 1995, Ingham
     1989 and 1996a.
41   *Ord.* prol., pars 5, n. 353.
42   *Lect.* 2, d. 25, n. 73.
43   On the relationship between will and nature, see, most recently,
     Hoffmann 1999.
44   Cf. *Ord.* prol., pars 5, qq. 1–2, n. 253.
45   "There are many necessary truths concerning contingents." *Ord.* prol.,
     pars 5, qq. 1–2, n. 350. On Scotus's understanding of practical knowledge
     as practical science, see Möhle 1995, 13–157.
46   Cf. the position Scotus criticizes in *In Metaph.* 9, q. 14, n. 5 ff., which
     he took to have been universally accepted up to that point.
47   On the meaning of this axiom, see Effler 1962.
48   *In Metaph.* 9, q. 14, nn. 122–4.
49   *In Metaph.* 9, q. 14, n. 47.
50   *ST* IaIIae.6.8.
51   "The will need not preserve in its acts the order that potential objects
     of willing (*volibilia*) are apt to have in virtue of their nature. Nor is the
     will's assent similar to that of the intellect, since there is necessity in the
     intellect on account of the evidentness of the object, which necessarily
     causes assent in the intellect; by contrast, it is not the case that the
     goodness of any object necessarily causes the assent of the will. Instead,
     the will assents freely to any given good, and it assents as freely to a
     greater good as it does to a lesser." *Ord.* 1, d. 1, pars 2, q. 2, n. 147.
52   *ST* I.82.1–2.

53 *Ord.* 4, d. 49, qq. 9–10, nn. 5–10. Cf. Spruyt 1998, especially 148–50. For
    more on this point and on what follows, see Möhle 1995, 389–414.
54 *Ord.* 1, d. 47, n. 9; cf. *Coll. par.* 17, n. 8.
55 *Add.* 2, d. 42, q. 1, nn. 10–11.
56 "Thus what is called good first and principally is being that is perfec-
    tive of another in the mode of an end; in a secondary sense, however,
    something is called good that leads [something else] to its end." *De
    veritate* 21.1.
57 *Quodl.* q. 18, n. 12.
58 "Moral goodness in an act bespeaks nothing other than a relation, since
    an act's being characterized by the requisite circumstances is not some-
    thing absolute [i.e., nonrelational] in the act, but merely the requisite
    relation of the act to the features that ought to characterize it." *Ord.* 1,
    d. 17, pars 1, qq. 1–2, n. 60.
59 Thus, moral goodness is, as it were, an adornment of the act. It
    comprises the requisite proportion to all those things to which the
    act ought to be proportioned (i.e., the power, object, end, time, place,
    and manner), and in particular as right reason dictates that these
    ought to be appropriate to the act. Thus, in place of all these we can
    say that it is the conformity (*convenientia*) of an act to right reason
    in virtue of which an act is good; if it is lacking, then no matter
    what else the act might bear a fitting relation to, it is not good.
    Therefore, the moral goodness of an act is chiefly the conformity of
    the act to right reason issuing a complete dictate regarding all the
    circumstances that ought to characterize the act.

    Ord. 1, d. 17, pars 1, qq. 1–2, n. 62; cf. *Ord.* 2, d. 7, n. 11. On this see
    Williams 1997 and Möhle 1995, 260–3, 278–329.
60 Aristotle, *Nic. Eth.* 6.13 (1144^{b}28–32); Thomas Aquinas, *In Eth.* 6.2.
61 *Ord.* 3, d. 36, n. 19. On this, see S. Dumont 1988.
62 *Lect.* 2, d. 25, nn. 69–80. On the underpinnings of Scotus's ethics in his
    account of the powers of the soul, see Möhle 1995, 158–212.

11 From Metaethics to Action Theory

Work on Scotus's moral psychology and action theory has been concerned almost exclusively with questions about the relationship between will and intellect and in particular about the freedom of the will itself. In this chapter I broaden the scope of inquiry. For I contend that Scotus's views in moral psychology are best understood against the background of a long tradition of metaethical reflection on the relationship between being and goodness. In the first section of this chapter, therefore, I sketch the main lines of that tradition in medieval thinking and examine the novel and sometimes daring ways in which Scotus appropriated them. In the sections that follow I elaborate on three areas of Scotus's action theory, very broadly conceived, in which his modifications of the medieval metaethical tradition can be seen bearing philosophical fruit. Thus, in the second section I examine his account of the goodness of moral acts, in the third his understanding of the passive dispositions of both sensitive appetite and will, and in the fourth his account of the active power of will.

I. BEING AND GOODNESS

Following Scott MacDonald we can distinguish two general approaches to the relation between being and goodness. The central claim of the *participation approach*[1] is that all beings are good because, and to the extent that, they participate in the Good itself. In *Republic* VI, for example, Plato argues that the Form of the Good is somehow responsible for both the being and the intelligibility of all the other Forms, and thereby of all other things whatsoever. As MacDonald notes, "Later Platonists, especially the neo-Platonists,

developed this strand of Plato's thought into a full-fledged cosmology"[2] according to which all things emanate from, and ultimately
return to, the Good. Although Christian thinkers saw that the doctrine of creation required them to deny emanationism, they saw no
theological reason to deny participation – in fact, they found in the
Platonist doctrine of participation a powerful theoretical tool for understanding creation. Both Augustine and Boethius, for example, held
that creatures are good because they participate in and are caused by
God, who is identified with the Good of Platonism. The participation approach makes goodness something extrinsic or relational: the
goodness of a being either is or depends on that being's relation to
something else. Consequently, this approach also requires some sort
of explicit theology or at least a doctrine of the Forms, since one
cannot explain the goodness of a being without making reference to
the nature of the Goodness in which that being participates and the
nature of the participation-relation itself.

The *nature approach*, by contrast, "starts from an identification
of the notion of the good with the notion of an end."[3] A thing is
good because, and to the extent that, it has attained the end or goal
characteristic of beings that have its nature. The characteristically
Aristotelian expression of this approach understands natures themselves as teleological. Thus, to *be* an *x* at all is to be aimed at the
characteristic end of *x*'s; to be a *good x* is to have attained that characteristic end. Unlike the participation approach, then, the nature
approach makes goodness something intrinsic: the goodness of a being is simply its having attained the end characteristic of things of
its kind. Consequently (and once again in distinction to the participation approach), the nature approach requires no explicit theology.
Since the standard of goodness is built into the nature of each kind
of thing, there is no need to refer to God or some Form of the Good
in order to explain the goodness of any particular being.

Both approaches generate what MacDonald calls "the universality
thesis," the claim that all things are good in virtue of their being.
But the two approaches arrive at the thesis differently and construe
it differently. On the participation approach, the important point is
that all things, other than God himself, have being only insofar as
they proceed from the Good and somehow imitate its goodness. On
the nature approach, the important point is that all things are good
exactly to the extent that they realize their nature, and of course

nothing can have being at all unless it realizes its nature to some extent.

The two approaches also have in common what we might call "the appetition thesis," the claim that all things aim at the good – in the case of beings with cognition, that all desire and intentional action are aimed at what the agent cognizes as good. Once again, the two approaches construe this claim in very different ways. On the participation approach, it is not clear whether the appetition thesis amounts to very much, since absolutely everything is good in the required sense.[4] On the nature approach, choosing what we take to be good means choosing what we take to be a good *for us*, that is, something perfective of us, something that actualizes our characteristic potentialities. Taken in this way, the appetition thesis is clearly substantive but far from obviously true. It requires an elaborate moral psychology, according to which all human appetites are aimed in some way at human perfection. It also naturally lends itself to a eudaemonistic virtue ethics, in which the virtues are understood as habitual dispositions of the various appetites by which they are aimed more reliably at the human good.

Even though the two approaches sometimes seem to pull in opposite directions, many medieval thinkers combined elements of both in their thinking about goodness. In Thomas Aquinas we see a brilliant attempt to synthesize the two approaches and to elaborate a normative ethics and moral psychology that does justice to both.[5] Aquinas defends the universality thesis in a way that unites the two approaches. He does so by understanding the act of creation as essentially teleological: God's creative activity is itself aimed at an end, and God brings into being creatures who are defined by their characteristic ends. And since the different sorts of creaturely being are simply different ways of imitating God, creatures participate in the divine goodness by attaining their characteristic ends. Aquinas also makes the appetition thesis plausible by showing in detail how human appetites – natural, sensitive, and intellectual – are aimed at human perfection. He identifies both appetitive and intellectual virtues by which the human good is more effectively discerned and attained in human actions and reactions.

In Scotus we see a strange fragmentation – not so much an unraveling of the Thomist synthesis as a deliberate dismantling. The creation approach remains, but the sort of goodness associated with it, which Scotus calls "essential goodness," has clearly lost its Platonic aura and is rigorously deemphasized. The sort of goodness associated with the nature approach, which Scotus calls "accidental goodness," is handled in a radically revisionist way. The notion of an end remains important, but that end is no longer the actualization of distinctively human potentialities. For Scotus argues that the ultimate end of human beings is not actually within our unaided grasp; barring supernatural intervention, no amount of action on our part will get us to that end. And although less ultimate ends are also good, accidental goodness does not consist in achieving those ends. Moreover, he severs the connection between appetite and the good in two ways. First, those appetitive powers that are indeed aimed at the good (that is, at characteristically human perfection) are devalued, since the accidental goodness of particular actions is, as I have said, not a matter of attaining any such good. And conversely, the appetitive power by which we attain such accidental goodness is, and indeed must be, aimed at something altogether distinct from human perfection.

II. THE HUMAN GOOD AND THE GOODNESS OF PARTICULAR ACTS

As I said in Section I, Thomas Aquinas developed his normative ethics out of the metaethical foundations provided by his fusion of the creation approach and the nature approach. For Aquinas "the human good is the state or activity in which the actualization of the potentialities specific to human beings consists."[6] His account of that state or activity is what gives content to his theory of natural law and his analysis of the virtues.

Scotus's account of these matters is distinctive in at least three ways. First, he insists that we cannot know by natural reason what the human good is, and a fortiori that we cannot elaborate any theory of normative ethics on the basis of our natural knowledge of the human good. Second, Scotus's account differentiates sharply between moral goodness and the goodness that is coextensive with being, thereby in effect cutting normative ethics loose from the metaethics on which many previous thinkers had founded it. Finally, he describes the moral goodness of an act as involving the perfection of the act rather than the perfection of the agent, and the perfection of an act in no way involves the act's tendency to perfect the agent. Our evaluation of acts is therefore unrelated to any theory about what human perfection consists in (even if such a theory were available).

I begin by discussing Scotus's views about our knowledge of our ultimate end. The first question of the Prologue to the *Ordinatio* asks "whether it is necessary for man in his present state to be supernaturally inspired by some special doctrine that he cannot attain by the natural light of the intellect." Scotus provides two main arguments for an affirmative answer. First, every agent that acts for an end needs an appetite for that end. In the case of human beings, that appetite is an intellectual appetite. In other words, it is an appetite that follows upon intellectual cognition. Therefore, if human beings are to act for their end, they need a distinct cognition of that end. But human beings cannot have a distinct cognition of their end through purely natural means. This is evident, first of all, because Aristotle himself, relying only on natural reason, could not settle conclusively what human happiness consists in:

The Philosopher, following natural reason, either asserts that perfect felicity consists in the acquired cognition of the separated substances, as he appears to say in Books I and X of the *Ethics*; or, if he does not definitely assert that this is the supreme felicity of which we are capable, he does not conclude by natural reason that anything else is. Thus, in relying solely on natural reason either he erred regarding the precise character of the end, or he remained in doubt about it.[7]

Now Aristotle's failure on this score was not attributable simply to carelessness or lack of insight. Scotus insisted that we do not (in our present state at least) know the proper end of *any* substance unless it has some act in which we see that end clearly exemplified as appropriate for that substance. And in our present state we do not experience any acts by which we know that a vision of the separated substances – or anything else, for that matter – is the appropriate end of human beings. Characteristically hedging his bets, Scotus goes on to say that *even if* natural reason were sufficient to establish what the end of human beings is, it would not be able to tell us the whole story about the end. For example, natural reason cannot tell us that the vision and enjoyment of God will last forever, or that it will involve human nature in its entirety, body and soul together. But both of these facts make our end more desirable.

Scotus's second argument for the insufficiency of natural reason is as follows. In order to act for an end on the basis of knowledge of that end, one needs to know three things: first, how the end is acquired; second, what the necessary conditions are on the part of the agent for the attainment of the end; and third, that these necessary conditions are sufficient for the attainment of the end. The first requirement is obvious, since if one does not know how the end is acquired, one will not know how to dispose oneself to achieve it. The second requirement is important, Scotus argues, because if one does not know everything that is necessary to the end, one could fail to achieve the end because of ignorance of something necessary. The third requirement is more of a psychological than a logical presupposition of striving for the end. If we suspect that we might do everything necessary to attain the end and nonetheless fail to attain it (because, for example, external agencies prevent us), we will be less likely to pursue the end wholeheartedly.

In fact, Scotus says, we cannot meet any of these three requirements by natural reason alone. We cannot know how happiness is attained because the connection between our activity and the attainment of happiness is altogether contingent. No human activity produces happiness; rather, God grants happiness as a reward for certain acts that he has contingently decided to regard as worthy of eternal happiness. Since the connection between our activity and our happiness is contingent and depends wholly on the divine will, we cannot know that connection by natural reason alone. For the same reason we cannot know by natural reason that certain actions are necessary or sufficient for the attainment of happiness. Therefore, knowledge of what our end is cannot guide us in the attainment of that end unless God provides us with certain crucial information about how the end is attained.

Now in a certain sense there is nothing terribly controversial about much of this. Aquinas makes it quite clear that our ultimate happiness is beyond our own power to achieve. He affirms that "neither human beings nor any other creature can attain happiness through their own natural abilities"[8] and that "human beings become happy by the action of God alone."[9] Furthermore, he holds that the precise character of our ultimate end, the beatific vision, is beyond our natural understanding.[10] So Aquinas would surely agree that we cannot have a clear conception of our ultimate end and that in some sense we cannot do anything to guarantee our attaining it.

But Aquinas, unlike Scotus, has more to say about this. For Aquinas distinguishes two sorts of happiness. The happiness that exceeds our natural abilities is perfect or supernatural happiness. But human beings are also directed toward an imperfect or natural happiness.[11] It is here that the nature approach to the metaphysics of being and goodness bears normative fruit. For it is this imperfect happiness that serves as the norm of morality. The good to which we are ordered by the moral virtues is natural happiness,[12] not supernatural happiness. And when Aquinas sets out to give specific content to the general principle that "good is to be done and pursued, and evil is to be avoided," he does so by examining those things to which human beings are naturally inclined, and which human reason therefore naturally apprehends as goods.[13] Again, these goods are the constituents of our natural happiness, not our supernatural happiness.

So there is for Aquinas, as there is not for Scotus, a sense of 'good' that is available to natural reason and is important in developing a detailed normative ethics. Now it might seem puzzling that Scotus does not here introduce something like Aquinas's imperfect happiness. For Scotus certainly does recognize that human beings have an intellectual appetite for their own good,[14] and if (to use his own argument against him) we cannot have an intellectual appetite for something we do not know, it seems to follow that we must have some sort of conception of our own good. As Aquinas says, reason naturally apprehends as goods all those things to which human beings are naturally inclined. Should not Scotus admit the same thing?

That Scotus is in some sense committed to the view that there is such a thing as natural happiness, and that we have some understanding of what it consists in, I have no doubt. What makes his ethics so distinctive is that he thinks natural happiness has nothing at all to do with morality. Right actions are right, not because of their relationship to human flourishing, but because God has freely commanded them.[15] This is why Scotus does not introduce natural happiness in the opening question of the *Ordinatio*. His question is whether our natural reason can tell us anything about how we ought to act. The fact that natural reason can tell us about the nature of imperfect happiness is, to Scotus's mind, not even relevant to the question, since imperfect happiness is not relevant to the moral norms that in fact obtain.

Now recall that according to the nature approach, the goodness of a thing is a matter of actualizing the potentialities that make it the sort of being it is; it is in that sense that goodness and being are "convertible."[16] For human beings, that state of actualization or full-being is called happiness, and normative ethics gets its content from the concrete conception of happiness and the ways in which it is attained. Since, as we have now seen, Scotus rejects the idea that happiness generates moral norms, he must also reject another characteristic thesis of the nature approach: that moral goodness is just a particular case or further refinement of the goodness that is convertible with being. And indeed Scotus draws a sharp distinction between the two.

According to *Metaphysics* 6, Scotus begins, 'good' is the same as 'perfect'. But 'perfect' has two meanings. In one sense, something is perfect when it has no intrinsic deficiency, that is, when it lacks nothing that is necessary to its being the sort of thing it is. Such a thing is said to be perfect by essential intrinsic perfection, or primary perfection: "The primary goodness of a being, which is called essential goodness, which is the integrity or perfection of the being in itself, implies positively the negation of imperfection, which excludes imperfection and diminution."[17] That this is the good that is convertible with being is made clear at *Reportatio* 2, d. 34, q. un., n. 18: "The subject of evil is not the good that is the contrary of evil, but the good that converts with being. For the evil that is the lack of secondary perfection denominates the good that is essential and primary perfection." In other words, something cannot be an evil thing unless it is, first of all, a thing – in other words, a being. So the subject of evil, the being that the evil is present in, is some being, and thus, given the convertibility of being with primary goodness, a primary good.

It follows that evil is not the contrary of primary goodness. The argument Scotus makes proceeds as follows:

Good in the first sense can have no contrary or privation in reality. For contraries are apt to qualify one and the same thing. Therefore, something that is not apt to be present in another thing has no contrary or privative opposite. But something that is good or perfect by primary perfection, insofar as it is a primary good, is not apt to be present in another thing. Even if it could be present in another thing as far as what-it-is is concerned (in the sense that an accident is in some way perfect by primary or intrinsic perfection, since it has an essence), nonetheless, insofar as it is a first good, it bespeaks perfection in itself and with respect to itself.[18]

The point of this admittedly obscure argument is that primary good-ness implies no relation to anything else, as an accident implies a relation to the subject in which it is present. Whiteness (for exam-ple) is present in a white thing, but primary goodness is not present in some other thing.[19] Contrast this with the kind of goodness that has evil as its contrary. That kind of goodness will involve a relation; it will be present in some other thing. Not surprisingly Scotus will call this kind of goodness "accidental goodness."

The important thing to note is that this understanding of primary goodness immediately rules it out of consideration as a useful con-cept for moral theory. For the good that is spoken of in moral theory needs not merely a contradictory, *not good*, but a contrary, *evil*. That is to say, 'good' must be a property that it is possible to be without. But nothing can be without essential perfection, since to be without essential perfection is not to be at all.

This is not to deny that essential perfection is a degreed property. It is possible for one thing to have more essential perfection than some other thing; what is not possible, however, is for two things *of the same kind* to have different degrees of essential perfection. An angel has more essential perfection (is better in terms of primary goodness) than a human being, but a good human being has no more essential perfection than a wicked human being.

Since primary good has no contrary and remains inviolate and undiminished so long as the nature survives, it is the second sense of 'good' that is important for moral theory. This is the good that has evil as its contrary, the good that is diminished by sin. Scotus calls it "secondary perfection" or "natural goodness."[20] The most useful characterization of secondary perfection is an analogy with beauty. The beauty of a physical object, Scotus says, is not some absolute (nonrelational) quality in the beautiful object. Rather, it is the aggre-gation of all the qualities that befit the object, such as size, shape, and color, together with the suitable relationship of those qualities to the object and to each other. In the same way, natural goodness is the secondary perfection of some thing that is constituted by all the qualities that befit it and each other. When all these qualities are present and suitably related, the object is perfectly good. If all of them are lacking but the nature that ought to be perfected by them remains, the nature is altogether bad. If some are lacking, the nature is bad, but not altogether so.

In *Quodlibet* 18 Scotus describes this "befitting" in much greater detail: "The secondary goodness of a being, which is accidental, or supervenient upon entity, is complete conformity: either the thing's complete conformity to some other thing to which it ought to conform, or the complete conformity of some other thing to it."[21] When a thing is good in the first way, in virtue of its conformity to some other thing, it is said to be good for, or a perfection of, the thing that it is good for. But it is not said to be good "denominatively," or accidentally good in itself. It is in this way that health is said to be good for a human being. Health is a perfection suited to human nature; we therefore call health 'good' because a human being who possesses health is to that extent good. So when this sense of 'good' is at issue, Scotus says, the form is denominated from the subject; that is, we call the form (health) 'good' because its presence makes the subject (the healthy person) good.

When a thing is good in the second sense, because it possesses the qualities that are appropriate to it, the thing is said to be good denominatively, or accidentally good in itself. For example, an attractive, smiling face is good because it has the qualities suitable to it. When this sense of 'good' is used, the subject is denominated from the form; that is, we call the subject (the face) 'good' because it possesses various qualities or forms (beauty and so forth) in virtue of which it is good.

A human act is by nature suited to be good in both ways. That is, it ought to bear a certain relationship to its agent, and various other things ought to bear a certain relationship to it. Now the striking thing here is that in discussing the natural goodness of an act, Scotus has almost nothing to say about the relationship of the act to the agent. That is, the natural goodness of an act does not seem to depend on whether the act is good for the agent. And since moral goodness turns out to be a kind of natural goodness, it follows that the moral goodness of an act does not depend on whether that act is good for the agent.

Now we have already seen that Scotus's rejection of the nature approach requires him to say something along these lines. But we should also notice that Scotus's general discussion of the two kinds of secondary goodness also naturally suggests that moral goodness will not depend on the perfection of the agent. For a thing is good in itself, not because it perfects some other thing, but because some other thing perfects it. This separation of the goodness of the agent from the goodness of the act is surely one of the most striking features of Scotus's moral theory. At *Ord.* 2, dd. 34–7, qq. 1–5, for example, Scotus describes sin as the privation of actual justice. But actual justice is defined in terms that have nothing whatever to do with the nature of the agent. The justice of an act is not a relation of the act to the agent – it apparently does not even involve such a relation as a constitutive part – but a relation of the act to a standard altogether external to the agent.

Moral goodness is simply the secondary perfection of a moral act, that is, an act elicited freely by an agent possessing will and intellect.[22] Moral acts have such goodness when they have an appropriate object, end, form, time, and place as judged by the agent's own reason. This is not to say that the agent's reason somehow constitutes the appropriateness of the object, end, and so forth. Instead, the object and end are appropriate or not independently of the judgment of reason; reason's task is simply to ascertain the moral facts. As I have argued elsewhere,[23] the appropriateness of an object or an end to a given action is, except for cases of metaphysical necessity, determined by God's free choice.

III. PASSIONS AND APPETITES

Scotus's rethinking of the relationship between being and goodness involves more than simply banishing natural happiness from moral reflection and redefining moral goodness so as to eliminate reference to the perfection of the agent. It also means a thorough overhaul of the moral psychology and action theory that grew out of the nature approach. Recall that according to the appetition thesis, all things aim at their own perfection. Human beings do so on the basis of cognition. Since human beings have both sensory and intellectual cognition, they also have sensory and intellectual appetites, which are inclinations to the human good as represented by the associated cognitive power. Very roughly speaking, we might say that the cognitive power "registers" a good in a certain way or under a certain description, and the appetitive power naturally inclines to that good. A detailed moral psychology can then be developed by exploring the various ways in which sense and intellect cognize goods, the corresponding inclinations of the appetitive powers, and the variety of ways in which both cognitive and appetitive activity contributes to or constitutes the human good. For the sake of brevity I shall call this moral psychology "the nature psychology" because it is associated with the appetition thesis as understood in accordance with the nature approach.

Now Scotus can happily accept a fair bit of the nature psychology, as far as it goes. He is certainly enough of an Aristotelian to agree that all things – human beings included – have an appetite for their proper natural end, and he accepts the distinction between sense and intellect and the associated distinction between sensory and intellective appetite. But his rethinking of the metaphysics of goodness requires him to say more. For the nature psychology aims to explain how our actions and reactions are aimed at the human good. Since Scotus denies that the moral goodness of particular acts is determined by their relation to the human good, he must supplement the nature psychology with some account of how we choose morally good acts. And more generally, since the nature psychology is concerned with natural happiness, which Scotus thinks is ultimately of no moral relevance, it plays a far less important role in his system than it does for philosophers who adopt the nature approach. In this section, therefore, I first lay out the parts of the nature psychology that Scotus can accept. I then consider the ways in which he finds that psychology deficient. In Section IV I show how he supplements the nature psychology so as to make room for morally good acts. I conclude by raising some questions about the relationship between the Scotist revisions, the nature psychology, and Scotus's larger project in action theory.

Scotus accepts the common view that sensory cognition is of particulars, whereas intellectual cognition is of universals.[24] Sensitive appetite, accordingly, is the passive power by which one is moved to some immediate response to particular objects as presented by the senses, with all their individuating conditions. Intellectual appetite, by contrast, is the passive power by which one is moved to a more reasoned response to particular objects as presented by the intellect, as falling under a generic concept like *good* or as consciously chosen for the sake of some end.[25] So appetitive inclinations are reactions or (in Scholastic jargon) passions; they are activated by the cognized object.

Scotus insists that there are passions in both sensitive and intellectual appetite.[26] Some passions concern things that by their very nature arouse desire or its opposite, and these belong to the concupiscible part of both sensitive and intellectual appetite. Other passions concern things that arouse desire or its opposite only on account of something else, and these belong to the irascible part of both sensitive and intellectual appetite. Suppose I like music and dislike writing papers. Music arouses the concupiscible passion of love and writing papers the concupiscible passion of hate. If someone insists on turning off my music and making me write a paper, I will feel the concupiscible passion of sadness over the silence and enforced work (it is a concupiscible passion because it is in effect a desire for the absence of the silence and enforced work). I will also feel the irascible passion of anger toward the person who has interfered with my pleasure. The aim of this irascible passion is not merely to get rid of that person but to exact revenge in some way. If I am trying to exact that revenge and have not yet succeeded, I will feel an irascible passion of sadness.[27] If I succeed, the passion of the irascible part is "assimilated to fruition on the part of the concupiscible part," as Scotus puts it. And if I believe that I will henceforth have uninterrupted enjoyment of the music, I will feel the irascible passion of *securitas*; but if I have reason to believe that more interference is on the way, I will feel the irascible passion of fear.[28]

Now all these passions, whether they arise in the sensitive or the intellectual appetite, are things that happen to us, not things that we do. The same is true of the general inclination of the intellectual appetite to the good. If the will – that is, the power by which one chooses and initiates actions – is merely intellectual appetite, then it will be nothing more than a passive response to whatever reason presents as good. My willing the good will be akin to my feeling flushed when I am aware that I have embarrassed myself or the rush of adrenaline that happens when I am suddenly confronted with what I recognize as a danger. Both these responses follow upon some sort of cognitive awareness, but I do not choose them and cannot control them. I just happen to be set up in such a way that I flush when I am embarrassed and release adrenaline when I am threatened. If I also just happen to be set up in such a way that I will something when the intellect presents it as good, I cannot control my acts of will either. Ultimate responsibility for them lies not with me but with whoever set up my intellectual appetite to be responsive to the good in that way.

So Scotus holds that the nature psychology makes the will entirely responsive, rather than active. Another problem with the nature psychology is that it leaves no room for us to will anything that is not in some way associated with the human good as registered by either sensory or intellectual cognition. And as we have seen, Scotus denies that moral norms derive their force or content from the human good; he also denies that the moral goodness of actions derives from any ordering to the human good. It follows that if the nature psychology is the whole story, human beings have no power to follow moral norms or to elicit morally good acts. That is, it might sometimes turn out that we choose what is in fact morally required, but only if by some happy accident the object presented by the intellect as perfective is also the object morality requires us to will. We would never be able to choose what is right *because* it is right. And even then our actions would not have moral goodness, since moral goodness is the goodness of an act elicited by a *free* agent[29]; we have already seen that if the will is merely intellectual appetite, it is not free, but merely a kind of passive response to intellectual cognition.

IV. THE WILL AS ACTIVE POWER

Scotus's solution to both problems is to posit two fundamental inclinations in the will: the *affectio commodi* and the *affectio iustitiae*.[30] The *affectio commodi* corresponds to intellectual appetite as understood in the nature psychology. The *affectio iustitiae* is much more difficult to characterize – a problem to which we will return – but one thing is certain: it provides the will with the freedom it could not have if it were merely intellectual appetite. It is, Scotus says, the "ultimate specific difference of a free appetite"[31]; that is, the *affectio iustitiae* is whatever distinguishes a free appetite from an unfree appetite. Scotus's favorite example of an unfree appetite is the sensitive appetite, and he often explains his theory of freedom by saying that if the will had only an *affectio commodi* – in other words, if it were merely intellectual appetite – it would be just as determined as the sensitive appetite in fact is: "An intellective appetite, if it lacked the *affectio iusti*, would naturally desire what is suited to the intellect, just as the sensitive appetite naturally desires what is suited to sense, and it would be no freer than the sensitive appetite."[32]

Often when Scotus discusses the two affections, he describes the role of the *affectio iustitiae* as being that of restraining or moderating the *affectio commodi*. In his discussion of the fall of Satan, for example, he says so repeatedly:

If, along the lines of Anselm's thought experiment in *On the Fall of the Devil*, one imagines an angel that had the *affectio commodi* and not the *affectio iustitiae* – i.e., one that had intellective appetite merely as that sort of appetite and not as free – such an angel could not refrain from willing advantageous things or from willing them in the highest degree.... Insofar as the will is merely intellective appetite it would actually be inclined in the highest degree to the greatest intelligible good. But insofar as the will is free, it can control itself in eliciting its act so that it does not follow its inclination, either with respect to the substance of the act, or with respect to its intensity, to which the power is naturally inclined. Therefore, that *affectio iustitiae*, which is the first controller (*moderatrix*) of the *affectio commodi* with respect to the fact that the will need not actually will that to which the *affectio commodi* inclines it, or will it to the highest degree, is the innate liberty of the will.... It is clear that a free will is not bound to will happiness in every way in which the will would will it if it were an intellective appetite without freedom. Rather, in eliciting its act the will is bound to moderate its appetite *qua* intellective appetite, that is, to moderate its *affectio commodi* so that it does not will immoderately.[33]

One has reason to restrain or moderate intellective appetite whenever the pursuit of happiness, if unchecked, would be immoral – or, in other words, would be counter to the divine will. According to Scotus, the rebel angels first sinned by willing their own happiness in a way that God had forbidden.[34] Because God had willed that they restrain their *affectio commodi*, they were bound to do so; because they had an *affectio iustitiae*, they were able to do so, and hence blameworthy when they refused to do so. God's will is in fact the rule or standard for every free appetite:

A free appetite ... is right ... in virtue of the fact that it wills what God wills it to will. Hence, those two *affectiones*, the *affectio commodi* and the *affectio iusti*, are regulated by a superior rule, which is the divine will, and neither of them is the rule for the other. And because the *affectio commodi* on its own is perhaps immoderate, the *affectio iusti* is bound to moderate it, because it is bound to be under a superior rule, and that rule ... wills that the *affectio commodi* be moderated by the *affectio iusti*.[35]

In other words, because it is not happiness but the divine will that grounds moral norms, we need to have the power to restrain the natural appetite for happiness so that we can will as God would have us will. The *affectio iustitiae* is what provides us with that power.

This much of Scotus's understanding seems to provide an answer to the two fatal shortcomings he saw in the nature psychology. A will endowed with the *affectio iustitiae* is no longer merely passive or responsive, as intellectual appetite is; and the *affectio iustitiae* enables us to will freely what is morally required of us without regard to happiness, so that we can elicit morally good acts. We might call this aspect of freedom "moral freedom." But Scotus's conception of freedom has another aspect, which we might call "metaphysical freedom"; and it is not at all clear how metaphysical freedom and moral freedom fit together.

The account of metaphysical freedom rests on the distinction Scotus makes between two basic kinds of active power: natural and rational. In contemporary terminology, the distinction is that the action of a natural power is necessary, given the circumstances and the laws of nature; the action of a rational power is contingent, given the circumstances and the laws of nature. (Scotus would not speak of laws of nature, but of the natures of the agent and patient, and in particular their active and passive causal powers.) For example, heat is determined by its very nature to cause heat. Unless it meets with some impediment to its action (some heat-resistant shield, say), it cannot help but cause heat. The will, however, is a rational power. There is nothing in the nature of the will that makes it act or not act in a given set of circumstances, nothing that makes it will in one way as opposed to another. Scotus hammers this point home in the *Lectura* discussion of contingency:

This logical possibility [of willing different objects] does not exist according as the will has acts successively, but in the same instant. For in the same instant in which the will has one act of willing, it can have an opposite act of willing in and for that very same instant.... Corresponding to this logical potency is a real potency, for every cause is prior in understanding with respect to its effect. Thus, the will, in the instant in which it elicits an act of willing, is prior in nature to its volition and is related contingently to it. Hence, in that instant in which it elicits a volition, it is contingently related to willing and has a contingent relation to willing-against – not because at some earlier time it had a contingent relation to willing, since at that time it was not a cause; but now, when it is a cause eliciting an act of willing, it has a contingent relation to the act, so that what is willing *a* can will-against *a*.[36]

From this passage alone it is not clear whether volition is always contingent or merely occasionally so. Some contemporary philosophers who agree with Scotus that freedom requires alternative possibilities hold that once our characters are fully formed, we are seldom free. For example, Peter van Inwagen argues that "there are at most *two* sorts of occasion on which the incompatibilist can admit that we exercise free will: cases of an actual struggle between perceived moral duty or long-term self-interest, on the one hand, and immediate desire, on the other; and cases of a conflict of incommensurable values. Both of these sorts of occasion together must account for a fairly small percentage of the things we do."[37] So if I have, say, the virtue of temperance, it is not really possible for me to take that third piece of cheesecake that is offered to me; refusing it will seem the only sensible thing to do, and "if we regard an act as the one obvious or the only sensible thing to do, we cannot do anything but that thing."[38] On van Inwagen's view, then, I am not acting freely when I refuse the cheesecake, although I would still be praiseworthy if my having the virtue of temperance is itself the result of prior free actions.

Scotus, however, does not agree. Whatever habits I may have developed, virtuous or vicious, the will is still free. Even the divinely infused habit of charity does not undermine freedom. Examining the dictum that "charity is to the will what a rider is to his horse,"[39] Scotus comments that the analogy works only if we think of the horse as free and the rider as "directing the horse in the mode of nature to a fixed destination." Then "the horse in virtue of its freedom could throw its rider, or else move itself toward something else, contrary to the rider's direction toward the destination."[40] Scotus even says that the blessed in heaven retain the power to sin, although God sees to it that they never exercise that power.[41] Presumably, then, the blessed dead are no longer free, since they no longer have alternative possibilities available to them. But Scotus's claims about the contingency of heavenly sinlessness show just how far he is prepared to carry the view that the will always remains a rational power. Even God cannot take away the will's power for opposites; he can only raise an impediment to its exercise.

This high view of the freedom of the will is surely not what one would have expected from the doctrine of the two affections. The *affectio iustitiae* is said to confer freedom by enabling us to overcome the passivity of intellectual appetite and will what is morally required of us without regard to happiness. This would give us alternative possibilities whenever we are confronted with a choice between happiness and morality, but surely not the seemingly unlimited alternative possibilities Scotus envisions. It is hard to see how the freedom of the blessed dead to abandon their perfect happiness and sin against God could be a manifestation of their power to will what is morally required without regard to happiness.

One might suggest a more complicated reading of the *affectio iustitiae*. Perhaps Scotus's idea is that (1) there can be no morality without freedom, (2) freedom requires alternative possibilities, and (3) if the nature of the will is such as to allow alternative possibilities sometimes, it will be such as to allow alternative possibilities all the time. In other words, moral freedom – the possession of an *affectio iustitiae* – entails metaphysical freedom. Somewhat paradoxically, then, the *affectio iustitiae* guarantees the will's power to sin. Unfortunately, there is no real evidence from Scotus's writings that he connected moral freedom with metaphysical freedom in quite this way. Moreover, (3) simply seems false. A view like van Inwagen's, in which the will is free sometimes but not always, is perfectly coherent.

It seems more likely that Scotus simply never thought through the connection between moral and metaphysical freedom. His case against the nature psychology leads him to posit an *affectio iustitiae*. A will that has an *affectio iustitiae* is certainly free in some sense. Now Scotus seems to have an *independent* intuition that freedom involves an unfailing power for opposites. So he talks as if it is obvious that an *affectio iustitiae* confers an unfailing power for opposites even though his arguments against the nature psychology suggest a far more restricted role for the *affectio iustitiae*.

NOTES

1 MacDonald also calls it the *creation* approach. See MacDonald 1988 and 1991b, 4–5.
2 MacDonald 1991b, 4.
3 MacDonald 1991b, 5.
4 Augustine, however, puts an ingenious spin on the appetition thesis when he argues in *Confessions* 2 that whatever we desire, we desire because it in some way imitates a divine perfection.
5 One reason many recent interpreters have downplayed Aquinas's natural law ethics in favor of his virtue theory – as if the two were in some sort of competition – is that they have failed to appreciate the richness

and complexity of Aquinas's metaethics. By bringing together the nature approach and the creation approach into one coherent system, Aquinas not only makes room for both natural law and virtue in his moral theory but makes each necessary to a full understanding of the other.

6 MacDonald 1991b, 19.

7 *Ord.* prol., pars 1, q. un., n. 14.

8 *ST* IaIIae.5.5.

9 *ST* IaIIae.5.6.

10 *ST* I.12.4.

11 For the significance of Aquinas's distinction between perfect and imperfect happiness, see Bradley 1997.

12 *ST* IaIIae.62.1, 63.2, 109.2.

13 *ST* IaIIae.94.2.

14 See the discussion of intellectual appetite in Sections III and IV.

15 The evidence for this claim would require far more space than I can give it here. See Williams 1998a.

16 Convertibility is best understood in contemporary terms as necessary coextension. Standard medieval accounts deny that 'being' and 'good' are synonymous: see, for example, Stump and Kretzmann 1991.

17 *Quodl.* q. 18, n. 5.

18 *Rep.* 2, d. 34, q. un., n. 3.

19 Scotus then seems to withdraw, or at least qualify, this point in the last sentence quoted. But all he means to convey there is that even if accidents, which do have contraries, are said to be primary goods (or to be good by primary goodness – his language is not consistent), we should not think that primary goodness has a contrary. We might say that a particular instance of whiteness is a primary good, since it has the appropriate sort of being. And certainly black is the contrary of white. But it is the contrary of white *qua* accidental form, not *qua* primary good; there *is* no contrary of white *qua* primary good. A particular instance of blackness will be every bit as much a primary good as a particular instance of whiteness.

20 At *Ord.* 2, d. 7, q. un., n. 11, Scotus uses "natural goodness" to refer to what is clearly primary or essential goodness, but this usage does not accord with his usual practice.

21 *Quodl.* q. 18, n. 3.

22 Human acts can also be considered without reference to the agent's will and intellect. The goodness of acts considered in this way is called "natural goodness." See Williams 1997.

23 Williams 1997 and 1998a.

24 In fact, Scotus's distinction between sensory and intellectual cognition is somewhat more complicated: see Robert Pasnau (ch. 9 in this volume,

Section IV). But this rough statement of the distinction is sufficient to motivate the distinction between sensory and intellectual appetite as Scotus understands it.

25 *Ord.* 3, d. 33, q. un., n. 6.

26 See especially *Ord.* 3, d. 33, q. un., n. 20; d. 34, q. un., nn. 10–13.

27 Scotus, that is, calls both the concupiscible and the irascible passion *tristitia*. Perhaps the concupiscible *tristitia* could best be called "discontent" and the irascible *tristitia* "frustration."

28 See *Ord.* 3, d. 34, q. un., nn. 10–13, for the clearest explanation of the distinction between the concupiscible and irascible passions, along with characterizations of *tristitia* and anger; see *Ord.* 4, d. 49, q. 6, nn. 22–3 for *securitas* and fear.

29 *Ord.* 2, d. 40, q. un., n. 3.

30 *Affectio commodi* is usually translated "affection for the advantageous" and *affectio iustitiae* (or *affectio iusti*) as "affection for justice." But both translations are misleading in various ways, and it seems safer to leave the expressions untranslated.

31 *Rep.* 2, d. 6, q. 2, n. 9.

32 *Rep.* 2, d. 6, q. 2, n. 9. See also *Ord.* 2, d. 6, q. 2, n. 8; 2, d. 25, nn. 22–3; 2, d. 39, q. 2, n. 5; and 3, d. 26, q. un., n. 17.

33 *Ord.* 2, d. 6, q. 2, nn. 8–9. The thought experiment to which Scotus refers is found in Anselm's *De casu diaboli* 12–14. Scotus borrowed the idea of the two affections from Anselm, but he puts them to very different use, and Scotus's understanding of the freedom that the *affectio iustitiae* confers is quite different from Anselm's. See Visser and Williams 2001 for discussion of Anselm's theory of freedom and in particular the argument of *De casu diaboli* 12–14.

34 *Ord.* 2, d. 6, q. 2, n. 9.

35 *Rep.* 2, d. 6, q. 2, n. 10.

36 *Lect.* 1, d. 39, qq. 1–5, nn. 50–51. See Calvin Normore (Ch. 4 in this volume) for a discussion of Scotus's modal theory.

37 van Inwagen 1989, 417–18. See O'Connor 2000, 101–7, for a discussion of van Inwagen's "restrictivism."

38 van Inwagen 1989, 406.

39 Scotus took this to be a saying of Augustine, but in fact it comes from the pseudo-Augustinian *Hypognosticon* III c. 11 n. 20 (PL 45, 1632).

40 *Ord.* 1, d. 17, pars 1, qq. 1–2, n. 155.

41 *Ord.* 4, d. 49 , q. 6, nn. 10–12.

12 Rethinking Moral Dispositions:

Scotus on the Virtues

Scotus's teachings on moral virtue have attracted little attention, in part because there is no single text where he presents them systematically, in part because scholars tend to associate Scotus with the ethics of freedom and right reason. Even those sympathetic to his views report, with apparent regret, his move away from the virtue-centered Aristotelian model of ethics.[1] This chapter attempts to explain the various roles that virtues do and do not play in his ethical theory. While Aristotle receives his share of criticism, so, too, does Augustine. The theory that emerges, striking in its originality, might be more appealing to some of today's readers than the better-known theory of Aquinas.

I. THIRTEENTH-CENTURY ETHICS: A LARGE, CONFUSING LEGACY

Ancient ethics takes as its starting point questions about the happiest human life and the virtues needed to live such a life. Virtues are thought to be dispositions developed only through many years of learning and practice, beginning in childhood. Vices, too, are dispositions; and like virtues, they gradually become "second nature" to the individual. For this reason Aristotle describes moral character as impossible, or at least exceedingly difficult, to change.[2] His definition of moral virtue as a disposition concerned with choice[3] does not imply, then, that people always remain free to choose actions "out of character." On the contrary, to perform a virtuous act as Aristotle recommends, the agent must not only choose the act but choose in accordance with "a firm and unchangeable disposition."[4]

The intellectual requirements for moral virtue are high. One needs not only expertise in acting but also the prudence to judge the best possible act in any given situation. Moral virtue requires in addition emotional responses in harmony with reason. Someone who judges the correct act to be done, but who must struggle to follow his rational judgment, does not meet the ancient standard of virtue.

Augustine's writings offer a radically different account of happiness and the virtues. He presents virtues as divine gifts, inseparable from faith in Christ, not dispositions that any human being might acquire through natural aptitude, learning, and practice. Virtue cannot bring happiness, for the only happiness properly so called is a reward provided by God in the afterlife. We can at most work to make ourselves more deserving of it. How might we do so? By exercising the virtues of faith, hope, and above all, charity. Where Aristotle makes prudence, an excellence of practical intellect, the foundation of all moral virtues, Augustine establishes as their foundation charity, a virtue of will. Only through charity are we able to love God and our neighbors as we should: according to their intrinsic worth, instead of in proportion to how well they serve our own interests or satisfy our own desires.[5]

From this perspective, then, even the most intelligent, accomplished pagan lacks any true moral virtue. However useful to others his actions might be, they are motivated by excessive self-love. Only God's gift of charity can transform a person's motivations. Charity, alas, does not eliminate the emotional disorder caused by original sin. The best human being on earth, even a saint, must still struggle to resist temptation.[6] But if no mortal is ever so virtuous as to be beyond temptation, neither is any so vicious as to be morally incurable. We all have the power of free choice. While Augustine believes we cannot use it rightly on our own, he emphasizes that we can do so with the help of God's grace.[7]

Despite their respect for Augustine, most Scholastic theologians refused to dismiss Aristotle's ethics as so much pagan folly. They worked instead to find ways of reconciling the two authorities. Thus they embraced the concept of virtue as a disposition, albeit only by stretching it wide enough to cover both naturally acquired virtues and the virtues of faith, hope, and charity, supernaturally "infused" by God.[8] The expanded concept of disposition created puzzles of its own, even as it left untouched a host of other difficulties, including a serious normative problem: the moral virtues described in the *Nicomachean Ethics* often differ strikingly from moral virtues described in the New Testament.

Is the model of fortitude the aggressive soldier who dies bravely while defending his country? Or is it the patient martyr who goes to his death rather than repudiate the faith? Rather than choose one and reject the other as representative of true fortitude, Thomas Aquinas postulated an entire species of Christian virtues with the same names as Aristotelian moral virtues (prudence, temperance, fortitude, etc.), but supernaturally infused by God together with the virtues of faith, hope, and charity. Following Aquinas, many other theologians posited infused moral virtues in addition to the three infused theological virtues and all the many naturally acquired virtues described by the ancients. The number of virtues soared; conceptual dilemmas endemic to the reconciliationist project remained.

This thumbnail sketch of Scholastic ethics as it stood in the late thirteenth century may help to explain Scotus's efforts to make it simpler and more coherent. He repeatedly applies some version of the principle of economy: a plurality should not be posited without necessity. Called "Scotus's rule" in the fourteenth century but today better known as "Ockham's razor," the principle encourages a theorist to postulate no more in the way of species, causes, or "entities" than he strictly needs to explain a given phenomenon. It works mainly to reduce ontological commitments so that the theorist will not posit the existence of a different "thing," much less a different kind or species of "thing," if he can provide a satisfactory explanation by appealing to a different aspect of the same thing or to the thing's relation to something else.

Scotus invokes the principle of economy to establish that, as far as this life goes, only seven virtues are necessary to make a human being perfect *simpliciter*: the theological virtues of faith, hope, and charity; the naturally acquired moral virtues of justice, temperance, and fortitude; and the naturally acquired intellectual virtue of prudence.[9] He sees no reason whatsoever to posit the infused moral virtues favored by Thomists.[10] At the same time, he underscores the variety of specific moral virtues that might combine to make a given individual a good person. Justice, temperance, and fortitude are not individual, specific moral virtues so much as genera of virtue.[11] To say, for instance, that no one can be a morally good person without temperance is to say that a good human being must have dispositions regulating her appetites for sex, food, and drink; it is not to say that there is only one form that temperance can take. A person might choose to drink wine in moderation, on appropriate occasions; she might equally choose complete abstinence. She might choose to live by a religious vow of chastity; she might equally choose to live by a vow of conjugal fidelity. By the same token, a person might acquire temperance and the prudence that temperance requires without acquiring fortitude and the prudence that fortitude requires.[12]

Scotus's effort to provide a simpler account of the virtues does not result in a cookie-cutter approach to morals. It does lead him to a dilemma: How can the conception of virtue as a second nature be reconciled with the freedom of the will?[13]

II. CAN VIRTUE MAKE AN ACT GOOD?

A common Scholastic dictum, drawn from Aristotle, declares that "a virtue perfects its possessor and makes his work good."[14] Scotus firmly supports the first part of the dictum. Like all leading masters of the period, he classifies virtues as dispositions that perfect the agent in one way or another. To explain what constitutes a good human being, he agrees, we must perforce speak of dispositions. For when we judge a person temperate or brave, instead of judging only some action of hers temperate or brave, we are referring to dispositions – that is, to how she habitually chooses to behave, regardless of how she might choose to act at this particular moment. Scotus nonetheless argues fiercely against the second part of the dictum: that virtue makes one's action morally good.

What does make an action morally good? Following Scotus, we divide the question into two parts: (1) What makes an action a moral action? and (2) What makes an action morally good?

II.1. Moral Actions Must Be Free

The first part of the question concerns not goodness or badness but what Scholastics call "imputability." It seeks to distinguish those actions within the individual's control, for which he can be held morally responsible, from the many actions, reactions, and mere movements not justifiably subject to praise or blame.[15] Rationality plainly matters. (Cats, infants, and lunatics cannot be held morally responsible for their behavior.) For Scotus, however, rationality is not enough. Moral actions require freedom, and the only free power of the soul is the will. All other powers, including the intellect, operate in their own right in the manner of nature: they are determined to act to the utmost and always act in the same way unless externally impeded.[16]

Consider, for example, the intellectual act of judging that $80 - 57 = 13$. If the erroneous judgment results from a weak knowledge of arithmetic, it is not a moral action. Now imagine a different case, in which a cashier spots this error on a customer's bill when giving change but chooses not to correct it, telling himself that it is the customer's responsibility to check her bill, not the store's responsibility to get it right. Such "rationalizing," an intellectual act, still has as its principal cause the cashier's will to shortchange a customer. It therefore qualifies as a moral action. Of course, the moral action par excellence, one entirely within the will's control, is the will's own act of choosing. Hence, Scotus defines moral virtue as "a disposition of the will to choose rightly, even as it was generated by right choices."[17]

In explaining the freedom crucial for moral action, Scotus ventures beyond metaphysical self-determination, relating the will's freedom to two general inclinations (or "affections"): to desire what is advantageous to oneself, and to love something according to its intrinsic worth.[18] Because the will's inclination to the advantageous includes the desire for both happiness and self-perfection, it might be construed as egocentric, but not necessarily egotistical or selfish. Even so, this represents only the natural aspect of the will. If the will had no other inclination, so that we were determined by nature to choose what we regard as the most advantageous of the available options, we would not be free, moral agents, regardless of how rational we might be in calculating and carrying out actions to our own advantage. All eudaemonistic ethical theories accordingly strike Scotus as disastrous failures. A moral agent must perforce have freedom of will, and this is rooted in the will's innate, inalienable inclination to justice.[19] In other words, moral responsibility requires that an agent be capable not only of different acts but also of significantly different motivations for acting.

Scotus consistently strives for symmetry in his analysis of moral responsibility. As a bad person must be able to choose a good act, so a good person must be able to choose a bad one. Philosophers today sometimes agree that moral responsibility requires the ability to choose a good act, yet deny that it requires the ability to choose a bad one.[20] Ordinary language appears to support this view. Suppose that we ask someone (call him George) why he told the truth on a particular occasion, and he responds, "I have always valued honesty highly; I simply cannot tell a lie." Do we interpret him as pleading for exemption from moral responsibility? Not at all: we regard his response as testimony to his excellent character. His truth telling, the argument goes, strikes us as all the more praiseworthy because he has lost the ability to lie.

Scotus would reply that we praise George's act because we interpret his professed inability to lie as a harmless exaggeration, or perhaps just a mistake about his own psychological makeup. We take it for granted that he could have lied, only that he finds lying so repugnant that in everyday life he never considers it a serious option. If years have passed without his encountering a situation in which he felt tempted to lie, he might even have drawn the erroneous conclusion that he no longer remains able to lie. Scotus might then try to raise George's consciousness by urging him to imagine situations in which there appear to be good moral reasons in favor of lying, so that the choice to be made cannot be reduced to a simple contest between honesty and self-interest.[21] It makes no difference whether George chooses (imaginatively) to tell the truth in the hypothetical situations presented to him. If he only agrees that he *could* choose to lie, Scotus has won his point.[22]

Now suppose that our first impression of George was mistaken. Suppose that, in fact, he is just as compulsive about truth telling, regardless of the circumstances, as a long-time alcoholic might be about drinking. Give him an opportunity to speak, and George cannot help but tell the truth. In such a case, Scotus would not consider the truth telling a moral action, and he certainly would not regard George as a model of virtue. Would we ourselves disagree? Many people, I think, would see a real-world character who cannot help but tell the truth as a rather frightening fanatic, or at least as a splendid candidate for psychotherapy.

II.2. Moral Growth Must Begin Somewhere

We turn now to the second part of our problem: What makes an action morally good? Can one reasonably claim that virtue, that is, a virtuous disposition, causes the agent's action to be morally good? Scotus thinks not. Even if one assumes that the only act in question is the will's choice, the thesis that "virtue makes one's action good" is false.[23]

That virtue cannot be sufficient to make one's act good seems evident. Suppose that a beggar asks St. Francis for alms, and Francis responds by kicking the fellow. Of course, we would find it hard to believe our eyes. Did Francis intentionally kick him, or was he only experiencing some kind of seizure or muscle spasm? Was the beggar wielding a knife that we failed to notice, perhaps threatening to attack, so that Francis responded with what amounts to an animal instinct for self-defense, instead of deliberately choosing to kick the man? There are many doubts that any observer familiar with Francis's character might entertain. Further reflection might even lead us to worry that we cannot be sure about our moral judgment of *anyone*'s actions. When intentions and motivations are crucial to the moral evaluation of an act, and we cannot know with certainty what goes on in another's mind, how are we in a position to judge his actions?

This is an important issue, but not an issue that Scotus and his colleagues discuss at length, for they all agree that God is the sole person entirely competent to serve as a moral judge.[24] When Scotus argues that even all the virtues combined are insufficient to ensure that the agent's act at this particular moment is good, he is not concerned with our own competence to judge whether the act of St. Francis or anybody else satisfies those requirements. The question is rather what the requirements *are*. Given the ineliminable human capacity to act out of character, he reasons, virtue cannot be a sufficient condition for the moral goodness of an act.

If one has trouble accepting that someone with a well-developed virtuous disposition can still choose a bad act, one might at least endorse a weaker thesis: that such a person remains able to choose morally neutral acts.[25] Her dispositions do not drive her into hyperactive "do-gooding," so that she never misses an opportunity to perform a virtuous deed. Even when she does perform a deed that observers take to be morally good, her end in acting might in fact make the action morally neutral. Imagine a person with the virtue of charity, someone strongly disposed to help others, who gives several large boxes of used clothes and books to the Salvation Army. However strong her disposition to helping others, it does not suffice to ensure that her donation is a morally good act. She might not have been thinking of others at the time. Preoccupied with spring cleaning, she might have donated the clothes and books simply to free up space in her closet and bookcases.

As virtue cannot be a sufficient condition for the moral goodness of one's action, neither can it be a necessary condition. Scotus thinks that Aristotle himself would have to endorse this thesis, lest his own theory become trapped in a vicious circle. If virtue is a disposition acquired from morally good acts, it must be possible to perform such acts without a virtue; otherwise, how could one develop the virtue in the first place? Since moral growth must begin somewhere, it can only begin with the choice of morally good acts by someone who has yet to acquire the virtues. Insist upon any moral virtue as a necessary condition, even insist upon the intellectual virtue of prudence, and one runs smack into circularity. Scotus concludes, then, virtue does not affect the moral substance of an action. An act is morally good because it conforms to all that the agent's right reason dictates: for example, the appropriate time and place, and above all, the appropriate end.[26]

As one might already guess, Scotus considers the end the most important factor determining the moral value of an act.[27] The act of giving money to a homeless person, for instance, would ordinarily be good if done from charity or generosity, bad if done from a desire to make the person feel inferior, and morally neutral if done to unburden one's own bulging pocket of coins. In a related but more tendentious vein, Scotus launches a defense of lying, at least in highly unusual circumstances. Set aside cases of perjury, where someone has sworn an oath before God to tell the truth; consider instead the moral dilemma much favored by modern ethics textbooks: What would you do if you were a German citizen during the Holocaust who had given Jews refuge in your home, but then found yourself faced with Nazis banging on your door, demanding to know whether there are any Jews on the premises? Both Augustine and Kant would urge you to say nothing, at most to dissemble, but definitely not to lie. In contrast, Scotus emphasizes that God gives full credit for the good will that motivates an action. Lying in the circumstances described would be a merely venial sin, for which punishment is strictly temporal; yet the motive could be so magnanimous that God judges it worthy of eternal reward.[28]

If his analysis ended here, Scotus might seem committed to the view that the virtuous dispositions he himself treats as moral perfections of the agent do nothing to make the agent choose good deeds with greater ease, promptness, and pleasure than a moral beginner. In fact, he claims that they do influence the manner in which a person acts, so that somebody with a virtue, all other things being equal, is able to act more perfectly than somebody without one. The arguments just sketched aim to prove only that virtue is neither necessary nor sufficient for the moral "substance" of an act, that it does *not* "make one's act good."[29] The positive role that virtues play in Scotus's ethical theory remains to be explored.

III. VIRTUE NATURALIZED

The idea that a person's dispositions do not determine her to act at all, much less to act virtuously, was widely accepted by Scholastics long before Scotus began teaching. Most took it for granted that mortals always have the power to choose actions contrary to their own moral character as so far formed. If Aristotle's works offered little support for this opinion, no matter: like Scripture, the Aristotelian corpus was ever open to interpretation. Less in the way of deliberately Christianizing interpretation was actually needed than one might assume, because virtually all Scholastics read Aristotle and his commentators in Latin translation. Owing partly to the translations, they believed that Aristotle's teachings on dispositions could be fitted into their own philosophical psychology without too much cutting and stretching.

Aquinas's *Summa theologiae* may serve for purposes of illustration. Quoting a commentary by Averroës on Aristotle's *De anima*, Aquinas declares that "a disposition is that whereby we act *when we will.*" The concept of a disposition alone, he contends, makes it plain that a disposition is *principally ordered to the will*.[30] This understanding of a disposition helps pave the way for a discussion of virtues, which Augustine says cannot be badly used – in contrast to a power of the soul, such as the will, which can be badly used.[31] Combine the expurgated Augustine with the expurgated Aristotle, and one arrives at the position defended by Aquinas and other leading Scholastic theologians: that a virtue is itself a disposition "determined to one" of opposite acts, but the power of will may or may not on any given occasion act in accordance with (alias "use") the virtue.

III.1. Acting with Ease and Pleasure

How does Scotus diverge from the consensus? On the one hand, he takes seriously the ancient idea of dispositions, including moral dispositions, as a second nature. On the other, his own basic dichotomy between free powers or causes and natural ones leads him to conclude that all dispositions, including the moral dispositions properly regarded as virtues, fall on the natural side of the line. Although they are produced by free acts of will, virtues themselves operate psychologically as other natural causes do. Same kind of cause, same kind of effect: precisely because virtues are dispositions, operating in their own own right they are determined ever to cause the same kind of actions that went to generate them.[32] For instance, if I repeatedly choose to give money when the collection basket at church is passed around, the disposition I thereby acquire inclines me to continue making such donations. It does not incline me to hand the basket on to my neighbor without making any contribution myself, much less to fish out a ten-dollar bill and pocket it. Were some disposition the total cause of my act, Scotus reasons – indeed, if it were merely the principal cause – the act would be merely natural, not moral, much less morally good.[33] I act virtuously only when I *choose* to act in accordance with my virtuous dispositions.

The requirement of choice should not be construed as a requirement that someone continue to engage in the extensive deliberation that she did as a moral beginner, lest she lose moral credit for her own virtuous actions. Scotus recognizes that virtue can lead the agent to deliberate and choose with such speed that she herself doesn't notice the time involved.[34] His theory in no way downgrades the swift, easy choices of a moral virtuoso. It aims rather to deny moral credit for truly "compulsive" actions, if there actually are any, such as those of our hypothetically fanatical truth-teller, George.

We know that the moral virtuoso's disposition enables him to act with greater ease, promptness, and pleasure than someone who lacks a virtuous disposition. We know the difference from experience, according to Scotus. While the moral substance of the two individuals' actions might be the same, the way in which they act is not. Virtues are postulated in ethical theory precisely to explain such differences.[35]

Here we must venture briefly into the thicket of complications characteristic of Scotus's work. In his view, a virtuous disposition inclines the will in the right direction, enabling it to act more promptly, more easily, and with greater pleasure than it would otherwise be able to (at least assuming equal effort on the part of the will). Promptness, ease, and pleasure are genuine differences in the mode of the action, rendering one's behavior more perfect in moral terms. But at the same time, the moral significance of these factors derives from differences in the way the will itself acts. The disposition, a natural cause operating as all natural causes do, figures rather in the *psychological* explanation of why the will acts more perfectly now than it did before it enjoyed the benefits of a virtue disposing it to choose rightly.

Scotus considers two psychological roles that the disposition might play: one as an active but secondary cause of the will's action; the other as a noncausal inclination, comparable to gravity, that inclines a heavy object to fall but hardly pushes it. He argues that both explanations could probably be sustained, for the second as well as the first could account for the phenomena of greater ease, pleasure, and so forth.[36] Whichever of the two psychological theories one prefers, note that neither suggests that differences in the manner of acting arise from the act as such; they arise instead from the agent's inclination to perform it. If I act with pleasure, it is not because there is something in the act that makes me enjoy doing it; I take pleasure in it because I myself have an inclination to perform this kind of act. If I act with ease, it is not because there is something intrinsically easy about the act. If the act itself were easy, it would stand to reason that one deserves less, not more, moral credit for performing it.

Though one must appeal to a disposition in order to give a full explanation of my behavior, Scotus does not think it strictly necessary to treat the disposition as a partial cause of my act – in effect, "pushing" me towards it. Applying the principle of economy, which advises against positing causality where it is unnecessary to explain the phenomena, we should therefore adopt the second position.[37] Scotus himself, however, favors the first, which attributes a greater role to the disposition. The disposition operates as a partial but secondary cause, enabling me to act more perfectly (in moral terms) than I could otherwise do – at least assuming an equal effort of will.[38] The best human behavior therefore combines the free choice of the will and the natural causality of dispositions.

III.2. Loving God above All

When Scotus turns to charity, he continues to favor a naturalistic approach, arguing that the disposition of charity – assumed by most of his colleagues to be produced in a person only by God's grace – is neither necessary nor sufficient to make an act charitable. On the contrary, someone by purely natural resources could even love God above all.[39] Argumentation for this thesis begins with natural theology: natural reason reveals a hierarchy of goods, that some good must be supreme among things to be loved, and that nothing other than the infinite good has this status. Hence, natural reason dictates that the infinite good be loved above all. But here Scotus introduces a moral principle, roughly to the effect that "ought" implies "can." Given natural reason's judgment that the divine good ought to be loved above all, the will must have the natural ability to carry out this act.[40] Whatever the effects of original sin, we cannot have lost the affection for justice that enables us to love some good according to its intrinsic worth. This is an inalienable feature of the will and a prerequisite for moral responsibility.

Scotus seizes upon the account of courage in Aristotle's *Ethics* as evidence that someone can by purely natural means love God above all.[41] Does not Aristotle himself say that the brave citizen should expose himself to death for the good of the republic? Given his doubts about the immortality of the soul, Aristotle cannot believe that the brave citizen will be motivated by hope of reward in some afterlife. He must believe that someone acting according to natural reason could rightly judge the public good a greater good than his own life, and so be willing to die in order to preserve it. What better testimony could one have for the capacities of human nature operating without special supernatural aid?

Even apart from the fact that loving one's country above all cannot be equated with loving God above all, Aristotle's value as a witness leaves much to be desired. In Book IX of the *Ethics* he casts the virtuous person as steadily motivated by self-love, albeit self-love of an enlightened, noble kind. Wherever the virtuous person appears to be giving something up, Aristotle describes him as seeking a greater share of honor or nobility for himself.[42] Unfortunately, the brave citizen's readiness to die in battle still poses a problem. Having no belief in an afterlife, he cannot expect an opportunity to enjoy whatever honors a heroic death might win him. Why, then, would he choose to risk dying? The best Aristotle can offer is the rather lame suggestion that quality trumps quantity, so that one hour of intense pleasure in performing some glorious deed should be preferred to many years of ordinary pleasures. Scotus insists upon a more flattering interpretation: "Such a brave person wills that both he himself and his act of virtue not exist rather than that evil befall the republic. Thus he simply loves the public good, which he wills to preserve, more than he does himself or his act of virtue. He exposes himself to death in order to preserve the republic, not in order to preserve his virtue."[43]

Augustine painted a far bleaker picture of fallen human nature. His writings labor to prove that only with God's grace, in the form of the God-given virtue of charity, can we be liberated from the excessive self-love produced by original sin. Because all moral virtues, even imperfect ones, depend upon charity, pagans have no true moral virtues at all. They may indeed willingly die in battle and thereby serve their countries, but what are their motivations? Augustine suggests that some pursue what they take to be the greatest available pleasure (a motivation he would think well evidenced by Aristotle's quality-trumps-quantity argument). Others, such as the Stoics, might be motivated by a desire for human praise; then again, they might be convinced that their own supposedly virtuous character is the highest good in the universe. Even the second interpretation reveals their grave moral errors. A virtuous person must perforce recognize God, not her own character, as the supreme good in the universe. She must recognize that virtue is itself a gift of God, not a triumph of human achievement. Finally, she must recognize that human beings cannot make themselves happy, that the most virtuous persons on the face of the earth remain vulnerable to illness, anxiety, grief, and all kinds of troubles. According to Augustine, pagan philosophers misdescribe happiness in order to make it seem attainable in this life and within the individual's own control. They all want to claim credit for making themselves happy. Not a single one teaches the truth: that happiness is a reward given by God in the afterlife to those he chooses.[44]

Scotus rejects Augustine's bleak moral picture in no uncertain terms. As he sees no reason in either conceptual analysis or human experience why a person should need some supernaturally infused virtue to perform a charitable act, so he sees no such reason why one should need some infused virtue to perform a charitable act with promptness, ease, and pleasure. If a non-Christian could perform an act with the same moral substance, could she not gradually acquire by natural means a disposition to choose such an act? Christians with God's grace are not the sole human beings able to love and choose some good greater than their own happiness and self-perfection; so why should they be the sole human beings able to do so easily, promptly, and with pleasure? Why should they not be able to develop, even to the level of perfection, the same virtues that God's chosen Christians can? Given his own preference for economy in theory construction, Scotus questions the necessity of even postulating supernaturally infused virtues.[45]

Suppose that one seeks to explain why God grants some persons rather than others the ultimate reward of eternal happiness. The true answer, to Scotus's mind, is that God chose to do so. Supernaturally infused virtues cannot explain why God chose these particular persons, because such virtues are themselves pure gifts of God, not something that an individual might earn by morally good behavior. If God has in fact ordained that infused virtues are necessary for salvation, he could have, by his absolute power, dispensed with them.[46] There is nothing about such virtues that makes them intrinsically necessary for a person's salvation. They have the status of secondary causes through which God in fact chooses to operate. Whatever he chooses to do in this indirect way, he could just as well have done directly. Any causal role that infused virtues play in salvation therefore arises strictly from the convenant God generously chose to make with mankind.

In sum, neither from conceptual analysis nor on the basis of experience would a theorist be driven to postulate the virtues of faith, hope, and charity routinely described by Scholastic theologians as supernaturally infused dispositions. Though Scotus himself firmly accepts their existence, he does so as a matter of religious belief. His arguments, then, do not aim to show that there are no God-given virtues; they aim to show that whatever causal role such virtues play in the process of salvation is one God chose to assign them. Should one protest that Scotus portrays God as opting for a comparatively elaborate scheme of salvation, in flagrant disregard of the principle of economy, Scotus would agree. God often acts more generously than frugally: an economist he is not.[47]

The repercussions that this innovative line of argument turned out to have in the history of Western theology would be hard to overstate. William of Ockham repeated and expanded Scotus's arguments against the theoretical necessity of infused virtues. The *via moderna* in theology associated with Ockham, in turn, happened to be the one in which a rebellious Augustinian monk named Martin Luther was schooled some two centuries later. Luther proceeded to deny that infused virtues are even de facto necessary for salvation. To him, the whole arcane apparatus of God-given dispositions reflects the disastrous influence of Aristotle on medieval theology. Far better that theologians refuse to posit dispositions of the human soul as intermediaries in the process of salvation and focus simply on the individual's relation to God.

Because Luther's dismissal of infused virtues can be traced backwards, through Ockham to Scotus, the first Scholastic theologian to subject this class of virtues to intense critical scrutiny, Scotus's innovations have come to play a large role in scholarly studies of Reformation theology.[48] Here, however, we shall focus on a few of the conclusions that Scotus himself drew. (Readers should consult Chapters 6 and 7 in this volume for a fuller explanation of his theology.)

III.3. Separating Moral Virtue from Happiness

A thesis pressed by Plato, Aristotle, and other ancient philosophers – that moral virtue brings happiness, or at least protects one from becoming miserable – never actually won strong support outside of philosophical circles. Even before Christianity entered the historical picture, ordinary people took it for granted that virtue requires actions disadvantageous to oneself, so that the most virtuous person would not be likely to lead the happiest possible life. They believed, too, that someone might have one moral virtue while lacking others.[49] In spurning the philosophers' vision of moral virtues as a

complete, indivisible system of psychic checks and balances, they
effectively removed one of the main grounds for asserting that virtue
brings happiness. Christian thinkers like Augustine did all the more
to undermine the claims of ancient ethics. Not only did they differ
from pagan philosophers in their conception of virtue, they differed
in their conception of happiness. With the standard of happiness (or
blessedness: *beatitudo*) raised to an all-time high, it became nearly
self-evident that nobody can attain happiness in this life. It became
equally hard to imagine how anyone could truly deserve happiness.
Realistically, what could a human being do to merit an eternity of
perfect fulfillment?

When Scotus discusses happiness, he adopts the high Christian
standard of what it amounts to. He follows Augustine in refusing
to lower the standard to include anything less than the complete,
eternal fulfillment of one's every desire. Thus, he argues that nobody
can attain happiness by natural means, no matter how virtuous she
might be. To claim that a person could attain happiness through her
own natural resources, Scotus adds, is an even greater heresy than
that of Pelagius.[50] Had God wanted us to attain happiness naturally,
he would have made us and our world differently. Instead he willed
that we attain happiness through grace, on the basis of merit.[51]

Here pause to recall that Scotus strongly opposes Augustine in
arguing that a person can acquire all of the moral virtues, can even
develop them to the level of perfection, through her own natural resources. She does not need the infused virtue of charity or any other
special gift of grace. While Scotus steadily downplays his criticisms
of this towering authority, the depth of the disagreement is impossible to miss. Having steadily opposed Augustine by describing moral
perfection in naturalistic terms, it becomes all the more important
that Scotus distinguish sharply between improving morally in this
life and attaining happiness in the afterlife. Failure to do so would not
only suggest that happiness lies within the individual's own control,
which Scotus himself believes plainly untrue, it might leave him
looking to conservative colleagues as if he were flirting with the
Pelagian heresy.[52] Small wonder, then, that he takes such pains to
support Augustine's view that *merit* requires a supernatural explanation. According to Scotus, our merit vis-à-vis happiness depends
strictly on what God himself chooses to accept as deserving of punishment or reward in the afterlife. Claim that God must welcome
individuals into heaven or consign them to hell on the basis of how

morally perfect or imperfect they have made themselves through their own natural resources, and one has reduced him to the level of a celestial bookkeeper – totting up the gains and losses of our mortal lives according to standards other than his own will, calculating the balance, and proceeding to dole out rewards and punishments accordingly.

What role, then, does the supernaturally produced virtue of charity play? What does it help to explain? In Scotus's view, it helps to explain how, but not why, some individuals attain the reward of happiness. This does not mean that the infused disposition of charity has some mysterious psychological effect. On the contrary, Scotus argues that it operates as a disposition in the same natural manner that naturally acquired dispositions do.[53] The will remains the primary cause of an action, the disposition itself only a secondary, subordinate cause. By the same token, the infused virtue of charity no more guarantees that the agent's act will be meritorious than a naturally acquired virtue guarantees that his act will be morally good. But where the moral goodness of an act comes from its conformity to reason, the merit of an act comes from its relation to God's will, from his decision to accept it as deserving of eternal reward. The act is accepted as meriting reward because God chooses to accept the person who performs it, not vice versa.[54]

The infused virtue of charity can therefore be considered a symptom, not a cause, of God's acceptance of the agent, as well as a necessary condition, but not a sufficient one, for an agent's action to be meritorious. If this virtue sufficed to make someone's actions meritorious, Scotus reasons, then they would be the actions of the disposition, or perhaps the actions of God, not the actions of the human agent. So even though charity, more than the human will, explains why an act has merit in God's eyes, the human will, more than charity, explains why the human agent chose the act.[55]

IV. CHOOSING AND FEELING

When moral virtue is defined as a disposition of the will to choose rightly, the relation between virtue and passion becomes puzzling. I may choose to stand my ground under enemy fire, but I cannot choose whether I feel terrified or reasonably composed at the time. One might conclude, then, that the virtue of fortitude disposes me to choose brave actions in appropriate circumstances, for the right reasons, yet it has nothing to do with how I feel, because I have no choice about how I feel.

Scotus's conclusion proves more nuanced. On the one hand, he argues that all moral virtues, as dispositions to choose, must belong to the will. On the other, he argues that the will can moderate the passions.[56] In struggling to stand my ground under fire, for example, I might compare the possible damage to myself with the damage done to my country when its soldiers flee or surrender. I might also try steering my thoughts away from present dangers, towards the pleasant prospect of winning the war and returning home. I can indeed exercise some control over what goes on in my mind. Over time I can thereby acquire a disposition to feel no more afraid than it is rational to feel in a given situation. If I do so – this is Scotus's point – the disposition is a psychological byproduct of the efforts I have made to moderate my passions. The moral significance it has, it owes to the will. In its own right a disposition to feel in certain ways can at most be a quasi-virtue, not a virtue strictly so called.[57]

This conclusion raises an interesting question: Could angels – which have reason and will but no bodies and hence none of the passions associated with bodies – acquire a virtue such as temperance or fortitude? Scotus argues at length that they could, then argues at length for the opposite view, refusing to take sides.[58] One might perhaps see this as evidence that he never worked out the details of his position.

V. MORALLY MIXED CHARACTERS

Aristotle and other ancient philosophers joined in defending a position no more compelling to ordinary people at the time than it is now: that the moral virtues are inseparable. No one can truly have justice, fortitude, or temperance without prudence, nor can one truly have prudence without justice and all the other moral virtues.[59] The idea that all moral virtues depend on an overarching practical wisdom becomes more plausible when one reflects upon three features of ancient ethics:

1. Virtue is supposed to be nearly impossible to lose and a source of pleasure to the agent – characteristics that virtue would

    be more likely to have if it were a complete, integrated sys-
tem of psychic checks and balances that eliminates internal
conflict.

2. Ancient ethics always considers the good life as a whole.
   Because the good life is regarded as an organic unity, the virtuous person must see it as such, so that the single, indivisible virtue of prudence becomes the foundation of all moral
   virtues.

3. Properly speaking, ancient virtue does not make a person
   good; it makes him *excellent*. By its very nature, virtue is an
   ideal that very few individuals will ever attain.

    As we know, Augustine rejected ancient teachings on the impor-
tance of prudence, adopting instead the God-given virtue of charity as
the foundation of all true virtues. In a letter to St. Jerome, Augustine
argued passionately against the related all-or-nothing conception of
moral virtue so favored by philosophers. Of special concern to him
were conclusions that Stoics had drawn from the unity of virtue: a
person has no wisdom at all until he has perfect wisdom; there are
no degrees of virtue and vice; the transition from vice to virtue must
therefore be complete and instantaneous, as when someone drowning suddenly bursts forth into the air. Augustine suggested that it is
un-Christian to treat virtue as an all-or-nothing affair, so that someone must be completely perfect to be considered virtuous at all.[60] In
his view, no Christian can attain moral perfection in the present life:
she can at most make steady progress. This letter was well known to
thirteenth-century theologians; those doubtful about ancient claims
for the indissoluble unity of virtue routinely cited it.[61] Remember,
though, that the same all-or-nothing view of moral character that
Augustine refuses to apply to Christians with the God-given virtue
of charity, he eagerly applies to all other human beings. Without
charity, a person has no true moral virtues, so that one of us differs
from others only in the particular combination of vices she happens
to represent.

    On the unity of the virtues as on so many other issues, Scotus
found some valuable insights in Aristotle, also some valuable insight
in Augustine, but insisted on charting his own path. Both authorities would richly dislike the conclusions he drew, albeit for different
reasons.

V.1. Prudence Required but Divided

Scotus rejects Aristotle's position on the unity of the virtues because he thinks it has two absurd implications: that a person progresses in an instant from having no true moral virtue to having them all, and that there is, at bottom, only one moral virtue, not a plurality of virtues that people develop piecemeal.[62] Scotus's arguments against both theses reprise a familiar theme (that moral growth must begin somewhere), while adding a new emphasis on the plurality of virtues. He gives Aristotle full credit for recognizing prudence as indispensable for moral goodness; he agrees that no moral virtue can be acquired without it. But at the same time, he refuses to treat prudence as a single, indivisible virtue, so that lack of prudence in any one area of life automatically proves the individual lacking prudence in all areas.

According to Scotus, it is impossible to acquire any moral virtue without the prudence related to it; but each moral virtue has its own prudence, and none of these specialized prudences has any necessary connection with any other. Thus, a person could not acquire the virtue of fortitude without the prudence related to fortitude, but she could acquire both of these virtues without acquiring temperance or the prudence related to temperance. The specialized prudences can indeed combine to form a harmonious "macroprudence." Such macroprudence must nonetheless be considered an aggregate, says Scotus, not the indivisible organic unity that Aristotle and his uncritical followers claim.[63]

V.2. Partial Perfections

Scotus stands firmly with Augustine in arguing that someone can have one moral virtue without another. Contrary to ancient philosophy, which treats each moral virtue as what amounts to an abstraction from the organic unity of a wholly virtuous character, Scotus insists that moral virtues can be separately acquired. Indeed, one virtue can even be developed to perfection without the development of another:

A virtue is a perfection of a human being, but not total perfection, else one moral virtue would suffice. But when something has several partial perfections, it can be perfect *simpliciter* as regards one perfection and imperfect *simpliciter* as regards another, as is apparent in the case of humans, to whom many organic perfections pertain, and who can have one perfection in the highest degree while not having another. For example, someone might be disposed in the highest degree as regards sight and touch while being unable to hear. Thus someone can have the highest degree of perfection in the subject matter of temperance while not having the perfection needed in the subject matter of another virtue, and can therefore be temperate *simpliciter*, even in regard to any act of temperance [although the person is not brave]. Nevertheless, nobody is moral *simpliciter* without all the virtues, just as nobody is sentient *simpliciter* without all the senses. But one is not less perfectly temperate, though one is less perfectly moral, just as one is not less perfect in seeing or hearing [from lack of other senses], though one is less perfectly sentient.[64]

If Scotus is right, would not a freestanding virtue, lacking other virtues to support it, sometimes produce bad actions? Imagine that a judge has the virtue of justice but lacks fortitude. When presiding at a Mafia trial, she receives an anonymous phone call threatening her life if she allows the accused to be convicted. The judge herself firmly believes the accused to be guilty; but being a rather spineless character, she does her best to ensure his acquittal. Would this not be an example of how justice without fortitude could produce an *un*just act?

The example proves nothing of the kind, according to Scotus. It is not the virtue of justice that goes wrong but the person who goes wrong, and not because of the virtue she has but because of the virtue she lacks. The judge's act is essentially an act of cowardice, chosen against her own disposition to justice. It is an act of injustice only incidentally (*per accidens*), chosen because a just act in these circumstances called for a fortitude that the judge, alas, did not have. Her lack of fortitude does not prove that she has not truly acquired the virtue of justice. Precisely because she has, she feels distressed about her own behavior, not indifferent, or worse, pleased with herself, as she would if she had the vice of injustice.[65]

Readers might be inclined to support this conclusion but still balk at the stronger thesis: that someone could develop one moral virtue (say, justice) to *perfection* without acquiring another moral virtue (say, fortitude). Considering how often in the course of ordinary life one needs fortitude in order to do what justice requires, it is hard to see how someone could become perfectly just without becoming brave at all. By the same token, how long could someone remain perfectly just if she goes wrong whenever justice demands fortitude?

Scotus points out that a single bad action does not destroy a virtue. It takes many bad acts, or at least a few seriously bad ones. He also agrees that a person having one virtue but not others would probably be at grave risk of losing it.[66] Other than this, he has little to offer as a response to the objections raised. He seems far more concerned to press a conceptual point than to explore issues of empirical psychology.

One might wonder, though, whether there are normative concerns hovering in the background. Scotus emphasizes that moral virtues might take various forms in different persons' lives. Moral diversity is important to him. Now consider the possibility that some individual – say, a cloistered nun who entered the convent at age five – has had ample opportunity to perform just and temperate acts but comparatively little occasion for brave acts. Her moral development might therefore be strikingly uneven, with far greater perfection in some areas than others. Although every human life will surely provide some occasion to exercise every moral virtue, the amount of exercise an individual gets in any particular virtue depends partly on circumstances.

Scotus toys with the idea that someone might acquire a virtue by imagining what she would do in various situations and making the right choices in these imagined scenarios. In such a way, he suggests, someone without a penny could nonetheless acquire the virtue of generosity. Against this, though, is Aristotle's judgment: however much I might wish for the impossible, I can only *choose* what is possible for me.[67] So in the end, Scotus does not insist upon the ability to make up for in imagination what one lacks in reality – a reasonable decision, since what hypothetical choices would appear to produce is hypothetical virtues, not real ones.

Scotus takes a firm position in arguing that a human being can acquire all the moral virtues and related prudences, even to the level of perfection, without God-given charity or any other infused virtue. Moral virtue is not less perfect in moral terms from the lack of infused charity. What charity adds is an *extrinsic* perfection, namely, an order to the ultimate end of happiness.[68] While God alone can make us happy, Scotus teaches, we can and should make ourselves good. If Augustine thought only those with God's grace are able to be good, then Augustine was mistaken.

NOTES

1 See, for example, Ingham 1989, 199–200. The most comprehensive treatment of Scotus's ethics remains the one presented in Wolter 1986, 3–123.
2 *Nic. Eth.* 3.5 $(1114^a15–22)$, 7.10 $(1152^a29–33)$.
3 Ibid. 2.6 $(1106^b36–1107^a2)$.
4 Ibid. 2.4 $(1105^a23–^b3)$.
5 *De civitate Dei* 5.19, 11.16, 14.25, 15.22, 22.30.
6 Ibid. 5.21, 19.4.
7 *De peccatorum meritis et remissione et de baptismo parvulorum* 2.6. For a brief overview of Augustine's ethics, see Kent 2001.
8 Lottin 1949; Nederman 1989–90; Colish 1993. Note that the Latin word *habitus*, here translated as "disposition," is sometimes translated by the cognate "habit."
9 *Ord.* 3, suppl. d. 34. (Wolter 1986, 348, 354).
10 *Ord.* 3, suppl. d. 36 (Wolter 1986, 414–16).
11 Ibid. (Wolter 1986, 354–6).
12 See Section V.1.
13 See Kent 1995 for late thirteenth-century controversies about freedom and virtue that help to place Scotus's views in their historical context.
14 *Nic. Eth.* 2.5 $(1106^a15–17)$.
15 *Quodl.* q. 18, n. 9.
16 *In Metaph.* 9, q. 15, nn. 20–41.
17 *Ord.* 3, suppl. d. 33 (Wolter 1986, 332).
18 *Ord.* 2, d. 6, q. 2 (Wolter 1986, 462–76). For more extensive discussion of the will's two "affections," see Thomas Williams in ch. 11 of this volume and Boler 1993.
19 Scotus, who thinks that ethical theory should begin by addressing the issue of moral responsibility, has reason to find Aristotle's theory inadequate. As Broadie observes, Aristotle does not even have a word meaning "responsible agent" any narrower than his word for "voluntary agent," which he applies to children and animals as well as adults. See S. Broadie 1991, 124–78, esp. 174n1.
20 For example, Wolf 1990.
21 *In Metaph.* 9, q. 15, n. 30, Scotus declares that a person who wills an act *experiences* that he could have refused. Because at least some persons deny experiencing such freedom, I suppose that Scotus would suggest "thought experiments" in an effort to change their minds.
22 *Ord.* 4, suppl. d. 49, qq. 9–10 (Wolter 1986, 192–6).

23 *Ord.* 1, d. 17, pars 1, qq. 1–2, nn. 56, 65–8; 4, suppl. d. 49, qq. 9–10 (Wolter 1986, 191). *Ord.* 1, d. 17, pars 1, qq. 1–2, often cited in the present essay, is nowhere available in a complete English translation. For useful excerpts and exposition, see Ingham 1989, 153–7, 185–96, 217–27.

24 In *Ord.* 4, d.17 (Wolter 1986, 262–8) Scotus uses this principle to attack remarks on confession in the leading textbook on canon law.

25 *Lect.* 2, d. 41, q. un., nn. 9–10. Brickhouse 1976 argues that the role Aristotle assigns to dispositions in the explanation of action rules out the possibility of changing one's character. Scotus, who prefers to read Aristotle as acknowledging the possibility, instead overhauls his account of how dispositions contribute to actions.

26 *Ord.* 1, d. 17, pars 1, qq. 1–2, nn. 60–62; *Quodl.* q. 18, nn. 3–6.

27 *Quodl.* q. 18, n. 6; *Ord.* 2, d. 40 (Wolter 1986, 224–8).

28 *Ord.* 3, suppl. d. 38 (Wolter 1986, 496). Cf. Kant 1993, 63–7, and the discussion of Augustine's views in Rist 1994, 191–4. Kant classifies lying as violation of a "perfect duty," hence as impossible to justify by appeal to the "imperfect duty" of helping one's neighbor. While Augustine's views are more obscure, he does (as Rist claims) seem to defend not only the position that it is better for me to suffer evil than do it, but also the position that it is better for someone else to suffer evil than for me to do it. Scotus nods to Augustine's authority in declaring the kind of lie in question a venial sin and then proceeds to urge a conclusion that Augustine would resist

29 *Ord.* 1, d. 17, pars 1, qq. 1–2, n. 100; 3, suppl. d. 33 (Wolter 1986, 326, 330–2).

30 *ST* IaIIae.49.3; 50.5 (emphasis added). Cf. Averroës, *In Aristotelis De anima* 3, n.18. For detailed exposition of *ST* IaIIae–IIaIIae, see Pope 2002.

31 *ST* IaIIae.55.4; 56.1. Cf. Augustine, *De libero arbitrio voluntatis* 2.19.

32 *Ord.* 1, d. 17, pars 1, qq. 1–2, nn. 24, 37; 3, suppl. d. 36 (Wolter 1986, 328–30, 342–6). A corollary of this position, defended in *Ord.* 4, d. 46, q. 1, (Wolter 1986, 246–50), is that God has no "virtues" strictly so called.

33 An oft-repeated point: see *Ord.* 1, d. 17, pars 1, qq. 1–2, nn. 29, 37, for just one example.

34 *Ord.* 3, suppl. d. 39 (Wolter 1986, 506).

35 *Lect.* prol., pars 4, qq. 1–2, n. 157; *Ord.* 1, d. 17, pars 1, qq. 1–2, n. 70; *Ord.* 3, suppl. d. 33 (Wolter 1986, 326, 332, 342–6).

36 *Ord.* 1, d. 17, pars 1, qq. 1–2, n. 53.

37 Ibid., nn. 47–52.

38 Ibid., nn. 69–70.

39 *Quodl.* q. 17; *Ord.* 3, suppl. d. 27 (Wolter 1986, 424–46).

40 *Ord.* 3, suppl. d. 27 (Wolter 1986, 434).

41 *Nic. Eth.* 3.6–9.

42 Ibid., 9.8 (1169^{a}12–^{b}2).

43 *Ord.* 3, suppl. d. 27 (Wolter 1986, 436).

44 *De trinitate* 13.7–8; *Sermo* 150; *De civitate Dei* 5.19–20, 14.28, 19.20.

45 *Ord.* 1, d. 17, pars 1, qq. 1–2, nn. 126–29; 3, suppl. d. 27 (Wolter 1986, 436); *Quodl.* q. 17, nn. 6–8, 13.

46 *Ord.* 1, d. 17, pars 1, qq. 1–2, nn. 160, 164.

47 Ockham expressly defends the same view. See Wood 1999, 358: "Does God Employ Ockham's Razor?"

48 For just two examples of the scholarly literature tracing Scholastic sources for Luther's theology, see Vignaux 1935 and McGrath 1998.

49 Irwin 1996. Section V, in this chapter, discusses the separability of virtues.

50 *Op. Ox.* 4, d. 49, q. ex lat., q. 11, n. 2.

51 *Ord.* 2, d. 6, q. 2 (Wolter 1986, 471–3).

52 Readers may find it helpful to consult Wood 1999 on the Pelagian angle. As she points out, some of the same doctrines that triggered charges of heresy against Ockham had previously been defended by Scotus.

53 *Ord.* 1, d. 17, pars 1, qq. 1–2, n. 188.

54 *Quodl.* q. 17, n. 4.

55 *Ord.* 1, d. 17, pars 1, qq. 1–2, nn. 139, 146, 152; *Quodl.* q. 17, n. 13.

56 *Ord.* 3, suppl. d. 33 (Wolter 1986, 330–4).

57 Ibid. (Wolter 1986, 332–4, 340).

58 Ibid. (Wolter 1986, 334–8).

59 *Nic. Eth.* 6.13 (1144^{b}30–1145^{a}2).

60 See Hauerwas 1997, 50, for a recent echo of the same judgment.

61 Augustine, *Epist.* 167, *Corpus Scriptorum Ecclesiasticorum Latinorum* 44, 586–609; Wood 1997b, 40–59.

62 *Ord.* 3, suppl. d. 36; *Coll.* 1.

63 *Ord.* 3, suppl. d. 36 (Wolter 1986, 392–412). For further discussion, see Ingham 1996b.

64 Ibid. (Wolter 1986, 388).

65 Ibid. (Wolter 1986, 388–90).

66 Ibid.

67 *Lect.* prol., pars 4, qq. 1–2, n. 176; *Ord.* 3, suppl. d. 33 (Wolter 1986, 338); *Nic. Eth.* 3.2 (1111^{b}20–25).

68 *Ord.* 3, suppl. d. 36 (Wolter 1986, 414); *Quodl.* q. 17, nn. 7–8.

BIBLIOGRAPHY

Adams, Marilyn McCord. 1987. *William Ockham*. 2 vols. Notre Dame, IN: University of Notre Dame Press.

——. 1992. "The Resurrection of the Body According to Three Medieval Aristotelians: Thomas Aquinas, John Duns Scotus, William Ockham." *Philosophical Topics* 20, 9–18.

Albert the Great. 1893. *Opera Omnia*, edited by S. C. A. Borgnet. Paris: Vivès.

Alexander of Hales. 1924–48. *Summa theologica*. Quaracchi: Collegium S. Bonaventurae.

Alluntis, Felix, ed. 1963. *Cuestiones cuodlibetales*. In *Obras del Doctor Sutil, Juan Duns Escoto*. Madrid: Biblioteca de Autores Cristianos.

——. 1965. "Demonstrability and Demonstration of the Existence of God." *Studies in Philosophy and the History of Philosophy* 3, 133–170.

Alluntis, Felix, and Allan B. Wolter, trans. 1975. *God and Creatures: The Quodlibetal Questions*. Princeton, NJ: Princeton University Press.

Ariew, Roger. 1985. *Medieval Cosmology: Theories of Infinity, Place, Time, Void, and the Plurality of Worlds*. Chicago: The University of Chicago Press.

——. 1999. *Descartes and the Last Scholastics*. Ithaca, NY: Cornell University Press.

Ashworth, E. J. 1991. "Signification and Modes of Signifying in Thirteenth-Century Logic: A Preface to Aquinas on Analogy." *Medieval Philosophy and Theology* 1, 39–67.

Avicenna. 1508. *Logica*. Venice: Octavius Scotus.

——. 1977/80. *Liber de philosophia prima sive scientia divina*, edited by S. Van Riet Louvain/Leiden: E. Peeters/E.J. Brill.

Bacon, Roger. 1905–40. *Opera hactenus inedita Rogeri Baconi*. Edited by Robert Steele and Ferdinand M. Delorme. 16 fasc. in 12 vols. Oxford: Clarendon Press.

_____. 1988. *Compendium studii theologiae*. Edited by Thomas S. Maloney. Leiden: E. J. Brill.

Balić, Carl. 1927. *Les commentaires de Jean Duns Scot sur les quatre livres des Sentences: Étude historique et critique*. Louvain: Bureaux de la Revue.

_____. 1929. "De collationibus Ioannis Duns Scoti, Doctoris Subtilis ac Mariani." *Bogoslovni Vestnik* 9, 185–219.

_____. 1939. *Ratio criticae editionis Operum omnium I. D. Scoti*. Rome: Schola typographica "Pio X."

Bauer, Ludwig, ed. 1912. *Die Philosophischen Werke des Robert Grosseteste, Bischofs von Lincoln*. Beiträge zur Geschichte der Philosophie des Mittelalters 9. Münster: Aschendorff.

Bérubé, Camille. 1964. *La connaissance de l'individuel au moyen âge*. Montreal: Presses de l'Université de Montréal.

Bettoni, Efrem. 1961. *Duns Scotus: The Basic Principles of His Philosophy*, ed. and trans. Bernardine Bonansea. Washington, DC: Catholic University of America Press.

Boler, John. 1993. "Transcending the Natural: Duns Scotus on the Two Affections of the Will." *American Catholic Philosophical Quarterly* 67, 109–126.

_____. 1996. "The Ontological Commitment of Scotus's Account of Potency in his *Questions on the Metaphysics*, Book IX." In Honnefelder et al. 1996, 145–160.

Bonansea, B. M. 1983. *Man and His Approach to God in John Duns Scotus*. Lanham, MD: University Press of America.

Bosley, Richard N., with Martin Tweedale, eds. 1997. *Basic Issues in Medieval Philosophy*. Peterborough, Ontario: Broadview Press.

Boulnois, Olivier. 1988. *Jean Duns Scot: Sur la connaissance de Dieu et l'univocité de l'étant*. Paris: Presses Universitaires de France.

_____. 1992. "Réelles intentions: nature commune et universaux selon Duns Scot." *Revue de Métaphysique et de Morale* 1, 3–33.

_____. 1995. "Représentations et noms divins selon Duns Scot." *Documenti e studi sulla tradizione filosofica medievale* 6, 255–280.

_____. 1999. "Si Dieu n'existait pas, faudrait-il l'inventer?" Situation métaphysique de l'éthique scotiste." *Philosophie* 61, 50–74.

Bradley, Denis J. M. 1997. *Aquinas on the Twofold Human Good: Reason and Human Happiness in Aquinas's Moral Science*. Washington, DC: The Catholic University of America Press.

Brady, Ignatius. 1954. "Comment on Dr. Wolter's Paper." In *Proceedings for the American Catholic Philosophical Association for 1954*, 122–130.

Brampton, C. K. 1964. "Duns Scotus at Oxford, 1288–1301." *Franciscan Studies* 24, 5–20.

Brickhouse, Thomas C. 1976. "A Contradiction in Aristotle's Doctrines Concerning the Alterability of *Hexeis* and the Role of *Hexeis* in the Explanation of Action." *Southern Journal of Philosophy* 14, 401–11.

Bridges, Geoffrey G. 1965. "The Problem of the Demonstrability of Immortality." In John K. Ryan and Bernardine M. Bonansea, eds. *John Duns Scotus, 1265–1965*, Studies in Philosophy and the History of Philosophy, 3. Washington, DC: Catholic University of America Press, 191–209.

Broadie, Alexander. 1995. *The Shadow of Scotus: Philosophy and Faith in Pre-Reformation Scotland*. Edinburgh: T. and T. Clark.

Broadie, Sarah. 1991. *Ethics with Aristotle*. Oxford: Oxford University Press.

Brown, O. J. 1979. "Individuation and Actual Existence in Scotus." *The New Scholasticism* 53, 347–61.

Brown, Stephen F. 1993. "Medieval Supposition Theory in Its Theological Context." *Medieval Philosophy and Theology* 3, 121–157.

———. 1994. "Henry of Ghent (b. ca. 1217; d. 1293)." In Gracia 1994.

Callebaut, André. 1928. "Le maîtrise du Bx. Jean Duns Scot en 1305; son départ de Paris en 1307 durant la préparation du procès des Templiers." *Archivum Franciscanum Historicum* 21, 214–39.

Catania, Francis J. 1993. "John Duns Scotus on *Ens Infinitum*." *American Catholic Philosophy Quarterly* 67, 37–54.

Colish, Marcia L. 1993. "*Habitus* Revisited: A Reply to Cary Nederman." *Traditio* 48, 77–92.

Copleston, Frederick. 1963. *History of Philosophy; Volume II*. New York: Image Books.

Craig, William Lane. 1988. *The Problem of Divine Foreknowledge and Future Contingents from Aristotle to Suarez*. Leiden: E. J. Brill.

Cress, Donald. 1975. "Toward a Bibliography on Duns Scotus on the Existence of God." *Franciscan Studies* 35, 45–65.

Cross, Richard. 1995. "Duns Scotus's Anti-Reductionistic Account of Material Substance." *Vivarium* 33, 137–170.

———. 1997a. "Duns Scotus on Eternity and Timelessness." *Faith and Philosophy* 14, 3–25.

———. 1997b. "Is Aquinas's Proof for the Indestructibility of the Soul Successful?" *British Journal for the History of Philosophy* 5, 1–20.

———. 1998. *The Physics of Duns Scotus: The Scientific Context of a Theological Vision*. Oxford: Clarendon Press.

———. 1999. *Duns Scotus*. Great Medieval Thinkers. Oxford: Oxford University Press.

Dahlstrom, Daniel A. 1980. "Signification and Logic: Scotus on Universals from a Logical Point of View." *Vivarium* 18, 81–111.

Dales, Richard C., ed. 1963. Robert Grosseteste, *Commentarius in VIII libros Physicorum Aristotelis*. Boulder, CO: University of Colorado Press.

Day, Sebastian. 1947. *Intuitive Cognition: A Key to the Significance of the Later Scholastics*. St. Bonaventure, NY: Franciscan Institute Press.

de Libera, Alain. 1991a. *César et le phénix. Distinctiones et sophismata parisiens du XIIIe siècle*. Pisa: Scuola Normale Superiore.

———. 1991b. "Roger Bacon et la référence vide. Sur quelques antécédents médiévaux du paradoxe de Meinong." In *Lectionum Varietates. Hommage à Paul Vignaux (1904–1987)*, edited by J. Jolivet, Z. Kaluza, and A. de Libera, 85–120. Paris: Vrin.

———. 1996. *La querelle des universaux: De Platon à la fin du Moyen-Age*. Paris: Éditions du Seuil.

de Muralt, André. 1991. *L'Enjeu de la philosophie médiévale*. Leiden: E. J. Brill.

Denifle, Heinrich, with Emile Chatelain, eds. 1889–1897. *Chartularium Universitatis Parisiensis*. 4 vols. Paris: Delalain.

Dolnikowski, Edith. 1995. *Thomas Bradwardine: A View of Time and a Vision of Eternity in Fourteenth-Century Thought*. Leiden: E. J. Brill.

Duhem, Pierre. 1913–59. *Le Système du monde. Histoire des doctrines cosmologiques de Platon à Copernic*. 10 vols. Paris: Hermann.

Dummett, Michael. 1991. *The Logical Basis of Metaphysics*. Cambridge, MA: Harvard University Press.

Dumont, Richard. 1965. "The Role of the Phantasm in the Psychology of Duns Scotus." *Monist* 49, 617–33.

Dumont, Stephen D. 1987. "The Univocity of Being in the Fourteenth Century (I): John Duns Scotus and William of Alnwick." *Mediaeval Studies* 49, 1–75.

———. 1988. "The Necessary Connection of Moral Virtue to Prudence According to John Duns Scotus – Revisited." *Recherches de Théologie Ancienne et Médiévale* 55, 184–206.

———. 1989. "Theology as a Science and Duns Scotus's Distinction between Intuitive and Abstractive Cognition." *Speculum* 64, 579–99.

———. 1992. "Transcendental Being: Scotus and Scotists." *Topoi* 11, 135–148.

———. 1995. "The Question on Individuation in Scotus's ≪Quaestiones super Metaphysicam.≫" In Sileo 1995, I:193–227.

———. 1996. "William of Ware, Richard of Conington and the *Collationes Oxonienses* of John Duns Scotus." In Honnefelder et al. 1996, 59–85.

———. 1998. "Henry of Ghent and Duns Scotus." In *The Routledge History of Philosophy, Volume III: Medieval Philosophy*, edited by John Marenbon. London: Routledge, 291–328.

———. 2001. "Did Duns Scotus Change His Mind on the Will?" *Miscellanea Mediaevalia* 28, 719–94.

Ebbesen, Sten. 1981. *Commentators and Commentaries on Aristotle's*

Sophistici Elenchi. A Study of Post-Aristotelian Ancient and Medieval Writings on Fallacies. Leiden: E. J. Brill.

———. 1988. "Concrete Accidental Terms: Late Thirteenth-Century Debates about Problems Relating to such Terms as 'album'." In *Meaning and Inference in Medieval Philosophy. Studies in Memory of Jan Pinborg*, edited by Norman Kretzmann, 107–74. Dordrecht: Kluwer.

———. 1991. "Doing philosophy the sophismatic way. The Copenhagen School, with notes on the Dutch School." In *Gli studi di filosofia medievale fra otto e novecento*, ed. by R. Imbach and A. Maierù, 331–59. Roma: Edizioni di storia e letteratura.

Effler, Roy. 1962. *John Duns Scotus and the Principle "Omne quod movetur ab alio movetur."* Louvain: Franciscan Institute Publications.

———. 1968. "Duns Scotus and the Necessity of First Principles of the [sic] Knowledge." In *De doctrina Ioannis Duns Scoti* 2, 3–20. Rome: Cura Commissionis Scotisticae.

Etzkorn, Girard J., with Allan B. Wolter, trans. 1997. *Questions on the Metaphysics of Aristotle by John Duns Scotus.* 2 vols. Saint Bonaventure, NY: Franciscan Institute Publications.

Frank, William A. 1982a. "Duns Scotus' Concept of Willing Freely." *Franciscan Studies* 42, 68–89.

———. 1982b. *Duns Scotus' Quodlibetal Teaching on the Will.* Ph.D. diss., Catholic University of America.

Frank, William A., and Allan B. Wolter. 1995. *Duns Scotus, Metaphysician.* West Lafayette, IN: Purdue University Press.

Gelber, Hester. 1974. *Logic and the Trinity: A Clash of Values in Scholastic Thought 1300–1335.* Ph.D. diss., University of Wisconsin.

Gilson, Etienne. 1952. *Jean Duns Scot: Introduction à ses positions fondamentales.* Etudes de philosophie médiévale 42. Paris: J. Vrin.

Godfrey of Fontaines. 1904–37. *Quodlibet I–XV.* Edited by Maurice de Wulf. Les philosophes belges: textes et études. Louvain: Institut supérieur de philosophie de l'Université.

Gorman, Michael. 1993. "Ontological Priority and John Duns Scotus." *Philosophical Quarterly* 43, 460–71.

Gracia, Jorge J. E. 1988. *Introduction to the Problem of Individuation in the Early Middle Ages.* 2nd rev. ed. Munich and Vienna: Philosophia Verlag.

———, ed. 1994. *Individuation in Scholasticism: The Later Middle Ages and the Counter-Reformation, 1150–1650.* Albany: State University of New York Press.

———. 1996. "Individuality and the Individuating Entity in Scotus's *Ordinatio*: An Ontological Characterization." In Honnefelder et al. 1996, 229–49.

Grajewski, Maurice. 1944. *The Formal Distinction of Duns Scotus: A Study in Metaphysics*. Washington, DC: Catholic University of America Press.

Grant, Edward, ed. 1974. *A Sourcebook in Medieval Science*. Cambridge, MA: Harvard University Press.

———. 1976. "The Concept of *Ubi* in Medieval and Renaissance Discussions of Place." *Manuscripta* 20, 71–80.

———. 1978. "Cosmology." In *Science in the Middle Ages*, edited by David C. Lindbergh. Chicago: The University of Chicago Press, 265–302.

———. 1979. "The Condemnation of 1277, God's Absolute Power, and Physical Thought in the Late Middle Ages." *Viator* 10, 211–44.

———. 1981. *Much Ado about Nothing: Theories of Space and Vacuum from the Middle Ages to the Scientific Revolution*. Cambridge, UK: Cambridge University Press.

Guyer, Paul. 1994. "Locke's philosophy of language." In *The Cambridge Companion to Locke*, edited by Vere Chappell, 115–145. Cambridge, UK: Cambridge University Press.

Hackett, Jeremiah M. G. 1994. "Roger Bacon (b. ca. 1214/20; d. 1292)." In Gracia 1994, 117–39.

Hamesse, Jacqueline. 1974. *Les Auctoritates Aristotelis: un florilège médiéval: étude historique et édition critique*. Louvain: Publications universitaires.

Harris, C. R. S. 1927. *Duns Scotus*. 2 vols. Oxford, UK: Clarendon Press.

Hauerwas, Stanley, with Charles Pinches. 1997. *Christians among the Virtues*. Notre Dame, IN: University of Notre Dame Press.

Henninger, Mark. 1989. *Relations: Medieval Theories 1250–1325*. Oxford, UK: Clarendon Press.

Henry, D. P. 1982. "Predicables and Categories." In Kretzmann et al. 1982, 128–42.

Henry of Ghent. 1979. *Henrici de Gandavo Opera Omnia*. Leiden: E. J. Brill.

Hissette, Roland. 1977. *Enquête sur les 219 articles condamnés à Paris le 7 mars 1277*. Louvain: Publications universitaires.

———. 1982. "Albert le Grand et Thomas D'Aquin dans la censure parisienne de 7 mars 1277." In *Studien zur Mittelalterlichen Geistesgeschichte und ihren Quellen*, 226–46. Berlin: Walter de Gruyter.

Hoeres, Wilhelm. 1965. "Wesen und Dasein bei Heinrich von Gent und Duns Scotus." *Franziskanische Studien* 47, 121–86.

Hoffmann, Tobias. 1999. "The Distinction between Nature and Will in Duns Scotus." *Archives d'Histoire Doctrinale et Littéraire du Moyen Age* 66.

Honnefelder, Ludger. 1979. *Ens inquantum ens: Der Begriff des Seienden als Solchen als Gegenstand der Metaphysik nach der Lehre des Johannes*

Duns Scotus. Beiträge zur Geschichte der Philosophie und Theologie des Mittelalters, NF 16. Münster: Aschendorff.

————. 1996. "Metaphysik und Ethik bei Johannes Duns Scotus: Forschungs-ergebnisse und -perspektiven. Eine Einführung." In Honnefelder et al. 1996, 1–33.

Honnefelder, Ludger, ed., with Rega Wood and Mechthild Dreyer, eds. 1996. *John Duns Scotus: Metaphysics and Ethics*. Studien und Texte zur Geistesgeschichte des Mittelalters 53. Cologne: E. J. Brill.

Hyman, Arthur, and James Walsh. 1973. *Philosophy in the Middle Ages*. Indianapolis: Hackett Publishing Company.

Ingham, Mary Elizabeth. 1989. *Ethics and Freedom: An Historical-Critical Investigation of Scotist Ethical Thought*. Lanham, MD: University Press of America.

————. 1996a. *The Harmony of Goodness: Mutuality and Moral Living According to John Duns Scotus*. Quincy, IL: Franciscan Press.

————. 1996b. "Practical Wisdom: Scotus's Presentation of Prudence." In Honnefelder et al. 1996, 551–71.

Irwin, T. H. 1996. "The Virtues: Theory and Common Sense in Greek Philosophy." In *How Should One Live? Essays on the Virtues*, edited by Roger Crisp, 37–55. Oxford, UK: Clarendon Press.

James of Viterbo. 1968. *Jacobi de Viterbio O.E.S.A. Disputatio Prima de Quodlibet*. Edited by Eelcko Ypma. Rome: Augustinianum.

John of Damascus (Damascene). 1864. *De Fide Orthodoxa*. Patrologia Graeca 94. Paris: J.-P. Migne.

————. 1955. *De Fide Orthodoxa: Versions of Burgundio and Cerbanus*. Edited by Eligius M. Buytaert. Franciscan Institute Publications: Text Series, 8. St. Bonaventure, NY: The Franciscan Institute.

Jordan, Michael Joseph. 1984. *Duns Scotus on the Formal Distinction*. Ph.D. diss., Rutgers University.

Kant, Immanuel. 1993. *Grounding for the Metaphysics of Morals*, 2nd ed., translated by James W. Ellington. Indianapolis: Hackett Publishing Company.

Kenny, Anthony and Jan Pinborg. 1982. "Medieval Philosophical Literature." In Kretzmann et al. 1982, 11–42.

Kent, Bonnie. 1995. *Virtues of the Will: The Transformation of Ethics in the Late Thirteenth Century*. Washington, DC: The Catholic University of America Press.

————. 2001. "Augustine's Ethics." In Kretzmann and Stump 2001, 205–33.

King, Peter. 1992. "Duns Scotus on the Common Nature and the Individual Differentia." *Philosophical Topics* 20, 50–76.

————. 1994. "Duns Scotus on the Reality of Self-Change." In *Self-Motion from Aristotle to Newton*, edited by Mary-Louise Gill and Jim Lennox, 227–90. Princeton: Princeton University Press.

Kluxen, Wolfgang. 1998. "Über Metaphysik und Freiheitsverständnis bei Johannes Duns Scotus." *Philosophisches Jahrbuch* 105, 100–109.

Knudsen, Christian. 1982. "Intentions and Impositions." In Kretzmann et al. 1982, 479–95.

Knuuttila, Simo. 1993. *Modalities in Medieval Philosophy*. London: Routledge.

Kretzmann, Norman. 1974. "Aristotle on Spoken Sound Significant by Convention." In J. Corcoran, ed., *Ancient Logic and its Modern Interpretations*. Dordrecht: Reidel.

——. 1982. "Syncategoremata, Exponibilia, Sophismata." In Kretzmann et al. 1982, 211–45.

Kretzmann, Norman, with Anthony Kenny and Jan Pinborg, ed. 1982. *The Cambridge History of Later Medieval Philosophy*. New York: Cambridge University Press.

Kretzmann, Norman, with Eleonore Stump. 1985. "Absolute Simplicity." *Faith and Philosophy* 2, 353–82.

——, ed. 1993. *The Cambridge Companion to Aquinas*. New York: Cambridge University Press.

——, ed. 2001. *The Cambridge Companion to Augustine*. New York: Cambridge University Press.

Lagerlund, Henrik. 1999. *Modal Syllogistics in the Middle Ages*. Ph.D. diss., Uppsala University.

Lang, Helen S. 1983. "Bodies and Angels: The Occupants of Space for Aristotle and Duns Scotus." *Viator* 14, 245–66.

Langston, Douglas C. 1986. *God's Willing Knowledge: The Influence of Scotus' Analysis of Omniscience*. University Park, PA: Pennsylvania State University Press.

——. 1993. "Scotus's Doctrine of Intuitive Cognition." *Synthese* 96, 3–24.

Lee, S. 1998. "Scotus on the Will: The Rational Power and the Dual Affections." *Vivarium* 36, 40–54.

Little, Andrew G. 1892. *The Grey Friars in Oxford*. Oxford: Oxford Historical Society Publications.

——. 1932. "Chronological Notes on the Life of Duns Scotus." *The English Historical Review* 47, 568–82.

Locke, John. 1975. *An Essay concerning Human Understanding*. Edited by P. H. Nidditch. Oxford, UK: Clarendon.

Lottin, Odon. 1949. "Les premières définitions et classifications des vertus au moyen âge." In *Psychologie et morale aux XIIe et XIIIe siècles* 3, section 2, part 1. Louvain–Gembloux: Abbaye du Mont César.

Loux, Michael. 1984. "A Scotistic Argument for the Existence of a First Cause." *American Philosophical Quarterly* 21, 157–65.

Lynch, J. E. 1972. *The Theory of Knowledge of Vital du Four*. St. Bonaventure, New York: Franciscan Institute Press.

MacDonald, Scott. 1988. "Boethius's Claim that all Substances are Good." *Archiv für Geschichte der Philosophie* 70, 245–79.

———, ed. 1991a. *Being and Goodness: The Concept of the Good in Metaphysics and Philosophical Theology*. Ithaca, NY: Cornell University Press.

———. 1991b. "The Relation between Being and Goodness." In MacDonald 1991a, 1–28.

Maier, Anneliese. 1982. "The Nature of Motion." In *On the Threshold of Exact Science*, ed. and trans. Steven D. Sargent. Philadelphia: University of Pennsylvania Press, 21–39.

Maierù, Alfonso. 1987. "Influenze arabe e discussioni sulla natura della logica presso i latini fra XIII e XIV secolo." In *La diffusione delle scienze islamiche nel medio evo europeo*, 243–67. Roma: Accademia Nazionale dei Lincei.

Major, John. 1892. *A History of Greater Britain as well England as Scotland Compiled from the Ancient Authorities by John Major, by name indeed a Scot, but by profession a Theologian*. Trans. Archibald Constable. Edinburgh: Edinburgh University Press.

Malcolm, J. 1979. "A Reconsideration of the Identity and Inherence Theories of the Copula." *Journal of the History of Philosophy* 17, 383–400.

Maloney, Thomas S. 1985. "The Extreme Realism of Roger Bacon." *Review of Metaphysics* 38, 807–37.

Mann, William E. 1982. "Divine Simplicity." *Religious Studies* 18, 451–471.

———. 1987. "Immutability and Predication: What Aristotle Taught Philo and Augustine." *International Journal for Philosophy of Religion* 22, 21–39.

———. 1992. "Duns Scotus, Demonstration, and Doctrine." *Faith and Philosophy* 9, 436–62.

———. 1993. "Hope." In *Reasoned Faith: Essays in Philosophical Theology in Honor of Norman Kretzmann*, edited by Eleonore Stump. Ithaca, NY: Cornell University Press, 251–80.

———. 1998. "Piety: Lending a Hand to Euthyphro." *Philosophy and Phenomenological Research* 58, 123–42.

———. 1999. "Believing Where We Cannot Prove: Duns Scotus on the Necessity of Supernatural Belief." In *The Proceedings of the Twentieth World Congress of Philosophy, Volume 4, Philosophies of Religion, Art, and Creativity*, edited by Kevin L. Stoehr. Bowling Green, KY: Philosophy Documentation Center.

———. 2001. "Augustine on Evil and Original Sin." In Kretzmann and Stump 2001.

Marenbon, John. 1987. *Later Medieval Philosophy (1150–1350). An Introduction*. London: Routledge.

Marmo, Costantino. 1989. "Ontology and Semantics in the Logic of Duns Scotus." In *On the Medieval Doctrine of Signs*, edited by Umberto Eco and Costantino Marmo. Amsterdam/Philadelphia: John Benjamins Publishing Co., 143–93.

_____, ed. 1997. *Vestigia, Imagines, Verba: Semiotics and Logic in Medieval Theological Texts (XIIth–XIVth Century)*. Turnhout: Brepols.

Marmura, Michael E. 1988. "Avicenna: Metaphysics." In *Encyclopaedia Iranica*, edited by Ehsan Yarshater. London/New York: Routledge and Kegan Paul, III: 75a–76b.

_____. 1992. "Quiddity and Universality in Avicenna." In *Neoplatonism and Islamic Philosophy*, edited by Parviz Morewedge. Albany, NY: SUNY Press, 77–87.

Marrone, Steven P. 1988. "Henry of Ghent and Duns Scotus on the Knowledge of Being." *Speculum* 63, 22–57.

_____. 2001. *The Light of Thy Countenance: Science and Knowledge of God in the Thirteenth Century*. Leiden: E. J. Brill.

Marston, Roger. 1932. *Quaestiones disputatae*. Biblioteca Franciscani Scholastica Medii Aevi 7. Quaracchi: Collegium Sancti Bonaventurae.

_____. 1994. *Quodlibeta quatuor*. Edited by Girard Etzkorn and Ignatius Brady, editio secunda. Biblioteca Franciscani Scholastica Medii Aevi 26. Grottaferrata: Collegium Sancti Bonaventurae.

Martin, Christopher. 1999. *Theories of Inference and Entailment in the Middle Ages*. Ph.D. diss., Princeton University.

Massobrio, Simona. 1991. *Aristotelian Matter as Understood by St. Thomas Aquinas and John Duns Scotus*. Ph.D. diss., McGill University.

McCarthy, Edward. 1976. *Medieval Light Theory and Optics and Duns Scotus' Treatment of Light in D. 13 of Book II of his Commentary on the Sentences*. Ph.D. diss., City University of New York.

McGrath, Alister. 1998. *Iustitia Dei: A History of the Christian Doctrine of Justification*. 2d ed. Cambridge, UK: Cambridge University Press.

Menn, Stephen. 1998. *Descartes and Augustine*. Cambridge, UK: Cambridge University Press.

Mercken, H. P. F. 1998. "Scotus's Interpretation of the *Lex Naturae* in the Perspective of Western Philosophical Ethics." In *John Duns Scotus (1265/6–1308): Renewal of Philosophy*, edited by E. P. Bos, 171–82. Amsterdam: Rodopi.

Möhle, Hannes. 1995. *Ethik als scientia practica nach Johannes Duns Scotus: Eine philosophische Grundlegung*. Beiträge zur Geschichte der Philosophie und Theologie des Mittelalters 44. Münster: Aschendorff.

_____. 1999. "Das Verhältnis praktischer Wahrheit und kontingenter Wirklichkeit bei Johannes Duns Scotus." In *Friedensethik im*

Spätmittelalter: Theologie im Ringen um die gottgegebene Ordnung, edited by Gerhard Beestermöller and Heinz-Gerhard Justenhoven, 47–61. Stuttgart: W. Kohlhammer.

Mondadori, Fabrizio. 2000. "'Quid Sit Essentia Creaturae, Priusquam a Deo Producatur': Leibniz' View." In *Unità e Molteplicità nel Pensiero filosofico e scientifico di Leibniz,* edited by Antonio Lamarra and Roberto Palaia. Florence: L. S. Olschki.

Morrison, Donald. 1987. "The Evidence for Degrees of Being in Aristotle." *Classical Quarterly* 37, 382–402.

Muckle, J. T., ed. 1933. *Algazel's Metaphysics.* Toronto: St. Michael's College.

Müller, Johannes P. 1974. "Eine Quästion über das Individuationsprinzip des Johannes von Paris O.P. (Quidort)." In *Virtus politica: Festgabe zum 75. Geburtstag von Alfons Hufnagel,* 335–55. Stuttgart in Bad Cannstatt: Friedrich Frommann Verlag.

Murdoch, John E. 1981. "*Scientia mediantibus vocibus:* Metalinguistic Analysis in Late Medieval Natural Philosophy." In *Sprache und Erkenntnis im Mittelalter,* Miscellanea Mediaevalia 13/1, ed. by W. Kluxen et al., 73–106. Berlin: W. de Gruyter.

———. 1982. "Infinity and Continuity." In Kretzmann et al. 1982, 564–91.

Nash, Peter E. 1950–1. "Giles of Rome, Auditor and Critic of St. Thomas." *The Modern Schoolman* 28, 1–20.

Nederman, Cary J. 1989 90. "Nature, Ethics, and the Doctrine of 'Habitus': Aristotelian Moral Psychology in the Twelfth Century." *Traditio* 45, 87–110.

Noone, Timothy B. 1995. "Scotus's Critique of the Thomistic Theory of Individuation and the Dating of the «Quaestiones in Libros Metaphysicorum», VII q. 13." In Sileo 1995, I:391–406.

———. 1998. "Scotus on Divine Ideas: *Rep. Paris.* I-A, d.36." *Medioevo* 24, 359–453.

Normore, Calvin G. 1993. "Peter Aureoli and His Contemporaries on Future Contingents and Excluded Middle." *Synthese* 96, 83–92.

Novak, Joseph A. 1987. "Aquinas and the Incorruptibility of the Soul." *History of Philosophy Quarterly* 4, 405–21.

O'Brien, Andrew J. 1964. "Duns Scotus' Teaching on the Distinction Between Essence and Existence." *The New Scholasticism* 38, 61–77.

Ockham, William. 1974. *Summa Logicae.* Edited by P. Boehner, G. Gál, and S. Brown. Volume 1 of *Opera philosophica.* St. Bonaventure, NY: Franciscan Institute.

O'Connor, Timothy. 2000. *Persons and Causes: The Metaphysics of Free Will.* Oxford, UK: Oxford University Press.

O'Donnell, J. Reginald. 1955. *Nine Mediaeval Thinkers: A Collection of Hitherto Unedited Texts*. Toronto: Pontifical Institute of Mediaeval Studies.

Owens, Joseph. 1957. "Common Nature: A Point of Comparison Between Thomistic and Scotistic Metaphysics." *Mediaeval Studies* 19, 1–14.

———. 1958. "The Accidental and Essential Character of Being in the Doctrine of St. Thomas Aquinas." *Mediaeval Studies* 20, 1–40.

Pasnau, Robert. 1995. "Henry of Ghent and the Twilight of Divine Illumination." *Review of Metaphysics* 49, 49–75.

———. 1997a. "Olivi on the Metaphysics of the Soul." *Medieval Philosophy and Theology* 6, 109–32.

———. 1997b. *Theories of Cognition in the Later Middle Ages*. New York: Cambridge University Press.

———. 1998. "Aquinas and the Content Fallacy." *The Modern Schoolman* 75, 293–314.

———. 2002. *Thomas Aquinas on Human Nature*. New York: Cambridge University Press.

Perler, Dominik. 1994. "What Am I Thinking About? John Duns Scotus and Peter Aureol on Intentional Objects." *Vivarium* 32, 72–89.

———. 1996. "Things in the Mind: Fourteenth-Century Controversies over 'Intelligible Species.' " *Vivarium* 34, 231–53.

Peter John Olivi. 1922. *Quaestiones in secundum librum Sententiarum*. Edited by Bernard Jansen. 3 vols. Bibliotheca Franciscani Scolastica Medii Aevi 4–6. Quaracchi: Collegium Sancti Bonaventurae.

———. 1998. *Epistola ad fratrem R.*, edited by C. Kilmer and E. Marmursztejn. *Archivum Franciscanum Historicum* 91, 33–64.

Petrus, Falcus. 1968. *Questions disputées ordinaires [par] Pierre de Falco*. Edited by A.-J. Gondras. Louvain, Éditions Nauwelaerts; Paris, Béatrice-Nauwelaerts.

Pinborg, Jan. 1971. "Bezeichnung in der Logik des XIII. Jahrhunderts." In Albert Zimmermann, ed., *Der Begriff der Repraesentatio im Mittelalter*, 238–81. Miscellanea Medievalia 8. Berlin: W. de Gruyter.

———. 1982. "Speculative Grammar." In Kretzmann et al. 1982, 254–69.

Pini, Giorgio. 1997. *La dottrina delle categorie nei commenti aristotelici di Duns Scoto*, tesi di perfezionamento. Pisa: Scuola Normale Superiore.

———. 1999. "Species, Concept, and Thing: Theories of Signification in the Second Half of the Thirteenth Century." *Medieval Philosophy and Theology* 8, 21–52.

———. 2001. "Signification of Names in Duns Scotus and Some of His Contemporaries." *Vivarium* 39, 20–51.

Plantinga, Alvin. 1974. *The Nature of Necessity*. Oxford, UK: Clarendon Press.

Pope, Stephen J., ed. 2002. *The Ethics of Aquinas*. Washington, DC: Georgetown University Press.

Porphyry. 1887. *Isagoge et in Aristotelis Categorias commentarium*. Edited by Adolfus Busse. Commentaria in Aristotelem Graeca, 4.1. Berlin: George Reimer.

———. 1966. *Porphyrii Isagoge translatio Boethii et anonymi fragmentum vulgo vocatum "Liber sex principiorum."* Edited by Lorenzo Minio-Paluello. Aristoteles Latinus, 1.6–7. Bruges-Paris: Desclée de Brouwer.

Prentice, Robert. 1967. "The Contingent Element Governing the Natural Law on the Last Seven Precepts of the Decalogue, According to Duns Scotus." *Antonianum* 42, 259–92.

Priest, Stephen. 1998. "Duns Scotus on the Immaterial." *The Philosophical Quarterly* 48, 370–2.

Prior, Arthur. 1970. "The Notion of the Present." *Studium Generale* 23, 245–8.

Pseudo-Dionysius the Areopagite. 1857. *De divinis nominibus*. Patrologia Graeca 3. Paris: J.-P. Migne.

Putnam, Hilary. 1975. "The Meaning of 'Meaning'." In Hilary Putnam, *Mind and Language*, Philosophical Papers, vol. 2. Cambridge: Cambridge University Press.

Read, Stephen, ed. 1993. *Sophisms in Medieval Logic and Grammar*. Dordrecht: Kluwer.

Rist, J. M. 1994. *Augustine. Ancient Thought Baptized.* Cambridge, UK: Cambridge University Press.

Robert Grosseteste. 1982. *Hexaëmeron*. Edited by Richard C. Dales and Servus Gieben. Oxford, UK: Oxford University Press.

Roest, Bert. 2000. *A History of Franciscan Education (c. 1210–1517)*. Leiden: Brill.

Rorty, Richard. 1979. *Philosophy and the Mirror of Nature*. Princeton, NJ: Princeton University Press.

Rosier, Irene. 1983. *La grammaire spéculative des Modistes*. Lille: Presses universitaires.

———. 1994. *La parole comme acte. Sur la grammaire et la sémantique au XIIIe siècle*. Paris: Vrin.

———. 1995a. "*Res significata* et *modus significandi*: Les implications d'une distinction médiévale." In *Sprachtheorien in Spätantike und Mittelalter*, edited by Sten Ebbesen, 135–68. Tübingen: G. Narr.

———. 1995b. "Henri de Gand, le *De Dialectica* d'Augustin, et l'institution des noms divins." *Documenti e studi sulla tradizione filosofica medievale* 6, 255–80.

Ross, James F. 1961. "Analogy as a Rule of Meaning for Religious Language." *International Philosophical Quarterly* 1, 468–502.

_____. 1968. *Philosophical Theology*. Indianapolis, IN: Bobbs-Merrill.

_____. 1989. "The Crash of Modal Metaphysics." *Review of Metaphysics* 43, 251–79.

_____. 1990. "Aquinas' Exemplarism, Aquinas' Voluntarism." *American Catholic Philosophical Quarterly* 64, 171–98.

Sagüez Azcona, P. 1968. "Apuntes para la historia del escotismo en España en el siglo XIV." In *De doctrina Ioannis Duns Scoti*, vol 4: *Scotismus decursu saeculorum*, 3–19. Rome.

Salmon, Wesley. 1977. "An 'At-At' Theory of Causal Influence." In *Philosophy of Science* 44, 215–24.

Schneider, J. H. J. 1996. "*Utrum haec sit vera*: Caesar est homo, Caesar est animal, Caesar non existente. Zum *Peri-Hermeneias*-Kommentar des Johannes Duns Scotus." In Honnefelder et al. 1996, 393–412.

Searle, John. 1969. *Speech Acts: An Essay in the Philosophy of Language*. Cambridge, UK: Cambridge University Press.

Shannon, Thomas A. 1995. *The Ethical Theory of Duns Scotus*. Quincy, IL: Franciscan Press.

Sharp, Dorothea E. 1930. *Franciscan Philosophy at Oxford in the Fourteenth Century*. London: Oxford University Press.

Siger of Brabant. 1974. *Écrits de logique, de morale et de physique*. Edited by B. Bazán. Louvain: Publications Universitaires.

Smart, J. J. C. 1963. *Philosophy and Scientific Realism*. London: Routledge and Kegan Paul.

Sileo, Leonardo, ed. 1995. *Via Scoti: Methodologica ad mentem Joannis Duns Scoti*. 2 vols. Rome: Antonianum.

Sondag, Gérard. 1993. *Duns Scot: L'Image*. Paris: J. Vrin.

_____. 1996. "Universel et *natura communis* dans l'*Ordinatio* et dans les *Questions sur le Perihermeneias* (une brève comparaison)." In Honnefelder et al. 1996, 385–91.

_____. 1997. "La solution scotiste au problème de l'individuation, avec une conjecture sur ses sources immédiates." In *Perspectives arabes et médiévales sur la tradition scientifique et philosophique grecque*. Actes du colloque de la Société internationale d'histoire des sciences et de la philosophie arabes et islamiques, edited by Ahmad Hasnawi, Abdelali Elamrani-Jamal, and Maroun Aouad, 505–21. Leuven/Paris: Peeters/Institut du Monde Arabe.

Sorabji, Richard. 1983. *Time, Creation, and the Continuum: Theories in Antiquity and the Early Middle Ages*. Ithaca, NY: Cornell University Press.

Spade, Paul Vincent, trans. 1994. *Five Texts on the Mediaeval Problem of Universals: Porphyry, Boethius, Abelard, Duns Scotus, Ockham*. Indianapolis, IN: Hackett Publishing Company.

Spruit, Leen. 1994. *Species intelligibilis: From Perception to Knowledge.* Leiden: E. J. Brill.

Spruyt, Joke. 1998. "Duns Scotus' Criticism of Henry of Gent's Notion of Free Will." In *John Duns Scotus (1265/6–1308): Renewal of Philosophy,* edited by E. P. Bos, 139–54. Amsterdam: Rodopi.

Steneck, Nicholas. 1970. *The Problem of the Internal Senses in the Fourteenth Century.* Ph.D. diss., University of Wisconsin.

Stella, Prospero. 1955. *L'Ilemorfismo di G. Duns Scoto.* Turin: Società editrice internazionale.

Stroick, Clemens. 1974. "Eine Pariser Disputation vom Jahre 1306: Die Verteidigung des thomistischen Individuationsprinzips gegen Johannes Duns Scotus durch Guillelmus Petri de Godino, O. P." In *Thomas von Aquino: Interpretation und Rezeption, Studien und Texte,* edited by Willehead Paul Eckert, 559–608. Mainz: Matthias-Grünewald Verlag.

Stump, Eleonore. 1982. "Theology and Physics in *De sacramento altaris*: Ockham's Theory of Indivisibles." In *Infinity and Continuity in Ancient and Medieval Thought,* edited by Norman Kretzmann. Ithaca, NY: Cornell University Press, 207–30.

———. 1995. "Non-Cartesian Substance Dualism and Materialism without Reductionism." *Faith and Philosophy* 12, 505–31.

———. 1985. "Absolute Simplicity." *Faith and Philosophy* 2, 353–82.

Stump, Eleonore, and Norman Kretzmann. 1991. "Being and Goodness." In MacDonald 1991a, 98–128.

Sylwanowicz, Michael. 1996. *Contingent Causality and the Foundations of Duns Scotus' Metaphysics.* Studien und Texte zur Geistesgeschichte des Mittelalters 51. Köln: E. J. Brill.

Tachau, Katherine. 1988. *Vision and Certitude in the Age of Ockham. Optics, Epistemology and the Foundations of Semantics, 1250–1345.* Leiden: E.J. Brill.

Tanner, Norman, ed. 1990. *Decrees of the Ecumenical Councils.* 2 vols. London: Sheed and Ward; Washington, DC: Georgetown University Press.

Thijssen, J. M. M. H. 1984. "Roger Bacon (1214–1292/97): A Neglected Source in the Medieval Continuum Debate." *Archives internationales d'histoire des sciences* 34, 25–34.

Thomas Aquinas. 1929. *In Sententias.* Edited by P. Mandonnet. Paris: Lethielleux.

———. 1989. *Expositio libri Peryermenias.* Editio Leonina I*/1. Rome and Paris: Commissio Leonina & Vrin.

Thomas of Sutton. 1969. *Quodlibeta.* Edited by Michael Schmaus. Munich: Bayerische Akademie der Wissenschaften.

Tweedale, Martin. 1993. "Duns Scotus's Doctrine on Universals and the Aphrodisian Tradition." *American Catholic Philosophical Quarterly* 67, 77–93.

Van Hook, Brennan. 1962. "Duns Scotus and the Self-Evident Proposition." *New Scholasticism* 36, 29–48.

van Inwagen, Peter. 1989. "When Is the Will Free?" *Philosophical Perspectives* 3, 399–422.

Vier, Peter. 1951. *Evidence and its Function According to John Duns Scotus.* St. Bonaventure, NY: Franciscan Institute.

Vignaux, Paul. 1935. *Luther: Commentateur des Sentences (Livre I, Distinction XVII).* Paris: J. Vrin.

Visser, Sandra, and Thomas Williams. 2001. "Anselm's Account of Freedom." *Canadian Journal of Philosophy* 31, 221–44.

Vos Jaczn, Antonie, H. Veldhuis, A. H. Looman-Graaskamp, E. Dekker, N. W. DenBok. 1994. *John Duns Scotus: Contingency and Freedom: Lectura I 39.* Dordrecht: Kluwer.

Waismann, Friedrich. 1959. *Introduction to Mathematical Thinking.* New York: Harper.

Ware, William. *Quaestiones in Sententias.* Vienna, Österreichische Nationalbibliothek, MS 1424.

Weidemann, H. 1994. *Aristoteles: Peri hermeneias.* Berlin: Akademie-Verlag.

White, Michael J. 1992. *The Continuous and the Discrete: Ancient Physical Theories from a Contemporary Perspective.* Oxford, UK: Clarendon Press.

Williams, Thomas. 1995a. *Monologion and Proslogion, with the Replies of Gaunilo and Anselm.* Indianapolis, IN: Hackett Publishing Company.

_____. 1995b. "How Scotus Separates Morality from Happiness." *American Catholic Philosophical Quarterly* 69, 425–445.

_____. 1997. "Reason, Morality, and Voluntarism in Duns Scotus: A Pseudo-Problem Dissolved." *The Modern Schoolman* 74, 73–94.

_____. 1998a. "The Unmitigated Scotus." *Archiv für Geschichte der Philosophie* 80, 162–81.

_____. 1998b. "The Libertarian Foundations of Scotus's Moral Philosophy." *The Thomist* 62, 193–215.

Wippel, John F. 1977. "The Condemnations of 1270 and 1277." *Journal of Medieval and Renaissance Studies* 7, 169–201.

_____. 1981. *The Metaphysical Thought of Godfrey of Fontaines. A Study in Late Thirteenth-Century Philosophy.* Washington, DC: Catholic University of America Press.

_____. 1984. *Metaphysical Themes in Thomas Aquinas.* Washington, DC: Catholic University of America Press.

_____. 1994. "Godfrey of Fontaines (b. ca. 1250; d. 1306/09), Peter of

Auvergne (d. 1303), and John Baconthorpe (d. 1345/1348)." In Gracia 1994, 222–8.

_____. 1998. "Thomas Aquinas and the Axiom that Unreceived Act is Unlimited." *Review of Metaphysics* 51, 558–61.

_____. 2000. *The Metaphysical Thought of Thomas Aquinas*. Washington, DC: Catholic University of America Press.

Wolf, Susan. 1990. *Freedom within Reason*. Oxford, UK: Oxford University Press.

Wolter, Allan B. 1946. *The Transcendentals and Their Function in the Metaphysics of Duns Scotus*. St. Bonaventure, NY: The Franciscan Institute.

_____. 1951. "Duns Scotus on the Necessity of Revealed Knowledge." *Franciscan Studies* 11, 231–72.

_____. 1954. "Duns Scotus and the Existence and Nature of God." In *Existence and Nature of God: Proceedings of the American Catholic Philosophical Association* 28, 94–121.

_____. 1966. *A Treatise on God as First Principle*. Chicago: Franciscan Herald Press.

_____. 1972. "Native Freedom of the Will as a Key to the Ethics of Scotus." Reprinted in Wolter 1990a, 148–62.

_____. 1986. *Duns Scotus on the Will and Morality*. Washington, DC: Catholic University of America Press.

_____. 1987. *Duns Scotus: Philosophical Writings*. Indianapolis: Hackett Publishing Company.

_____. 1990a. *The Philosophical Theology of John Duns Scotus*. Edited by Marilyn McCord Adams. Ithaca, NY: Cornell University Press.

_____. 1990b. "Duns Scotus on Intuition, Memory, and Our Knowledge of Individuals." In Wolter 1990a, 98–122.

_____. 1990c. "The Realism of Scotus." In Wolter 1990a, 42–53.

_____. 1990d. "Scotus's Individuation Theory." In Wolter 1990a, 68–97.

_____. 1990e. "Duns Scotus on the Natural Desire for the Supernatural." In Wolter 1990a, 125–47.

_____. 1993. "Reflections on the Life and Works of Scotus." *American Catholic Philosophical Quarterly* 67, 1–36.

_____. 1995. "Duns Scotus at Oxford." In Sileo 1995, I.183–91.

_____. 1996. "Reflections about Scotus's Early Works." In Honnefelder et al. 1996, 37–57.

Wolter, Allan B., with Marilyn McCord Adams. 1982. "Duns Scotus' Parisian Proof for the Existence of God." *Franciscan Studies* 42, 248–321.

_____. 1993. "Memory and Intuition: A Focal Debate in Fourteenth Century Cognitive Psychology." *Franciscan Studies* 53, 175–230.

Wood, Rega. 1987. "Scotus's Argument for the Existence of God." *Franciscan Studies* 47, 257–77.

_____. 1996. "Individual Forms: Richard Rufus and John Duns Scotus." In Honnefelder et al. 1996, 251–72.

_____. 1997a. "Roger Bacon: Richard Rufus' Successor as a Parisian Physics Professor." *Vivarium* 35, 222–50.

_____. 1997b. *Ockham on the Virtues*. West Lafayette, IN: Purdue University Press.

_____. 1999. "Ockham's Repudiation of Pelagianism." In *The Cambridge Companion to Ockham*, edited by Paul Vincent Spade, 350–73. Cambridge, UK: Cambridge University Press.

Zimmermann, Albert. 1967. "Eine anonyme Quaestio: 'Utrum haec sit vera: homo est animal homine non existente'." *Archiv für Geschichte der Philosophie* 49, 183–200.

CITATIONS OF WORKS ATTRIBUTED TO JOHN DUNS SCOTUS

As new volumes of the critical edition appear — and one appeared while this volume was in production — some citations in the text and in this index will no longer match the canonical citation forms. If a reference in this volume leads to what appears to be the wrong passage in a critical edition, the reader should look up the passage in the Wadding edition and then locate the corresponding passage in the critical edition. Both the Vatican edition and the Bonaventure edition reproduce the marginal numbering of the Wadding edition in square brackets in the inside margin. The Vatican edition of the *Ordinatio* also offers tables showing the correspondence between questions in the Wadding edition and those in the Vatican edition.

Add.

2, d. 25, q. 1: 236
2, d. 42, q. 1: 331
2, d. 42, q. 4: 236, 327

Coll.

1: 376
3: 58, 236
13: 58
17: 331
36: 68, 308

De primo princ.

1: 38–40, 64, 137, 158, 228
2: 40, 42, 64
3: 43–5, 64, 65, 136, 137, 138, 139, 140, 159, 227
4: 65, 136, 141, 157, 224, 227, 228, 229, 232, 234, 309

In De an.

q. 5: 304, 305
q. 6: 278, 279, 304, 305, 307
q. 9: 279, 304
q. 10: 279, 304
q. 11: 304, 305, 310
q. 12: 306
q. 13: 66, 304
q. 14: 304
q. 17: 304, 305, 306
q. 18: 305, 308
q. 19: 307, 308, 310
q. 21: 58, 307, 308
q. 22: 308

In Metaph.

prol.: 27, 57, 228
1, q. 1: 45, 57, 58, 63
1, q. 3: 279
1, q. 4: 304, 310, 311
1, q. 6: 124
2, qq. 2–3: 58, 304, 307, 308, 309
2, qq. 4–6: 64, 65
4, q. 2: 60, 281, 284
5, q. 1: 64
5, qq. 5–6: 32, 33, 62
5, q. 7: 35
5, q. 8: 63, 64
5, q. 9: 62
5, q. 10: 97, 98
5, q. 11: 34, 36, 37, 62, 63

In Periherm. I

In Periherm. II

Ord./Op. Ox.

Quodl.

Rep.

1A, prol., q. 1, a. 4: 158
1A, prol., q. 3, a. 1: 57
1A, d. 2, qq. 1–4: 65
1A, d. 35, q. 1: 232, 233
2, d. 1, q. 3: 227, 234
2, d. 1, q. 6: 281
2, d. 3, q. 2: 67
2, d. 3, q. 8: 67
2, d. 6, q. 2: 351
2, d. 12, q. 2: 67
2, d. 16, q. un.: 304
2, d. 34, q. un.: 339, 350
4, d. 17, q. un.: 329
4, d. 33, qq. 1–3: 330
4, d. 44, q. 1: 65

Theor.

9, prop. 5: 197
16, prop. 3: 197

INDEX

Medieval authors are indexed according to their given names.